COMMEMORATIVE EDITION

Newman's

BIRDS

OF SOUTHERN AFRICA

REVISED BY
Vanessa Newman

SCIENTIFIC CONSULTANT: FAANSIE PEACOCK

sappi

D1500692

Tribute to Kenneth Newman

He was a wonderful guy. Only now, after Ken's death, are his contributions to humanity and Nature beginning to be fully appreciated. Apart from being Africa's 'Mr Birdman', his achievements were many and his influence global, in some respects.

Ken grew up in England, yet when he arrived here shortly after World War II, he soon gathered as much knowledge about this continent's natural wonders as any individual in Africa. It was he, as much as anyone in the world, who taught people how to identify – in an almost subconscious instant – shapes flying in the air. As a boy too young to enlist for service early in World War II, he was recruited to teach Allied airmen, plane-spotters and anti-aircraft gunners his arcane skill which allowed them to tell the difference between Allied aircraft and the enemy flying over Britain.

His favourite place was in a makoro on the waters of the Okavango Delta. Or in a glider soaring above the highest vultures on the Highveld. His most memorable place was probably an unnamed patch of equatorial jungle beyond the Congo, on the road to Timbuktu. It was near Lake Chad in the 1950s that the jalopy in which Ken and his wife were travelling broke down irretrievably. As night fell the lost couple were marooned, without food, human contact or any form of communication. In the gloom they suddenly saw a face at their window, heavily scarred

with patterned cuts. It smiled, and they saw in the torchlight two rows of file-sharpened teeth. Ken had met an unknown tribe. 'The women as well as the men were quite naked, except for a little flap they wore; they were primitive and wonderful people. Some of the nicest we ever met.'

Ken was a true gentleman in the best, old-fashioned sense; one who believed self-importance and self-interest were anathema to the spirit.

His life was dedicated to sharing with others those so-called 'moments of magic' which he had discovered in a special area of life on this planet. In propagating to the world awareness of this 'life force' he was exceeded in the past century by only one man I believe: Roger Tory Peterson who had, 30 years previously, through his art and obsession, popularised birding and turned it into a tourist industry in the United States.

Ken would spurn as irrelevant my attempt at listing his achievements in this same field. But his work was highly relevant, and all the world should be aware of and grateful for it. He pioneered a popular form of bird guides which outsold all other books in Africa except, until quite recently, the Bible. His books followed a clear, instantly grasped formula inspiring similar bird guides here and in many other countries. If you go back to his simple step-by-step route to bird identification, set out in different words in almost all his works, you will see how effective his teaching is and how big his influence has been.

Fortunately he will be with us, and our children and our children's children for a long time. His daughter Vanessa is among the first to hold the torch that illuminates his work, his advice, his paintings and his unspoken philosophy. Hers is an important mission, for birding has become one of the most effective ways of re-introducing 'civilised' mankind to the joys and benefits of our natural environment. The form of widespread public interest in birdlife which Ken encouraged so joyously provides a constant reminder of the growing threats to our environment. Vanessa's work will benefit all of us. It should help other birders – scientific, scholarly and people of the earth – to carry the torch in greater and greater numbers.

HARVEY TYSON (former Editor of *The Star*)
Hermanus 2010

DEDICATION

To the memory of Kenneth, who loved his birds,
and to Ursula, who loved the trees they perched in.
They will continue living in our hearts
and be remembered by all who knew them.
From Vanessa, Nicholas and Pamela.

Struik Nature (an imprint of Random House Struik (Pty) Ltd)
Reg. No. 1966/003153/07
80 McKenzie Street, Cape Town, 8001
PO Box 1144, Cape Town, 8000 South Africa
www.randomstruik.co.za

Log on to our photographic website **www.imagesofafrica.co.za**
for an African experience.

First published by Macmillan South Africa (Publishers) (Pty) Ltd in 1983
Published by Southern Book Publishers (Pty) Ltd in 1988
Published by Struik Publishers (Pty) Ltd in 2000
Commemorative Edition published by Struik Nature in 2010

3 5 7 9 10 8 6 4 2

Softcover edition ISBN: 978 1 77007 876 5
PVC edition ISBN: 978 1 77007 878 9

Also available in Afrikaans as *Newman se Voëls van Suider-Afrika*
Softcover edition (Afrikaans) ISBN: 978 1 77007 877 2
PVC edition (Afrikaans) ISBN: 978 1 77007 879 6

Publishing manager: Pippa Parker
Managing editor: Helen de Villiers
Editor: Ian Parsons
Ornithological consultant: Faansie Peacock
Designer: Louise Topping
Design assistant: Jennifer Addington
Reproduction: Hirt & Carter
Printed and bound by: Craft Print International Ltd

SPONSOR'S FOREWORD

It is with mixed feelings that I am introducing this revised edition of Sappi-sponsored *Newman's Birds of Southern Africa*. I am delighted to present an updated version of this definitive field guide; on the other hand, I am saddened that Ken is not here to witness its re-launch. His death in October 2006 was a loss not just for the birding community, but for anyone interested in conservation.

Ken played a pivotal role in the popularisation of bird watching through the publication of his many books. His commitment was reflected through his presidency of both the South African Ornithological Society and BirdLife South Africa, and he was President of the BirdLife Sandton branch at the time of his death. Ken was the first non-scientist to receive the prestigious Gill Memorial Medal, for a lifetime's contribution to ornithology in southern Africa. He was also awarded a BirdLife South Africa Owl Award for promoting the enjoyment, conservation, study and understanding of wild birds and their habitats.

Ken had a rich canvas from which to draw: over 900 bird species occur in southern Africa, of which 179 are either full or near endemics. The region also hosts a number of intra-African migrants such as cuckoos and kingfishers, as well as birds from the Arctic, Europe, Central Asia, China and Antarctica. Of the 10 families of birds found only in Africa and related islands, nine are found in southern Africa.

Sappi's association with Ken – and with birding – goes far back. Between 1997 and 2007, Sappi Forests held the Sappi Great Birding Adventure annually: teams of watchers recorded bird species sighted on Sappi's lands within a given period of time, and those frequently recorded were compared with unusual, infrequent sightings. This showed that 286 species (63%) were recorded regularly (five or more times); and 74 species (16%) were recorded only once, and are regarded as rare on these estates. Every year, an average of 15 Red Data species were recorded, with two Critically Endangered species, the Blue Swallow and Wattled Crane, frequently listed.

Together with our strategic partner, WWF, we are also involved in several community-owned avi-tourism projects on our land, centred around threatened, biodiversity-rich indigenous forests and wetlands in KwaZulu-Natal and Mpumalanga. The objective is to protect sensitive biomes and establish sustainable business ventures for rural communities. These include the Wakkerstroom Birding Centre in Mpumalanga, the Ongonye Forest Birding Camp in KwaZulu-Natal and the Southern KwaZulu-Natal Birding Route.

In a world characterised by speed and urgency, birding offers the antithesis – a chance to sit still, unwind and simply observe – whether in one's own garden or in a remote area of bush. Little wonder that it is one of the fastest growing hobbies in the world and that, for many, sighting the birding Big Six – the Ground Hornbill, Kori Bustard, Saddlebilled Stork, Pels Fishing Owl, Lappet-faced Vulture and Martial Eagle – is more important than sighting the Big Five game animals.

Benjamin Franklin said, 'An investment in knowledge always pays the best interest'. Whether you're a committed twitcher intent on adding yet another 'lifer' to your list, or a beginner, you'll find this field guide invaluable.

It has been predicted that paper usage would die out in the 21st century. This revised edition is proof of the integral role paper still plays in education, in preserving our collective memory and in providing the tactile and visual experience that only paper can offer. Ken's commitment to and his passion for his subject are alive on every page of this field guide.

I hope you enjoy reading it and using it as much as I plan to.

RALPH BOËTTGER
Chief Executive Officer • Sappi Limited

ACKNOWLEDGEMENTS

Newman's Birds of Southern Africa was my father's chief labour of love, an ongoing project which he began when I was a small child and one I'm proud to continue for him, on behalf of my brother Nicholas and sister Pamela. Even towards the end of his life, when he knew there would soon come a time when he could no longer work on his books, I sensed only a deep satisfaction that he'd had an opportunity to share his love and immense knowledge of birds with others while he could. Dad never once insisted that any of us take up the reins, but I always knew I couldn't abandon his legacy. Once my decision was made and I announced to him my intention not to let his long years of hard work simply end, he just smiled in that quiet, gentle way that he had, saying, 'well then, I'd be very happy with that'. I'm not the only person to wish there was some way of downloading a person's knowledge to access after they've gone, because no matter how often I picked his brains I continued to learn from him right up to the end. While I'm lucky enough to be able to draw and paint as he did, there is so much accumulated expertise that he took with him. It has therefore been a vast boon to have had the invaluable help of ornithologist Faansie Peacock to fill the gaps of my knowledge in bringing this Commemorative Edition to life; my sincere and heartfelt thanks go to him.

The Commemorative Edition is not only a tribute to my father's work and achievements, but is a natural evolution following recent DNA research and ornithological re-classification, much of which has been achieved by the Percy FitzPatrick Institute in Cape Town. Subsequent alterations to groupings and scientific names have, in many instances, affected common names. While there will always be debate on the 'suitability' or 'accuracy' of the vernacular, I've taken the decision to make name changes in accordance with the International Ornithological Committee (IOC) list. These changes are also in line with those common names used in other parts of Africa and the rest of the world.

My father's original motivation was to produce an informative but easy-to-use field guide that both beginners and expert birders could use. In the Commemorative Edition my objective has been to enhance it as a reference tool, a challenge in itself for a field guide, which, by its very nature, shouldn't be too complicated! However, when I considered the little gems of information on recognition, calls, behaviour, etc. that I've hand written in my own treasured and well-leafed copy over the years, I felt it would really add something. So, in the trend adopted by other field guides around the world, the plates are now annotated. All distribution maps are updated according to the latest recordings and incorporate a new two-toned theme indicating species' abundance. There is also more detail on rarities, vagrants, endangered and endemic species, which is vitally important to our general understanding of our fragile and very threatened ecology.

On behalf of my father, grateful thanks must of course go to everyone who helped him bring this field guide together in its original form over the years: his friends, colleagues, museums and ornithological institutions. My own thanks go to Nick, Pam and my husband Edward, for their continued support over the many months I've been working on this. Thanks also to Banie Penzhorn who, once again, has taken on the massive task of translating information and names into Afrikaans. My thanks go also to Pippa Parker of Struik Nature, a font of knowledge and experience, who has guided me through this revision from the start. Naturally, my biggest thanks are to my beloved father for being the best, most patient teacher, quietly training me for when I would take up the torch and run with it.

VANESSA NEWMAN, for Kenneth Newman (1924–2006)

CONTENTS

SCOPE OF THIS FIELD GUIDE

This field guide covers the whole of the southern African subregion and the subantarctic region adjacent to the continent. Southern Africa is generally accepted as being that part of Africa lying south of the Zambezi, Okavango and Kunene rivers, or approximately 17°S. It embraces several national states and a diversity of geophysical regions, ranging from tropical coasts to the most arid desert, and its bird fauna is correspondingly diverse. As might be expected, the birds show strong affinities with the avifauna of the rest of Africa south of the Sahara Desert (the Afrotropical region). The majority of birds found in the subregion therefore also occur north of its limits.

Emperor and Adelie penguins

In addition to the wide variety of mainland birds, numerous pelagic sea birds, many of which breed on islands in the southern oceans, visit the southern African coasts. These sea birds, ranging in size from the diminutive storm-petrels to the enormous albatrosses, are often difficult to identify. Many are only identified by small details of plumage or flight pattern and, in addition, they are normally glimpsed from the pitching deck of a ship or from wind-blasted and rain-lashed shores as they mount upwards briefly from a wave trough before descending out of sight again. Such are the difficulties of getting to grips with sea bird identities that, for many years, the average bird-watcher showed little interest in them. Even so, the birds of the northern seas have always been better known than those of the southern oceans through their more frequent contact with land.

Since the 1960s, a gradual change has come about because of a new interest by leading nations of the world in the southern islands and in Antarctica itself. Permanent stations have been established for, amongst other things, weather monitoring. Teams of scientists are permanently or temporarily stationed in these inhospitable regions for the purpose of studying the ocean and its resources. As an example, the Percy FitzPatrick Institute of African Ornithology in Cape Town has for many years been studying sea-bird life in the seas adjacent to southern Africa. A succession of its researchers has been based on Marion Island, from where periodic visits are made to other islands as far afield as the Tristan da Cunha group.

Much has been learned about the population dynamics, feeding ecologies and breeding of some sea birds. Stemming from this new interest in the southern sea birds, and the increased need for a specific guide to those found in southern African seas, the entire region south to the pack ice has been included in this field guide. Not only does it embrace all sea birds known to reach the shores of southern Africa, but also those that will be seen on or in the vicinity of Tristan da Cunha (Tristan, Nightingale and Inaccessible islands), Gough, Bouvet, Marion and Prince Edward islands. There is a total of 19 additional species, including some land birds. South Africa's territorial waters now extend to 200 nautical miles offshore, and this has led to an increase in sightings of sea birds that now qualify for inclusion in the southern African species list.

IDENTIFYING BIRDS

With the array of birds that can be seen in southern Africa (around 1 000 species), identifying the bird you have seen can be extremely challenging. To this end, you need the right equipment, you need to use the equipment you have correctly and you need to notice the features of the bird and its environment that will lead to an accurate identification.

WHAT YOU NEED TO IDENTIFY BIRDS

Binoculars

A pair of binoculars is an essential part of a bird-watcher's equipment; hardly any bird can be properly studied without it. Many good makes are available and 7 x 30, 8 x 35 or 10 x 40 are recommended. The first figure indicates the magnification and the second, the diameter of the front, or objective, lens.

Generally speaking, the greater the diameter of the objective lens in proportion to the eyepiece, the more light is gathered and transmitted, and so the brighter the image. Many people also use a telescope to study distant, difficult-to-identify species.

Field guides and handbooks

A field guide is the next essential part of the bird-watcher's equipment. The field guide concept originated in the late 1930s in response to the need for portability coupled with ease of reference. First was the now famous series by Roger Tory Peterson, covering the birds of the United States of America. Later the idea caught on in Britain, Europe and elsewhere. For the serious bird-watcher, a field guide is only a supplement to a more comprehensive and informative bird handbook, the latter usually being too bulky and cumbersome for normal fieldwork. The main purpose of a field guide is to help the observer identify a species speedily from an illustration and a brief description of plumage and song. More comprehensive information about the bird may then be sought at leisure from an appropriate handbook.

Bird call recordings

When learning the songs and calls of birds the use of bird-call recordings can help tremendously. A wide range of CDs and mp3s is available and many are linked to this field guide.

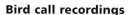

WHAT TO LOOK FOR WHEN IDENTIFYING BIRDS

The following six guidelines will help you to identify a bird; try to memorise them. With practice, they will come to mind automatically when you look at a new bird and will help you to remember its important features. If possible, write what you have seen in a notebook at the time of sighting.

■ Relative size

Compare the bird with common ones that are well known to you. Is it larger or smaller than a sparrow? If larger, is it larger or smaller than a pigeon? If larger, is it larger or smaller than a guineafowl?

| 14–15 cm | 33 cm | 53–58 cm |

■ Bill shape and colour

The shape of a bird's bill is a guide to what it eats and, therefore, to the kind of bird it is. Is its bill short, stout and conical like that of a sparrow, or is it small and slender, long and slender, long and curved, powerful and hooked? What colour is its bill? Many birds have black or dark bills, but some bills are brightly coloured.

Insect-eater

Flower-prober

Ground-prober

Fish-eater

Omnivore

Fruit-eater

Seed-eater

Flesh-eater

■ Length and colour of the bird's legs

Does the bird have unusually long legs, such as are found in many that wade in water or walk in long grass, or short legs as seen in swallows and swifts? Are its legs a distinctive colour?

■ Plumage colours or markings

If the bird has bold markings on its head, wings, body or tail, these should be noted, as should any bright colours. Many birds have white wing-bars or tail-bars; others have distinct eyebrows or breast-bands.

Communal nests of Red-billed Buffalo-weavers in a mixed thornveld habitat.

◼ Habitat

Is it in the garden, in water, in grassland, bushveld or forest? The habitat in which the bird is seen is another important clue to the kind of bird it is (see description of habitats on pp. 26–32).

◼ Activity

Is it walking, hopping, wading or swimming? Does it peck at the ground, feed in the air or in a tree, or probe in the mud? Try to detail its behaviour as closely as possible.

Often the details of a bird's structure, plumage or behaviour are soon forgotten and the observer may spend much time trying to recall them. If these six points are remembered or noted at the time of the observation, an analysis can be made after the bird has flown away.

HOW TO USE THIS BOOK

Once you have used the guidelines above to identify the bird's features, it is time to consult the field guide. Follow the six steps below to identify the bird you have seen accurately. These identification methods are further explained on pp. 14–33.

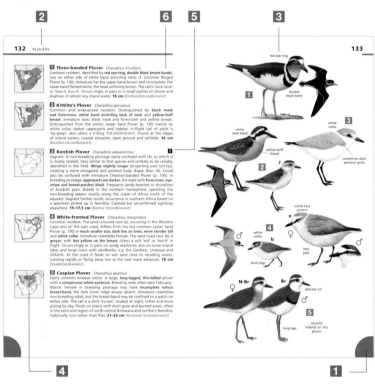

1 Three-banded Plover *Charadrius tricollaris*
Common resident. Identified by **red eye-ring, double black breast-bands**, one on either side of white band encircling neck; cf. Common Ringed Plover (p. 130). Immature has the upper band brown and incomplete, the lower band flecked white, the head uniformly brown. The call is 'wick-wick' or 'tiuu-it, tiuu-it'. Occurs singly, in pairs or in small parties on shores and shallows of almost any inland water. **18 cm** (Driebandstrandkiewiet)

2 Kittlitz's Plover *Charadrius pecuarius*
Common and widespread resident. Distinguished by **black mask and forecrown, white band encircling back of neck and yellow-buff breast**. Immature lacks black mask and forecrown and yellow breast. Distinguished from the similar Lesser Sand Plover (p. 130) mainly by white collar, darker upperparts and habitat. In-flight call of adult a 'tip-peep'; also utters a trilling 'trit-tritritritritrit'. Found at the edges of inland waters, coastal estuaries, open ground and airfields. **16 cm** (Geelborsstrandkiewiet)

3 Kentish Plover *Charadrius alexandrinus*
Vagrant. In non-breeding plumage easily confused with (4), to which it is closely related. Very similar to that species and unlikely to be reliably identified in the field. **Wings slightly longer** (projecting past tail-tip), creating a more elongated and pointed body shape than (4). Could also be confused with immature Chestnut-banded Plover (p. 130). In breeding plumage, **upperparts are darker**, the male with **forecrown, eye-stripe and breast-patches black**. Frequents sandy beaches or shorelines of brackish pans. Breeds in the northern hemisphere, spending the non-breeding season mostly along the coasts of Africa north of the equator. Vagrant further south; occurrence in southern Africa based on a specimen picked up in Namibia. Claimed but unconfirmed sightings elsewhere. **15–17,5 cm** (Kentse Strandkiewiet)

4 White-fronted Plover *Charadrius marginatus*
Common resident. The sand-coloured race (a), occurring in the Western Cape and on the east coast, differs from the less common Lesser Sand Plover (p. 130) in **much smaller size, dark line on lores, more slender bill and white collar**. Immature resembles female. The west coast race (b) is **greyer, with less yellow on the breast**. Utters a soft 'wit' or 'twirit' in flight. Occurs singly or in pairs on sandy seashores; also on some inland lakes and large rivers with sandbanks, e.g. the Zambezi, Limpopo and Olifants. At the coast it feeds on wet sand close to receding waves, running rapidly and flying away low as the next wave advances. **18 cm** (Vaalstrandkiewiet)

5 Caspian Plover *Charadrius asiaticus*
Fairly common summer visitor. A large, **long-legged, thin-billed** plover with a **conspicuous white eyebrow**. Breeding male often seen February–March. Female in breeding plumage may have **incomplete rufous breast-band**, the dark lower edge always absent. Immature resembles non-breeding adult, but the breast-band may be confined to a patch on either side. The call is a shrill 'ku-wit', loudest at night, softer and more piping by day. Flocks on plains with short grass and burned areas, often in the semi-arid region of north-central Botswana and northern Namibia. Habitually runs rather than flies. **21–23 cm** (Asiatiese Strandkiewiet)

1 Using the colour coding (see pp. 14–17), identify in which section of the book you are most likely to find the bird.

2 Using the running head at the top of the page, decide on which page or group of pages you should be looking.

3 Examine the pictures of the birds and decide which looks most like the bird you have seen.

4 Check the selected bird's distribution map and see whether the bird occurs in the area, and whether it is present all year round or only some of the year. Text below the map indicates the bird's status, e.g. endangered, vulnerable, etc.

5 Symbols (see p. 21) indicate whether the bird is endemic/near-endemic/introduced/vagrant/rare.

6 Read the text to pick up additional information and confirm the identification.

1 and **2** WHICH GROUP DOES THE BIRD BELONG TO?

The colour coding in the field guide divides the bird species into 12 distinct groups. By placing the bird you have seen into one of the 12 groups, you immediately limit the number of species you need to consider in determining

Ocean, offshore and Subantarctic birds

Habitat is your best clue to placing birds in this group.
The exceptions are some of the gulls, the African Skimmer and some of the terns, all of which are also seen on inland waters.

EXTRA-LIMITAL SPECIES: Cormorants 34 • **Penguins** 34 •
Storm Petrels 36 • **Diving Petrels** 36 • **Terns** 26 • **Petrels** 38 •
Sheathbills 38 • **Moorhens & Rails** 38 • **Buntings** 40 • **Thrushes** 40
OFFSHORE SPECIES: Penguins 42–45 • **Albatrosses** 46–51 •
Petrels & Fulmars 52–58 • **Prions** 58–60 • **Shearwaters** 60–63 •
Storm Petrels 64–67 • **Boobies & Gannets** 68 • **Tropicbirds** 70 •
Frigatebirds 70 • **Jaegers & Skuas** 72 • **Gulls & Kittiwakes** 74–77 •
Skimmers • 78 • **Terns** 78–85

Inland waterbirds

Habitat is the defining feature once again (see also the next group).

Pelicans 86 • **Cormorants** 88 • **Darters** 108 • **Herons, Egrets
& Bitterns** 90–99 • **Storks** 100–104 • **Hamerkops** 104 •
Flamingos 106 • **Ibises & Spoonbills** 106–108 • **Finfoots** 108

Ducks, wading birds and shorebirds

These birds are also found on inland and coastal waters; the wading birds generally have long legs adapted for feeding in shallow water or on the shoreline.

Geese & Ducks 110–119 • **Greves** 120 • **Coots, Gallinules & Moorhens** 120–123 • **Flufftails, Crakes & Rails** 124–127 • **Painted-Snipes** 128 • **Plovers, Snipes & allies** 128–133 • **Sandpipers and allied waders** 134–146 • **Golden Plovers** 146 • **Jacanas** 148 • **Lapwings** 148–151 • **Oystercatchers** 152 • **Phalaropes** 152 **Crab Plovers** 154 • **Avocets & Stilts** 154

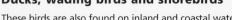

its identity. Once you have located the right group of birds, headings at the tops of pages will tell you which family group (or groups) is dealt with on each page. Use this to find the page that probably features the bird you have seen.

Terrestrial birds

These include the long-legged birds that inhabit grasslands.

Thick-Knees 156 • Pratincoles & Coursers 156–159 • Bustards & Korhaans 160–165 • Cranes 166 • Quails, Francolins & Spurfowl 168–175 • Buttonquails 176 • Guineafowl 176 • Ostriches 178 • Secretarybirds 178

Raptors

Birds of prey all have bills and talons adapted for killing and eating meat.

Vultures 180–185 • Milvus Kites 186 • Snake-Eagles 186–189 • True Eagles 190–199 • Buzzards 200–204 • Goshawks & Sparrowhawks 204–210 • Harriers & Marsh-Harriers 210–213 • Hawks 214–216 • Falcons & Kestrels 216–223

Colourful, medium-sized birds

This group is comprised of colourful, medium-sized birds with distinctive calls.

Sandgrouse 224 • Pigeons & Doves 226–231 • Parrots & Lovebirds 232–234 • Trogons 234 • Turacos & allies 236 • Cuckoos 238–242 • Coucals 242–245

Nocturnal birds

Very distinctive nocturnal birds. Most also have identifying calls.

Owls 246–252 • **Nightjars** 252–257

Aerial feeders, hole-nesters and sociable birds

A diverse group comprising species that catch their prey in flight, such as swifts, swallows and martins; the distinctive mousebirds; the hole-nesting species (barbets, bee-eaters, hornbills and hoopoes); and the honeyguides.

Swallows 258–264 • **Martins** 264–268 • **Swifts** 269–273 • **Mousebirds** 274 • **Bee-eaters** 274–279 • **Kingfishers** 280–285 • **Rollers** 286 • **Wood Hoopoes** 288 • **Hoopoes** 288 • **Hornbills** 290–294 • **Barbets & Tinkerbirds** 294–298 • **Woodpeckers** 298–302 • **Wrynecks** 302 • **Honeyguides & Honeybirds** 304–306 • **Creepers** 306 • **Broadbills** 302 • **Pittas** 306

Insect-eaters

The slender-billed, insect-eating birds of this group have similarities of shape and behaviour.

Larks 308–319 • **Long-billed Larks** 316 • **Sparrow-Larks** 320 • **Pipits, Longclaws & Wagtails** 322–333 • **Drongos** 334 • **Cuckooshrikes** 336 • **Crows** 338 • **Orioles** 338–341 • **Bulbuls & allies** 342–345 • **Tits** 346 • **Babblers** 348 • **Thrushes, Chats & Robins** 350–371

Insect-eaters, fruit-eaters and omnivores

This group contains a variety of insectivorous, frugivorous or omnivorous species that can be recognised from their jizz.

Warblers & allies 372–388 • **Cisticolas** 388–397 • **Prinias** 398–400 • **Flycatchers** 400–405 • **Batises & small Flycatchers** 406–409 • **Shrikes** 410–414 • **Boubous** 414 • **Tchagras** 416 • **Bush-Shrikes** 418–420 • **Helmet-Shrikes** 420 • **Starlings** 422–427

Specialised feeders

This is a small group of specialised feeders. The oxpeckers have very distinctive feeding behaviour, white-eyes are specialised leaf-gleaners, and the other species all feed on nectar.

Sugarbirds 428 • **Oxpeckers** 428 • **Sunbirds** 430–441 • **White-Eyes** 442

Seed-eaters

The seed-eaters are distinguished by their strong, conical bills.

Weavers, Sparrows & Queleas 442–455 • **Widowbirds & Bishops** 456–459 • **Finches, Waxbills, Twinspots & Mannikins** 460–470 • **Cuckoo Weavers** 470 • **Whydahs** 472–474 • **Indigobirds** 476–483 • **Canaries, Siskins & Buntings** 476–483

3 COLOUR PLATES

Use the colour illustrations to find the bird that looks most like what you have seen (watch out for colour variations). The birds have been painted, so far as is possible, in such a way as to reveal their characteristic shapes, colours, markings and stance (or 'jizz' as it is known in birding parlance). Where several species on a plate closely resemble each other, they are all drawn in a similar stance to facilitate direct comparison. All the main figures on a plate are in approximate proportion to each other and, wherever possible, all birds in a family are drawn to the same proportions whether on the same plate or not. In a few cases it has been necessary to depict larger birds of a family to a smaller scale than the others on the same plate. Secondary figures showing birds in flight or performing some other characteristic action are not drawn to the same proportions as the main figures.

It is customary in bird books to present species in strict taxonomic order, that is to say, in the order used by the national checklist. This usually means that one starts with the ostrich and the grebes, continues with sea birds, herons, ducks, and so on, and finishes with canaries and buntings. In this field guide, this order of presentation has been applied with elasticity. Because its basic purpose is to help with bird identification, and in the knowledge that many users may not be familiar with the various bird families and their characteristics, some species that have a visual resemblance to birds of another family have been illustrated with those they most closely resemble.

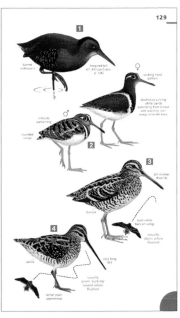

Symbols used on the colour illustrations

♂	denotes MALE
♀	denotes FEMALE
J	denotes a juvenile or immature bird
Br	denotes breeding plumage
N-Br	denotes non-breeding plumage

4 DISTRIBUTION MAPS

Each bird description is accompanied by a small distribution map showing the areas in which it is likely to be found. These species ranges are rough guides only, based on present-day knowledge of the bird's occurrence.

All maps are two-toned: each species' relative abundance is indicated by dark pink (common) and light pink (less common). In some cases, light pink may also indicate where a species occurs during part of the year only. In certain cases, notably among the waterbirds, light-pink areas have been added to indicate temporary range extensions that occur under favourable weather conditions.

Vagrants are indicated by small open circles, while the known local ranges of isolated populations are shown with coloured spots. Arrows have been liberally applied to highlight small populations or vagrants. For pelagic species, distribution is given for a wide oceanic region.

Because birds are highly mobile creatures, they frequently appear in the most unlikely places and one should be ever watchful for species occurring beyond the range shown on the maps. Comparison with the master maps (p. 20) will provide an accurate key to the locations shown on the distribution maps or in the text.

Key to distribution maps

OCEAN DISTRIBUTION
The broad area of colour over the ocean indicates a bird of the open seas, rarely found along the coast.

COASTAL DISTRIBUTION
The narrow band indicates a bird found along the coast.

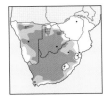

POPULATION DENSITY
The dark area indicates where a bird is more common, the pale area indicates where it is less common or ranges for only part of the year.

OPEN CIRCLES AND ARROWS
A circle indicates where a bird has been recorded but is not regular. An arrow points to an area where there is a known population, be it resident or visiting.

SUBANTARCTIC REGION
An arrow indicates where there is a known resident population. The other distribution indicators apply as for southern Africa.

Southern African subregion

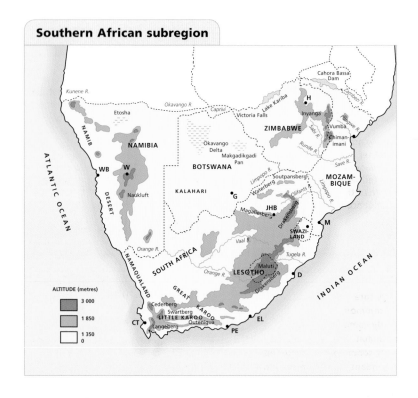

ALTITUDE (metres)

3 000
1 850
1 350
0

Subantarctic region

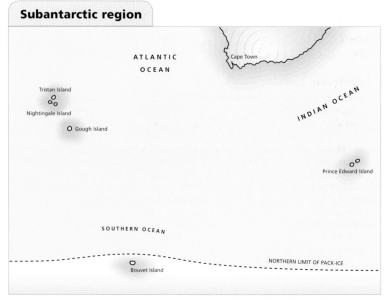

5 STATUS OF THE SPECIES

The status of a bird as an endangered species (near threatened, vulnerable, endangered or critically endangered) is indicated below the distribution map.

NEAR THREATENED	likely to become endangered in the near future
VULNERABLE	high risk of endangerment in the wild
ENDANGERED	high risk of extinction in the wild
CRITICALLY ENDANGERED	extremely high risk of extinction in the wild

Following the bird's names is a brief statement about its relative abundance, whether it is rare or endemic, and whether it is a seasonal visitor, a resident or a vagrant. Endemic, near-endemic, introduced, vagrant and rare species are marked with symbols, as shown below. (Note that terms indicating abundance relate to the bird's status within its preferred or normal habitat, and not to its abundance in the entire region.)

E	endemic: found exclusively in the area indicated
N E	near-endemic: almost exclusively inhabits the area indicated
I	introduced from other parts of the world by humans
V	vagrant: not normally seen in southern Africa
R	rare: recorded 10 times or less in any year in suitable habitat
Very rare	recorded 5 times or less in any 5-year period
Uncommon	recorded 30 times or less a month in suitable habitat
Fairly common	recorded 1–10 times a day in suitable habitat
Common	recorded 10–50 times a day in suitable habitat
Very common	recorded 50–100 times a day in suitable habitat
Abundant	recorded 100 times or more a day in suitable habitat
Seasonal	seen at certain times of the year only
Winter	April–August
Summer	September–March
Localised	seen only in restricted areas of suitable habitat
Resident	breeds in southern Africa
Visitor	non-breeding (Palearctic or intra-Africa migrant)

E Endemic species

Of special interest are the endemics: those species found in southern Africa and nowhere else. There are 100 endemics in the region and 76 near-endemics (species whose distribution extends just beyond southern Africa).

African Black
   Oystercatcher
African Penguin
African Rock Pipit
Agulhas Long-billed Lark
Ant-eating Chat
Bank Cormorant
Barlow's Lark
Barratt's Warbler
Black Harrier
Black-eared Sparrowlark
Black-headed Canary

Blue Crane
Blue Korhaan
Botha's Lark
Brown Scrub Robin
Buff-streaked Chat
Burchell's Courser
Bush Blackcap
Cape Batis
Cape Bulbul
Cape Canary
Cape Clapper Lark
Cape Grassbird

Cape Long-billed Lark
Cape Longclaw
Cape Parrot
Cape Rock jumper
Cape Rock-Thrush
Cape Shoveler
Cape Siskin
Cape Spurfowl
Cape Sugarbird
Cape Vulture
Cape Weaver
Cape White-Eye

Chirinda Apalis
Chorister Robin-Chat
Cinnamon-breasted
   Warbler
Crowned Cormorant
Denham's Bustard
Drakensberg Prinia
Drakensberg Rockjumper
Drakensberg Siskin
Dune Lark
Eastern Long-billed Lark
Fairy Flycatcher
Fiscal Flycatcher
Forest Buzzard
Forest Canary
Greater Double-collared
   Sunbird
Grey Tit
Grey-winged Francolin
Ground Woodpecker
Gurney's Sugarbird
Hartlaub's Gull
Jackal Buzzard

Karoo Eremomela
Karoo Korhaan
Karoo Lark
Karoo Long-billed Lark
Karoo Prinia
Karoo Scrub Robin
Karoo Thrush
Kimberley Pipit
Knysna Turaco
Knysna Warbler
Knysna Woodpecker
Large-billed Lark
Layard's Warbler
Melodious Lark
Namaqua Warbler
Neergaard's Sunbird
Orange River White-Eye
Orange-breasted Sunbird
Pied Starling
Pink-throated Twinspot
Protea Canary
Red Lark
Roberts's Warbler

Rudd's Lark
Rufous-eared Warbler
Sclater's Lark
Sentinel Rock-Thrush
Short-clawed Lark
Sickle-winged Chat
Sociable Weaver
South African Shelduck
Southern Bald Ibis
Southern Black Korhaan
Southern Boubou
Southern Double-collared
   Sunbird
Southern Pied Babbler
Southern Tchagra
Swee Waxbill
Victorin's Warbler
White-backed Mousebird
White-bellied Bustard
White-quilled Bustard
White-throated Robin-Chat
Yellow-breasted Pipit

N E Near-endemic species (including breeding endemics)

Acacia Pied Barbet
African Red-eyed Bulbul
Ashy Tit
Barred Wren-Warbler
Benguela Long-billed Lark
Black-chested Prinia
Black-faced Babbler
Bokmakierie
Boulder Chat
Bradfield's Hornbill
Bradfield's Swift
Burchell's Sandgrouse
Burchell's Starling
Burchell's Coucal
Cape Bunting
Cape Cormorant (BE)
Cape Gannet (BE)
Cape Penduline Tit
Cape Sparrow
Cape Starling
Carp's Black Tit
Chat Flycatcher
Chestnut-vented Warbler
Cloud Cisticola
Crimson-breasted Shrike
Damara Red-billed
   Hornbill
Damara Tern (BE)

Double-banded
   Sandgrouse
Dusky Sunbird
Eastern Clapper Lark
Fawn-coloured Lark
Gray's Lark
Great Sparrow
Grey-backed Cisticola
Grey-backed Sparrow Lark
Hartlaub's Spurfowl
Herero Chat
Kalahari Scrub Robin
Karoo Chat
Lark-like Bunting
Lemon-breasted Canary
Ludwig's Bustard
Marico Flycatcher
Monotonous Lark
Monteiro's Hornbill
Mountain Wheatear
Namaqua Sandgrouse
Natal Spurfowl
Olive Bush-Shrike
Pale-winged Starling
Pink-billed Lark
Pririt Batis
Red-billed Spurfowl
Red-crested Korhaan

Red-headed Finch
Rockrunner
Rosy-faced Lovebird
Rudd's Apalis
Rufous-winged Cisticola
Rüppell's Parrot
Sabota Lark
Scaly-feathered Weaver
Shaft-tailed Whydah
Short-toed Rock-Thrush
South African Cliff
   Swallow (BE)
Southern Pale Chanting
   Goshawk
Southern White-crowned
   Shrike
Southern Yellow-billed
   Hornbill
Spike-heeled Lark
Stark's Lark
Swainson's Spurfowl
Tractrac Chat
White-tailed Shrike
White-throated Canary
Woodward's Batis
Yellow Canary

■ Introduced species

Many birds have been introduced into southern Africa in past years, but only 11 species survive today. They are:

Chukar Partridge	Common Starling	Mallard
Common Chaffinch	House Crow	Mute Swan
Common Myna	House Sparrow	Rose-ringed Parakeet
Common Pigeon	Indian Peafowl	

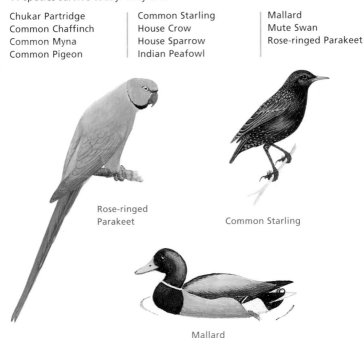

Rose-ringed Parakeet

Common Starling

Mallard

6 SPECIES DESCRIPTIONS

The final step is to read the text about the bird you think you have identified to check whether the description matches its behaviour, call and habitat. The species descriptions have several components.

Status   English common name(s)   Scientific name

Description

3 Blue-cheeked Bee-eater *Merops persicus*
Uncommon to locally common summer visitor. Distinguished from (4) by **pale blue forehead, eyebrows and cheeks**, and **yellow-and-brown throat and upper breast**. Told from European Bee-eater (p. 276) by green (not gold-and-brown) mantle. A large bee-eater of generally **green appearance**. The short, liquid call is 'prruik' or 'prree-oo, prree-oo'. Usually occurs in small flocks near large rivers, dams, floodplains and coastal grassland, where it often hawks from a dead tree standing in water. **27–33 cm** (Blouwangbyvreter)

Voice

Habitat

Measurement   Afrikaans common name   Behaviour

Bird names

In the descriptive text for each species, on the page facing the illustration of that species, the bird's common English name is given first in bold letters. In some cases a second common English name in wide use is also given in brackets. Immediately following the common name is the scientific name by which the species is known throughout the world regardless of language. This appears in italic type and consists of the bird's genus and species, in that order. The Afrikaans common name is given in brackets at the end of the text.

Scientific names call for some explanation for the benefit of those unaccustomed to them. The accepted common names of species tend to vary from country to country. Therefore, based on the international system of scientific nomenclature originated in the 18th century by the Swedish naturalist, Carl Linnaeus, all animals (and this includes birds) have been placed in clear groups or taxa, using names based on Latin or ancient Greek, which obviates any risk of confusion. No two birds can have the same binomial (two-part) scientific name. First, all animal life is placed in classes, and birds belong to the class Aves, mammals to the class Mammalia, insects to Insecta, and so on. These classes are then divided into major groups known as orders. The orders are subdivided into families, the families into genera (genus is the singular), and the genera into one or more species. A species can further be divided into races or subspecies.

When the above system of scientific nomenclature is applied to the common House Sparrow, its credentials look like this:

Class:	Aves
Order:	Passeriformes
Family:	Passeridae
Genus:	*Passer*
Species:	*domesticus*

Description of the species

This is a brief description of the bird, enlarging on what is shown in the illustration and, where possible, comparing it with other species with similar plumage. It is important to be familiar with certain terms used to describe a bird's anatomy. These are clearly indicated in the illustrations opposite.

Voice

After the description is a rendition of the bird's call or song, written as closely as possible to the sound heard. If it cannot be written, a general description is given of the type of song uttered. The transcription of birdsong into words is no easy matter, and no two people hear it or describe it in quite the same way. These descriptions should, therefore, be regarded as approximations only, and reference to one of the popular bird-call recordings is recommended.

Southern Red Bishop (p. 456):
'zik-zik-zik... ayzayzayzayzay'

Bird anatomy

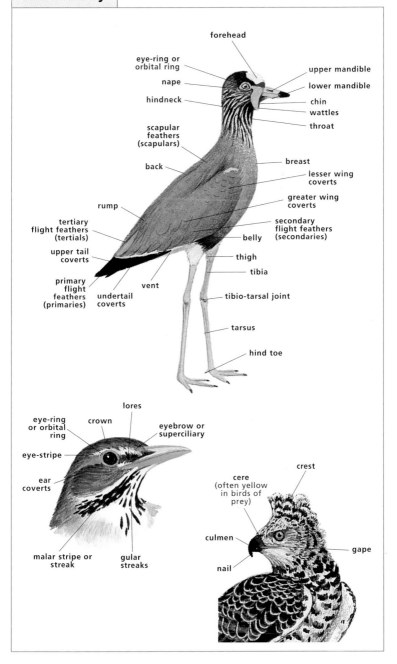

forehead

eye-ring or orbital ring

upper mandible

nape

lower mandible

hindneck

chin

wattles

throat

scapular feathers (scapulars)

breast

back

lesser wing coverts

greater wing coverts

rump

secondary flight feathers (secondaries)

tertiary flight feathers (tertials)

belly

upper tail coverts

thigh

tibia

primary flight feathers (primaries)

vent

undertail coverts

tibio-tarsal joint

tarsus

hind toe

lores

crown

eye-ring or orbital ring

eyebrow or superciliary

eye-stripe

crest

ear coverts

cere (often yellow in birds of prey)

culmen

gape

malar stripe or streak

gular streaks

nail

Bird habitats

The bird's usual habitat is described next and provides a vital clue to its usual haunts. All birds have a preferred habitat, often with a specialised niche within that habitat, and many will disappear entirely if their habitat is destroyed or degraded, because they are unable to adapt to different living conditions. Thus, in order to see many bird species it is necessary to know and seek their preferred habitat, often a very restricted area or one difficult to access. There are several major habitat types in southern Africa.

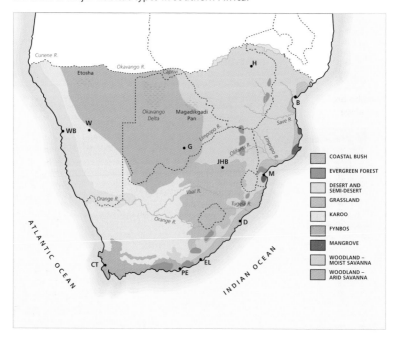

WOODLAND: The moist and arid tree savannas of southern Africa together make up its richest bird habitat. This variable habitat, covering about three-quarters of the region and supporting most of its bird species, can be further divided into areas known as bushveld, woodland, savanna, mopane-veld and miombo. Bushveld is a somewhat loose term applied to the woody veld found over much of the far northeastern lowveld areas of southern Africa. It is comprised of various types of deciduous, small-tree woodland and mixed bush varieties and may include such diverse vegetation as scrub mopane, mixed thorn and broad-leaved bushes and even small patches of pure thornbush. The presence of all these bush types is dictated by variations in soil types, so that one sees frequent changes, each type intergrading with another. Woodland is made up of broad-leaved trees, usually deciduous, with wider spacing than is found in bushveld, so that their canopies do not touch. Perhaps the richest woodland type in terms of bird populations and species numbers is miombo woodland, a broad-leaved biome in which deciduous trees, especially *Brachystegia* and *Julbernardia* species, are dominant. In miombo woodland, a major veld type of Zimbabwe above 1 200 m, the tree canopies do actually touch. However, the trees are so spaced as to allow sufficient sunlight to penetrate for the rich growth of grasses and shrubs.

Miombo broad-leaved woodland in Zimbabwe

White Stork in Mopane-veld, Kruger National Park

Mixed woodland in southern Botswana

Bushveld near the Limpopo River, a common mixed woodland

Mature thorn savanna, a woodland habitat on Kalahari sands

Coastal bush in the Eastern Cape

COASTAL BUSH: This consists of dense evergreen vegetation with thick undergrowth and some tall trees. It grows on sandy soils in a narrow strip along the east and south coasts and shares many characteristics and bird species with evergreen forest.

FOREST: Throughout Africa indigenous forests are being increasingly cut back for fringe agriculture, or the trees felled for charcoal production. These evergreen, animal-rich regions have taken millions of years to reach their present-day climax, and are irreplaceable. As they disappear the birds that depend on them, and much other animal life besides, disappear too. Pockets of riverine evergreen forest occur in the midst of many other, more arid, habitats. Alien plantations of eucalyptus or pine trees should not be confused with indigenous evergreen forests.

Evergreen forest interior

Commercial plantation in Limpopo province, a man-made forest

Riverine forest in Mpumalanga province

Dune forest, an evergreen forest habitat surrounding a coastal lagoon

FYNBOS: Fynbos is home to a number of endemic bird species, including Victorin's Warbler, Cape Sugarbird, Orange-breasted Sunbird, Protea Canary and many other species with a wider habitat tolerance. Unfortunately runaway fires tend to devastate large areas of fynbos almost annually.

Montane fynbos (above) and coastal fynbos (below) in the Western Cape

Montane grassland interspersed with evergreen forest, southern African escarpment

GRASSLAND: There are wide expanses of grassland, where trees are sparse or absent, in the central high-altitude regions of southern Africa. These apparently wide expanses of unspoiled 'grassveld' have become a rapidly diminishing biome through the spread of crop farming, human settlements, multi-carriageway roads, opencast mining, commercial forestry and other industries. Montane grassland, an apparently pristine, inaccessible and inhospitable region for settlement or farming, has also been reduced in recent years by the often ill-judged encroachment of commercial timber plantations with their inevitable network of access roads. Steep grass slopes on shallow soils that were once held stable are now exposed to soil erosion after heavy rains following clear-felling.

A typical Karoo landscape

KAROO: The semi-arid south-central and west-central areas are comprised of stony plains, either flat or undulating and sparsely dotted with succulent plants, shrubs and small trees. Rocky, scrub-covered, flat-topped hills may also be present. Annual rainfall is 150–300 mm except in the more arid regions where it may be as little as 50–200 mm and where desert grasses predominate. Birdlife is mostly comprised of korhaans, larks, warblers and canaries plus raptors, including Verreaux's and Martial eagles and kestrels.

SEMI-DESERT: As typified by the semi-arid scrub and bush savanna of southwestern Namibia, it is home to a surprisingly wide variety of birds, both resident and seasonal. Residents most in evidence are the White-quilled Bustard, Pale Chanting Goshawk, Greater Kestrel, Double-banded Courser, Cape Crow, African Red-eyed Bulbul, Capped Wheatear and Marico Flycatcher. During summer Red-backed and Lesser Grey shrikes, Caspian Plovers and various migrant warblers arrive. Since the region suffers from high temperatures and a serious lack of standing water it is surprising that so many insectivorous birds are able to make a living in the region. The secret is that the numerous stunted broad-leaved bushes harbour a thriving insect community that provides adequate moisture for those that feed on it.

Semi-desert in Namibia

Namibian dune desert (foreground) and stony desert intersected by riverine forest

WETLANDS: The inland waters of southern Africa, including rivers, streams, dams, pans, estuaries, marshes and floodlands, are one of the most vulnerable habitat types. They are all too frequently drained or filled for industrial development or agriculture. Wetlands are very productive for the birdwatcher.

Floodlands, a wetland habitat

A pan, a temporary wetland habitat

MANGROVE: Mangroves are a threatened habitat confined to isolated pockets on the northeast and east coasts. These specialised communities of estuarine and intertidal fauna and flora are dominated by mangrove trees.

Mangroves in northern Mozambique, an east-coastal wetland habitat

COASTLINE: The southern African coastline stretches for over 5 000 km and supports a wide variety of resident and migrant bird populations.

A river estuary, a coastal wetland habitat

Intertidal zone of a south coastal habitat

Behaviour

Where relevant there is a description of the typical behaviour of the species, which is often a useful guide to its identity. Many species that closely resemble one another can be accurately identified by small traits of behaviour, such as wing-flicking, tail-wagging or by their display procedure.

Lilac-breasted Rollers perform a tumbling, rolling display flight.

Male Southern Masked Weavers often flutter their wings excitedly at their nests.

Measurement

Size is often difficult to gauge but the measurements are useful for comparison. It is a good idea to remember the size of three common birds and then to use that as a yardstick when looking at the sizes in the book: a House Sparrow is 14–15 cm, a Common Pigeon is 33 cm and a Helmeted Guineafowl is 53–58 cm (see p. 10).

The measurements given for each bird in this field guide represent those of a dead bird lying flat on a table, neither stretched nor compressed. If the bird has long legs that project beyond the tail, these are included in the total measurement. In a few cases only, where a species has seasonally long tail-plumes, the total measurement with and without the tail is given. The reason for measurements being taken in this way is that it is not practicable to measure a bird while it is standing, perched or swimming because various species hold themselves in different ways at different times. A long-necked bird may hold its head and neck outstretched or tucked in, some birds have a hunched posture while others of similar size may habitually stand erect.

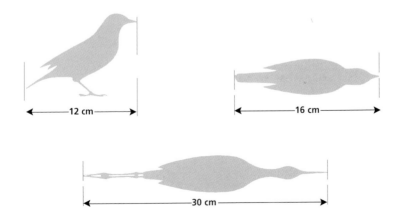

12 cm

16 cm

30 cm

EXTRALIMITAL SUBANTARCTIC BIRDS
(This section does not include birds that are vagrant to the subantarctic region.)

CORMORANTS
Web-footed, long-necked, hook-billed, fish-eating waterbirds that hunt their prey under water, and surface to swallow it. They swim with body partially submerged and habitually stand out of water with wings spread. Normally silent. See also p. 88.

1 Imperial Cormorant *Phalacrocorax atriceps*
Common on Marion Island. **The only cormorant in the subantarctic region.** Gregarious; breeds in small colonies on rocky headlands and low cliffs. **61 cm** (Keiserduiker)

PENGUINS
Flightless marine birds of the southern oceans. Characterised by **stocky build, flipper-like wings, short legs** and an **erect stance**. They dive to considerable depths in pursuit of fish. On the surface they swim with most of the body submerged, head held high. See also pp. 42–44.

NEAR THREATENED

2 Gentoo Penguin *Pygoscelis papua*   **V**
Common, but vagrant to southern Africa. **Bright red bill, orange feet** and **triangular white ear-patches** diagnostic. Immature resembles adult but has duller bill and grey-mottled throat. Occurs in small breeding colonies on Marion and Prince Edward islands. Unlike other penguins shows fear of humans and makes off when approached. **76 cm** (Witoorpikkewyn)

3 Chinstrap Penguin *Pygoscelis antarcticus*
Common. **Thin black line across throat** diagnostic at all ages. Found with (4) in small groups in pack ice. Very common breeder on Bouvet Island; vagrant to Marion Island. **76 cm** (Kenbandpikkewyn)

4 Adelie Penguin *Pygoscelis adeliae*
Common. Identified by **short, stubby bill, black head** and **white eye-rings**. At long range immature resembles (3), but the black of the face extends below the eyes. Most often seen in small groups in the pack ice, resting out of water or porpoising at speed through the water. **71 cm** (Adéliepikkewyn)

5 Emperor Penguin *Aptenodytes forsteri*
Uncommon. **Largest penguin in the world.** Distinguished from smaller King Penguin (p. 44; breeds on Marion and Prince Edward islands) by **creamy yellow, not orange, patches on sides of head** and **shorter, more decurved bill**. Confined to the ice shelf and pack ice within the Antarctic; rarely seen at sea. Mostly found singly or in small groups. **112 cm** (Keiserpikkewyn)

N-Br

1

Br

white ear-patch
extends over cap

2

orange
feet

mostly white
face

thin black
chin-strap

3

creamy
yellow
ear-patch

decurved
bill

5

white
eye-ring

short
bill

J

dark
face

4

STORM PETRELS

Swallow-sized petrels of generally dark appearance, some with white rumps or underparts, all with **long, delicate legs**. They fly with a bat-like motion or an erratic bounding motion, or with more direct, swallow-like movement. Many **feed from the water's surface with feet pattering in the sea, and appear to walk on the water**. Specific identification is difficult except at close range. See also pp. 64–66.

1 Grey-backed Storm Petrel   *Garrodia nereis*   Ⓡ

Uncommon in offshore waters at Gough, Marion and Prince Edward islands. **Dark head and flight feathers** with **ash-grey back and rump**. Only storm petrel in the region with uniformly grey back and rump; cf. (2). Usually solitary. Flight swallow-like; hovers buoyantly when feeding and skips from side to side low over the water. **17 cm** (Grysrugstormswael)

2 White-faced Storm Petrel   *Pelagodroma marina*   Ⓡ

Common offshore at Tristan group. Only storm petrel in the region with **white throat and breast** and **distinctive head markings**. Pale grey rump (not white as in most other storm petrels) contrasts with dark back. **Legs very long and projecting beyond tail**. Occurs in small groups of 2–4 that fly in ships' bow waves, and has a **peculiar, fast swinging action** as it skips and trails its long legs through the waves. **21 cm** (Witwangstormswael)

DIVING PETRELS

Very small, short-necked, short-winged and short-tailed sea birds. They fly close to the water's surface with rapid wing beats, bouncing off the waves like flying fish or **plunging through them** with no perceptible change in wing beats or speed. When settled on the water, they float high like grebes (p. 120) and take off after a short run across the surface.

3 Common Diving Petrel   *Pelecanoides urinatrix*

Common resident on Tristan group, Marion and Prince Edward islands. **At sea indistinguishable from (4)**, differing mainly in bill shape and size (see illustrations). Otherwise seen as small black-and-white birds with fast, direct flight on **short, whirring wings**. Occurs singly or in small groups around islands. **20 cm** (Gewone Duikstormvoël)

4 South Georgian Diving Petrel   *Pelecanoides georgicus*

Common resident on Marion and Prince Edward islands. **At sea indistinguishable from (3)**; cf. bill illustrations. At sea behaviour identical to (3). Breeds at higher elevations than (3) on islands, usually on non-vegetated cinder cones, where it digs small, rat-like tunnels deep into the scoria. **19 cm** (Kleinduikstormvoël)

TERNS

Smaller than gulls, with more slender proportions. Most species have **forked tails**. They plunge-dive for fish. See also pp. 78–84.

5 Kerguelen Tern   *Sterna virgata*

Resident on Marion and Prince Edward islands. **Darker grey** than Arctic Tern (p. 82), with **grey tail, grey underwings** and **shorter, thinner bill**. Immature darker and more heavily barred than immature Antarctic Tern. **Flight buoyant**; cf. *Chlidonias* terns (p. 84). Regularly feeds on insects taken from the ground on open grassy plains. **31 cm** (Kerguelensterretjie)

NEAR THREATENED

contrasting ash-grey rump

1

pale grey rump

very long legs protrude beyond tail

distinctive head markings

2

white underwing coverts

white underparts

dark head

white undertail coverts

short, thin bill

5

cf. Arctic and Antarctic terns (p. 82)

grey underwings

Br

N-Br

3

hard to distinguish at sea, and bill shape differences discernible only at close range

4

3 & 4

dives right through waves

short wings

PETRELS

Pelagic birds ranging in size from the tiny prions (15 cm) to the giant petrels and small albatrosses. See also pp. 52–60.

1 **Snow Petrel**   *Pagodroma nivea*
Common in pack ice and adjacent seas. **Unmistakable, all-white bird.** Flight rapid over sea and ice. More agile on land than other petrels. Sometimes runs over pack ice in the manner of a shorebird. Breeds on Bouvet Island. **34 cm** (Witstormvoël)

SHEATHBILLS

White, pigeon-like, scavenging birds of the southern islands and ice floes. They fly laboriously and reluctantly, but they can swim.

2 **Black-faced Sheathbill**   *Chionis minor*
Common resident on Marion and Prince Edward islands. Told by its **plump, white appearance**, with **black bill and facial skin** and **pink legs**; cf. (3). Frequents penguin rookeries and grassy coastal plains in pairs or small groups. Feeds on penguin corpses, eggs and regurgitated food, which it obtains by disturbing penguins feeding their young. **38 cm** (Kleinskedebek)

3 **Snowy Sheathbill**   *Chionis albus*   **V**
Differs from the Black-faced Sheathbill (p. 38) in **pink cere, yellow bill with black tip** and **grey legs**. A conspicuous terrestrial scavenger from the Antarctic, from where it migrates northwards to the southern tip of South America. Unafraid of humans. Birds recorded in our region have most probably been ship-assisted. **40 cm** (Grootskedebek)

MOORHENS AND RAILS

Smallish, long-legged, large-footed, mainly terrestrial or water-associated birds. See also pp. 120–122, 128.

VULNERABLE

4 **Gough Island Moorhen**   *Gallinula comeri*
Common on Gough Island; reintroduced to Tristan Island following past extirpation. Similar to Common Moorhen (p. 122) but has **red (not yellow) legs**. Most frequent on the coastal plateau; but more often heard than seen. Very secretive; keeps within thick tangles of tree fern and bracken to avoid predation by skuas (p. 72). Wings small but can flap for a short distance when disturbed. **27 cm** (Goughwaterhoender)

5 **Inaccessible Island Rail**   *Atlantisia rogersi*   **E**
Common endemic on Inaccessible Island. The smallest living flightless bird. Unmistakable; the **only small rail on the island**. Very vocal, the call 'pseep' heard all over the island. Individuals frequently glimpsed as they **race, rodent-like, between tussock clumps**. Inquisitive, coming into open areas to inspect unusual objects. **17 cm** (Inaccessible-riethaan)

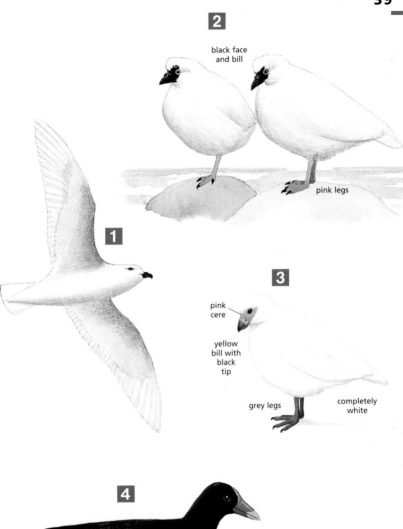

2

black face
and bill

pink legs

1

3

pink
cere

yellow
bill with
black
tip

grey legs

completely
white

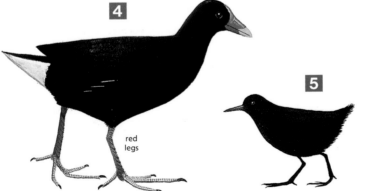

4

red
legs

5

BUNTINGS

The so-called buntings of the Tristan group and Gough Island differ from mainland buntings (p. 482) in several ways, being more closely related to the Fringillidae of South America.

VULNERABLE

1 Inaccessible Island Finch *Nesospiza acunhae* and Nightingale Island Finch *Nesospiza questi*

Common resident. Confined to Inaccessible and Nightingale islands. Distinguished from (3) by **smaller, thinner bill.** Song is a melodious twittering or chirping 'chickory-chikky', followed by a wheezy 'tweeyer'. Birds on Inaccessible Island have larger bills and are more buffy on the breast. Pairs or small flocks forage on the ground or clamber over *Phylica* bushes in search of insects. **16 cm** (Inaccessible/Nightingale-streepkoppie)

CRITICALLY ENDANGERED

2 Gough Bunting (Gough Finch) *Rowettia goughensis*

Common resident on Gough Island, where it is the only bunting. **Sexes markedly different.** Immature resembles female, but more richly coloured (orange-buff). Has a penetrating 'tissik' call; utters a soft 'pseep' while feeding. Pairs and small groups forage on the ground or clamber over tussocks and *Phylica* bushes. Inquisitive and unafraid of humans, but dives for cover when a skua passes overhead. **16 cm** (Goughstreepkoppie)

VULNERABLE

3 Wilkins' Bunting (Wilkins' Finch) *Nesospiza wilkinsi*

Common resident on Inaccessible and Nightingale islands. Occurs alongside (1) but is **more heavily built** and has **a massive, thick bill** used for cracking open hard *Phylica* nuts. The call of Nightingale Island birds is a clear 'tweet-twee-yeer, tweet-tweeyer'. Inaccessible Island birds have a similar but harsher call. Occurs mostly in the *Phylica* bush and tree-fern zone; less often in open grassy and tussock areas. **18 cm** (Wilkinsstreepkoppie)

THRUSHES

Largely terrestrial, **insectivorous** birds. The sexes are alike. See also pp. 350–352.

NEAR THREATENED

4 Tristan Thrush *Nesocichla eremita*

Common resident on Tristan, Inaccessible and Nightingale islands. Unmistakable **orange-brown thrush with heavy overlay of dark brown blotches, the wings showing much orange at rest and in flight.** Immature has more orange spotting and streaking on the upperparts and smaller, more clearly defined spots on the underparts. Birds on Nightingale Island have a more streaky breast. The song is 'chissik, chissik, trrtkk, swee, swee, swee' or 'pseeeooee, pseeeooee, pseeeooee, pseep-tee'. It hides beneath canopies of *Phylica* bushes. Found in clearings in undergrowth where it hops about with typical thrush-like stance, turning over moss and leaf litter in search of food. Birds on Tristan Island are more secretive than those on Inaccessible and Nightingale islands. **22 cm** (Tristanlyster)

1 streaked, thin bill, slender body

only bunting on Gough Island

black lores, ♂, black bib, plain

2 ♀, heavily marked

3 thick bill, heavily built

orange edges on wing-feathers, **4**, dense blotches

BIRDS OF SOUTHERN AFRICA

PENGUINS

Flightless marine birds of the southern oceans. They are characterized by **stocky build, flipper-like wings, short legs** and, **on land, an erect stance**. They walk with a shuffling gait or, on rough terrain, a series of hops and slides in which the bill and stiff tail may be used as props. On snow and ice penguins may lie prone and propel themselves with their feet and flippers. In water the flippers are used in an oar-like action, and the feet as an aid to steering. They dive to considerable depths in pursuit of fish. **On the surface they swim with most of the body submerged, head held high.** Colours basically black and white. Sexes are alike.

VULNERABLE / ENDANGERED

1 Rockhopper Penguin *Eudyptes chrysocome* **V**

Vagrant. Distinguished by **short, stubby red bill** and **pale yellow stripe** from in front of the eyes to the nape, where it ends in a **shaggy plume**. Differs from (2) in **plain black forehead**, wholly dark rump and fairly stiff lateral head-plumes. Individuals, usually moulting birds, occasionally seen ashore on southern mainland coast (c. 50 records); otherwise not normally at sea in southern African waters. A summer breeder on Tristan group, Marion and Prince Edward islands. Sometimes considered to be three separate species: Western Rockhopper Penguin (*E. chrysocome*), Eastern Rockhopper Penguin (*E. filholi*) and Northern Rockhopper Penguin (*E. moseleyi*), which are distinguished by the patterns on the undersides of the flippers. **61 cm** (Geelkuifpikkewyn)

VULNERABLE

2 Macaroni Penguin *Eudyptes chrysolophus* **V**

Rare vagrant. Distinguished from (1) by **more robust bill** and **orange-yellow eyebrow plumes** that meet on the forehead. The plumes are **loose and floppy**. At sea distinguished from (1) with difficulty; however, in addition to the plumes, the **pale, fleshy sides of the gape** and **white rump-spot** are diagnostic. Immature differs from immature of (1) in yellow stripe starting above eye (not in front of eye). At sea utters a harsh, nasal bark. A few individuals ashore on southern mainland coast, but not normally seen in southern African waters. Summer breeder on Bouvet, Marion and Prince Edward islands. **71 cm** (Langkuifpikkewyn)

3 Little Penguin *Eudyptula minor* **V**

Rare vagrant. World's smallest penguin. Easily identified by its **white or silvery iris** and **indigo upperparts**. Could be confused with dark-backed juvenile African Penguin (p. 44), which is much larger and has a dark eye. Immature has paler upperparts and greyish chin and throat. On the breeding grounds utters soft cat-like mewing, trumpeting calls and high-pitched screams. Breeds along the coasts of southern Australia, Tasmania, New Zealand and the Chatham Islands. Also recorded in Chile, where it has been suggested that an undiscovered breeding population may exist. In southern Africa, sole record is of a single adult, found on Ichaboe Island off Lüderitz, Namibia, in Apr 2005. **35–42 cm** (Kleinpikkewyn)

1

black
forehead

pale yellow
eyebrow plumes do
not join above bill

black
rump

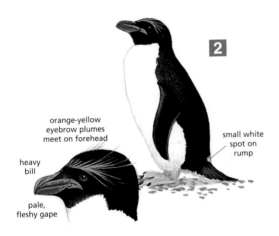

2

orange-yellow
eyebrow plumes
meet on forehead

heavy
bill

pale,
fleshy gape

small white
spot on
rump

3

pale eye

tiny; stands
around 40 cm
high

distinctive
indigo sheen

AKA Jackass ...

1 African Penguin *Spheniscus demersus* E

Very common to locally abundant endemic resident. Black and white facial pattern and white underparts with **encircling black bar** diagnostic. Individuals **sometimes with double bar** as (a). Chick (b) and immature (c) as illustrated. The call is a donkey-like braying, heard mostly at night. Occurs singly or in groups in coastal waters or colonies on offshore islands and mainland beaches. **63 cm** (Brilpikkewyn)

VULNERABLE

2 King Penguin *Aptenodytes patagonicus* R V

Rare vagrant. **Large size, long, pointed bill** and **bright orange ear-patches** distinguish it from all other penguins in southern African waters. In Antarctic waters distinguished from larger Emperor Penguin (p. 34) by orange, not pale yellow, ear-patches. At sea utters a monosyllabic 'aark'. Rarely ashore on southern mainland coast. Breeds on Marion and Prince Edward islands. **94–100 cm** (Koningpikkewyn)

rarely shows
double
black band

a

1

c

b

bright orange
ear-patch

long, slim,
pointed bill

2

large
size

cf. Emperor Penguin (p. 34)

ALBATROSSES

Huge, narrow-winged marine birds identified by their **wing patterns** and **bill coloration**. Immatures frequently different to adults. Several races of well-known species have been elevated to full-specific status, but some authorities still consider many of these taxa to fall under a few, wide-ranging species. The genus *Diomedea* contains the Wandering, Tristan, and Southern and Northern Royal Albatrosses, which all show white backs in the adult stage. All the smaller albatrosses can be identified by their **dark upper bodies forming a bridge with their dark upperwings**.

VULNERABLE

1 Wandering Albatross *Diomedea exulans*

Uncommon in offshore waters. In its adult stage differs very little from the confusingly similar (2) and (3), but has a pink bill with a yellowish tip, which **lacks the black cutting edge** of other species. Young birds undergo a lengthy process of age-related body whitening. Juveniles leave the nest all-brown except for a white facial mask, and retain similar white underwings to the adult at all subsequent stages. Upperwings whiten **from the centre outwards towards the wing tips and forward towards the leading edge** (b–d). Stage (d) retains a greyish crown-patch and upper breast while the upperwing shows distinct whitening. Breeding may occur from this stage onwards. In stage (e) the entire body is white, while the whitening of the upperwing is well advanced. Old birds of this species (f) become entirely white except for a narrow black trailing edge on the wing, the so-called 'Snowy' stage. **107–135 cm** (Grootalbatros)

CRITICALLY ENDANGERED

2 Tristan Albatross *Diomedea dabbenena* **R**

(NOT ILLUSTRATED) Status in southern African waters uncertain. Previously regarded as a race of the Wandering Albatross. Breeds on Tristan and Gough islands. Older birds probably indistinguishable at sea from (1), but young birds have a more prolonged sequence of age-related plumages, yet to be clearly defined. (Tristangrootalbatros)

VULNERABLE

3 Southern Royal Albatross *Diomedea epomophora* **V**

Rare vagrant. A diagnostic feature at all life stages is a **black cutting edge to the bill**. Young birds (a, b) identified by **dark upperwings** (not extending across the back), **small whitening patches on the inner wing** and no dark markings on the head. The **white tail has a black tip**. Stage (c) is separable from young (1) by the whitening process of the upperwing surface, which **commences from the leading edge and gradually extends backwards**. Adults (d) closely resemble the 'Snowy' stage of (1), except for the pinkish-yellow bill with black cutting edge, visible at close range. Sexes are alike. **107–122 cm** (Witvlerkkoningalbatros)

ENDANGERED

4 Northern Royal Albatross *Diomedea sanfordi* **V**

Rare vagrant. Previously known as the northern Pacific race of the 'Royal Albatross', it also has a **black cutting edge to the bill**, but is distinguished from (2) by having **black leading edges to the underwings** extending from the carpal joints to the primaries (a) and **full black upperwings at all life stages**. Immatures (b) have indistinct brownish mottling on the crown, pencil-like vermiculations on the lower back and **black tips on the tail-feathers**. **107–122 cm** (Swartvlerkkoningalbatros)

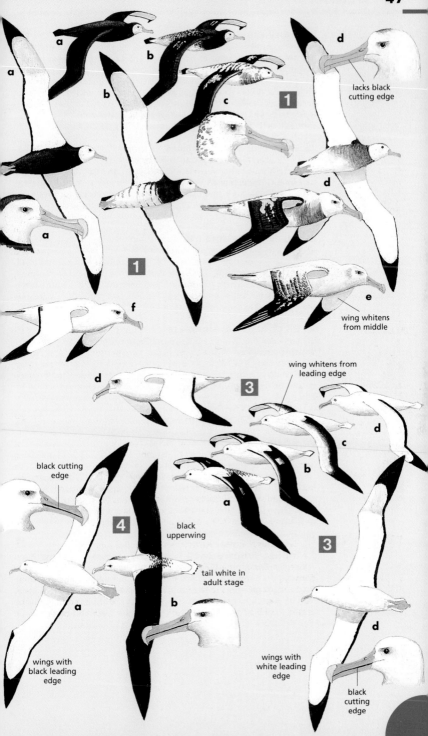

1

lacks black
cutting edge

1

wing whitens
from middle

3

wing whitens from
leading edge

black cutting
edge

4

black
upperwing

tail white in
adult stage

3

wings with
black leading
edge

wings with
white leading
edge

black
cutting
edge

ENDANGERED

1 Sooty Albatross *Phoebetria fusca* **R**

Rare in southern offshore waters. **All-dark, slender** albatross with **narrow wings** and **long, wedge-shaped tail**. Differs from (2) in having a **uniformly dark back**, which rarely shows contrast with upperwings except in very worn plumage, and then never as pale as (2). At close range, **pale yellow cutting edge on bill** is diagnostic. At sea, difficult to distinguish between the immature of this and (2), but this species shows a **pale buffy collar** that does not extend to the lower back. Could also be confused with either of the giant-petrels (p. 52). **86 cm** (Bruinalbatros)

NEAR THREATENED

2 Light-mantled Albatross *Phoebetria palpebrata* **V**

Very rare vagrant. Adults differ from (1) in **ash-grey mantle and body**, which contrast sharply with **dark head, wings and tail**. At close range, **pale blue cutting edge on bill** is diagnostic. The immature has a slightly mottled, all-pale back, and pale underbody. Could also be confused with either of the giant-petrels (p. 52). **86 cm** (Swartkopalbatros)

VULNERABLE

3 Laysan Albatross *Phoebastria immutabilis* **V**

Very rare vagrant. Upperwings, mantle, back and upper tail blackish; head, rump and body white. Underwings are white with narrow black trailing edge margins and **variable dark patches on the coverts**. Adult and immature are alike except for bill colours: **dull yellow with a black tip in adult**, but duller in immature. The pink **feet protrude beyond the tail** in flight. **80 cm** (Swartwangalbatros)

ENDANGERED

4 Black-browed Albatross *Thalassarche melanophrys*

Common summer visitor; all-year in southern offshore waters. **Blackish-brown upperwings, mantle and upper tail** contrast with pure white head and body. The white underwings show black margins, the **leading edge being particularly broad**. At close range, **black brows** and **orange-yellow bill with pink tip** are distinctive. Immature plumage similar to adult, but shows duskier underwings and a greyish nape that extends to form a collar; the bill dusky-horn with black tip (cf. Grey-headed Albatross on p. 50). **80–95 cm** (Swartrugalbatros)

ENDANGERED

5 Atlantic Yellow-nosed Albatross
Thalassarche chlororhynchos

Regular visitor to west coast waters. This species and (6) are the smallest, most slender albatrosses. The adult has a **grey wash on the head** and white body; upperwings, mantle and upper tail blackish brown, **underwings show narrow black margins** (cf. other grey-headed albatrosses). The bill is black with a **broad yellow upper ridge**. Immatures of this and (6) have white heads and all-black bills and cannot be told apart at sea. **75–81 cm** (Atlantiese Geelneusalbatros)

ENDANGERED

6 Indian Yellow-nosed Albatross *Thalassarche carteri*

The Indian Ocean equivalent of (5) and a common winter visitor to east coast waters. Exactly as the Atlantic species, but with a **white head**; at close range may reveal a **grey suffusion to the cheeks**. The bill is black with a **yellow upper ridge** that tapers towards the tip. Immature same as immature of previous species. **71–85 cm** (Indiese Geelneusalbatros)

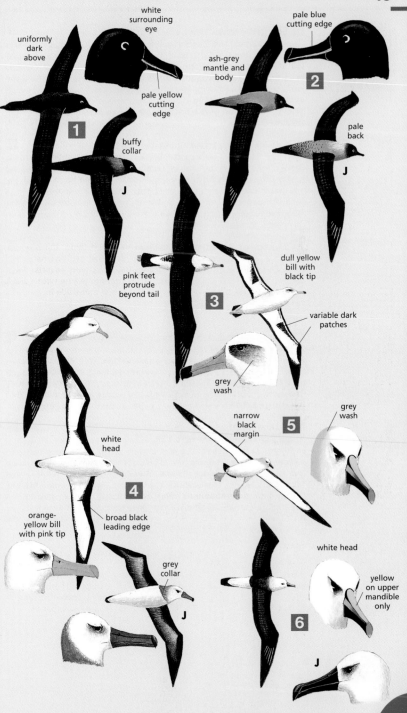

uniformly dark above

white surrounding eye

pale yellow cutting edge

1

buffy collar

J

pale blue cutting edge

ash-grey mantle and body

2

pale back

J

pink feet protrude beyond tail

dull yellow bill with black tip

3

variable dark patches

grey wash

narrow black margin

5

grey wash

white head

4

orange-yellow bill with pink tip

broad black leading edge

grey collar

J

white head

yellow on upper mandible only

6

J

NEAR THREATENED

1 Shy Albatross *Thalassarche cauta*

Common winter and uncommon summer visitor. The **largest black-browed albatross**. Apart from dark upperwings, mantle and upper tail, the head and body are white in adults. Underwings have **narrow black margins** and a diagnostic **black patch or 'thumbprint' where the leading edge of each wing joins the body**. The black brow and **grey bill with yellow tip** are visible at close range. Immature like adult but with blue-grey head and **grey bill with black tips** on both mandibles. **95 cm** (Bloubekalbatros)

VULNERABLE

2 Salvin's Albatross *Thalassarche salvini* V

Very rare vagrant. Formerly considered a race of (1). The underwing pattern same as (1), but the dark wing-tip region is more extensive. It also differs in having a grey-brown head with **white forehead** and **ash-grey mantle extending to the upper breast**. Bill ivory-horn, with a yellowish upper and lower ridge. **Tip of upper bill yellow; tip of lower mandible black**. Immature as adult but bill grey with black tips on both mandibles. **90 cm** (Salvinalbatros)

CRITICALLY ENDANGERED

3 Chatham Albatross *Thalassarche eremita* V

Very rare vagrant. Formerly considered a race of (1). Exactly as the previous species but with a **completely grey head and neck, the head without a white cap**. Bill **yellow with a dark spot at the tip of the lower mandible**. **90 cm** (Chathamalbatros)

VULNERABLE

4 Grey-headed Albatross *Thalassarche chrysostoma* R

Rare winter visitor. Told by grey head and black bill with **yellow ridges to both mandibles** (cf. other grey-headed albatrosses). The underwings have a **broad blackish margin on the leading edge** and a narrow margin on the trailing edge. Tail dark above and below. Immature has dark underwings and a variable extent of grey on the head and breast, but has a **black bill with a dull yellow tip**. **80–90 cm** (Gryskopalbatros)

VULNERABLE

5 Buller's Albatross *Thalassarche bulleri* V

A rare vagrant to Cape waters. Can be confused with other albatrosses with grey-brown heads, but has a **contrasting white forehead** and **narrow underwing margins**. The bill is black with a **broad yellow culmen and narrow yellow ridge to the lower mandible** (cf. Yellow-nosed Albatrosses, p. 48). Young birds start with a dark bill that gradually becomes **dull yellow or horn colour on the ridges** before assuming full adult bill colouring. **76–81 cm** (Witkroonalbatros)

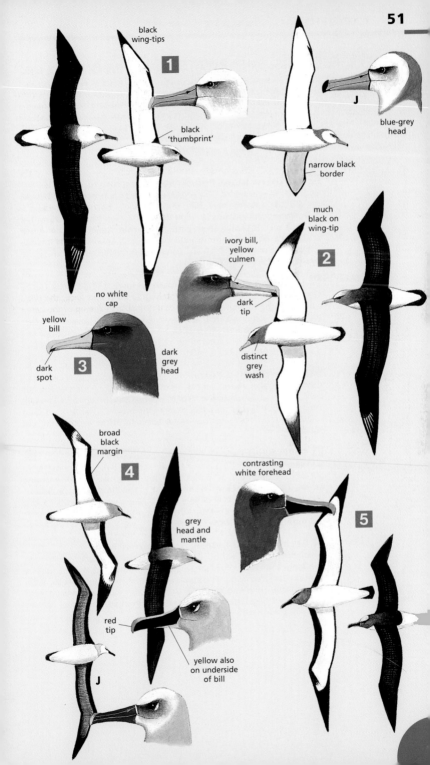

black
wing-tips

1

black
'thumbprint'

J

blue-grey
head

narrow black
border

much
black on
wing-tip

ivory bill,
yellow
culmen

2

dark
tip

distinct
grey
wash

no white
cap

yellow
bill

dark
spot

3

dark
grey
head

broad
black
margin

4

contrasting
white forehead

5

grey
head and
mantle

red
tip

yellow also
on underside
of bill

J

PETRELS, FULMARS, SHEARWATERS AND PRIONS

A large and varied group of **long-winged pelagic birds**, ranging in size from the small prions (14–20 cm) to the giant-petrels, which are comparable in size to albatrosses. They are characterised by a **single nasal tube surmounting the upper mandible that encloses both nostrils**, which open obliquely or vertically. They show **drab plumage colours** and have a typically **stiff-winged mode of flight**. All species breed on islands in the subantarctic and visit southern African offshore waters mainly during the winter months, when they may be seen foraging for offal around fishing trawlers.

NEAR THREATENED

1 **Northern Giant Petrel**   *Macronectes halli*

Common all-year visitor. This and (2) distinguished from Sooty Albatross (p. 48) by **massive pale bill, thicker wings, bulkier body** and a **humpbacked appearance in flight**. Difficult to tell from (2) unless bill colour is seen: **creamy yellow with a darker tip**. Adult has some white around the face but never as extensive as in (2). Immature identifiable only at close range by bill colour. Congregates around seal islands on the west coast. **75–90 cm** (Grootnellie)

NEAR THREATENED

2 **Southern Giant Petrel**   *Macronectes giganteus*

Common all-year visitor. Two morphs: (a) more common variant with **extensive area of white** or speckled-white on head extending to upper breast (more extensive than in (1)); (b) **entirely white except for a few scattered black feathers. Bill pale cream with greenish tip.** Immature can be confused with (1). Found singly or in small flocks, especially around trawlers. **75–90 cm** (Reusenellie)

VULNERABLE

3 **White-chinned Petrel**   *Procellaria aequinoctialis*

Common all-year visitor. Differs from all other dark petrels except (1) and (2) in much larger size, darker colour and pale **greenish-yellow bill**. The white chin is small in adult; absent in immature. Gregarious; found in large numbers around trawlers. **A common offshore petrel. 58 cm** (Bassiaan)

VULNERABLE

4 **Spectacled Petrel**   *Procellaria conspicillata*   **R**

Uncommon non-breeding visitor. Closely similar to the previous species, but smaller and told by **dark-tipped bill, extensive white markings on the head**, and **lack of white throat patch**. Breeds on the Tristan group and, when not breeding, mostly disperses westwards to the waters of southern Brazil. Very infrequent off the coast of Namibia. An endangered species. **51 cm** (Brilbassiaan)

5 **Great-winged Petrel**   *Pterodroma macroptera*

Uncommon all-year visitor. Characterised by large head, short neck and **long, thin wings held at sharp angle at the carpal joint**. Differs from similar-sized Sooty Shearwater (p. 62) in **dark underwings**, from (3) in smaller size and **short black bill**. Solitary at sea, moving with **dashing, twisting flight**, often towering high above the water. **42 cm** (Langvlerkstormvoël)

creamy yellow bill with darker tip

1

greenish bill tip

a

plumage variable

a

2

rounded tail (cf. Sooty Albatross, p. 48)

b

J

3

white chin patch

dark underwings

3

pale ivory yellow

dark underwings

4

white 'spectacles'

dark-tipped bill

dark underwings

short black bill

5

sharply angled wings

1 Southern Fulmar *Fulmarus glacialoides* **R**

Rare winter visitor. Identified by **pale grey upperparts, white patches at the base of the primaries** and **dark-tipped bill**. Underparts white except for **grey trailing edge to wings** (cf. Snow Petrel, p. 38, which is entirely white). Occurs singly, most often around trawlers. **46 cm** (Silwerstormvoël)

2 Antarctic Petrel *Thalassoica antarctica* **V**

Rare vagrant. Resembles Pintado Petrel (p. 56) but is larger and lacks white patches and chequered pattern on the upperwings. Instead, it has a **broad white area** on trailing edge of upperwings. Underparts are white, except for **brown head**, bold brown leading edge to wings and **tail narrowly tipped brown**. General appearance browner than Pintado Petrel. Common in the pack ice, where they gather in large flocks and rest on icebergs and ice floes. Vagrant to Marion Island and southern offshore waters. **43 cm** (Antarktiese Stormvoël)

ENDANGERED

3 Atlantic Petrel *Pterodroma incerta* **R**

Rare winter visitor. An all-dark, brown petrel except for **white lower breast and belly**. In worn plumage, throat and breast can appear mottled. **Upperparts uniformly dark brown.** Superficially resembles Soft-plumaged Petrel (p. 56) but is larger and lacks the white throat and breast-band of that species. Also much darker above than Grey Petrel (p. 60), and with a **short black bill** (not slender pale bill). Solitary at sea. **43 cm** (Atlantiese Stormvoël)

4 White-headed Petrel *Pterodroma lessonii* **R**

Rare winter visitor. **Snow-white head** with **dark eye-patches, entirely white underbody and tail** and **dark underwings** render this species unmistakable. The upperparts are grey-brown with a conspicuous, dark open **'M'-shape across the back and wings**. Solitary at sea and **does not forage near trawlers**. **45 cm** (Witkopstormvoël)

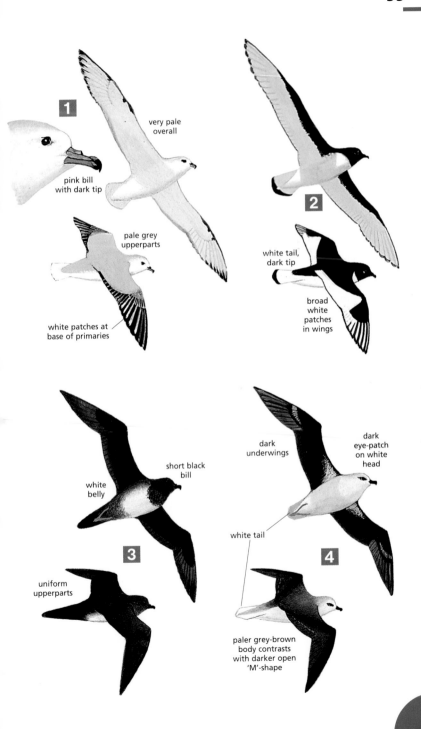

1

very pale
overall

pink bill
with dark tip

pale grey
upperparts

white patches at
base of primaries

2

white tail,
dark tip

broad
white
patches
in wings

short black
bill

white
belly

3

uniform
upperparts

dark
underwings

dark
eye-patch
on white
head

white tail

4

paler grey-brown
body contrasts
with darker open
'M'-shape

1 Soft-plumaged Petrel *Pterodroma mollis* R

Uncommon winter visitor. Resembles Atlantic Petrel (p. 54) but is smaller, has **dusky breast-band** on otherwise **entirely white underparts**. Faint shadow of open **'M'-pattern across upperwings and back**. Rare dark morph differs from larger Great-winged Petrel (p. 52) in less uniform, slightly mottled underparts, and from (3) in these features plus less grey appearance. At sea occurs singly or in pairs; **does not scavenge around trawlers**. 32 cm (Donsveerstormvoël)

2 Barau's Petrel *Pterodroma baraui* V

Rare vagrant, but possibly overlooked. Larger and darker above than pale form (1), from which it is easily distinguished by its mostly **white (not dark) underwings** with a conspicuous **black diagonal bar** extending from the wing bend to the middle of the underwing coverts. **White forehead** gives it a capped appearance. **Collar is partially grey**; does not form a complete breast-band. Recent pelagic trips off the coast of northern KwaZulu-Natal and Mozambique have produced several records, Sep–Nov. 38 cm (Baraustormvoël)

ENDANGERED

3 Kerguelen Petrel *Lugensa brevirostris* R

Rare offshore visitor occasionally wrecked in large numbers on eastern coast. Similar in shape and outline to Great-winged Petrel (p. 52), but much smaller and **grey**, not dark brown. The head appears unusually **large. Underwings have a thin, pale leading edge** from body to carpal joint, noticeable at close range. Differs from the dark phase of (1) in greyer coloration and more uniform underparts. Flies very fast with rapid wing beats interspersed with long glides over the waves; sometimes towers high above the sea, **much higher than any other petrel**. 36 cm (Kerguelense Stormvoël)

4 Cape Petrel *Daption capense*

Abundant winter visitor. An unmistakable **pied petrel** with two white patches on each upperwing and a **chequered pattern on back and rump**. Underparts white with **dark brown borders to wings (bolder on the leading edge) and tail-tip** (cf. Antarctic Petrel, p. 54). Occurs singly or in vast flocks around trawlers; regularly seen from shore in stormy weather. 36 cm (Seeduifstormvoël)

5 Bulwer's Petrel *Bulweria bulwerii* V

Rare vagrant. **Prion-sized, dark brown petrel** with long wings and **long, wedge-shaped tail that appears pointed**. Pale diagonal wing-bar on **upperwings** visible at close range. No similar-sized, all-dark petrel occurs in the southern African region; cf. prions (p. 58). Flight action prion-like but much more erratic, **staying closer to wave surface**. Seen rarely in southwestern offshore waters. 26–28 cm (Bleekvlerkkeilstert)

6 Jouanin's Petrel *Bulweria fallax* V

Rare vagrant to the east coast, from the northwest Indian Ocean. Closely similar to (5). **Dark blackish brown** like that species, with a **long, pointed tail**, but **lacks the pale wing-panels**. Also slightly larger, with **broader wings** and **rounded wing-tips**. Flies low over the water with rapid, shallow wing beats followed by long glides in calm sea conditions. Flies higher and more erratically in strong winds. 30–32 cm (Donkervlerkkeilstert)

NEAR THREATENED

7 Antarctic Prion

Included only as a size comparison: see p. 58.

dusky breast-band

white throat

white forehead, black cap

pale underwings

no breast-band

2

mottled underparts

1

pale, narrow leading edge on wing

appears large-headed

3

rare dark morph

uniform grey body

pale grey primaries

4

dark brown tail

chequered pattern on back and rump

pale diagonal wing-bar

long, pointed tail

5

slender, pointed wings

broad wings with rounded tips

long, pointed tail

6

all-dark underwing

Antarctic Prion

7

1 Blue Petrel *Halobaena caerulea*

Offshore winter visitor. Occasionally blown ashore in large numbers. A small blue-grey petrel **resembling a prion** (see below), but larger and with **black markings on the crown, nape and sides of breast**, and a **square, white-tipped tail**. The open 'M'-pattern across upperwings and back is fainter than in prions. Often seen **in company with flocks of prions**, but faster flight action makes it stand out. **30 cm** (Bloustormvoël)

PRIONS

Small blue-grey petrels that breed in the subantarctic and disperse throughout the southern seas when not breeding. These erratic, non-breeding visitors to our shores have such closely similar plumage patterns as to be specifically almost indistinguishable at sea. **All have a dark open 'M'-pattern across their upperwings and mantle, their tails wedge-shaped and dark-tipped.** Prions fly fast, twisting from side to side and alternately revealing their white underparts and dark upperparts. They are occasionally blown ashore and wrecked, large numbers of corpses then littering beaches. In the hand specific identification is possible by examination of bill shape and size; see illustrations. The three species and three subspecies at present all have separate common names, but the taxonomy of the group is complex and future reclassifications are possible.

2 Broad-billed Prion *Pachyptila vittata*　R

Uncommon visitor, mostly to the west coast. In the hand, its **black (not blueish), extremely broad and flattened bill** is diagnostic. Its body is bulky and the **tail is only slightly tipped black**. Usually shows fairly broad and **dark patches on the sides of its breast**. **30 cm** (Breëbekwalvisvoël)

3 Antarctic Prion *Pachyptila desolata*

Uncommon visitor, mostly in winter. This is the smallest and most abundant prion. Shows a distinct **dark 'M'-pattern on the upperwings**, a well-defined **white eyebrow** and a fairly **narrow blueish bill**. **27 cm** (Antarktiese Walvisvoël)

4 Salvin's Prion *Pachyptila salvini*　R

Very uncommon visitor, mostly to the east coast. Very similar to (2), but **bill blueish (not black)**. However, it is doubtful whether these two species can be distinguished at sea. **28–30 cm** (Marionwalvisvoël)

5 Slender-billed Prion *Pachyptila belcheri*　V

Irregular winter-visiting vagrant to southern African shores; occasionally irrupts in large numbers. Stranded individuals have been recorded on Western Cape and Indian Ocean coasts. Generally **paler than other prions** and shows a weaker bill, less distinct dark 'M'-pattern on the upperwings and paler head and face than (3). **27 cm** (Dunbekwalvisvoël)

6 Fairy Prion *Pachyptila turtur*　R

Rare visitor between June and November, with strandings occurring on all coasts. Small and **pale in colour**, with the head especially pale. Lacks a dark line through the eye and has a **broader black tail-tip** than other prions. **23–25 cm** (Swartstertwalvisvoël)

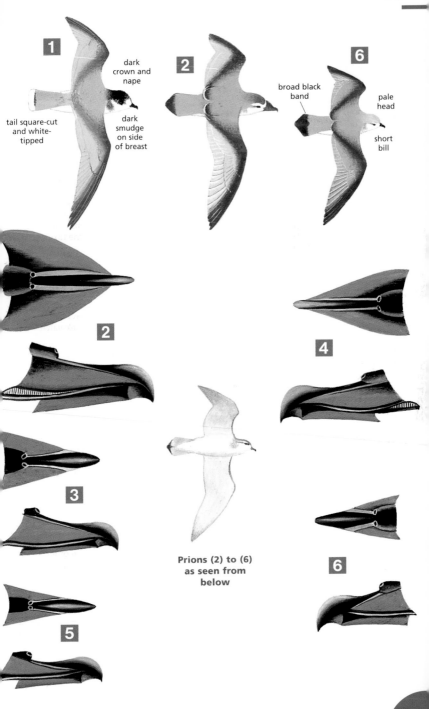

1

dark crown and nape

tail square-cut and white-tipped

dark smudge on side of breast

2

6

broad black band

pale head

short bill

2

4

3

Prions (2) to (6) as seen from below

6

5

1 Grey Petrel *Procellaria cinerea* **R**

Rare visitor to southwestern offshore waters. A large **grey-and-white** petrel that resembles (3) but differs in **conspicuous dark underwings and undertail**. Flight action stiff with shallow wing beats on straight, ridged wings. Solitary at sea; rarely scavenges around trawlers. **48 cm** (Pediunker)

SHEARWATERS

Shearwaters differ from other petrels in having **long, thin bills** and, with a few notable exceptions, **short, rounded tails**. They fly with short bursts of rapid wing beats alternated with long, stiff-winged banking glides low over the water.

2 Great Shearwater *Puffinus gravis*

Common visitor. Similar in size to (3), from which it differs in darker upperparts, **distinctive black cap**, **white collar** and **dark smudge on belly**. At close range, the **white sickle shape on rump** and **dark bill** may be seen. Usually in small flocks, but gather in large groups on feeding grounds in western offshore waters. **45–50 cm** (Grootpylstormvoël)

3 Cory's Shearwater *Calonectris diomedea*

Common summer visitor. **Ash-brown upperparts**, uncapped appearance (owing to lack of white collar) and **yellow bill** distinguish it from (2). Its flight is also slower and more laboured. In worn plumage can show a **thin white sickle-shape on rump**. Gregarious in small numbers and regularly seen from the shore. Most common race in southern African waters is *C.d. borealis*; the nominate Mediterranean race *C.d. diomedea* (sometimes considered a separate species, Scopoli's Shearwater) has also been recorded. **46 cm** (Geelbekpylstormvoël)

4 Streaked Shearwater *Calonectris leucomelas* **V**

Very rare offshore visitor. Previously regarded as a race of (3), but differs in being **whiter about the face** and having **pronounced streaking on the head and nape**. Upperparts also greyer (less brown). **45–48 cm** (Gestreepte Pylstormvoël)

5 Manx Shearwater *Puffinus puffinus* **R**

Rare summer visitor. The second smallest shearwater in the region. **All-black upperparts. Underparts and underwings are white**, extending almost to the wing-tips. Distinguished from Little and Tropical Shearwaters (p. 62) by larger size, more extensive **black on the head extending below the eyes** and **white undertail coverts**. Flight action less fluttering than that of Little and Tropical Shearwaters, with longer glides between wing beats. Occurs singly in flocks of Sooty Shearwaters (p. 62). **35–37 cm** (Swartbekpylstormvoël)

6 Balearic Shearwater *Puffinus mauretanicus* **V**

Very rare offshore visitor. Sometimes considered to be a race of (4), and very similar to that species. In the field appears less contrastingly black and white, showing more **brown tones to the plumage**, and **dusky (not white) underwings, breast and undertail coverts**. **32–38 cm** (Baleariese Pylstormvoël)

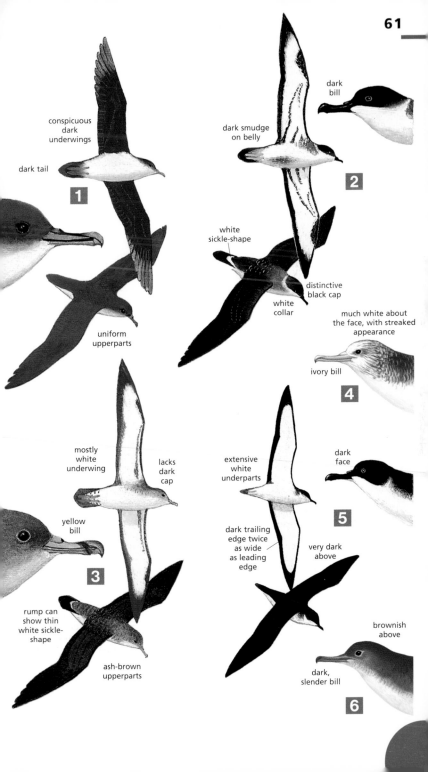

conspicuous dark underwings

dark tail

dark bill

dark smudge on belly

white sickle-shape

1

uniform upperparts

distinctive black cap

white collar

2

much white about the face, with streaked appearance

ivory bill

4

mostly white underwing

lacks dark cap

extensive white underparts

dark face

yellow bill

3

5

dark trailing edge twice as wide as leading edge

very dark above

rump can show thin white sickle-shape

ash-brown upperparts

brownish above

dark, slender bill

6

NEAR THREATENED

1 Sooty Shearwater *Puffinus griseus*
Abundant all-year visitor. Sooty-brown with **conspicuous pale areas on the underwings**, which distinguishes it from all other dark petrels in southern Africa. **Dark bill** and **slender, pointed wings** that are held straight and stiff in flight. Feeds in mixed flocks of Cape Gannets (p. 68) and Cape Cormorants (p. 88), sometimes in thousands. Often seen close inshore. Less commonly forages around deep-sea trawlers. **46–53 cm** (Malbaartjie)

2 Wedge-tailed Shearwater *Puffinus pacificus*
Infrequent visitor to Mozambique coast; rare off KwaZulu-Natal coast. Closely resembles (3) but differs in **dark bill. Tail wedge-shaped (not rounded)** and appears pointed when not spread. Also occurs in a less common pale morph resembling Great Shearwater (p. 60), but lacks white rump and collar, and has a **dark vent** but **unmarked white belly.** Wings broad at the base and held slightly bowed, not straight and stiff as in (1). Found singly or in small groups. **42 cm** (Keilstertpylstormvoël)

3 Flesh-footed Shearwater *Puffinus carneipes*   **R**
Rare winter visitor to east coast. Larger than (1) and differs in **dark underwings.** Smaller than White-chinned Petrel (p. 52), the **bill pink with a dark tip** (not greenish yellow). Differs from (2) in larger size, narrower, longer wings, **rounded (not wedge-shaped) tail** and **pinkish (not black) legs and bill** (the latter with a darker tip). At long range, pink legs and feet when extended appear as a pale vent. Accompanies foraging flocks of Cape Gannets (p. 68) in Agulhas current. **45 cm** (Bruinpylstormvoël)

4 Little Shearwater *Puffinus assimilis*   **R**
Rare visitor, chiefly to southwestern coast in summer. A **very small black-and-white shearwater** which, in calm conditions, **flies close to the surface with rapid wing beats** interspersed with **long glides on bowed wings.** Much smaller size, white face of (a), *P.a. tunneyi*, and flight action separate it from Manx Shearwater (p. 60). *P.a. elegans* (b) has dark grey upperparts; cf. (5). Occurs singly, occasionally around trawlers. **28 cm** (Kleinpylstormvoël)

5 Tropical Shearwater *Puffinus bailloni*   **V**
Rare vagrant to east coast. Previously considered a subspecies of Audubon's Shearwater (*Puffinus lherminieri*). Similar in size to (4) and with similar flight action, but differs in **dark brown upperparts** (not dark grey) and **dark undertail.** Race (4b) has dark grey upperparts that can appear brown; dark undertail is therefore the best identifying characteristic for Tropical Shearwater. Occasional inshore sightings, but occurs in the Mozambique Channel. **30 cm** (Tropiese Kleinpylstormvoël)

6 A storm petrel
Included for size comparison with shearwaters. See p. 64.

pale areas on underwing

1

dark bill

dark bill

2

wedge-shaped tail

smaller than (3)

slender wings held straight and stiff

pale bill, dark tip

trailing edge as broad as leading edge

a

a

white cheeks

blue-black tinge to upperparts

a

rounded tail

conspicuous pinkish feet

3

dark grey upperparts

b

b

4

wide dark edges

dark undertail

5

dark brown tinge to upperparts

Storm petrel

6

STORM PETRELS

Swallow-sized petrels of generally dark appearance, some with white rumps, underbodies or underwings, all with **long, delicate legs**. Many feed from the surface with **feet pattering in the sea; they appear to walk on the water** while remaining airborne with raised wings. Specific identification best at close range, but specific flight actions often diagnostic. See also p. 36 for subantarctic storm petrels.

■ European Storm Petrel   *Hydrobates pelagicus*
Common summer visitor. The **smallest seabird** in the region. Identified from (3) by **white stripe on underwing, wing-tips not pointed** and **legs that do not project beyond the tail in flight**. Flight bat-like and direct. Occasionally patters feet on water. Occurs in large flocks and is frequently found wrecked on beaches. **14–18 cm** (Europese Stormswael)

■ Leach's Storm Petrel   *Oceanodroma leucorhoa*   R
Uncommon summer visitor. Differs from (1) and (3) in slightly larger size, **longer, pointed wings**, more slender appearance and **forked tail**. Flight erratic, bounding over the waves and sometimes flying like a small shearwater. Unlike other storm petrels, **does not patter feet on water**. Occasionally seen in small flocks, but usually solitary at sea. A small population breeds on offshore Cape islands. **22 cm** (Swaelstertstormswael)

■ Wilson's Storm Petrel   *Oceanites oceanicus*
Common visitor and rare resident. Best identified by **rounded wings**, uniformly dark underwing pattern and **long, spindly legs projecting well beyond square tail**. Has yellow-webbed feet, but these are almost impossible to see at sea. **Flight action more swallow-like**, not bat-like as (1). **16–19 cm** (Gewone Stormswael)

■ Matsudaira's Storm Petrel   *Oceanodroma matsudairae*   V
Rare vagrant. A dark brown storm petrel, slightly larger than others in the region. Upperwings show small but **clear white patch at base of primaries** and distinct crescent shape formed by **pale wing covert edges**. Tail is deeply forked, like (2). **Flight mostly leisurely with frequent gliding action**. A wanderer from islands near South-east Asia and Indonesia. **25 cm** (Oosterse Stormswael)

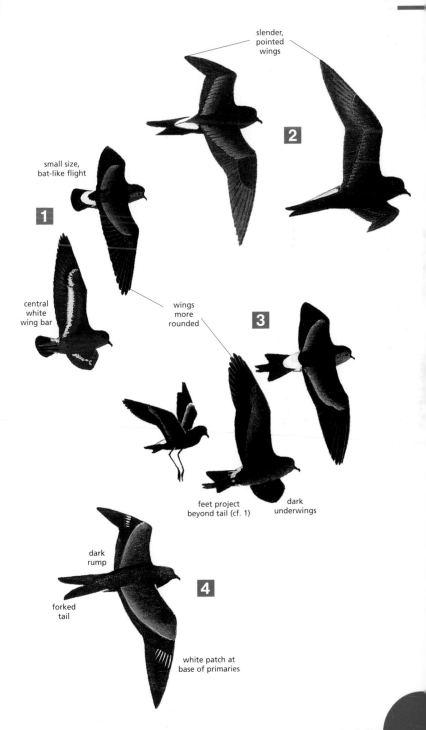

slender,
pointed
wings

2

small size,
bat-like flight

1

central
white
wing bar

wings
more
rounded

3

feet project
beyond tail (cf. 1)

dark
underwings

dark
rump

4

forked
tail

white patch at
base of primaries

1 Madeiran Storm Petrel *Oceanodroma castro* V

Rare vagrant. A large storm petrel, closest in shape to Leach's Storm Petrel (p. 64). Differs in **less deeply forked tail** (appears square in flight), **less obvious pale panel on upperwing** and overall **darker coloration**. White rump appears wide rather than long, and lacks the narrow darker stripe down the middle. Larger than Wilson's Storm Petrel (p. 64), with **longer, narrower wings** and **longer tail**. Feet do not project beyond tail. Typical flight action buoyant and zigzagging, with occasional glides low over the water. Unlike Leach's Storm Petrel, does not execute erratic changes in speed and direction and has shallower wing beats. Breeds on islands in the Atlantic (e.g. Azores and Madeira) and Pacific (e.g. Galapagos). Fairly common off West African coast, but first recorded in southern African waters in Nov 2008. **19–21 cm** (Madeirastormvoël)

2 Black-bellied Storm Petrel *Fregetta tropica* R

Uncommon winter visitor. Larger than Wilson's Storm Petrel (p. 64), differing in **white underwings** and **white belly with black stripe down the centre** that broadens on the vent and encompasses entire undertail coverts. Habitually flies in front of or alongside ships and has a **bounding flight action**, occasionally bouncing off waves on its breast; cf. (3). Solitary at sea. **20 cm** (Swartpensstormswael)

3 White-bellied Storm Petrel *Fregetta grallaria* R

Uncommon winter visitor. Difficult to tell from (2) unless seen at close range, but has **entirely white belly, with the white extending to the undertail coverts**. Mantle and wing coverts tipped grey, giving **paler-backed appearance** than (2). Habitually flies in front of or alongside ships with **bounding flight**, occasionally bouncing off waves on its breast; cf. Matsudaira's Storm Petrel (p. 64). Solitary at sea. Occurs from southern Namibia to the east coast, but is most common in the south Feb–Mar. **20 cm** (Witpensstormswael)

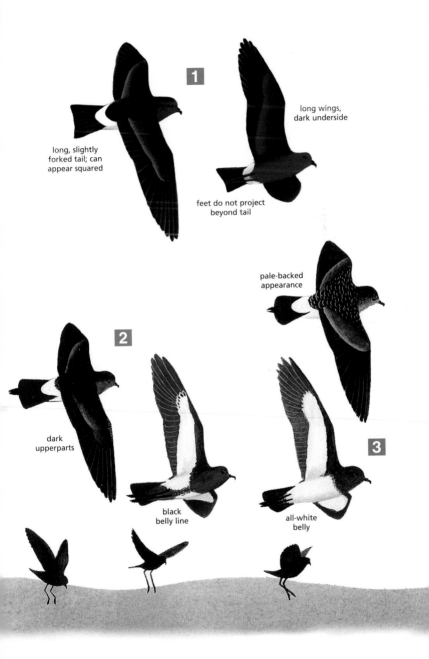

1

long wings, dark underside

long, slightly forked tail; can appear squared

feet do not project beyond tail

pale-backed appearance

2

dark upperparts

black belly line

3

all-white belly

BOOBIES AND GANNETS

Large, robust seabirds with **long, thick necks** and **straight, conical bills**. The smaller boobies have a tropical distribution, while gannets prefer a temperate climate. All **catch fish by plunge-diving** from about 20 m above the sea. Flight stiff-winged with powerful, fairly rapid wing beats, **head and neck stretched forward**.

1 Red-footed Booby *Sula sula*
Fairly common in Mozambique Channel; a rare visitor further south. Adults variable, usually **all-white** except for **black flight feathers** and **small black underwing spot near carpal joint**. Cheeks have a faint yellow wash. Other features are a **two-toned blue-grey and pinkish bill**, brown eyes and **red feet**. Less common morph shows all-brown plumage; cf. (2). Could be confused with larger and more robust (4), but tail longer and all-white. Immature **all-brown** with **yellowish feet**. 66–77 cm (Rooipootmalgas)

2 Brown Booby *Sula leucogaster*
A very rare visitor to northwest and east coast waters, often after a cyclone. Brown with **white central underwings and belly**; the bill yellow. Cf. immature (3), which has speckled upperparts; body shape of Brown Booby more slender and elongated. **78 cm** (Bruinmalgas)

3 Cape Gannet *Morus capensis* N E
Common to locally abundant endemic resident. Unmistakable, large black and white seabird with **yellow head and hindneck**. At close range, distinctive black lines on the bill and face and a long **black line down the centre of the throat** are visible. **Tail is normally black**; rare individuals have white outer tail feathers. Immature all-dark, heavily spotted all over. Body, head and neck become white in that sequence; finally wings become white at about two years. Seen singly or in straggling flocks offshore; **large aggregations over fish shoals**. Individuals plunge-dive repeatedly. Roosts at night in colonies on offshore islands or at sea. **87–100 cm** (Witmalgas)

VULNERABLE

4 Australasian Gannet *Morus serrator* V
Rare vagrant to southern African coastal waters. Almost identical to (3), but has **much shorter central throat stripe, slightly darker iris** and **white outer tail feathers**. Not easily distinguishable from (3) at sea, but often roosts ashore with flocks of that species. **84–92 cm** (Australiese Malgas)

VULNERABLE

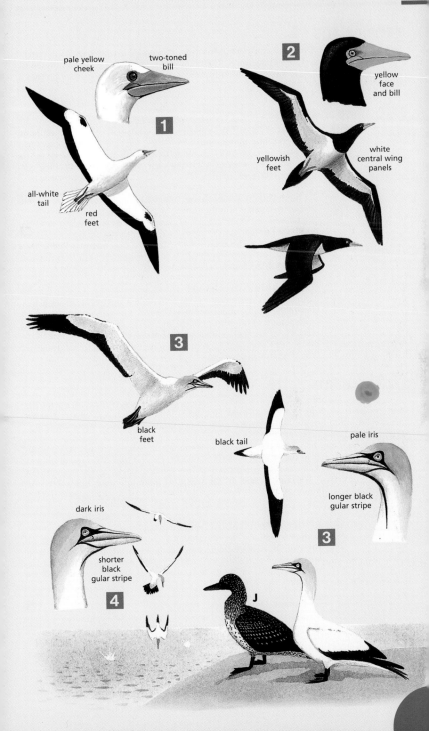

pale yellow cheek

two-toned bill

1

all-white tail

red feet

2

yellow face and bill

white central wing panels

yellowish feet

3

black feet

black tail

pale iris

longer black gular stripe

3

dark iris

shorter black gular stripe

4

J

TROPICBIRDS

Tern-like seabirds with the **two central tail feathers elongated into streamers**, lacking in immatures. They are usually seen singly. Their flight is fluttering, interspersed with long glides, and they catch fish by plunge-diving from a height of 12–16 m above the sea. They are distributed across the tropics.

1 **White-tailed Tropicbird** *Phaethon lepturus* **R**
Uncommon visitor. Has a **yellow bill, white tail-streamers** and **black marks on the upperwings**. Immature has blacker wing-tips than immature of (2). Occurs in Indian Ocean waters; occasional visitor on the east coast; infrequent on the west coast. **40 cm** (excluding tail-streamers) **(Witpylstert)**

2 **Red-tailed Tropicbird** *Phaethon rubricauda* **R**
Uncommon visitor. Distinguished by **red bill** and **red tail-streamers**. Plumage **almost entirely white** or flushed pink when breeding; lacks the black outer primaries of (1) and (3). Immature has a distinctive **black bar through the eye**. The bill is initially black and later becomes yellow, then orange. Occurs in Indian Ocean waters; occasional visitor on the east coast. **46 cm** (excluding tail-streamers) **(Rooipylstert)**

3 **Red-billed Tropicbird** *Phaethon aethereus* **V**
Rare vagrant. Adults have a diagnostic **red bill** and **white tail-streamers**. Underparts white; **upperparts well barred**, resembling the upperparts of immatures of other tropicbirds. Immature has a dull yellow bill and a black eye-stripe that extends to its nape, and lacks tail-streamers. Seen off the west coast and Cape peninsula. **50 cm** (excluding tail-streamers) **(Rooibekpylstert)**

FRIGATEBIRDS

Huge, blackish, aerial-feeding seabirds with very **long, pointed wings that are normally held swept back from the carpal joint**; diagnostic in flight. They have deeply forked tails and short red legs, so are unable to walk. They **clamber about in trees when on land**. Males usually have an inflatable red throat sac; females show more white on the body; both have grey bills. They cannot settle on water but in flight they **soar effortlessly (often very high above the sea)**, are highly manoeuvrable and feed mostly by harassing other sea birds to make them disgorge food, or snatch fish (e.g. flying fish) and food from the surface of the sea. They can **remain on the wing for days at a time**, but will return to shore to roost.

4 **Great Frigatebird** *Fregata minor*
Fairly frequent on the Mozambique coast; rarely seen further south. The **male is all-black** while the **female has a white throat and belly**; immatures have white or tawny heads and necks. Often snatch fishermen's bait or their catch, and harass other birds. **86–100 cm**; wingspan **180–210 cm** (Grootfregatvoël)

5 **Lesser Frigatebird** *Fregata ariel* **V**
Rare vagrant to the Mozambique coast following cyclones. Male is all-black except for **white 'armpits'**, while females and immatures have a **white throat extending to the 'armpits'**. Size difference between (4) and (5) not discernible unless directly compared. **71–81 cm** (Kleinfregatvoël)

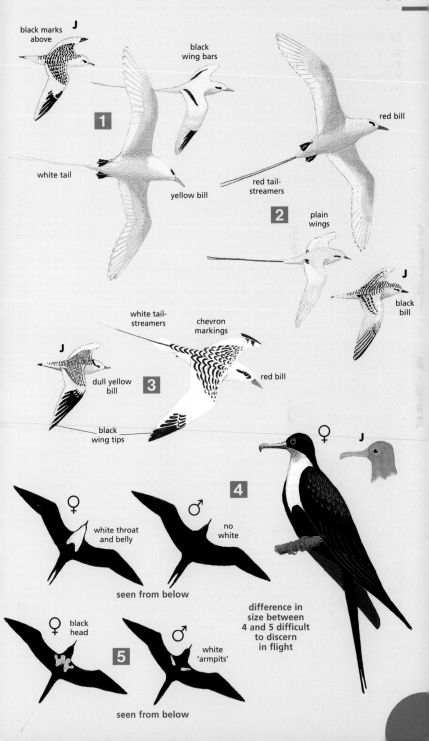

black marks above

J

black wing bars

red bill

1

white tail

yellow bill

red tail-streamers

2

plain wings

J

black bill

white tail-streamers

chevron markings

J

dull yellow bill

3

red bill

black wing tips

♀

J

4

♀

white throat and belly

♂

no white

seen from below

difference in size between 4 and 5 difficult to discern in flight

♀ black head

5

♂

white 'armpits'

seen from below

JAEGERS AND SKUAS

Skuas are robust, predominantly brown, predatory seabirds with **characteristic white flashes at the base of their primaries, wedge-shaped tails with the two central feathers elongated**, and **dark bills and feet**. Immatures are all very similar and their bodies are **heavily barred**. The field identification of skuas (especially non-breeding birds, which resemble immatures, and birds with worn, damaged or absent tail extensions) is challenging. All species are variable, with dark, pale and intermediate morphs and several age-related plumage stages. Identification (particularly of the smaller *Stercorarius* genus, known as jaegers – the common name derived from the German for 'hunter') requires careful study of the proportions, structure and flight action in addition to plumage details.

1 Parasitic Jaeger *Stercorarius parasiticus*
Common summer visitor. Plumage very variable between (a) pale and (b) dark morph birds. Differs from (3) in smaller size, **narrower wings** and **more agile flight**. In adults, **pointed central tail feathers project 3–4 cm beyond tail tip**. A **falcon-like** species that chases small gulls and terns. Occurs close inshore; singly or in small groups. **46 cm** (Arktiese Roofmeeu)

2 Long-tailed Jaeger *Stercorarius longicaudus*
Uncommon summer visitor. Adults in summer unmistakable with pale, grey-brown upperparts, **dark trailing edge to upperwings** and **long, pointed tail projections**. A rare dark morph also occurs. In winter, adults and immatures lack tail projections and may be difficult to distinguish from (1), but are **more slender** and **tern-like in flight**. Less parasitic than other skuas and regularly scavenges at trawlers in Cape waters. **54 cm** (Langstertroofmeeu)

3 Pomarine Skua *Stercorarius pomarinus*
Uncommon summer visitor. Pale (a) and dark (b) morphs occur. Larger than (1), approaching size of Kelp Gull (p. 76). **Broader wings, bulkier body** and longer-tailed appearance also help to distinguish it. In breeding plumage, central tail feathers project 4–8 cm beyond tail and are **blunt and twisted**. Usually in pairs or small groups that chase gulls and terns. **50 cm** (Knopstertroofmeeu)

4 South Polar Skua *Catharacta maccormicki*   **V**
Rare vagrant. Pale morph told by its **whitish head**, golden nape and pale body **contrasting with dark brown upperparts**. Rare dark morph and immatures difficult to distinguish from (5) but are smaller and more compact and have smaller bills and heads. Solitary at sea; chases Cape Gannets (p. 68) at trawlers. Common in pack ice and on ice shelf. **52 cm** (Suidpoolroofmeeu)

5 Subantarctic (Southern) Skua *Stercorarius antarcticus*
Common all-year visitor. Superficially like immature Kelp Gull (p. 76), but larger and darker, with **conspicuous white flashes at base of primaries**. Bill more robust than (3). Distinguished from other skuas by **bulky, broad-winged appearance** and **short, wedge-shaped tail**; cf. (4). Usually solitary at sea, but gathers in flocks around trawlers. Regularly seen from shore. **58 cm** (Bruinroofmeeu)

a

long, pointed
tail projections

narrow
wing base

1

no distinct
white patch

2

a

short,
pointed tail
projections

b

b

3

broad
wing base

blunt, twisted
tail projections

a

whitish
head

4

short,
wedge-
shaped
tail

wings
markedly
broader than
(1–3)

robust bill

5

wings
darker
than body

prominent
white
flashes

GULLS AND KITTIWAKES

A well-known group of scavenging shore and sea birds, most with **white underparts** and **grey or black upperparts**. Their tails are rounded or shallowly forked, their bills and feet yellowish or reddish. Gulls **do not dive into the water**, but pluck offal or refuse from the surface or from land. Flocks utter loud screaming sounds when feeding.

1 Hartlaub's Gull *Chroicocephalus hartlaubii* **E**

Common to abundant endemic resident. Slightly smaller than (5). In breeding plumage, differs in having **faint traces of a grey hood, dark eyes** (as in juvenile (5)) and **deeper red bill and legs**. At other times **head is entirely white**. Juvenile also has all-white head; bill and legs dark brown; sometimes only a few black spots show on tail-tip when close to attaining full adult plumage. The most common small gull of the west coast. **38 cm** (Hartlaubmeeu)

2 Franklin's Gull *Leucophaeus pipixcan* **V**

Rare summer vagrant. Breeding adult has **all-black head with white eyelids** and **rosy flush on breast**. Grey wings with a **white bar separating the grey from a black wing-tip** are diagnostic. Non-breeding adult's head is grizzled black and white. Immature has a dark mantle and wings, white underparts and rump, broad black tail-tip and dark smudges on nape. Solitary or in company with other gulls. **33 cm** (Franklinmeeu)

3 Sabine's Gull *Xema sabini*

Common summer visitor. A small but distinctive, mostly pelagic gull with a striking **upperwing pattern** and tern-like flight. Combination of **all-black forewing, white wedges on inner wing** and **forked tail** diagnostic. In breeding plumage, whole head is dark grey and, at close range, **black bill with yellow tip** is visible. Non-breeding adults and immatures lack dark grey head, but have a **dark patch on nape and hindneck**. Solitary or in very large flocks at sea; rarely seen ashore. **33 cm** (Mikstertmeeu)

4 Black-headed Gull *Chroicocephalus ridibundus* **V**

Rare vagrant. Dark **chocolate-brown head** of breeding adult unmistakable. Otherwise differs from (1) and (5) in smaller size, shorter, thinner bill, **much greater expanse of white on forewing** and **white (not grey or dusky) underwing**. Occurs singly, often in company with (5). **35–38 cm** (Swartkopmeeu)

5 Grey-headed Gull *Chroicocephalus cirrocephalus*

Common to abundant resident. Breeding adult has **all-grey hood, pale yellow eyes** and **bright red bill and legs**. Non-breeding adult has a **grey smudge on the ear coverts only**; cf. (1). Immature has the front half of the head pale grey with a **darker ear-patch that extends over the crown**, a **dark eye** and either a dark-tipped bill with orange-pink base or a wholly dark bill (latter very rare variation). A gull of our **inland waters** (where it breeds) and coasts. **42 cm** (Gryskopmeeu)

6 Black-legged Kittiwake *Rissa tridactyla* **V**

Rare vagrant. **Yellow bill** and **grey upperwing with small black tip** diagnostic of adult. Immature very similar to (3) but larger. It also lacks the forked tail, has a dark bar across hindneck and a conspicuous open 'M'-pattern across upperwings. Solitary at sea or in company with (3). **41 cm** (Swartpootbrandervoël)

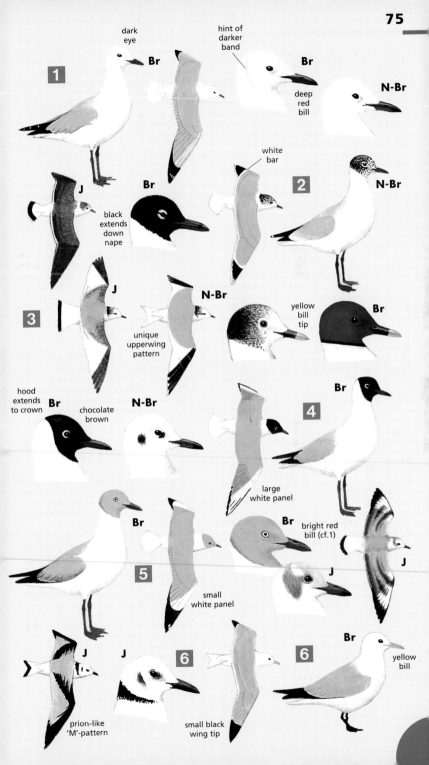

dark eye

Br

hint of darker band

Br

deep red bill

N-Br

1

white bar

J

Br

black extends down nape

2

N-Br

3

J

N-Br

unique upperwing pattern

yellow bill tip

Br

hood extends to crown

Br

chocolate brown

N-Br

4

Br

large white panel

5

Br

Br

small white panel

Br

bright red bill (cf.1)

J

J

J

prion-like 'M'-pattern

J

6

small black wing tip

6

Br

yellow bill

1 Kelp Gull *Larus dominicanus*

Very common resident. Adult has **dark eyes** and **whitish-yellow feet**; cf. (2). Immature (a) initially **mottled dark brown with paler barred rump** and **dark brown legs**; could be mistaken for a skua (p. 72), but lacks white patches at bases of primaries). With age becomes paler (b). Occurs singly or in small groups that scavenge along coasts, especially harbours; rarely inland. Local race *L.d. vetula* sometimes considered a separate species (Cape Gull); vagrant nominate race *L.d. dominicanus* has subtly different head shape and paler eyes, but very similar overall. **60 cm** (Swartrugmeeu)

2 Lesser Black-backed Gull *Larus fuscus* **R**

Uncommon visitor. Very similar to (1) but smaller and more slender, with **wings projecting well beyond tail at rest**. Bill less robust, thinner and more slender, eyes pale straw in colour (not dark), legs and feet bright chrome-yellow. In flight shows a **narrower white trailing edge to the wing**. Immature similar plumage sequence to (1) but generally paler, with same slender shape as adult and light pink (not dark brown) legs and feet. Occurs singly or in small groups at river estuaries and inland waters. Grey-backed *L.f. heuglini* often considered a separate species (Heuglin's Gull); this form occasionally recorded on east and south coast. **53–56 cm** (Kleinswartrugmeeu)

3 Heuglin's Gull *Larus fuscus heuglini* **V**

Rare vagrant to southern African coast. Migrates from northern Europe and Russia to overwinter in southwest and southeast Asia as well as East Africa. A large gull, very similar to (2) in appearance and, until recently, considered a subspecies of that and (4). Adult has a **pale yellow iris** (dark in juvenile) with a **dark-red orbital ring** and **long, bright yellow legs** (dull pinkish in juvenile), **slate-grey back and wings** (mottled brown in juvenile), with the **blackish wing-tips extending well beyond tail**. Differs from (2) in being larger and having a generally paler, more slender appearance; hind-head usually more heavily streaked brown due to late moulting. **58–60 cm** (Heuglinmeeu)

4 Slender-billed Gull *Chroicocephalus genei* **V**

Very rare vagrant from the Mediterranean and southern Asia, first recorded in Durban in 1999. **Slender, elegant-looking gull** with **pale grey wings and back**, with only the **tips of the outer primaries black** in adult bird. **Slender, slightly decurved bill is dark reddish brown; legs dark orange-red.** Differs from Hartlaub's Gull (p. 74) in being larger, has pale eye (dark in Hartlaub's), and lacks the white 'spots' on black primaries. **41–43 cm** (Dunbekmeeu)

a

J

takes several years to acquire adult plumage

b

J

dull greenish-grey or whitish-yellow feet

J

chrome-yellow feet

J

N-Br

black

1

usually dark eye

heavy bill

pale eye

slender bill

2

chrome-yellow feet

3

usually mottled head and neck, dark red eye-ring

N-Br

slender, dark reddish-brown bill, sloping forehead

some non-breeding adults with greyish hood

white outer primaries

pale grey back and wings

4

dark orange-red legs

SKIMMERS

Tern-like birds with **specialised bills** and feeding behaviour.

NEAR THREATENED

1 African Skimmer *Rynchops flavirostris* R

Fairly common, localised resident. A black and white **tern-like** bird with **distinctive bill structure**; this and feeding action diagnostic. Immature has streaked forehead, buff-edged feathers on upperparts and blackish bill with red base. Call is a harsh, lapwing-like 'krreh' or 'kweh' repeated. Feeds by flying low over the water's surface in a skimming action with the **long lower mandible immersed in the water**. Rests on sandbanks. Small flocks on large permanent rivers, lakes and lagoons. **38 cm** (Waterploeër)

TERNS

More slender, more agile than gulls and, in most species, with deeply forked tails. The majority feed at sea, **plunge-diving for fish**. A few – such as the marsh terns (p. 84) – feed mainly on insects **caught in dipping flight or plucked from the surface** of inland ponds, lakes and rivers. Calls are mostly similar and rather nondescript, typically 'kee-vit' or 'krit'.

2 Royal Tern *Thalasseus maximus* V

Rare vagrant to northern Namibian waters. Differs from very similar (4) in **black cap extending to bill** in breeding plumage and **orange (not yellow) bill**. In non-breeding plumage has almost white head, orange bill and **paler grey upperparts**. Usually solitary. **48–50 cm** (Koningsterretjie)

NEAR THREATENED

3 Caspian Tern *Hydroprogne caspia*

Common resident. **Largest tern** in southern Africa. **Massive red bill** and overall size render it unmistakable. In pairs or small flocks at coastal lagoons and large inland waters. **52 cm** (Reusesterretjie)

Great Crested ...

4 Swift Tern *Thalasseus bergii*

Common resident. Intermediate in size between (3) and Sandwich Tern (p. 80). **Bill is yellow**, not orange as in Lesser Crested Tern (p. 80) and (2). Immature has **heavily barred back and tail**, pale yellow bill and sometimes yellow legs. Occurs in small groups in coastal waters. Roosts on beaches and estuaries. **50 cm** (Geelbeksterretjie)

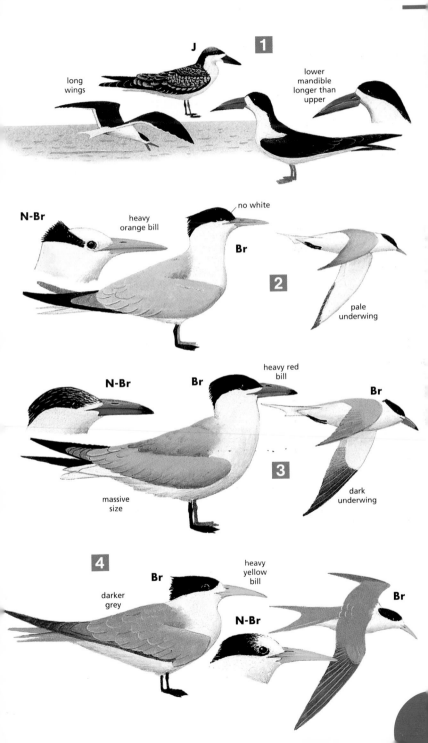

1

long wings

J

lower mandible longer than upper

N-Br

heavy orange bill

no white

Br

2

pale underwing

N-Br

Br

heavy red bill

Br

massive size

dark underwing

3

4

Br

darker grey

heavy yellow bill

N-Br

Br

1 Little Tern *Sternula albifrons*

Non-breeding summer visitor. With Damara Tern (p. 82) the **smallest tern** in the region. In breeding plumage distinguished from Damara Tern by **well-defined white forehead, yellow legs** and **black-tipped yellow bill**; in non-breeding and immature plumage, by shorter black bill and darker grey back; in flight by **dark leading edge of wings**, which contrasts with pale secondaries. Has **very fast wing beats** and frequently hovers when feeding. Small flocks mostly on the east coast. **24 cm** (Kleinsterretjie)

2 Black-naped Tern *Sterna sumatrana* ▐V▌

Rare vagrant. Intermediate in size between (1) and Common Tern (p. 82). A **small, very pale tern** with diagnostic **black line running from eyes** and broadening to form a **black patch on nape**. First primary feather noticeably black in flight, forming a **thin black line on leading edge of wing**. Immature resembles (1) but is larger, has longer, slightly decurved bill and pink flush on breast at close range. Associates with (1) and Common Tern (p. 82) on KwaZulu-Natal coast. **33 cm** (Swartneksterretjie)

3 Gull-billed Tern *Gelochelidon nilotica* ▐V▌

Rare vagrant. Similar in size to (4) but differs in having a **thick, stubby, black bill** unlike that of any other tern. At rest, reveals **unusually long legs** and stands higher than other terns. Occurs **mostly over inland waters** and feeds like a marsh tern (p. 84), often pursuing insects. **38 cm** (Oostelike Sterretjie)

4 Sandwich Tern *Thalasseus sandvicensis*

Common summer visitor. Much larger than Common Tern (p. 82), its **back paler** than other similar-sized terns. Differs from (3) in much slimmer appearance and **long, thin bill**, which is **black with a yellow tip**. Call is a loud 'kweet'. Occurs in small groups along the coast; feeds just offshore and rests on beaches. **40 cm** (Grootsterretjie)

5 Lesser Crested Tern *Thalasseus bengalensis*

Common summer visitor. Similar in size to (4) but has darker back and **orange bill**. Differs from (6) in smaller size (difficult to judge if not directly compared) and **orange bill**, and from much larger Royal Tern (p. 78) in size and darker grey back. Feeds in small numbers over estuaries and open sea, mostly from Durban northwards. The most common coastal tern in Mozambique. **40 cm** (Kuifkopsterretjie)

6 Elegant Tern *Thalasseus elegans* ▐V▌

Rare vagrant. Most similar to (5), distinguished by **slightly downcurved upper mandible**, and **slightly longer and thinner bill**. Bill also slightly brighter **reddish orange**; sometimes shows a yellower tip and culmen. **Long crest** gives the head a shaggy appearance. Rump and tail paler grey than (5) (may look white in the field). In non-breeding plumage, black crown more restricted, but retains a black patch around eye; cf. non-breeding (5). Juvenile has shorter and more yellowish bill. Could also be confused with larger, more robust and stronger-billed Royal Tern (p. 78), which has shorter crest and usually more white on forehead. To date recorded only twice in the subregion: Strandfontein, Jan 2006, and Swakopmund, Feb 2007. Normally breeds off the Pacific coast of the southern USA and Mexico, wintering in Central and South America. Favours coastal habitats; likely to be encountered in mixed tern roosts. Call similar to that of (4): a loud 'kweet'. **40–43 cm** (Elegante Sterretjie)

NEAR THREATENED

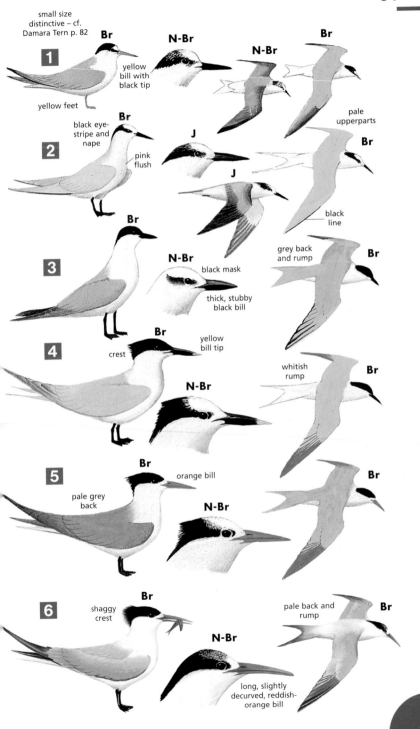

1 small size distinctive – cf. Damara Tern p. 82

Br   N-Br   N-Br   Br

yellow bill with black tip

yellow feet

pale upperparts

2 black eye-stripe and nape

Br   J   J   Br

pink flush

black line

3 Br   N-Br

black mask

thick, stubby black bill

grey back and rump   Br

4 Br   N-Br

crest   yellow bill tip

whitish rump   Br

5 Br   N-Br

orange bill

pale grey back

Br

6 Br   N-Br

shaggy crest

pale back and rump   Br

long, slightly decurved, reddish-orange bill

1 Damara Tern *Sternula balaenarum* **E**
Uncommon endemic resident. **Small size** and **all-black cap** diagnostic of breeding plumage. At other times differs from Little Tern (p. 80) in **longer, slightly decurved bill**, **paler grey back** and **dumpier body shape**. In flight, the leading edge of wings not as dark as in Little Tern; at long range **appears almost white**. Small groups on southern and west coast, feeding offshore and in bays and estuaries. Frequently hovers and flies with very fast, flicking wing beats. **23 cm** (Damarasterretjie)

2 White-cheeked Tern *Sterna repressa* **V**
Rare vagrant. In breeding plumage almost identical to (5), differing in **uniformly dark grey back, rump and tail**. Also difficult to tell from (3), but is slightly smaller and much darker; **underparts are grey**. Flies like a marsh tern (p. 84). Occurs singly in roosts of (3). **33 cm** (Witwangsterretjie)

3 Common Tern *Sterna hirundo*
Abundant summer visitor. Distinguished from (4) and (5) by **longer bill** and, at rest, **noticeably longer legs**; in flight in non-breeding plumage by **grey rump and tail** (not white), and by only the **inner primaries appearing translucent**. In breeding plumage, red bill has black tip. Occurs in thousands offshore, roosting in estuaries and on beaches. **35 cm** (Gewone Sterretjie)

4 Arctic Tern *Sterna paradisaea*
Common summer visitor. Differs from (3) in much **whiter appearance, very short legs, shorter, thinner bill** and more buoyant flight. In non-breeding plumage, **grey back contrasts with white rump and tail. All primaries appear translucent.** Frequents roosts of (3) on beaches and in estuaries. **35 cm** (Arktiese Sterretjie)

5 Antarctic Tern *Sterna vittata*
Common winter visitor. Breeding plumage unmistakable: **overall dark grey with long white cheek-stripe** and **black cap** (cf. Whiskered Tern, p. 84). Differs from rare (2) in white (not grey) rump and tail and from (6) in darker grey colour, plumper body and **thicker, more robust bill.** Non-breeding plumage retains much of the grey underparts; **bill remains dark red with black at tip and along ridges.** Immature heavily barred buff on mantle. Roosts on rocky shorelines and sandy beaches. Feeds far out at sea. **38 cm** (Grysborssterretjie)

6 Roseate Tern *Sterna dougallii* **R**
Uncommon resident. Differs from all other small terns in **much paler back** (looks wholly white at long range) and **red bill with dark tip**. In breeding plumage, **breast is suffused with pink** but looks white at a distance. **Tail-streamers very long.** Occurs singly or in small groups at coast; found in roosts of (3). **38 cm** (Rooiborssterretjie)

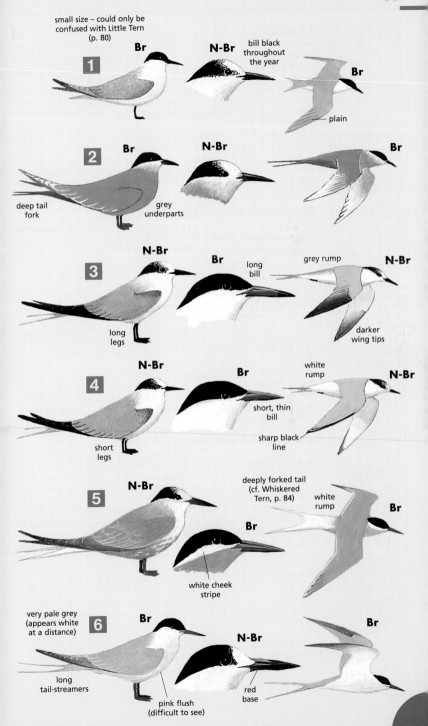

small size – could only be confused with Little Tern (p. 80)

1

Br

N-Br

bill black throughout the year

Br

plain

2

Br

N-Br

Br

deep tail fork

grey underparts

3

N-Br

Br

long bill

grey rump

N-Br

long legs

darker wing tips

4

N-Br

Br

white rump

N-Br

short, thin bill

sharp black line

short legs

5

N-Br

deeply forked tail (cf. Whiskered Tern, p. 84)

white rump

Br

Br

white cheek stripe

6

very pale grey (appears white at a distance)

Br

N-Br

Br

long tail-streamers

pink flush (difficult to see)

red base

1 Sooty Tern *Onychoprion fuscata*
Uncommon visitor. Very similar to (2) but has **dark brown (not grey-brown) back** and small triangular white forehead-patch with **no white stripe over the eyes**. Immature is sooty-brown above and below, with buff speckling on back, a pale vent and white outer tail feathers. The call is a harsh 'wekawek'. Normally seen only in small numbers after cyclonic weather off the east coast, but very common over deeper waters of the Mozambique Channel. **42 cm** (Roetsterretjie)

2 Bridled Tern *Onychoprion anaethetus*   **V**
Rare vagrant. Slightly smaller than (1), differing in **grey-brown back** that contrast with **darker wings and tail**. White on forehead is narrower and extends as **white eyebrow-stripe above and behind eyes**. Immature is white below; upperparts are barred buff, not speckled as in (1). Occurs on east coast with (1) after cyclones. **38 cm** (Brilsterretjie)

3 Common (Brown) Noddy *Anous stolidus*   **V**
Rare vagrant. Main differences between this species and (4) are **size, bill length** and **extent of white on crown**. Occurs singly, from Mozambique to southwestern Cape. Is sometimes mobbed by Hartlaub's Gulls (p. 74), which mistake it for a skua. **41 cm** (Grootbruinsterretjie)

4 Lesser Noddy *Anous tenuirostris*   **V**
Rare vagrant. Differs from (3) in **size, bill length** and **extent of white on crown**. Immature very similar to adult but has whiter forehead. Occurs on east coast in roosts of Common Terns (p. 82) after storms. **36 cm** (Kleinbruinsterretjie)

5 Black Tern *Chlidonias niger*
Uncommon summer visitor. In non-breeding plumage differs from other marsh terns in slightly smaller size and generally much **darker appearance**. The back, rump and tail are uniformly dark. More extensive black on head and diagnostic **black smudges on sides of breast**. Rarely seen inland over fresh water; occurs on coast alongside Common Terns (p. 82) and feeds at sea. **23 cm** (Swartsterretjie)

6 Whiskered Tern *Chlidonias hybrida*
Uncommon resident. In breeding plumage differs from White-cheeked Tern (p. 82) in **short tail with a shallow fork** and **white vent**; from Antarctic Tern (p. 82) in **short grey (not white) tail**. In non-breeding plumage differs from other marsh terns in less extensive black on head, plainer upperwings, pale grey (not white) rump, **thicker, heavier bill** and less buoyant flight. Call is a characteristic dry 'kerk'. Occurs (and occasionally breeds) **on freshwater pans and lakes**. **23 cm** (Witbaardsterretjie)

7 White-winged Tern *Chlidonias leucopterus*
Common summer visitor. Unmistakable in breeding plumage, with wholly **black body and underwing coverts** and **pale grey to white wings**. In non-breeding plumage differs from (5) in paler head, whitish-grey rump, the tail being paler than the back and **lack of dark smudges on sides of breast**. Its buoyant flight, more contrasting upperwings, paler rump, weaker bill and **black ear-spot** distinguish it from (6). Occurs **over fresh water, sometimes in large numbers**. **23 cm** (Witvlerksterretjie)

white limited to forehead

dark brown back

white eyebrow

1

grey-brown back

contrasting grey mantle

2

thick bill

3

extensive white on crown

thin bill

4

solid black cap

grey rump

Br

5

N-Br

N-Br

dark grey wing

black smudge

heavy bill

white stripe

Br

6

Br

plain wings

short tail

grey wing

N-Br

(cf. Antarctic Tern, p. 82)

black ear-spot

weak bill

Br

7

Br

whitish-grey rump

N-Br

pale grey to white wing

darker wing tips

PELICANS

Huge white waterbirds with large bodies, **short legs with webbed feet**, long necks, **long bills** and a **naked distensible pouch beneath the lower mandible**. They catch fish by gathering in flocks and driving the shoals into shallow water, where they scoop the fish up in their bill-pouches. They walk awkwardly but **soar effortlessly, sometimes to great heights**.

VULNERABLE

■ Pink-backed Pelican *Pelecanus rufescens*

Uncommon, localised resident. Adult in non-breeding plumage has **grey upperparts** and a **greyish-white head and underparts**. The bill is **pale yellow with a pink tip**; legs are buff. In flight told from (2) by **greyish underwings** and **dark grey (not black) flight feathers**. Adult in breeding plumage has a rich yellow bill-pouch with a pink edge to the upper mandible, rich orange-yellow legs and feet, and pinkish feathers on the back (visible only at close range). Immature has a rust-brown head, neck and upperparts, white underparts, and pale yellow bill and pouch. Breeding populations occur in KwaZulu-Natal and northern Botswana; a vagrant elsewhere. **135 cm** (Kleinpelikaan)

NEAR THREATENED

② Great White Pelican *Pelecanus onocrotalus*

Common, localised resident. Adult in non-breeding plumage told from (1) by larger size and **all-white appearance**. The bill is pale yellow and pink, and the **bill-pouch and legs are yellow**. In flight the **white underwings contrast with black flight feathers**. Adult in breeding plumage has a pink flush to the body and a yellow patch on the upper breast; the upper mandible remains pink and grey and the pouch yellow, but the **legs and feet turn pink**. Head and neck of immature dusky in various degrees (darkest when young); has dark-brown wings and tail and yellowish underparts. Occurs in flocks on coastal islands (including artificial guano islands), estuaries, bays, lagoons and occasionally on large dams. Locally common in the vicinity of Cape Town, Walvis Bay and Swakopmund in Namibia and in northern Botswana. **180 cm** (Witpelikaan)

white area
around eye

1

N-Br

overall greyer
than (2)

J

greyish
underwings

1

Br

pink back
(difficult to
see)

pink area
around eye

Br

yellow
patch

black-
and-white
wings

J

2

pink legs
and feet

yellow
face

N-Br

overall whiter
than (1)

CORMORANTS

Waterbirds with **webbed feet, long necks** and **hooked bills**. They hunt for fish and frogs **under water**, surfacing to swallow prey. Their bodies are partially submerged when they swim, and they habitually **stand out of the water with wings outspread**. They are mostly silent, except for raucous squabbling at breeding colonies.

NEAR THREATENED

1 Cape Cormorant *Phalacrocorax capensis* ⬛ N E

Common to abundant near-endemic resident. Breeding adult told by entirely **glossy green-black plumage, head without crest** and **base of bill orange-yellow**. Non-breeding adult and immature dusky brown; paler on belly. Occurs singly or in flocks in coastal waters, roosting on offshore islands. **Groups habitually fly in long lines over the sea** and feed in flocks. **64 cm** (Trekduiker)

ENDANGERED

2 Bank Cormorant *Phalacrocorax neglectus* ⬛ E

Common endemic resident. Told by **heavy-bodied appearance, crested head** and a **white rump when breeding**. Wings dark brown. Rest of body is **black with bronze sheen**. Immature duller black. Occurs singly or in small groups in coastal waters; often seen **standing on small islands and offshore rocks**. **75 cm** (Bankduiker)

NEAR THREATENED

3 Crowned Cormorant *Microcarbo coronatus* ⬛ E

Fairly common endemic resident. A small **marine cormorant** told from (4) by an overall **blacker appearance, permanent crest** and shorter tail. Immature is brown. Occurs singly or in small groups on rocky coastlines and coastal islands; occasionally lagoons. **54 cm** (Kuifkopduiker)

4 Reed Cormorant *Microcarbo africanus*

Common resident. Adults have **all-black bodies** (male with small crest on forehead), **grey-brown speckled wings, yellow to reddish facial skin** and ruby-red eyes. The **bill is yellow**. The brownish immature has **off-white (never pure white) underparts**. Upper breast is more buffy (cf. (5)). Female illustrated is a sub-adult, at which stage it is able to breed. Occurs singly or in groups on any **inland water**. Occasionally seen at the coast; cf. (2). **60 cm** (Rietduiker)

5 White-breasted Cormorant *Phalacrocorax lucidus*

Common or localised resident. Identified by **large size, white throat and breast** or, in immature, **entirely white underparts** (much whiter than immature of considerably smaller (4)). Adult has **green eyes**, pale grey bill with a darker culmen and **yellow facial skin**. Occurs singly or in groups on coastal rocks, islands and estuaries, and in large inland waters. **90 cm** (Witborsduiker)

DARTERS

Slender-necked, straight-billed diving birds.

6 African Darter *Anhinga rufa*

Common resident. Long, thin neck with a **characteristic kink, straight (not hooked) bill**, rufous coloration and slender appearance. Male has **grey bill**; blacker than female, with silvery-beige plumes on mantle when breeding. Female browner; bill creamy-white. Immature similar to female, with indistinct head and wing markings. Swims with only head and neck above water; perches with outstretched wings after swimming. May call a guttural 'ger-ge-ger-ger-gerkgerr-ger' for long periods while perched. Occurs singly or in small groups on large inland waters. **79 cm** (Slanghalsvoël)

small crest

appears large-headed with thick neck

no yellow on throat

J

1

orange-yellow at base of bill

no crest

2

white rump in breeding plumage

heavy-set

crest present year-round

3

♂

4

♀

J

off-white to buffy breast

pointed bill

5

J

pure white throat and breast

6

J

long, snake-like neck

silvery-beige plumes on mantle when breeding

HERONS, EGRETS AND BITTERNS

Water-associated birds with **long bills and necks** and long legs. When breeding, many species have long, filamentous plumes on their back or lower breast (or both), while others have more or less permanent long plumes on their napes. **In flight, they tuck their heads into their shoulders**, thus differing from storks, ibises and cranes. They seldom soar. Many herons are solitary in habit and secretive, while others are gregarious and seen more frequently. Most perch in trees and nest in trees or reeds, or even on the ground. All have harsh, squawking voices heard mostly when flushed. The four comparative silhouettes on the page opposite represent (a): Dwarf Bittern (1); (b): Squacco Heron (p. 92); (c): Little Egret (p. 96); and (d): Grey Heron (p. 98).

1 **Dwarf Bittern** *Ixobrychus sturmii*
Uncommon summer resident and visitor. Told by **slate-grey upperparts** and **heavily streaked underparts**; orange-yellow legs and feet often hang down in flight. Immature is rufous below with rufous-tipped feathers above. Flight is direct and pigeon-like. Usually solitary and largely crepuscular or nocturnal. Frequents well-wooded rivers and **bushes or thickets standing in floodwaters.** When disturbed may adopt a sky-pointing posture, as illustrated. **Perches in a tree when flushed.** Nomadic. **25 cm (Dwergrietreier)**

2 **Little Bittern** *Ixobrychus minutus*
Uncommon resident and visitor. **Bold black-edged wings** of male unmistakable; female recognised by **buffy neck** and **black cap**. Immature differs from that of (1) mainly in paler, less rufous underparts and **olive (not orange-yellow) legs**; from immature of (4) in **tawny (not dark) folded wings.** Solitary or scattered in **reed beds or sedges.** A diurnal species. Difficult to flush; adopts sky-pointing posture to avoid detection. In flight, the **bold black and buff wings** are unmistakable. Nomadic. **26 cm (Kleinrietreier)**

CRITICALLY ENDANGERED

3 **Great Bittern** *Botaurus stellaris* 　　　　　　　**R**
Rare resident. Similar to immature of Black-crowned Night-Heron (p. 92), but a **much larger bird** with a more **thickset appearance.** More **heavily streaked overall**, with **black cap** and **yellow or red-brown eyes.** In flight, **feet project entirely beyond tail.** Flies with slow wing beats on broad, owl-like wings. Normal take-off call is 'squark'; otherwise utters a **deep booming call day or night** during the summer breeding season. Solitary and highly secretive in seasonal flood plains, permanent marshes and streams in grassland, where it remains mostly concealed in reed beds and similar dense vegetation. When alarmed, adopts an **upright, sky-pointing stance** that blends well with a background of dry reeds; it is not easily flushed. **64 cm (Grootrietreier)**

4 **Striated Heron** *Butorides striata*
Common resident. Its **upperparts appear grey-green**, with **creamy feather edges.** Sides of neck and flanks grey, **cap black; yellow feet** prominent on take-off. Immature identified by dark upperparts with **whitish spots on folded wings**; cf. immatures of (1) and (2). When flushed, gives a sharp and startling 'kew'! A common small heron, usually found singly on well-wooded rivers, large dams, pans, estuaries and lagoons with mangroves. Active by day, hunting from a low branch or dead tree in water or on shoreline. Perches in a tree when flushed. Not as secretive as others on this page, often standing in exposed positions. **41 cm (Groenrugreier)**

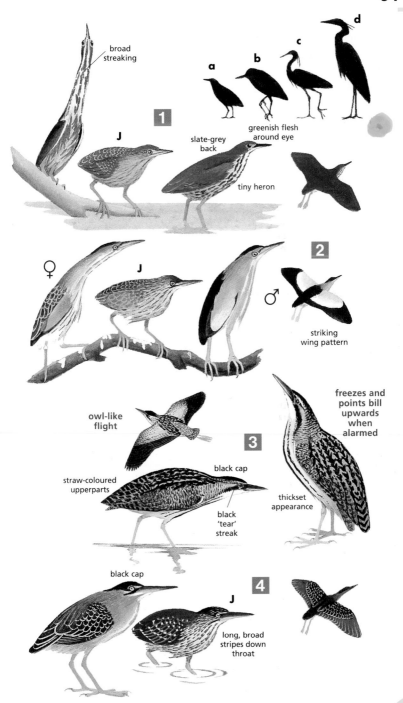

broad streaking

1

a   b   c   d

greenish flesh around eye

J

slate-grey back

tiny heron

♀   **J**   ♂

2

striking wing pattern

owl-like flight

3

freezes and points bill upwards when alarmed

black cap

straw-coloured upperparts

black 'tear' streak

thickset appearance

black cap

4

J

long, broad stripes down throat

ENDANGERED

1 **Malagasy Pond-Heron** *Ardeola idae* **V**
Rare winter vagrant. Occurs only in non-breeding plumage, when very difficult to distinguish from (2). Differs in **darker brown upperparts,** contrasting strongly with white wings in flight, **broader and bolder neck streaks** and heavier bill. **Bill greenish** with **black tip and culmen.** Recorded occasionally in eastern Zimbabwe and especially in wetlands in Mozambique; regular in East Africa. **47 cm** (Madagaskar-ralreier)

2 **Squacco Heron** *Ardeola ralloides*
Common to very common resident. In non-breeding plumage differs from (1) in **paler, less contrasting upperparts, yellowish bill** and **blackish culmen. Legs normally pale yellow** but pinkish red for a few days when breeding. Young birds can be quite dark above and have broader neck streaks; appear very similar to (1). In flight **looks like a white egret** unless **biscuit-coloured or pale orange upperparts** are visible. Solitary at lakes, lagoons, marshes, sewage ponds and streams. **43 cm** (Ralreier)

3 **Rufous-bellied Heron** *Ardeola rufiventris*
Uncommon summer resident and visitor. A robust, all-dark heron; in good light the **maroon wings and belly** are diagnostic. Non-breeding adult has **pale yellow bill (upper mandible grey), facial skin and legs.** When breeding the bill, facial skin and legs become coral-pink. Immature has **buff-edged feathers on its upperparts.** Nomadic, solitary and secretive near secluded waters with ample fringing and surface vegetation. When flushed, perches in a tree or drops into dense vegetation. **58 cm** (Rooipensreier)

VULNERABLE

4 **White-backed Night-Heron** *Gorsachius leuconotus* **R**
Uncommon resident. **Dark hood, white facial markings, yellow legs** and **rufous body** diagnostic. Upperparts grey in male, dark brown in female and immature. **White back-plumes** present at all ages. When alarmed into flight, utters a toad-like 'kraak'. Occurs singly or in pairs, sparsely distributed on quiet rivers and dams. **Secretive, hiding by day in dense waterside vegetation** and emerging only at night. Most frequent at Lowveld rivers and on the panhandle of the Okavango River in northern Botswana. **53 cm** (Witrugnagreier)

5 **Black-crowned Night-Heron** *Nycticorax nycticorax*
Common resident and visitor. Adult has characteristic **black cap and back** contrasting with **white and grey wings and underparts**; nape-plumes may be absent. Immature can be mistaken for adult of Great Bittern (p. 90) but is smaller, with **orange eyes** and **white spots to the tips of the feathers** on the upperparts. Single birds, pairs or groups occur on river backwaters, dams and lagoons. Roosts in trees or waterside vegetation by day. Some roosts may harbour many of the birds at a time. It emerges late afternoon in preparation for nocturnal hunting, and is often heard flying overhead at night, uttering a high-pitched and slightly rasping 'wok'. Nomadic when not breeding. **56 cm** (Gewone Nagreier)

darker above than (2)

1

heavy
bill

N-Br

bold
streaking

completely white
in breeding
plumage

fine
streaking
down sides
of neck

N-Br

2

Br

biscuit-
coloured

white wings
revealed in
flight

Br

appears quite
dark

3

maroon
panels

N-Br

dark hood

4

conspicuous white
area around eye

J

small white
patch most
visible in flight

black cap

whitish
spots

J

broad
wings

black
back

5

1 Black Heron *Egretta ardesiaca*

Uncommon to locally common resident. Differs from (2) in more robust proportions, uniform overall colouring, **dark eyes** and **dark legs with bright yellow feet**. Has **unique habit of forming a canopy with its wings** when fishing. Single birds or groups – sometimes large flocks – found at the fringes of lagoons, floodpans and dams, less often on rivers. Nomadic. **66 cm** (Swartreier)

VULNERABLE

2 Slaty Egret *Egretta vinaceigula*

Uncommon, localised resident. In proportions like a slate-grey Little Egret (p. 96). Distinguished from (1) by **yellow lower legs and feet** and, at close range, **buff foreneck** and **yellow eyes and facial skin**. Plumes on the nape sometimes absent. Seen mostly singly in shallow, well-vegetated floodpans and river backwaters of the Okavango Delta, Linyanti and Chobe River regions of northern Botswana; a vagrant elsewhere. **60 cm** (Rooikeelreier)

3 Little Blue Heron *Egretta caerulea* V

Rare vagrant. A wanderer from the Americas. A single bird has been recorded on several occasions in the Western Cape. Best told by its **prune-coloured head and neck, with blue-grey body and long plumes along its back**. Legs and feet greeny-grey (not yellow as in Little and Snowy Egrets, p 96); **pale yellow eye**. Immature completely white; can have slate-grey blotching as it attains adult plumage. Both adults and juveniles have a two-toned bill: greyish with dark tip. Found close to waters-edge in lagoons, swamps and estuaries. **64–74 cm** (Kleinbloureier)

4 Western Reef Heron *Egretta gularis* V

Rare vagrant. Occurs in two colour morphs, the dark morph (a) being the more common. Best told by its **blue-grey plumage with white chin and upper throat**, the **rather heavy, blackish bill, and the legs with thick tarsi and yellow feet**. The less common white morph (b) can be confused with the Little Egret (p. 96) but differs (usually) in having some grey in the plumage. It also has a heavier, yellow-and-black bill and **shorter, olive-green legs and feet**; the lower legs (tarsi) are heavier than in Little Egret. A heron of rocky shorelines in West and East Africa, the white morph being most frequent on Indian Ocean shorelines. **56–66 cm** (Westelike Kusreier)

dark eye

1

blackish

adopts unique
'canopy' posture
when fishing

dark legs

yellow feet

yellow
eye

buff
foreneck

dark grey
with blueish
tinge

longer winged
than (1)

2

J

yellow
lower legs

bill has deep base
and is slightly
decurved

usually some
yellow on tip
and on culmen

4

3

maroon-red
head and neck

white
upper
throat

dark horn-
coloured bill

J

a

b

two-toned
bill (both ad.
and juv.)

greenish-
grey legs

thick
tarsi

often olive-tinged
(not black)

dull
yellow
feet

bill and legs more
robust-looking than
Little Egret (p. 96)

1 Cattle Egret *Bubulcus ibis*

Very common resident, with numbers increasing in summer when resident birds are augmented by a migratory influx from central Africa. **Buff plumes** present on the head, back and breast of breeding adults from October to March only. **Bill short and yellow** (coral when breeding); legs the same. **Feet are dusky.** Immature differs from (2) in **smaller size, shorter, thicker neck** and **black feet. Flocks of varying sizes attend grazing cattle** or wild animals (especially buffaloes) in reserves. Flies to and from regular roosts mornings and evenings. Large numbers breed in reeds or in trees over water; **may rest on shorelines but seldom feed in water. 54 cm** (Veereier)

2 Little Egret *Egretta garzetta*

Fairly common resident. Larger, **longer-necked** and **more slenderly proportioned than (1). Bill and legs longer and black; feet yellow.** Head-plumes normal in adults, breast-plumes and back-plumes briefly present when breeding. Immature lacks plumes. Solitary on quiet inland waters, estuaries and coastal pools; always near water. Stands quietly in shallows or walks forward slowly, stealthily hunting, occasionally darting forwards or doing a quick 'dance' when pursuing prey. **64 cm** (Kleinwitreier)

3 Snowy Egret *Egretta thula* ▮V

Rare vagrant. Very difficult to distinguish from (2) and variation in both species causes further complications. Typically shows **bright yellow lores, which extend between the eye and base of the bill.** In (2), this area is mostly grey, but may be pink, orange or dull yellow in breeding season. In breeding plumage, shows **bushy tuft of short plumes,** compared to the long, drooping plumes on hindcrown of (2). Legs and feet variable, but in non-breeding plumage has **yellow colour extending up to knee-joint (or higher) on back of legs,** a pattern very rarely shown by (2). Juvenile and non-breeding birds have contrasting **grey or even pale yellow lower mandible.** Note that some birds (particularly juveniles) are probably indistinguishable from (2) in the field. Usually silent, but may utter a typical egret croak while foraging. A rare but possibly overlooked vagrant from the Americas. **55–65 cm** (Sneeuwitreier)

4 Intermediate Egret *Egretta intermedia*

Uncommon resident. Larger than (1) and (2), more heavily built, but smaller than (5). Plumes usually absent or reduced when not breeding. **Bill and upper legs yellow** (orange-red when breeding); **lower legs and feet blackish green.** The neck has the characteristic kink of the larger herons and, in profile, the **long lower neck feathers tend to hang proud of the body;** cf. (5). Often confused with (5), but can be told by the **short gape that finishes below the eye (not behind it).** Usually solitary on quiet, well-vegetated pans and floodlands. **68 cm** (Geelbekwitreier)

5 Western Great Egret *Ardea alba*

Fairly common resident. Almost the size of Grey Heron (p. 98). **Long-necked, long-legged egret** with **orange-yellow bill;** frequently misidentified as (4), but is much larger with **entirely black legs and feet.** The **line of the gape extends behind the eye;** cf. (4). For a few weeks when breeding, the bill is black, often with a yellow base, and filamentous plumes are present on the back. Single birds usually seen standing motionless in shallows of large rivers, dams, estuaries and floodpans. Dispersive and nomadic. **95 cm** (Grootwitreier)

Br

N-Br

short yellow bill

short neck

J

1

short legs, black feet

pointed, slender black bill

Br

2

N-Br

black legs

yellow lores

short, shaggy plumes

3

gape extends behind eye

yellow feet

yellow bill

Br

about size of Grey Heron (p.98)

N-Br

long neck

shorter neck than (5)

4

yellowish upper legs difficult to see

5

all-black legs

1 Grey Heron   *Ardea cinerea*

Common resident. At rest, appearance of adult differs from that of (4) in the **white crown above a broad black band** that extends from forehead to nape; head and neck otherwise white. **Bill and legs yellow** (reddish when breeding). In flight, shows **entirely grey underwings**. Immature is much paler than adult and immature of (4), also differing in having yellow (not pale grey) bill and legs. Solitary, **feeding in the shallows of quiet dams, pans, rivers, lagoons and estuaries**. May sometimes forage in coastal rock pools. Stands motionless for long periods or creeps forward stealthily in a crouched attitude. **100 cm** (Bloureier)

2 Purple Heron   *Ardea purpurea*

Fairly common resident. Often confused with (3) but is **much smaller, more slender**. The striped **neck snake-like**, the **bill thin**. Immature entirely rufous with darker feathers on the upperparts and rufous patches on upperwings visible in flight; similar size as adult. Solitary and secretive, preferring the shelter of reeds and other emergent vegetation fringing quiet dams, pans and marsh pools. May visit garden fish ponds. Nomadic. **89 cm** (Rooireier)

3 Goliath Heron   *Ardea goliath*

Uncommon resident. **Larger than all other herons** and more robustly proportioned, with **slate-grey upperparts** and **rich rufous underparts**. The **heavy bill and long legs are slate-grey**. Immature similar to adult, but rufous areas are paler. Occurs singly or in pairs on rivers, lakes, pans and estuaries. **Hunts in deeper water than most other herons**, standing motionless for long periods or walking slowly. Flies with **very slow wing beats**. **140 cm** (Reusereier)

4 Black-headed Heron   *Ardea melanocephala*

Common resident. Differs from the superficially similar (1) in **entirely black (or dark blue-grey) cap and back of neck**, and **slate-grey bill and legs**. In flight told by **black and grey underwings**. Immature greyer than immature of (1); bill and legs pale grey (not yellow). Occurs singly or in scattered groups in grassland (especially pastures), grassy road verges, farmlands and marshes. **Seldom feeds in water** but roosts and breeds in trees or in reeds over water. **97 cm** (Swartkopreier)

J

dark streak

yellowish bill

1

mostly aquatic habitats

uniformly grey underwings

yellow legs

thin, pointed bill

striped neck

2

J

black cap and back of neck

4

mostly dry land habitats

two-tone underwings

thick brown neck

heavy bill

3

world's largest heron

J

pale grey legs

STORKS

Large to very large **long-legged and long-necked birds** with **straight, stout bills**. Plumage mostly **black and white**; bills and legs whitish, reddish or dark. Storks walk with a stately gait and frequently rest on the ground with the **lower parts of their legs stretched forward** (see illustration of immature Marabou (2)). **In flight, the neck is stretched out** (unlike herons, which fly with retracted necks) and the legs may trail down at a slight angle to the body. Most storks **sometimes soar to great heights** during the heat of the day; many are communal in habit and most frequent water or damp places to some extent. Diet ranges from large insects, reptiles, frogs and other waterlife to carrion in one species. They make **guttural sounds and hisses** at nests, and **bill-clapping is used as a greeting between pairs**. The nests are large stick structures placed in trees or on rocks, cliffs or the ground.

ENDANGERED

1 Saddle-billed Stork *Ephippiorhynchus senegalensis*
Uncommon resident. A large, **strikingly coloured stork** unlikely to be confused with any other either at rest or in flight. Male has **small yellow wattles** and **dark iris**; female **lacks wattles** and shows **yellow iris**. Immature has grey instead of black markings, the white areas mottled with black; bill dull, blackish. Occurs singly or in pairs in the shallows of large rivers, lakes, dams, flood plains and marshes. **145 cm** (Saalbekooievaar)

NEAR THREATENED

2 Marabou Stork *Leptoptilos crumeniferus*
Uncommon to locally common visitor and resident. A **huge, bare-headed, bare-necked stork** with a **distensible fleshy pouch** on the lower foreneck. Unlike other storks, **flies with the neck tucked in**. Immature has a woolly covering to the head. Generally occurs in groups, numbering from a few individuals to larger flocks, frequently **associating with vultures at animal carcasses and refuse dumps**. Mostly found in wildlife sanctuaries where many congregate at kills or around camps. Groups also gather on river sandbanks to bathe and rest. Sometimes soars to great heights. Otherwise spends much time standing inactive or perched. **152 cm** (Maraboe)

yellow iris

bold black-and-white pattern

♀

dark iris

unmistakable bill and saddle

♂

small yellow wattles

1

red 'knees'

bare fleshy pouch

2

J

defecates on legs, which gives white colour

1 White Stork *Ciconia ciconia*

Common summer visitor and resident. Unmistakable large black-and-white stork with **red bill and legs**. In flight distinguished from Yellow-billed Stork (p. 104) by **white tail**. In summer large flocks feed in grassland, farmlands and bushveld, often mixing with (3). Tend to avoid large, permanent floodplains and marshes. Flocks often soar at great heights on hot days. May suddenly appear in a district and remain a few days to feed, then depart, this behaviour especially linked to infestations of agricultural pests. Seen singly or in small groups. Annual influxes vary from year to year. **117 cm** (Witooievaar)

NEAR THREATENED

2 Black Stork *Ciconia nigra*

Uncommon resident. Similar to (3) but differs in **larger size, red bill** and **longer, red legs**. In flight differs in **black (not white) rump**. Immature has yellowish-green bill and legs, and duller black plumage. Occurs singly or in pairs but groups sometimes gather to roost in trees at night. Frequents cliffs and gorges when breeding, otherwise forages around rivers, dams and estuaries. **122 cm** (Grootswartooievaar)

3 Abdim's Stork *Ciconia abdimii*

Common non-breeding summer visitor. Smaller, shorter-legged than (2), with **tawny bill, blue face** and **pink legs with red joints and feet**. In flight this species and (2) are difficult to tell apart. **White rump** is diagnostic at close range. Usually occurs in flocks, sometimes in hundreds. Feeds in grassland, agricultural lands and bushveld, often mixing with (1). Flocks soar to great heights when moving and, like (1), move about in response to insect outbreaks. **76 cm** (Kleinswartooievaar)

white head

red bill

red legs

1

white tail

red bill and face mask

2

red legs

blue face mask

white rump

tawny bill

3

pinkish legs with red joints and feet

NEAR THREATENED

1 **Yellow-billed Stork** *Mycteria ibis*

Fairly common to locally common resident and visitor. Told by **white plumage, yellow bill** and **red face, forehead and legs**. When breeding, white plumage has a pink tinge and red face becomes more vivid. Juveniles and immatures are illustrated at bottom of this page. Small groups or large flocks occur on floodpans, large rivers, lakes and estuaries, usually near woodlands. Feeds by wading constantly and probing with the bill immersed and partly open. **97 cm** (Nimmersat)

NEAR THREATENED

2 **Woolly-necked Stork** *Ciconia episcopus*

Sparse resident and common summer visitor. Identified by **woolly white neck and head**, the **black face** contrasting with **chocolate-brown body**. Undertail coverts project beyond the tail. Immature similar but duller, the bill horn-coloured. Usually solitary but large influxes occur during summer at floodplains, pans and rivers in well-wooded regions of northern Botswana and the Zambezi Valley in Zimbabwe. **86 cm** (Wolnekooievaar)

NEAR THREATENED

3 **African Openbill** *Anastomus lamelligerus*

Uncommon to locally common resident and visitor. A **small stork** appearing **all-black** with a **tawny bill**. At close range the **gap between the mandibles** is visible; this is lacking in the immature. Occurs singly or in flocks at large rivers, floodlands and pans in wooded regions. Feeds on freshwater mussels and snails caught while wading. Rests at the waterside or in trees. Nomadic; flocks on the move soar to great heights. Breeds opportunistically when water levels are suitable, building nests colonially in reeds or trees in floodlands. **94 cm** (Oopbekooievaar)

HAMERKOP

A long-legged freshwater bird, widespread in Africa south of the Sahara and having no close relatives.

4 **Hamerkop** *Scopus umbretta*

Common resident. A **small dull-brown waterbird** with a **large, backward-projecting crest** and **heavy, conical black bill**. Sexes are alike, immature similar. In flight sometimes utters a nasal 'wek… wek… wek…'; at rest may repeatedly utter a wavering, high-pitched 'wek-wek-warrrrk'. Occurs singly, but sometimes in groups when feeding, at almost any freshwater locality and at estuaries. Feeds in the shallows, shuffling its feet to disturb frogs and fish. At deeper waters of large lakes may hover briefly before swooping down to seize fish near the surface. Builds huge, domed nests in waterside trees (see illustration) or on cliffs. **56 cm** (Hamerkop)

Young Yellow-billed Storks

Imm.   J

red face

yellow bill

black tail

1

white, woolly neck

black face

dark brown

2

all black

3

4

raptor-like in flight

FLAMINGOS

Occur in flocks of many thousands or singly. The two species described below may be found together. They prefer **shallow saline pans, dams and estuaries**, as well as **sheltered coastal bays**, but are nomadic and remain in one place only for as long as conditions are suitable. Over most of the region they are infrequently seen. Both species have a **honking call** which, in flocks, sounds like babbling. Immatures are grey-brown with a bill pattern similar to that of adults. They feed on algae or aquatic invertebrates which are filtered from the water with specialised bills, the feeding birds walking in a **characteristic posture with the head held upside down**.

NEAR THREATENED

1 Lesser Flamingo *Phoenicopterus minor*
Locally abundant nomadic resident and visitor from other parts of Africa. Distinguished by **evenly coloured dark maroon bill, which looks black at a distance. Pinker, more evenly coloured** than (2). In flight, the wing coverts appear **mottled with dark red**. Immature is dull grey-brown; see illustration below. Frequents shallow, brackish water and saltpans. **102 cm (Kleinflamink)**

NEAR THREATENED

2 Greater Flamingo *Phoenicopterus roseus*
Locally abundant nomadic resident and visitor from other parts of Africa. Distinguished by **pink bill** (not dark maroon as (1)) with **black tip**. Prefers shallow lakes, brackish water, saltpans and coastal lagoons. May be in company of (1) and can be told apart in being **much taller and whiter**. In flight, the **wing coverts are a uniform scarlet**. Immature grey and black, with blue-grey bill; see illustration below. **140 cm (Grootflamink)**

IBISES AND SPOONBILLS

Fairly large birds with longish legs. Ibises have long, decurved bills for **probing in the ground** for insects, worms and other invertebrates, as well as small reptiles and mammals on occasion. Spoonbills have spatulate bills used to **catch small fish and aquatic invertebrates**. All but the Hadeda Ibis are normally silent.

3 African Spoonbill *Platalea alba*
Fairly common resident. Distinguished from other white waterbirds by **pink legs** and **pink, spoon-shaped bill**. Immature's **wings and head are streaked brown**. Occurs singly or in groups on seasonal pans, floodplains, dams, lagoons and rivers. It **feeds by moving its partially open bill in a sideways action** below water. It breeds colonially in reed beds or in trees. Nomadic when not breeding. **91 cm (Lepelaar)**

Imm.

Imm.

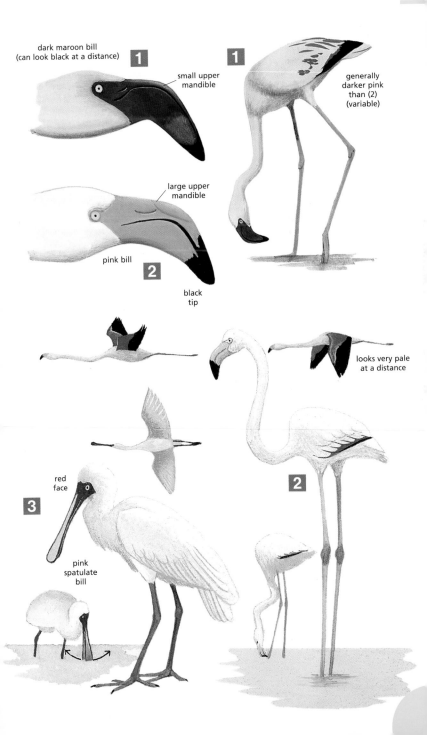

dark maroon bill
(can look black at a distance) **1**

small upper
mandible

1

generally
darker pink
than (2)
(variable)

large upper
mandible

pink bill **2**

black
tip

looks very pale
at a distance

3

red
face

pink
spatulate
bill

2

1 African Sacred Ibis *Threskiornis aethiopicus*
Common resident. **Decurved black bill** and **black head, neck and legs** contrast with otherwise white plumage. At close range, **loose, fluffy plumes on the back** are visible. In the immature, black head and neck are speckled white, front of the neck white. Groups or flocks forage in marshy ground, dams, on shorelines, agricultural lands, **rubbish dumps** and in breeding colonies of other large birds. Migratory to some degree within Africa. In southern Africa, most common in summer. **89 cm** (Skoorsteenveër)

2 Hadeda Ibis *Bostrychia hagedash*
Common resident. Identified by **heavy brown body with fairly short legs, decurved bill with red culmen, iridescent pink shoulder** and **white cheek-stripe**. Shows broad wings in flight. Immature is dull and fluffy-headed. **Very noisy**, especially early morning and evening; when perched or in flight utters a raucous 'Ha! ha-a-a… ha-ha-a-a…'. Often, several pairs call in unison. Pairs or small groups feed on damp ground, near water or in vleis, plantations, agricultural lands, playing fields and suburban gardens. Roosts in tall trees and flies to and from feeding grounds early and late in the day. **76 cm** (Hadeda)

VULNERABLE

3 Southern Bald Ibis *Geronticus calvus*　**E**
Uncommon to locally common endemic resident. Distinguished by **bright red bald head, red bill** and **pink legs**. Iridescent plumage **appears black at a distance**. Immature is duller, the head and neck covered in greyish feathers. Sometimes utters a high-pitched 'keeauw-klaup-klaup'. Small flocks frequent montane grassland in the eastern high-rainfall region, breeding and roosting on cliffs. Feeds singly or in groups in dry or burned grassveld and agricultural lands. **79 cm** (Kalkoenibis)

4 Glossy Ibis *Plegadis falcinellus*
Locally common resident and visitor. More **slender and lighter-bodied** than other ibises. **Bronze-brown** with **iridescent green wings** when breeding; at other times the head and neck are **flecked with white**. Immature is a paler brown, the throat whitish. Single birds or small flocks frequent grassland, farmlands, vleis, pans, sewage works and lake shores. **71 cm** (Glansibis)

FINFOOTS

Three species occur worldwide; one in Africa. They resemble ducks and cormorants but are unrelated to these groups.

5 African Finfoot *Podica senegalensis*
Uncommon resident. Differs from ducks and cormorants in **bright orange-red bill and legs.** Has no characteristic call, but sometimes utters a harsh croaking sound. Found singly or in pairs on **quiet, tree-fringed rivers** where it swims quietly beneath the overhanging branches. **Swims with much of the body submerged**, head and neck stretched forward with each foot-stroke. Shy and retiring. If disturbed, flies low across the water and paddles with its feet, making a distinctive splashing sound. Seldom flies. Roosts at night over water on a low, overhanging branch. **63 cm** (Watertrapper)

1

pink

J

black, unfeathered neck

loose, fluffy plumes

2

broad wings

paler head than (1)

short legs

white cheek-stripe

J

3

slender wings

thin bill

N-Br

4

Br

more slender build than (2)

long legs

5

white line down side of neck

spotted back ♀

♂

♂

cf. cormorants (p. 88)

bright orange-red feet and legs

GEESE AND DUCKS

Most of the region's ducks are either migratory to some extent or locally nomadic, their movements being dictated by food, rainfall and breeding requirements. Many show **marked plumage differences between the sexes**. Ducks and geese undergo a flightless four-to-eight-week period each year when they moult all their flight feathers simultaneously.

The large Spur-winged and Egyptian Geese (p. 112) differ from geese of the northern hemisphere in having **longer bills and legs**, the African Pygmy-Goose (p. 112) being our only representative of the 'true' geese.

Ducks of the genus *Dendrocygna* (whistling ducks), which include the White-faced and Fulvous whistling ducks on this page, differ from those of other genera in having **close-set legs placed well back on the body**. This enables them to **stand erect** and **walk without waddling**. In addition they show **no sexual dimorphism** and have whistling voices. In contrast, ducks of the genus *Anas*, often referred to as dabbling ducks, have **widely spaced legs placed centrally on the body**. This causes them to **stand with the body horizontally** and to **walk with a waddle**. They are further typified by quacking voices.

1 **White-faced Whistling Duck** *Dendrocygna viduata*
Common resident. Only other species with white face is female South African Shelduck (p. 112), from which it can be told by **black head and neck, darker plumage** and **erect stance**. Immature has brown-smudged face. The call is a loud, shrill 'swee-swee-sweeoo', often by many birds in a flying flock. Large flocks often occur on large rivers, lakes, dams, estuaries, floodplains and sewage ponds, especially where there is surface and emergent vegetation. Spends much of the day resting on shorelines or sandbanks. It is locally nomadic and also makes long-range movements northwards in winter. **48 cm** (Nonnetjie-eend)

2 **Fulvous Whistling Duck** *Dendrocygna bicolor*
Fairly common resident. **Cream-coloured flank-feathers** on **golden-brown plumage** diagnostic. Immature resembles adult. Less vocal than (1), it repeats two resonant notes 'tsoo-ee'. In pairs or small flocks on a variety of quiet waters, often with (1). Spends much time swimming during the day. Nomadic when not breeding. **46 cm** (Fluiteend)

3 **White-backed Duck** *Thalassornis leuconotus*
Uncommon resident. **White back visible only in flight**. Best told while swimming by **pale spot at the base of the bill, sharply tapering bill with deep base** and a **humped back** sloping down to the submerged tail. Immature resembles adult. Utters a soft whistle 'cur-wee'. In pairs or small groups on secluded pans, lagoons and dams with ample surface and emergent vegetation. Seldom seen out of water; often difficult to spot – swims low in water and hides amongst vegetation. Dives readily. Nomadic when not breeding. **43 cm** (Witrugeend)

peaked crown

barred

1

wings more rounded than other ducks

orange face

2

cream flank feathers

white back usually only visible in flight

3

tortoiseshell pattern

extensive dark speckling on head

pale spot at base of bill

tawny patch

1 no white

2 white crescent

3 white

1 **African Pygmy-Goose**   *Nettapus auritus*

Locally common resident. Identified by **small size, dark green upperparts, orange body** and **short yellow bill. White wing panels diagnostic in flight.** Immature resembles female. Male utters a soft twittering whistle 'choo-choo' or 'pee-wee' and a repeated, subdued 'tsu-tswi… tsu-tswi…'; female a weak quack and a twittering whistle. Pairs or groups on quiet, sheltered pans, dams and pools with clear water and water lilies. When alert, remains motionless among the surface vegetation and is difficult to detect. Dives readily and perches in trees. **33 cm (Dwerggans)**

2 **South African Shelduck**   *Tadorna cana*   E

Common endemic resident. A long-bodied duck with horizontal stance. Male told by **solid grey head.** Female shows higly **variable amount of white on the face**; differs from White-faced Whistling Duck (p. 110) in **grey (not black) head and neck.** In flight similar to (3), but both sexes differ in **richer rufous body** and **grey head**; female distinguished by white face. Immature is duller than adult. Female initially has white circles around eyes, which extend over the face with maturity. Male utters a deep 'hoogh', 'how' or 'honk', the female alternating with a harsher 'hark'. Females hiss while accompanying immatures. Courting pairs are noisy and aggressive. Pairs or flocks frequent brackish pans, dams and lakes, and large deep waters (especially when in wing-moult). Dives if pursued. May also be seen away from water when breeding. Mostly restricted to drier southern and western areas; rarely recorded in the moister northeast. Nomadic when not breeding. **64 cm (Kopereend)**

3 **Egyptian Goose**   *Alopochen aegyptiaca*

Abundant resident. Distinguished from (2) by **long neck, long pink legs, pink bill** and **rufous eye-patches.** Immature is duller. **Very noisy** in social interactions; male utters a husky wheezing sound, female a harsh, nasal, high-pitched 'hur-hur-hur-hur'. Both sexes extend the head and neck when calling. Pairs occupy small waters or sections of rivers, but large numbers often gather on deep waters to moult their wing feathers or on sandbanks when large rivers are in spate. Often flies in the evening to communal grazing grounds. Common even in built-up areas, as long as some open water surfaces are available. **71 cm (Kolgans)**

4 **Spur-winged Goose**   *Plectropterus gambensis*

Common resident. **Very large size** and **glossy black plumage** diagnostic. Male has **fleshy caruncle on the forehead** and a **variable amount of white on the face and underparts**, least in southern populations. In flight the **prominent white forewings** distinguish this species from Knob-billed Duck (p. 118). Immature is brown, showing little or no white. Not very vocal; male utters a soft, high-pitched 'cherwit' in flight; either sex a four-syllable 'chi-chi-chi-chi'. Occurs in flocks in a variety of wetlands in bushveld, especially favouring floodplains. They fly in 'V'-formations or staggered lines. Perches in dead trees. Very large numbers may gather on deep waters during winter wing-moult, diving if pursued. **102 cm (Wildemakou)**

white wing panels

emerald-green patch

tiny yellow bill

♂ ♀

♂

♀

orange body

variable white on face

grey head

2 ♂

rich brown flanks

black bill

♀

pink bill

rufous eye-patch

dark line on wing

breast-patch may be absent in younger birds

3

greyish flanks

long pink legs

variable white on face

♀

4

♂

J

very large size

1 Hottentot Teal   *Anas hottentota*

Common resident. Differs from (2) in **very small size** (almost as tiny as African Pygmy-Goose, p. 112), **grey-blue (not pinkish-red) bill** and absence of any speckling on rear part of the body. When swimming, the **flank feathers usually overlap the wing** to form a zigzag dividing line. Normally silent. Pairs and groups frequent shallow freshwater marshes, pans and dams, especially sewage ponds. Spends much of the day resting out of water. **35 cm** (Gevlekte Eend)

2 Red-billed Teal   *Anas erythrorhyncha*

Very common resident. Larger than (1), differing in **pinkish-red bill** and **completely spotted body**. In flight shows a **creamy speculum**. The few sounds made by this species are soft, audible only at close range, but female may utter a louder series of quacks that decrease in volume. Frequently in large flocks on lakes, floodplains, dams and sewage ponds. Smaller numbers during the rainy season, when there are widespread long-distance dispersals. **48 cm** (Rooibekeend)

3 Southern Pochard   *Netta erythrophthalma*

Common resident. With its **blue-grey bill**, male superficially recalls (4), but differs in darker coloration with **uniform head and back, distinctive crimson eye, longer neck** and more elegant proportions. Female differs from (4) in **whitish crescent on sides of head** and **white throat and bill-base**. In flight, the **whitish speculum extends the full width of the wing**. No distinctive call. Pairs or flocks occur on deep fresh water. Regular long-distance migrations have been recorded from as far afield as Kenya. **51 cm** (Bruineend)

NEAR THREATENED

4 Maccoa Duck   *Oxyura maccoa*

Uncommon, nomadic resident. A **small, squat species**, with a **bright-blue broad-based bill**. **Chestnut-coloured breeding male** unmistakable. Female and male in non-breeding plumage differ from female of (3) in **horizontal facial stripes** and **squat appearance**. Generally silent. Occurs on dams and lakes with extensive fringing reed beds – usually more females than males. Seldom seen out of water during the day. **Swims low in the water** with tail trailing, the **tip submerged, or with tail stiffly erect**. In courtship the male often swims with head and neck stretched forward, the neck inflated and the bill in the water making bubbles, tail erect. Both sexes dive frequently. Nomadic during spring and summer. **46 cm** (Bloubekeend)

1

white trailing edge

grey-blue bill

tiny size

2

large, creamy panel on inner wing

pinkish-red bill

3

pale, C-shaped crescent

pale area at base of bill

dark brown above

♀

♂

crimson eye

♀

pale blue-grey bill

♂

horizontal pale stripe on face

♀

bright blue bill

♂

often swims low in water

often holds tail erect

♂

contrasting dark head

♀

chestnut body

1 Cape Shoveler *Anas smithii* **E**

Common endemic resident. A dull brownish duck identified by **large black spatulate bill** and **yellow-orange legs**; cf. (2). In flight shows a **dark green speculum** and **pale blue forewings**. Male has yellow eye; eye dark in female. Immature is duller. Normally silent but male sometimes utters an explosive 'rrar' or a series of quiet, hoarse 'cawick' sounds with rising pitch, sometimes interspersed with a fast, rattling 'ra-ra-ra-ra-ra'. Female may utter a series of notes with downward inflection, a rippling chatter 'cha-cha-cha-cha-cha' or a persistent quacking. Pairs or flocks in shallows of tidal estuaries, lagoons and sewage ponds; indifferent to large open waters. Most common in the southwestern Cape and southeastern region of southern Africa, moving between the two regions. **53 cm** (Kaapse Slopeend)

2 Northern Shoveler *Anas clypeata* **V**

Very rare vagrant. Male most likely to occur in non-breeding plumage as illustrated; then differs from (1) in **larger, pale buff (not black) bill** and paler overall appearance. Single birds and pairs occur occasionally in widely separated localities, mostly Jul–Dec. Males in breeding plumage are probably escapees from private wildfowl collections. **51 cm** (Europese Slopeend)

3 Garganey *Anas querquedula* **V**

Very rare visitor. Male most likely to occur in non-breeding plumage, which resembles that of female. A **small brownish duck** with **distinct streaks above and below the eyes**. Differs from female Maccoa Duck (p. 114) in this and a more slender bill. Often confused with young Knob-billed Ducks (p. 118), which also show pale eyebrows but are much larger and have longer necks and pale rumps. Sits low in the water when swimming. Occurs occasionally Dec–Mar in Zimbabwe, Botswana and northern South Africa. **38 cm** (Somereend)

4 Cape Teal *Anas capensis*

Common resident. A **small, pale duck** with **pink upturned bill**; looks almost white at a distance. In flight shows a predominantly **white speculum** with a **dark green central patch**. Immature resembles adult. Usually silent. In flocks (large flocks when in wing-moult) on coastal lagoons, saltpans, sewage ponds and tidal mudflats. Has a preference for brackish waters and soda lakes. Long-distance movements have been recorded within southern Africa. **46 cm** (Teeleend)

5 Northern Pintail *Anas acuta* **V**

Rare vagrant. Male in breeding plumage unmistakable, but more likely to occur in non-breeding plumage, resembling the female. Then told by **slender proportions, dull grey bill** and **pale, grey-brown plumage; long tail may not be present**. In flight **wings appear pointed**. Underbody, wing linings and trailing edge of secondaries white; **upperwing shows green speculum**. May occur on any inland waters. Recorded in Zimbabwe and Namibia Nov–Feb. Most sightings are probably of escaped aviary birds. **51–66 cm** (Pylsterteend)

N-Br ♂ ♀ · 5 ♀ · blackish-brown head · Br ♂ · long, pointed tail

pale blue

spatulate bill ♂

♂

dark green speculum

dark tail

♀

yellow-orange legs (brownish in female)

yellow eye ♂

dark eye ♀

1

♂

♀

N-Br ♂

2

bill heavier and even more spatulate than (1)

yellow edges to bill

♀

N-Br

♂

long white eyebrow

striped head ♀

Br ♂

elongated plumes

♀

♀

3

pink bill

bird appears very pale from a distance

4

1 African Black Duck   *Anas sparsa*

Uncommon resident. Characterised by **dark grey-brown plumage** with **bold white spots on wings and back** and **iridescent blue speculum** with white border. Immature browner, spots buffy, belly barred white. When swimming appears short-necked and long-bodied. Mostly calls when flying in pairs: female utters a persistent loud quacking, male an almost imperceptible 'weep… weep… weep'. During daytime, pairs inhabit streams and rivers with stony bottoms (often in well-wooded valleys), moving to larger, open waters at sunset to roost. **51–54 cm** (Swarteend)

2 Yellow-billed Duck   *Anas undulata*

Very common resident. **Bright yellow bill with black central patch** diagnostic. Feathers are brown but edged with white, broadly on flanks and underparts, giving **ashy appearance**. **Head and neck dusky**. In flight shows **iridescent emerald speculum**. Immature has buff-edged feathers; underparts more heavily spotted. No distinctive call, but on take-off female utters loud, evenly spaced quacks. Pairs and flocks occur on various open waters: estuaries, lakes, dams, flooded lands, pans and slow-running rivers with pools. In the dry season, large numbers often congregate on open waters, but disperse widely during rains. **53–58 cm** (Geelbekeend)

3 Mallard   *Anas platyrhynchos*

Fairly common introduced species. Male has **metallic-green head and neck, dull-yellow bill** and **orange legs**; both sexes show **iridescent violet speculum** edged white. Domestic varieties may have different colour combinations. A common European duck introduced into southern African wildfowl collections, from where escapees are frequent. Has become feral in many regions and can interbreed with indigenous ducks, especially (2). Hybrids show a mixture of characteristics of both species. Usually seen in pairs on any open inland water, most often near human habitation. **50–60 cm** (Mallard)

4 Knob-billed (Comb) Duck   *Sarkidiornis melanotos*

Uncommon to locally common resident. Male much larger than female; distinguished by **glossy dark blue upperparts, white underparts, black-speckled head and neck** (washed yellow when breeding) and a **large fleshy caruncle on forehead and bill**. Female duller and lacking caruncle. Immature quite different from adult. In first year (a) has dark brown upperparts, pale buff underparts and **distinct eye-stripe**; sub-adult (b) is more like female but underparts orange-buff, with heavier spotting on head and neck. Mostly silent. Flocks, often large in the dry season, frequent marshes, temporary bushveld pans, floodplains and estuaries. Often perches in dead trees. **64–79 cm** (Knobbeleend)

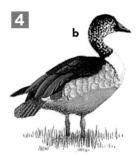

iridescent
blue
speculum

1

dark bill

white spots

iridescent
green
speculum

2

yellow
bill

dark olive
legs

iridescent
violet
speculum

3

♂

♀

orange legs

densely
speckled

♂

♀

4

'comb'

buff yellow
wash

♂ **Br**

N-Br
♂

white or
pale grey
underparts

GREBES

Small, **almost tailless** waterbirds. They **feed beneath the surface by diving**, remaining submerged for 20–50 seconds. They are **seldom seen on land**, but fly long distances at night to new waters. Breeding and non-breeding plumages differ. Small chicks are **striped on the upperparts**, the head-stripes remaining until nearly fully grown. Chicks ride on parents' backs.

1 Little Grebe   *Tachybaptus ruficollis*
Common resident. Smaller than any duck. **Rufous neck and creamy spot at base of bill** diagnostic of breeding bird; at other times differs from (2) in **dull (not white) underparts** and **dark eyes**. The call is a descending, laughing trill. Single birds or loose groups occur on inland waters, seldom large rivers. Dives frequently and skitters across the water when chasing rivals. **20 cm** (Kleindobbertjie)

2 Black-necked Grebe   *Podiceps nigricollis*
Locally common resident. Larger than (1). **Black plumage** and **golden flanks and ear coverts** of adult in breeding plumage unmistakable; when not breeding has a **white throat and foreneck. Eyes are red.** Utters a quiet 'poo-eep' and a rapid chattering. Small groups on quiet saline waters or densely wintering flocks in sheltered bays on the southern and west coast. When preening, habitually exposes its white belly by rolling to one side on the water. Nomadic. **28 cm** (Swartnekdobbertjie)

3 Great Crested Grebe   *Podiceps cristatus*
Uncommon resident. Unmistakable, with **long crests** when breeding and **long, flattened cheek-feathers**. In non-breeding plumage differs from (2) in **white head with black cap only, darker ruby-red eyes, larger bill** and **larger size**. Normally silent. Pairs occur on large inland waters bordered by low, emergent vegetation. On water, when preening, habitually exposes its white underparts like (2). **50 cm** (Kuifkopdobbertjie)

COOTS, GALLINULES, MOORHENS, CRAKES AND RAILS

Small to fairly large, long-legged, large-footed, mainly freshwater-associated birds. A few species inhabit grassland, vleis or lush forest undergrowth. Most water-associated species habitually **flick their tails to reveal white undertail coverts**. Coots and moorhens are **blackish** with **brightly coloured frontal shields (foreheads) and bills**. Gallinules have **blue-green plumage**, while crakes and rails have mostly cryptic colouring. The minute flufftails or pygmy crakes show marked sexual dimorphism. Many species are extremely secretive and almost impossible to see, except when they fly clumsily with feet hanging low over vegetation.

4 Red-knobbed Coot   *Fulica cristata*
Very common resident. The **only all-black waterbird with white frontal shield and bill; legs and lobed (not webbed) feet grey**. Immature is ash-brown, no white shield. Normal call 'clukuk' or 'cronk'. Solitary or in groups on open inland waters with reed beds. Swims, occasionally dives, or walks at edges of reed beds or on shoreline, occasionally further afield in marshlands. Habitually stands on floating nest mounds. Frequently pursues other coots in noisy overwater chases. **43 cm** (Bleshoender)

1

rufous neck

Br

creamy spot

dumpy shape

N-Br

dirty buff (never white as in (2))

red eye

clear black-and-white face pattern

sharp and slightly upturned bill

N-Br

golden ear coverts

Br

long-necked and elegant apprearance

crisp, pure white

2

Br

white face (cf. White-faced Whistling Duck p. 110)

crested head

striped head pattern shared by all juvenile grebes

3

long neck

J

wholly black

4

knobs more conspicuous during breeding

white frontal shield and bill

1 American Purple Gallinule *Porphyrio martinica* **V**

Rare vagrant. Adult differs from (2) in small size, **pale blue frontal shield, yellow-tipped bill** and **lemon-yellow legs**. Most arrivals are immatures: mainly dull khaki-brown with a greenish flush on the back and wings, belly dull blue. At least 20 records for the southwestern coast. A transatlantic vagrant from the Americas. **33 cm** (Amerikaanse Koningriethaan)

2 African Purple Swamphen *Porphyrio madagascariensis*

Common resident. *P. madagascariensis* sometimes lumped as a subspecies of *P. porphyrio*, which occurs in other parts of the world. Large and bulky, with predominantly **purple-blue and dark green** coloration. Larger than (1), differing in **red frontal shield** and **pink legs**. Immature is duller; brownish with red-brown legs. Has a deep, explosive bubbling call varied with various shrieks and groans. Occurs singly or in pairs in marshes and the vegetation surrounding inland waters, especially sewage ponds. Walks about on mudflats and reed-bed fringes, sometimes clambering about tangled reeds. Can swim and is not secretive. **46 cm** (Grootkoningriethaan)

3 Lesser Moorhen *Gallinula angulata*

Uncommon summer resident. Small, secretive waterbird similar to the more common and confiding (5). Differs from that species in **paler grey or greenish plumage**, mostly **yellow bill with red only on the culmen** and **pointed (not rounded) frontal shield. Legs greenish or red-brown** but lack the red tibial rings of (5). Immature much duller. The call is three to five rapid hoots 'tu-tu-tu…'. Occurs singly or in pairs on shallow ponds with surface and fringing vegetation, vleis and flooded grassland. Erratic and secretive, arriving in large numbers in temporarily suitable habitats. **23 cm** (Kleinwaterhoender)

4 Allen's Gallinule *Porphyrio alleni*

Uncommon and irregular late summer resident. Small, **large-footed waterbird** with **green upperparts, dark blue body, neck and head,** and **red bill and legs. Frontal shield varies in colour from dull apple-green to blueish.** Immature as illustrated; cf. immature of (3). The call is a series of rapidly delivered clicks 'dik-dik-dik-dik…' or a melodious, rolling 'purrrrr-pur-pur-pur' during courtship. A shy bird; occurs singly or in pairs on secluded ponds with dense fringing vegetation where it climbs about tangled reeds, walks on water lilies or swims. **25 cm** (Kleinkoningriethaan)

5 Common Moorhen *Gallinula chloropus*

Common resident. Larger than (3), with **bright red bill** and **rounded frontal shield. Tip of bill and legs yellow; flank feathers white.** Legs yellow or greenish yellow with **red band around tibia.** Immature is browner. The call is a high-pitched, descending 'kr-rrrrk'. Frequents dams, pans and quiet rivers with fringing reed beds, singly or in pairs. Swims more in open water than (3) but also feeds out of water in vleis and marshlands. **30–36 cm** (Grootwaterhoender)

pale blue frontal shield

yellow tip

J

1

red bill and frontal shield

lemon-yellow legs

large size

2

more yellow than (5)

3

pale grey or greenish-grey

frontal shield blue in male; green in female

Br

♂

small size

shy and usually remains hidden in cover

4

dark green

red bill with yellow tip

J

bold white flank feathers

5

yellow legs

often quite tame

FLUFFTAILS AND CRAKES

Smallest of the crakes. They are highly secretive and difficult to flush, but once airborne fly a short distance with legs dangling before dropping back into cover; they can seldom be flushed a second time. Calls are usually the only indication of a species' presence.

CRITICALLY ENDANGERED

1 White-winged Flufftail *Sarothrura ayresi* **R**
Very rare and highly localised. Status unclear: possibly a non-breeding visitor from Ethiopia. On the ground, shows a **chestnut tail with black bars** and a **whitish belly**. **White wing-panels** visible when flushed. **Flushes more easily than other flufftails and flies higher and further once airborne.** The call is a soft, deep 'woop, woop, woop, woop, woop…', often several birds calling simultaneously. Occurs in a handful of high-lying marshes in southern Africa, with occasional records from scattered localities. **14 cm (**Witvlerkvleikuiken)

VULNERABLE

2 Striped Flufftail *Sarothrura affinis* **R**
Rare, localised resident. Male has **chestnut head and tail**; female probably indistinguishable from female of Buff-spotted Flufftail (p. 126). The call is loud and distinctive: a drawn-out 'huuuuuuuuuuuuuuu', the length of the note between those of Red-chested and Buff-spotted flufftails (p. 126). Also gives a sharp, piercing 'ke-ke-ke-ke… weh-weh-weh…' in a long series. Frequents rank montane grassland, dense fynbos and bracken patches, not necessarily near water. **15 cm** (Gestreepte Vleikuiken)

3 Streaky-breasted Flufftail *Sarothrura boehmi* **R**
Rare summer resident. When flushed shows a **dark tail** and a **pale throat**, but best identified by its call: a deep and rapid 'booooo' at two-second intervals and repeated about 12 times; also a high-pitched 'bee' about 12 times with no appreciable pause. Occurs in vleis, flooded grassland and grass bordering lakes and swamps. Most records from eastern Zimbabwe. **15 cm** (Streepborsvleikuiken)

4 Spotted Crake *Porzana porzana* **R**
Uncommon summer visitor. Differs from African Crake (p. 126) in having generally paler colouring, **less boldly barred flanks** and **yellow bill with red base**. Differs from (5) in **more spotted, less streaked** appearance and yellow bill. The call is a series of whip-like notes 'hwitt-hwitt-hwitt', seldom heard in southern Africa. Occurs in dense vegetation in shallow water, occasionally in fringing vegetation around pans in dry regions. **24 cm** (Gevlekte Riethaan)

5 Striped Crake *Aenigmatolimnas marginalis* **R**
Uncommon summer visitor. Best identified by **orange-buff undertail coverts** and **white lines on mantle and wings**. Differs from (4) in **more streaky, less spotted upperparts, paler underparts** and **thicker, darker bill**. Female shows diagnostic blue-grey underparts; rich buff in male. The call (often heard at night) is a constant ticking like a wristwatch 'tak-tak-tak-tak-tak…'. Extremely secretive dweller of flooded grassland and small pools. Occasionally breeds in southern Africa in years of good rainfall, and probably overlooked. **24 cm** (Gestreepte Riethaan)

chestnut tail with black bars

♂ ♀ **1** ♂

conspicuous white wing panels in both sexes

whitish belly

2 chestnut tail ♂

♀

plain chestnut tail

♂

3 ♂

pale throat

black tail

♂ pale chin

♀

chestnut colour extends to mid-breast

4

greyish face

yellow bill with red base

white spots

undertail usually plain buff

orange-buff undertail

♂

5

white streaking

♀

♂

rich buff

blue-grey

1 Red-chested Flufftail *Sarothrura rufa*

Fairly common resident. Very similar to (2), but seldom overlaps in habitat. Further distinguished by **reddish colouring of male extending onto its mantle and lower breast, mostly black tail** and **streaked (not spotted) upperparts**. Female is much darker but paler on chest and throat. The normal call is a much-repeated 'ooo-ooo-ooo-ooo-dueh-dueh-dueh…', but also utters a quail-like 'ick-kick-kick-kick…' and a loud, rapid squeaking 'dui-dui-dui…' up to 40 times, fading at the end. A secretive bird of marshes, damp valleys and vleis, where it remains concealed in dense vegetation. **15–17 cm** (Rooiborsvleikuiken)

2 Buff-spotted Flufftail *Sarothrura elegans*

Fairly common resident. A tiny, dumpy terrestrial forest bird, usually located by distinctive foghorn-like call. Male has **rounded buff spots** (not streaks like other flufftails) and a **chestnut tail barred with black**. Female is paler and uniform. The call is a long, drawn-out and mournful 'wooooooooooo-eeeeeeeee', rising at the end, and can be heard from a good distance away. Frequents the moister areas of evergreen forests, overgrown wastelands and long grass. Occasionally in well-wooded suburban gardens, but very secretive. **17 cm** (Gevlekte Vleikuiken)

3 Baillon's Crake *Porzana pusilla*

Uncommon resident and visitor. Male illustrated. Female has **whitish throat and central breast**. Barely bigger than a flufftail. Most resembles (5), but **barring on flanks less pronounced**, and **upperparts have white streaks**. Utters a low, piping 'quick-quick'. Highly secretive, inhabiting marshes, lush waterside vegetation and flooded grassland. Sometimes emerges into the open but dives into cover again at the least disturbance. **18 cm** (Kleinriethaan)

4 Corn Crake *Crex crex* [R]

Uncommon summer visitor. A **short-billed, tawny** crake with **blackish upperparts, barred flanks** and **chestnut wing coverts**. Silent in southern Africa; on European breeding grounds gives a rasping 'krrek-krrek', as suggested by scientific name. Found in lucerne, rank grass, fallow fields and airfields, sometimes near streams. When flushed flies off with legs dangling, the chestnut wings conspicuous. **37 cm** (Kwartelkoning)

NEAR THREATENED

5 African Crake *Crecopsis egregia* [R]

Uncommon summer visitor. **Heavily mottled upperparts** and **boldly barred underparts** distinctive. **Bill pinkish, eye red** and often with **narrow white eyebrow**. Could also be confused with longer-billed African Rail (p. 128). Utters a high-pitched chittering trill of eight or nine notes. Found in grassland, vleis and thickets, usually but not necessarily near water. Secretive but will emerge to visit rain puddles on roads. It flushes easily. **20–23 cm** (Afrikaanse Riethaan)

6 Black Crake *Amaurornis flavirostris*

Common resident. Unmistakable with **red legs** and **bright yellow bill**. Immature is a duller version of the adult, with dark bill and legs. The call is an explosive, harsh 'rr-rr-rr' ending in a resonant croak; also various clucking sounds. Single birds or scattered individuals at the waterside on quiet rivers, lakes, dams and floodplains, or walking on floating vegetation. Not secretive. **20–23 cm** (Swartriethaan)

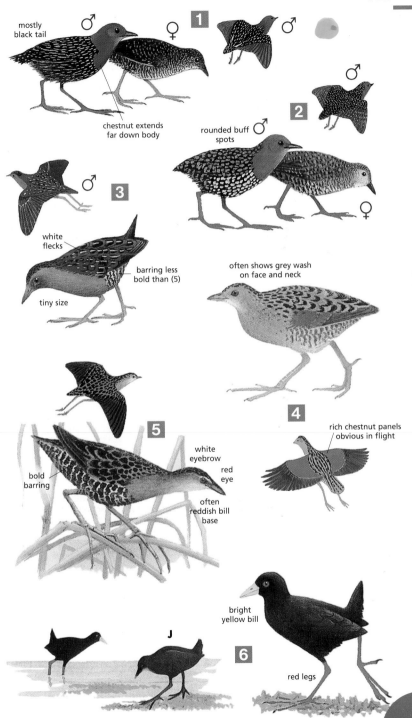

mostly
black tail

♂ ♀ **1** ♂

chestnut extends
far down body

rounded buff ♂
spots

2 ♂

♂ **3**

white
flecks

barring less
bold than (5)

tiny size

often shows grey wash
on face and neck

♀

4

white
eyebrow

red
eye

5

bold
barring

often
reddish bill
base

rich chestnut panels
obvious in flight

bright
yellow bill

J

6

red legs

1 **African Rail** *Rallus caerulescens*
Fairly common resident. Identified by **long red bill and legs, brown upperparts** and **barred underparts**. Immature is sooty-brown, white of throat extending to central breast, flanks barred rufous. The call is a shrill, trilling rattle 'creeea-crak-crak-crak…'. A shy, skulking bird of reed beds and thick swamp vegetation, only occasionally emerging at pool fringes. Moves with stealth and speed, flicking its tail continuously. **36 cm** (Grootriethaan)

PAINTED-SNIPES

Not related to true snipes, painted-snipes are more colourful. They use the unusual breeding strategy of polyandry, in which males incubate the eggs and raise the chicks.

NEAR THREATENED

2 **Greater Painted-Snipe** *Rostratula benghalensis*
Uncommon nomadic resident. Told by **white patches surrounding eyes** and distinctive curving **white band extending from breast and reaching over wings onto the back**. Immature resembles male. Female utters a soft, hollow-sounding 'wu-koo' and 'boo-hu-hu'. Pairs and groups are found on muddy shorelines of dams, pans and swamp pools, usually where reeds or other waterside vegetation offer immediate refuge. When walking, bobs its hindquarters up and down. Much more shy and retiring than true snipes. **28–32 cm** (Goudsnip)

PLOVERS, SNIPES AND ALLIES

Terrestrial and waterside birds. Large plovers are **long-legged** and **stand erect**; small plovers and most shorebirds **hold their bodies horizontally, postures hunched**.

NEAR THREATENED

3 **Great Snipe** *Gallinago media* ▉R
Rare summer visitor. Differs from (4) in **shorter bill, spotted upperwing coverts, more heavily barred underparts** and **flight behaviour**. Silent in Africa, but may give soft and weak-sounding croak when flushed. Flushes reluctantly but then rises silently and flies straight before dropping down again. Solitary in marshy localities. Sparsely distributed, with strong populations in central Zimbabwe, northern Namibia and north of Beira in Mozambique. **35 cm** (Dubbelsnip)

4 **African Snipe** *Gallinago nigripennis*
Common resident. Differs from (3) in **whiter underparts, extraordinarily long bill**, and **distinctive flight behaviour**: when flushed takes off with a sucking 'chuck' call and zigzags at low level before resettling. In breeding display the male flies high, then zooms down steeply with fanned tail feathers vibrating to make a soft whinnying sound known as drumming. Occurs singly or in pairs in marshy localities. **32 cm** (Afrikaanse Snip)

1

barred underparts

long red bill (cf. African Crake, p. 126)

♀

striking head pattern

distinctive curving white bands extending from breast and reaching over wings onto the back

♂

intricate patterning

rounded wings

2

3

bill shorter than (4)

barred

bold white bars on wings

usually silent when flushed

4

white

very long bill

usually gives 'sucking' sound when flushed

rather plain upperwings

1 Lesser Sand Plover *Charadrius mongolus*
Summer visitor. Difficult to distinguish from (2) unless seen side by side. Differs in **less heavy bill**, shorter, usually **dark green-grey legs** and the lack of any clear mark between bill and eye. Could also be confused with juvenile Kittlitz's Plover (p. 132). Utters 'chitic, chitic' on take-off and, occasionally, a short, soft trill. Occurs singly or in small groups, mostly on east coast tidal flats. **20 cm** (Mongoolse Strandkiewiet)

2 Greater Sand Plover *Charadrius leschenaultii*
Rare summer visitor. Differs from (1) in **much heavier bill, longer, paler legs** and **larger size**. Cf. also immature of Kittlitz's Plover (p. 132), which is **smaller** and has a **white collar**. Flight call is a short 'drrit'; also utters a trill 'chirrirrip', longer than that of (1). Occurs singly or in small groups on tidal mudflats, especially east coast estuaries and lagoons. **22 cm** (Grootstrandkiewiet)

3 Chestnut-banded Plover *Charadrius pallidus*
Common resident. **Chestnut breast-band** diagnostic in male; fainter in female. Female also lacks the **black crown and lores**. Utters a soft 'chuck' on take-off. Occurs singly, in pairs and in scattered flocks on saltpans, coastal lagoons and sandflats, less frequently singly or in pairs inland at pans, gravel pits, dams and banks of large rivers. Inland records widespread but irregular. **15 cm** (Rooibandstrandkiewiet)

NEAR THREATENED

4 Common Ringed Plover *Charadrius hiaticula*
Uncommon summer visitor. A dumpy, short-billed plover; **yellow-orange legs** and a **single bold black breast-band** extending around neck diagnostic. In flight it differs from Three-banded Plover (p. 132) in distinct **white wing-bar**. The call is 'coo-eep' or 'too-li'. Occurs singly or in small parties, often with Three-banded Plover, on shorelines of coastal lagoons, estuaries and inland waters. **18 cm** (Ringnekstrandkiewiet)

5 Little Ringed Plover *Charadrius dubius*
Rare vagrant. In breeding plumage, told from (4) by its **bright yellow eye-ring, wholly dark and finer bill, pale brown or greyish-pink (not yellow-orange) legs** and **white eyebrow** extending up as a band over the forehead. Slightly smaller, appearing longer-legged with more pointed rear end and less robust body. In non-breeding plumage, black face-mask and chest-band become brownish, and the forehead and eyebrow buff, but paler eye-ring is usually still discernible. In flight distinguished from (4) by much less obvious (or absent) white wing-bar. Calls 'pew' in flight. Breeds across a large expanse of central and western Palearctic region, wintering in Africa south of the Sahara. Solitary specimens recorded at inland wetlands in northern part of the subregion. **16–18 cm** (Kleinringnekstrandkiewiet)

1

toes barely project beyond tail

shorter and slightly weaker bill than (2)

N-Br

short tibia

dark green-grey legs

2

disproportionately large bill

N-Br

toes project beyond tail

long tibia

legs usually pale green

3 ♂

chestnut band

very pale overall

J

stout bill, often with orange base

♀

lacks black markings (cf. White-fronted Plover p. 132)

3

single broad black band

4

yellow-orange legs

5

brown breastband with pale eyebrow

N-Br

brown rump, indistinct whitish wing bars

pale legs

Br

1 Three-banded Plover *Charadrius tricollaris*

Common resident. Identified by **red eye-ring, double black breast-bands**, one on either side of white band encircling neck; cf. Common Ringed Plover (p. 130). Immature has the upper band brown and incomplete, the lower band flecked white, the head uniformly brown. The call is 'wick-wick' or 'tiuu-it, tiuu-it'. Occurs singly, in pairs or in small parties on shores and shallows of almost any inland water. **18 cm** (Driebandstrandkiewiet)

2 Kittlitz's Plover *Charadrius pecuarius*

Common and widespread resident. Distinguished by **black mask and forecrown, white band encircling back of neck** and **yellow-buff breast**. Immature lacks black mask and forecrown and yellow breast. Distinguished from the similar Lesser Sand Plover (p. 130) mainly by white collar, darker upperparts and habitat. In-flight call of adult is 'tip-peep'; also utters a trilling 'trit-tritritritritrit'. Found at the edges of inland waters, coastal estuaries, open ground and airfields. **16 cm** (Geelborsstrandkiewiet)

3 Kentish Plover *Charadrius alexandrinus* ▮V

Vagrant. In non-breeding plumage easily confused with (4), to which it is closely related. Very similar to that species and unlikely to be reliably identified in the field. **Wings slightly longer** (projecting past tail-tip), creating a more elongated and pointed body shape than (4). Could also be confused with immature Chestnut-banded Plover (p. 130). In breeding plumage, **upperparts are darker**, the male with **forecrown, eye-stripe and breast-patches black**. Frequents sandy beaches or shorelines of brackish pans. Breeds in the northern hemisphere, spending the non-breeding season mostly along the coasts of Africa north of the equator. Vagrant further south; occurrence in southern Africa based on a specimen picked up in Namibia. Claimed but unconfirmed sightings elsewhere. **15–17,5 cm** (Kentse Strandkiewiet)

4 White-fronted Plover *Charadrius marginatus*

Common resident. The sand-coloured race (a), occurring in the Western Cape and on the east coast, differs from the less common Lesser Sand Plover (p. 130) in **much smaller size, dark line on lores, more slender bill** and **white collar**. Immature resembles female. The west coast race (b) is **greyer**, with **less yellow on the breast**. Utters a soft 'wit' or 'twirit' in flight. Occurs singly or in pairs on sandy seashores; also on some inland lakes and large rivers with sandbanks, e.g. the Zambezi, Limpopo and Olifants. At the coast it feeds on wet sand close to receding waves, running rapidly or flying away low as the next wave advances. **18 cm** (Vaalstrandkiewiet)

5 Caspian Plover *Charadrius asiaticus*

Fairly common summer visitor. A large, **long-legged, thin-billed** plover with a **conspicuous white eyebrow**. Breeding male often seen February–March. Female in breeding plumage may have **incomplete rufous breast-band**, the dark lower edge always absent. Immature resembles non-breeding adult, but the breast-band may be confined to a patch on either side. The call is a shrill 'ku-wit', loudest at night, softer and more piping by day. Flocks on plains with short grass and burned areas, often in the semi-arid region of north-central Botswana and northern Namibia. Habitually runs rather than flies. **21–23 cm** (Asiatiese Strandkiewiet)

red eye-ring

double black band

1

3

white collar

white neck band

yellow-buff breast

sometimes dark pectoral spots

2

J

subtle face pattern

a

♀

4

white collar

b

♂

very pale

short legs

♂

N-Br

Br

♀

delicate bill

♂

5

long legs

usually inland on dry plains

SANDPIPERS AND ALLIED WADERS

A group of small birds usually found along shorelines and wading in shallow water. They usually have longish legs and bills for probing mud, feeding on small insects and invertebrates. Species breed in northern regions and during this time the males assume richly coloured plumage. They migrate south in drab non-breeding plumage at the start of the southern hemisphere summer. Illustrations depict the species in non-breeding plumage, unless otherwise indicated.

1 Marsh Sandpiper *Tringa stagnatilis*

Common summer visitor. **Clear white underparts** diagnostic. Differs from (2) in **smaller size, straight, slender bill** and **yellowish legs**. In flight shows **white back and rump** as (2), but its **feet protrude further**. When put to flight, calls a soft rapid 'tjuu-tjuu-tjuu'. Occurs singly or in small groups on coastal lagoons and estuaries or inland waters. Feeds by probing in shallows. **23 cm (Moerasruiter)**

2 Common Greenshank *Tringa nebularia*

Common summer visitor, a few all year. A large, long-legged wader. Has **clear white underparts** like (1) but is **larger**, with more robust, **slightly upturned bill** and **green-grey legs**. In flight, also shows extensive **white back and rump**, its **feet slightly protruding**. On take-off calls a diagnostic, loud triple 'tew-tew-tew'. Usually found singly on coastal or inland waters. Shy and difficult to approach. When flushed towers up and utters its triple call before flying off some distance. **32 cm** (Groenpootruiter)

3 Lesser Yellowlegs *Tringa flavipes* ▨

Vagrant. Could be confused only with Wood Sandpiper (p. 136), from which it differs in having **bright lemon-yellow legs**. Also larger, longer-legged and much more slender than Wood Sandpiper. **23–25 cm** (Kleingeelpootruiter)

4 Greater Yellowlegs *Tringa melanoleuca* ▨

Vagrant. Occurs in non-breeding plumage. Larger than (3) with **longer, Greenshank-like bill** and **orange-yellow (not lemon-yellow) legs**. Compared with (2), the **bill is straighter** with **greenish or yellowish base**, the **body is generally browner** (less greyish), while the **breast has greyish streaking**. In flight, the **very long wings** and **square, white tail-patch** (which does not extend up onto the back) are diagnostic. A wanderer from the Americas. **29–33 cm** (Grootgeelpootruiter)

narrow

1

long, white eyebrow

2

broad

long, yellowish legs

pale overall, with distinctive white shoulder patch

thin, straight bill

bill long and thick-based, slightly upturned

subtle patterning

green-grey legs

short eyebrow

3

dark back

long lemon-yellow legs

long, slender wings

more brown than grey

4

overall, slightly lighter coloration than (3)

bright orange-yellow legs

1 Common Redshank *Tringa totanus* **R**

Rare summer visitor. Differs from (2) in less lanky, **browner appearance**; from most other shorebirds in **red or orange legs** and **reddish base to moderately long, straight bill**. Differs from (3) in plain upperparts and bill shape. In flight the **only shorebird with white triangular patches on the wings,** plus white back, rump and tail, the latter faintly barred. Calls 'teu-he-he' on take-off. Flight erratic with jerky, deliberate wing beats, feet slightly protruding beyond the tail. Usually occurs singly, often with other shorebirds, on coastal mudflats, estuaries, lagoons and inland waters. **25 cm (Rooipootruiter)**

2 Spotted Redshank *Tringa erythropus* **V**

Rare summer vagrant. Lankier and more gracefully proportioned than (1). **Bill and legs longer. Overall appearance greyish**, usually with some **spotting on the upperparts; whitish underparts**. Further differs from (1) in **clear (not diffuse) white eyebrow, finer bill**, which droops slightly at the end and which has the **red restricted to the lower mandible only**, and different wing pattern. In flight shows no wing-bar and has **oval white patch on back**; feet protrude more than in (1). Posture fairly erect. The call is a deep 'chee-wit'. May occur at either inland or coastal waters. **30 cm (Gevlekte Rooipootruiter)**

3 Ruff *Philomachus pugnax*

Abundant summer visitor. **Male much larger than female** (known as a reeve). Told by **short, slightly decurved bill with slightly bulbous tip,** featureless face, except for a **small white patch at the base of the bill**, and **boldly scaled or mottled upperparts. Legs orange** in adult, grey-green in immature. Male may be seen in spring or autumn with traces of its breeding plumage. In flight it shows **white oval patches on sides of dark tail**. Birds in a flock may call 'chit' in a twittering chorus. Occurs singly, in groups or in large flocks in shallows of coastal and inland waters, flooded fields and farmlands. Takes flight in dense flocks. **24–30 cm (Kemphaan)**

4 Green Sandpiper *Tringa ochropus* **R**

Uncommon summer visitor. Differs from (5) in **darker, less obviously spotted upperparts, longer bill, white eyebrow only in front of eye, grey or greenish (not dull yellow) legs** and clear border between streaked breast and white belly. In flight shows **larger white rump, broadly barred tail** and **dark underwing coverts; the toes project only slightly past the tail**. When flushed it towers up, uttering a loud, shrill 'weet-a-weet', then makes off with erratic, snipe-like flight. Solitary on quiet streams and grassy ponds. **23 cm (Witgatruiter)**

5 Wood Sandpiper *Tringa glareola*

Common summer visitor, some all year. Has **well-spotted upperparts, broad, distinct eyebrow extending behind the eye**, short, straight bill and fairly long, **dull yellow legs**. In flight shows **pale grey underwing coverts**, differing mainly in this and bill length from (4); **feet protrude well beyond tail**. When flushed towers up and calls a flat, triple 'chiff-iff-iff'; also has a high-pitched alarm call 'tchi-tchi-tchi-tchi-tchi'. Occurs singly or in small groups on most shallow inland waters, flooded grassland and coastal estuaries. **20 cm (Bosruiter)**

1

diffuse eyebrow

N-Br

white

densely mottled

Br

red legs

2

clear eyebrow and face pattern

N-Br

fine bill drops slightly towards tip

red legs

Br

bulbous bill tip

Br

Br

Br

3

♂

male much larger than female

white ovals

3

♀

boldly scaled upperparts

N-Br

bright orange legs

4

dark with some white spots

eyebrow faint behind eye

dark underwings

white

broad bars

grey or greenish legs

5

distinct white eyebrow behind eye

densely spotted white

dull yellow legs

NEAR THREATENED

1 Black-tailed Godwit *Limosa limosa* **R**

Rare summer visitor. Despite **straight (or only very slightly upturned) bill** and **longer legs** (especially tibia), it is not easily distinguished from (2) at rest, but head, neck and breast are of **uniform tone, not streaked**. In flight the **broad black tail-band** and **prominent white upperwing-bars** are distinctive. When flying may call a loud 'wicka-wicka-wicka'. Usually occurs singly, **mostly at inland waters**, but a few coastal sightings have been made. **40–50 cm** (Swartstertgriet)

2 Bar-tailed Godwit *Limosa lapponica*

Fairly common summer visitor. Stockier appearance with **shorter legs** (especially tibia) than (1); **bill long** (longest in female) and **gently upcurved (not straight)**. Head, neck and breast more **obviously streaked**. In flight the tail shows numerous light bars at close range; the wings lack bars. The call is a deep 'god-whit'. Occurs singly or in flocks on tidal mudflats and sheltered coastal bays; occasionally on inland waters. **36–39 cm** (Bandstertgriet)

3 Hudsonian Godwit *Limosa haemastica* **V**

Vagrant. Occurs in non-breeding plumage, when similar to (1) and (2). Most diagnostic features are seen in flight when **black underwing coverts** are apparent; **rest of underwing grey**, except for narrow white region at base of secondaries and inner primaries (the other godwits have mostly white underwings; dark-edged in (1)). The **black tail** also distinguishes it from (2). May mix with other godwits. Breeds in northern Canada. **37–42 cm** (Hudsonbaaigriet)

4 Whimbrel *Numenius phaeopus*

Common summer visitor, a few all year. Differs from (5) in markedly **smaller size, shorter decurved bill** (about two and a half times length of head) and **dark cap with pale central line**. In flight shows extensive **white back and rump**. Call is a twittering 'peep-eep-eep-eep-ee'. Occurs singly or in small groups on coastal lagoons, rocky shorelines, estuary and harbour mudflats; less frequently on inland waters. **43 cm** (Kleinwulp)

NEAR THREATENED

5 Eurasian Curlew *Numenius arquata*

Uncommon summer visitor. Much larger than (4) with **extremely long, decurved bill**. Shows **no distinctive pattern on crown**. In flight shows similar large white area on back and rump to (4), but generally **paler overall appearance**. From a distance could also be confused with an ibis (p. 108). Utters various calls, including 'cur-lew' or 'coorwe-coorwe' and 'quee-quee-quee'. Groups, up to about 50 or 60, occur on coastal shorelines (especially southern and western coasts), estuaries, coastal lagoons, tidal rivers and harbours. A vagrant to inland waters. **59 cm** (Grootwulp)

NEAR THREATENED

6 Asiatic Dowitcher *Limnodromas semipalmatus* **V**

Rare vagrant. **Exceptionally long bill** and **large size** eliminate confusion with most wader species, but could be confused with godwits on this page, which have slightly upturned bills with contrasting paler bases and finer tips. In non-breeding plumage usually shows **dark chevrons on flanks** (lacking in godwits). In flight shows a **finely barred rump**, lacking the striking white rump and back of (2) and the distinctive black-and-white pattern of (1). In breeding plumage whole body suffused with **deep rufous** (brighter and more extensive in male). Calls include a quiet, repeated 'che-up' note. Breeds sparsely in western Siberia and Mongolia, wintering primarily in coastal wetlands in southeast Asia. Recorded once at Leeupan, Benoni, in Nov 2004. **34–36 cm** (Asiatiese Snipgriet)

1

long eyebrow

N-Br

quite plain

long, slightly upturned bill

black tail

long legs

Br

plain head and neck

bold flight pattern

2

short eyebrow

very long, noticeably upturned bill

♀ N-Br

mottled upperparts

barred tail

short tibia

Br

3

pinkish base of bill

black underwings

black tail coverts

black legs

4

diagnostic pale stripe down middle of crown

darker than (5)

5

lacks bold head markings

bill longer than (4), longest in females

may superficially resemble an ibis

paler than (4)

6

N-Br

uniform upperparts

long, straight bill

1 Little Stint *Calidris minuta*
Common summer visitor. A tiny, active wader. Extremely similar to (2), differing in **slightly longer, more slender bill** and more **heavily blotched upperparts** (dark feather centres). Well-worn plumage may appear paler, so bill shape is the best guide. Utters a sharp 'chit' or rapid 'chit-chit-chit…'. Occurs singly, in small flocks or occasionally in large numbers at coastal estuaries and lagoons and various inland waters. Feeds on shorelines and in shallows with hunched, head-down posture. **14 cm** (Kleinstrandloper)

2 Red-necked Stint *Calidris ruficollis* V
Rare summer visitor. Told from (1) only with care: **bill slightly shorter, more robust and less tapered; upperparts paler (not blotched); feathers more grey with dark central shafts.** General appearance longer but with **shorter legs** than (1). Breeding plumage diagnostic: **rufous head, neck and breast** (chin and central throat usually white in (1)). Call a weak, short 'chit'. Occurs singly on coastal estuaries and lagoons, especially along the east coast. **15 cm** (Rooinekstrandloper)

3 Long-toed Stint *Calidris subminuta* V
Rare vagrant. Appears slightly taller than (1), from which it is best distinguished **by yellow (not black) legs** and **richer, darker brown upperparts streaked with pale buff.** Differs from (4) in richly marked (not uniform) upperparts. Unlike other stints, the feet project past the tail in flight. Adopts characteristic stance, **stretching its neck and standing very upright. 13–15 cm** (Langtoonstrandloper)

4 Temminck's Stint *Calidris temminckii* V
Rare vagrant. Very similar to (1) but has **yellowish (not black) legs and feet** and **fairly uniform, unmarked grey upperparts.** In flight the **outer tail feathers are white**, not grey as in (1). **13–15 cm** (Temminckstrandloper)

5 Baird's Sandpiper *Calidris bairdii* V
Rare vagrant. Larger than (1) but smaller than Curlew Sandpiper (p. 142). Has characteristic upperparts, **appearing very scaled.** Like (7), overall **body shape slender and streamlined, wingtips projecting well beyond tail.** Differs in **dark-centred, not white, rump.** Head shape diagnostic, appearing squarish like a Green or Wood Sandpiper (p. 136), rather than a stint. **14–16 cm** (Bairdstrandloper)

6 Broad-billed Sandpiper *Limicola falcinellus* R
Rare summer visitor. Identified by fairly **long bill with a flattened, decurved tip, streaked head** and **short legs.** In breeding plumage shows additional stripes on mantle, these and head-stripes giving **snipe-like flight pattern.** Call is a soft trill. Occurs singly on coastal estuaries, quiet bays, lagoons and pans; rarely inland. **17 cm** (Breëbekstrandloper)

7 White-rumped Sandpiper *Calidris fuscicollis* V
Rare vagrant. Similar in shape and size to (5) but has **longer, very slightly decurved bill** and **lacks the scaled upperparts.** Told from Curlew Sandpiper (p. 142), which also has a **white rump**, by much smaller size and shorter bill. **15–17 cm** (Witrugstrandloper)

1

white

Br

smaller than (2) with darker, more contrasting colour

extremely similar

slightly shorter bill than (1)

marginally shorter legs and longer body than (1)

Br

2

3

richly marked above

4

yellowish legs

5

usually has streaked breast-band

long wings project past tail

boldly streaked head

bold patterning

short legs

6

Br

7

white

long wings

1 Common Sandpiper   *Actitis hypoleucos*

Common summer visitor, a few all year. Has diagnostic **white pectoral region showing above folded wing. Medium-short, robust bill** and habit of **frequently bobbing its hindquarters**. In flight shows no white rump, but **faint wing-bar** and **white outer tail feathers**. When flushed, utters a shrill 'twee-wee-wee' and flies away; flies low with **stiff, downward-bowed wings, flapping with sporadic flicking action** below the horizontal. Occurs singly on shores of rivers, lakes, dams, estuaries and rocky coasts. **20 cm** (Gewone Ruiter)

2 Curlew Sandpiper   *Calidris ferruginea*

Abundant summer visitor. The most common small shorebird with a **decurved bill**. Differs from very similar but rare (3) in **gently tapering bill** and, in flight, **broad white rump**. Differs from rare Broad-billed Sandpiper (p. 140) in **evenly decurved bill** (not curved at the tip only), longer legs, less contrasting upperparts and broad white rump. Calls 'chiet-chiet' in flight. Occurs in small flocks at inland pans and dams (especially sewage ponds) and in very large flocks at coastal lagoons, estuaries and west coast bays. **19 cm** (Krombekstrandloper)

3 Dunlin   *Calidris alpina*   V

Vagrant. Can be confused with (2), but is smaller and has a **dark (not white) rump, shorter, less decurved bill** and **browner, more marked upperparts**. In breeding plumage shows a diagnostic **black belly patch**. **15–22 cm** (Bontstrandloper)

4 Pectoral Sandpiper   *Calidris melanotos*   R

Rare summer visitor. With **richly patterned upperparts** recalls a small Ruff (p. 136). Best told by **well-streaked buffy breast terminating in a sharp line**, contrasting with **pure white underparts**, and a **dark crown**. In flight shows snipe-like streaks on back. Usual call is 'prritt', one or more times. Takes off with erratic snipe-like action, then flies straight. Occurs singly on coastal estuaries, inland sewage works and in moist grassland, often with other shorebirds. **Can be quite tame. 20–23 cm** (Geelpootstrandloper)

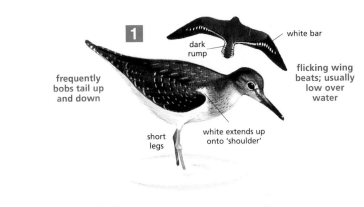

1

white bar

dark rump

flicking wing beats; usually low over water

frequently bobs tail up and down

short legs

white extends up onto 'shoulder'

rather pale, plain grey-brown

2

white rump

Br

bill distinctly decurved

bill shorter than (2) and less decurved

3

dark rump

short legs

4

richly patterned

streaked breast ends in definite line

white underparts

yellowish legs

1 Red Knot *Calidris canutus*
Common summer visitor. Differs from other short-billed shorebirds in **plump-bodied appearance. Straight, short and rather blunt bill.** In flight the wings appear long and pointed, the **white wing-bars** conspicuous; cf. (2). Calls 'knut', sometimes in a series. Flocks at coastal lagoons, estuaries and rocky shores, especially along the west coast; individuals rarely inland. Feeds with a slow forward movement while probing mud several times between steps. Flocks fly in dense packs, twisting and turning at speed. **25 cm** (Knoet)

2 Great Knot *Calidris tenuirostris* ▉V
Rare vagrant. Largest *Calidris* sandpiper; can only be distinguished with care from (1). Appears **larger** and **longer-legged**, with a longer, more tapered body shape owing to **longer neck**, proportionately **smaller head** and **long wings** that project beyond the tail. The bill is longer than the head and slightly decurved, and has a deeper base but finer tip than (1). Upperparts less uniform, with **darker feather centres** and more brown than grey in tone. More pronounced **spotting on breast sides** and **chevrons on flanks**. Leg colour variable, although often darker than (1). In breeding plumage, breast is almost black, with rufous spangling on scapulars. Rump white with isolated grey marks on upper rump (unlike fully grey-speckled rump of (1)). Usually silent but may call 'knut-knut' in flight. Breeds in northeastern Siberia, wintering from India through southeast Asia to Australia. Four records from southern Africa to date, but probably overlooked. **26–28 cm** (Grootknoet)

3 Sanderling *Calidris alba*
Common summer visitor. A small shorebird with **very white appearance with dark shoulder-patch** and **short, thick bill. White wing-bars** conspicuous in flight. Larger and paler than any stint (p. 140). When flushed calls a liquid 'blt-blt'. Flocks, mostly on open seashores, characteristically run along the water's edge and feed where the waves have receded. An uncommon passage migrant on inland waters. Feeds in a hunched, head-down posture, probing wet sand hurriedly, continuously. Flight is low and direct. **19 cm** (Drietoonstrandloper)

4 Terek Sandpiper *Xenus cinereus*
Common summer visitor. Distinguished by **long upcurved bill, short, orange-yellow legs** and **pale grey-brown upperparts** with a **dark shoulder.** In flight shows **white secondaries** and **grey rump.** Calls a fluty 'tur-lip'. Occurs singly or in flocks on coastal estuaries and lagoons. Bobs its rear up and down like Common Sandpiper (p. 142). Sometimes runs at speed between bouts of deep probing with its bill. **23–25 cm** (Terekruiter)

5 Ruddy Turnstone *Arenaria interpres*
Common summer visitor. Characterised by **long body, hunched, head-in-shoulders appearance**, horizontal stance and **striking plumage pattern;** all stages between full breeding and non-breeding plumages occur. In flight reveals **extensive white back and wing-bars.** Flight or contact call 'ktuk-a-tut'. Flocks of five to 20 frequent coastal mudflats and shorelines, especially rocky shores; occasionally on inland waters. Feeds by turning over small stones, shells, caked mud and debris. If flushed, flies off low. **22 cm** (Steenloper)

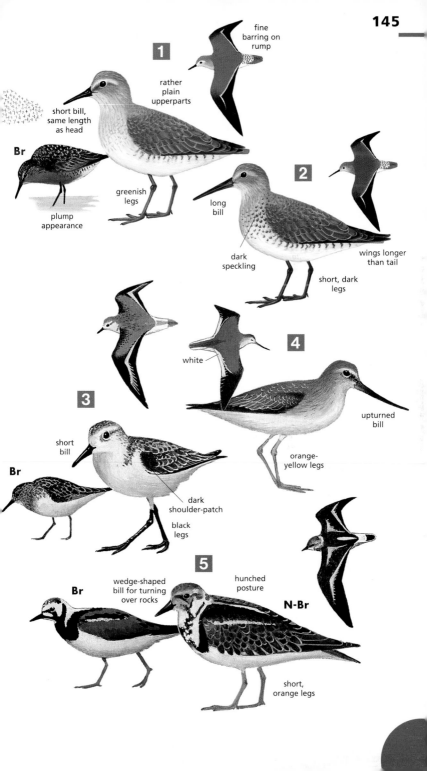

1

fine barring on rump

rather plain upperparts

short bill, same length as head

Br

greenish legs

plump appearance

2

long bill

dark speckling

wings longer than tail

short, dark legs

3

white

4

upturned bill

orange-yellow legs

short bill

Br

dark shoulder-patch

black legs

5

wedge-shaped bill for turning over rocks

hunched posture

Br

N-Br

short, orange legs

NEAR THREATENED

1 Buff-breasted Sandpiper *Tryngites subruficollis* **V**
Vagrant. Looks like a richly coloured, diminutive Ruff (p. 136). The **short, straight bill** and **small, rounded head**, combined with **the lack of wing-bars or white oval patches on the sides of the tail**, should rule out confusion with the Ruff. In flight shows **silvery underwings** with a **diagnostic dark 'comma'**. Occurs more in moist grassland than on shorelines. **18–19 cm** (Taanborsstrandloper)

2 Grey Plover *Pluvialis squatarola*
Common summer visitor, a few all year. Non-breeding plumage resembles (4), but more **chunky with greyish overall appearance**. Larger size, **short, stout bill** and **fairly long legs** distinguish it from smaller shorebirds. **In flight shows black 'armpits'**. Both partial breeding plumage (a) and full breeding plumage (b) occur in spring and autumn. Has a far-carrying whistle 'tlui-tlui' or 'pee-u-wee'. Occurs singly or in flocks on tidal flats and secluded seashores; occasionally inland. **28–30 cm** (Grysstrandkiewiet)

GOLDEN PLOVERS

Previously known as the Lesser Golden Plover, with two races, but now given full specific status as American Golden Plover and Pacific Golden Plover. **Rare vagrants** that reach our shores in **non-breeding plumage** when their specific identity can be problematic. They differ from the similar Grey Plover (2) in their non-breeding plumage in having **dull grey (not black) 'armpits'**, fairly long upper legs, **golden-spangled upperparts**, more elegant proportions and an upright stance.

3 Pacific Golden Plover *Pluvialis fulva* **V**
Rare visitor. Slightly smaller and less robust than (4). The **eyebrows and head have a yellow wash**; rest of **upperparts grey-brown spotted golden-yellow**. Greyish throat, neck and breast feathers edged yellow, **belly pure white**. In flight and seen from above, wings show a barely visible **white wing-bar**; the **rump is dark** and **feet protrude slightly beyond tail**; **underwings are grey**. The call is the same as that of (4) plus a repeated 'chu-leek'. **23–26 cm** (Asiatiese Goue Strandkiewiet)

4 American Golden Plover *Pluvialis dominica* **V**
Rare late summer visitor. Appears slightly more robust than (3) and differs also in having a **clear white eyebrow** that becomes wider posteriorly, a **darker crown** and a **dull greyish breast with white (not yellow) mottling**; the **belly drab (not white)**. Upperparts are dull grey-brown with all feathers edged buff-yellow. In flight differs from (2) in having a **dark rump** and **plain grey underwings**; its **feet do not protrude beyond its tail**. The call is a melodious 'tu-ee' or 'tee-tew'. Few records of single birds in coastal regions. **24–28 cm** (Amerikaanse Goue Strandkiewiet)

1

scalloped

rich buff

obvious silvery underwing

dark 'comma'

pale rump

black 'armpits'

N-Br

heavy bill

heavy-set appearance

2

a

b

Br

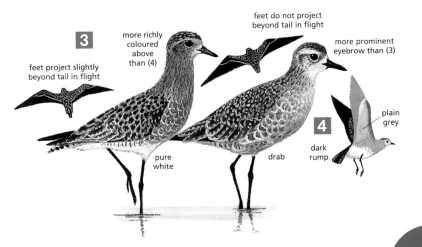

3

more richly coloured above than (4)

feet do not project beyond tail in flight

more prominent eyebrow than (3)

feet project slightly beyond tail in flight

pure white

drab

plain grey

dark rump

4

JACANAS

Distinctive waterbirds with long legs and very long toes, perfectly evolved for walking on floating or semi submerged vegetation. Always found in freshwater habitats such as lagoons, slow flowing rivers and pans, especially those with waterlillies. Both species are highly nomadic according to abundance of water and seasonal flooding. Diet consists mainly of aquatic insects and small crustaceans.

1 African Jacana *Actophilornis africanus*

Common resident. Adult unmistakable with **exceptionally long toes**, **chestnut body** and **blue frontal shield and bill**. Immature has a **black stripe through the eye** and **black crown**; cf. (2). The call, uttered while standing or flying, is 'kyowrrr'. Individuals or scattered groups **walk on floating vegetation** on lily-covered pans, dams and river backwaters. Frequently chases others in short dashes or in low flight while calling loudly. **40 cm** (Grootlangtoon)

NEAR THREATENED

2 Lesser Jacana *Microparra capensis*

Uncommon, localised resident. **Very much smaller than (1): sparrow-sized minus feet.** Differs from immature of (1) in **pale feather edges to brown upperparts** giving scaled effect; **central mantle and back deep bronze-brown; forehead brown; crown and eye-stripe chestnut** and **underparts white**. In flight, easily distinguished from (1) by **white trailing edge on upperwings**. Immature has a dark crown, the nape golden-chestnut. Silent except for an occasional 'kruk'. Occurs on lily-covered ponds, dams and river backwaters. **20 cm** (Dwerglangtoon)

LAPWINGS

Long-legged terrestrial birds with characteristically black, white and brown colouring. Usually found in pairs or small groups, favouring short grassland areas never far from fresh water. Lapwings breed during the winter season, laying their well camouflaged eggs into a shallow scrape on the ground, which they aggressively and noisily defend from humans and other predators.

3 Senegal Lapwing *Vanellus lugubris*

Uncommon resident. Closely resembles (4) but **upperparts olive-brown** (not warm brown), the **white forehead forward of the eye**, the **dark lower breast-band usually narrow, legs dark brown or blackish**. Upperwing and underwing patterns diagnostic (see illustration). The call is a piping 'thi-wit'. Small parties in dry grassland and open woodland. **23 cm** (Kleinswartvlerkkiewiet)

NEAR THREATENED

4 Black-winged Lapwing *Vanellus melanopterus*

Fairly common visitor and resident. Differs from (3) in **white forehead extending to above the eye**, a **bright red eye-ring**, a **broad dark band on the lower breast** and **dark red legs**. Upperwing and underwing patterns diagnostic (see illustration). The normal call is a harsh 'tlu-wit', the alarm call a shrill 'che-che-che-cherek', rising to a scream when highly agitated. Usually in flocks in hilly grassland, and on golf courses and playing fields where grass is short. **29 cm** (Grootswartvlerkkiewiet)

uniform
chestnut body

1

blue frontal
shield and bill

chestnut
crown

2

small size

lacks black
nape of adult

J

plain chestnut
back, rump and wings

less extensive white on
forehead than (4)

3

smallish and
'leggy'

narrow,
dark breast-
band

more white
than on (3)

bright red
eye-ring

white

dark
brown or
blackish
legs

4

broad dark
breast-band

white wing-
bar

dark
red legs

1 Long-toed Lapwing *Vanellus crassirostris*

Uncommon, localised resident. Striking pied appearance: **white front half of head, neck and upper breast** contrast with **black nape, rear neck and breast-band**. **Very long toes.** In flight reveals **mostly white underwings**. The call is 'wheet' and, in flight, a clicking 'kick-k-k-kick-k-k-k'. Mostly solitary on large rivers and backwaters, lakes and floodplains; feeds while walking on floating vegetation. **30 cm** (Witvlerkkiewiet)

2 Blacksmith Lapwing *Vanellus armatus*

Very common resident. A pied plover with **grey wings and mantle**. Immature has the **basic plumage pattern of adults, but in tones of speckled brown**. The call is a metallic 'klink, klink, klink' (hence its name) repeated loudly and continuously when disturbed. Pairs and scattered individuals frequent the shores of a wide variety of inland waters, marshy ground, flooded fields and other moist places. **30 cm** (Bontkiewiet)

3 Crowned Lapwing *Vanellus coronatus*

Very common resident. Distinguished by **white circle surrounding a black cap, black-tipped red bill** and **red legs**. Eyes usually **pale yellow**, sometimes dark brown. Very noisy, calling 'kie-weeet' on the ground or a repeated 'kree-kree-kreeip-kreeip' in flight, day or night. Pairs and groups found on dry, open ground with short or burned grass, especially on airfields, traffic islands and sports fields; also in lightly wooded country. Often fly about in small groups at some height, calling repeatedly. **30 cm** (Kroonkiewiet)

4 African Wattled Lapwing *Vanellus senegallus*

Common resident. **Bright yellow bill, wattles and legs** distinguish it from all but (5), from which it differs in **shorter wattles, white patch only on forecrown**, a **streaked neck, lack of white bars on folded wings** and **brown breast and underparts** (except for the belly). The call is a shrill 'kwep-kwep-kwep-kwep', speeding up with increased agitation. Pairs and small groups frequent grassy waterside localities, riverbanks, dam walls, fringes of sewage ponds and vleis. **35 cm** (Lelkiewiet)

NEAR THREATENED

5 White-crowned Lapwing *Vanellus albiceps*

Uncommon, localised resident. Distinguished from (4) by **longer wattles** (longer than the bill), a **broad white band** (dark-edged in males) extending from the bill over the crown, **entirely white underparts** and a black wing bordered with white above. In flight the **underwings appear mainly white**. A noisy species, the call a sharp 'peep, peep-peep, peep…' uttered at rapid speed if the bird is flushed. Pairs and groups frequent the shores and sandbanks of large perennial rivers. **30 cm** (Witkopkiewiet)

6 Spur-winged Lapwing *Vanellus spinosus* Ⅴ

Vagrant. Differs from the superficially similar (2) in lacking any grey plumage, having the **entire cap black; upper breast to neck white** with an **expanding black stripe from chin to black lower breast; upperparts dull brown**. When alarmed calls a sharp, metallic 'pick' repeatedly. Several records from the northern and eastern parts of the subregion. Could occur on any wetland, especially shorelines of large rivers. **25–28 cm** (Spoorvlerkkiewiet)

black
hindneck

1

mostly
white
underwings

immature shows
same basic
plumage patterns
as adult

white

white
throat-patch

J

2

long toes for
walking on floating
vegetation

distinctive
white
'crown'

3

red legs

short
wattles

conspicuous
white bar

broad
white band

streaked
neck

long
wattles

4

prominent
wing-spur

5

black
underparts

white
underparts

bright
yellow
legs

black
cap

dull brown
upperparts and
wings

6

OYSTERCATCHERS

A group of striking black or pied birds with red bills and legs. Their long, strong bills are perfect tools for prying open molluscs and probing in the mud for insects, worms or small crustaceans. Pairs can be very territorial, noisily defending the nest, which is a shallow scrape on the ground – with a piping, plover-like call. Their flight is rapid and direct.

1 **Eurasian Oystercatcher** *Haematopus ostralegus* **V**
Rare visitor. Fairly large, pied shorebird with **orange bill** and **pink legs**. Usually occurs in southern Africa as non-breeding or immature, the latter with **dark tip to bill**. **In breeding plumage lacks white throat**. The call is a shrill 'kleeep' and a shorter 'pic, pic'. Occurs singly or in small groups on sandy coastlines, river mouths and lagoons. Sometimes in company with the larger (2). **43 cm** (Bonttobie)

NEAR THREATENED

2 **African Black Oystercatcher** *Haematopus moquini* **E**
Common endemic resident. The only **entirely black shorebird with red bill, eyes and legs**. Immature is browner. Normal call 'klee-weep, klee-weep'; alarm call a sharp 'ki-kik-kiks'. Occurs singly or in small groups on rocky coastlines, estuaries and coastal lagoons. Is most common on the Cape and Namibian coastlines, but is threatened by human disturbance of habitat. **51 cm** (Swarttobie)

PHALAROPES

Long-legged oceanic 'sandpipers'. They **swim buoyantly like small gulls** and, with the exception of (5), feed from the surface with **pirouetting action**. They sometimes occur on inland waters, otherwise well offshore in Atlantic waters. Female breeding plumages are brighter than those of males; non-breeding plumages identical.

3 **Red-necked Phalarope** *Phalaropus lobatus*
Rare non-breeding summer visitor. Identified by **thin bill** (about same length as head) and **dark grey upperparts**, often with a white 'V'-shape; may have dark cap. In breeding plumage shows darker brown upperparts with striking facial pattern, as illustrated. In flight shows a dark rump and narrow white wing-bar, cf. (5). Occurs in flocks at sea or singly on coastal lagoons and shallow ponds. **17 cm** (Rooihalsfraiingpoot)

4 **Red Phalarope** *Phalaropus fulicaria*
Uncommon non-breeding summer visitor. Identified by **short, fairly robust bill** with (usually) **yellow base** and **pale uniform upperparts**. Breeding plumage as illustrated. In flight shows **grey rump** and **broad white wing-bar**. Occurs in flocks at sea or singly on deep inland waters. **20 cm** (Grysfraiingpoot)

5 **Wilson's Phalarope** *Phalaropus tricolor*
Summer vagrant. Identified in non-breeding plumage by **long, needle-like bill, lack of eye-patch, straw-coloured legs** (black when breeding) and **no wing-bar**. Breeding plumage is dark russet brown above, with a striking facial pattern, as illustrated. Occurs singly on shallow inshore waters. May feed by wading in shallows on partially flexed legs while lunging rapidly from side to side with bill. If swimming, stabs rapidly at surface, occasionally spinning. **22–24 cm** (Bontfraiingpoot)

Br

N-Br

red eye

red bill

1

pink legs

red legs

2

3

dark grey upperparts

thin bill; always black

narrow white bar

♀ **Br**

white 'V'-shapes usually visible on folded wing

N-Br

broad white bar

uniform pale upperparts

short thick bill

N-Br

plain

♀ **Br**

4

pale rump

no eye-patch

long needle-like bill

no white wing-bar

♀ **Br**

5

N-Br

black legs

cf. Marsh Sandpiper (p. 134)

CRAB PLOVER

The Crab Plover is a monotypic species confined to the East African coast from the Red Sea to northern Mozambique. It is a vagrant further south.

1 Crab Plover *Dromas ardeola* R

Rare visitor. **Long-legged, mainly white shorebird**; immature browner. Differs from other similar black-and-white birds in **heavy, thick bill**. Flies stiff-winged, the legs protruding well beyond the tail. Utters a harsh 'crook' or 'cheeruk' when flushed. Occurs in small flocks (usually up to around 30 individuals, but occasionally 200 or more) on east coast mudflats, lagoons, estuaries and mangroves. Most frequent in Mozambique. **38 cm** (Krapvreter)

AVOCETS AND STILTS

Elegant, **long-legged, long-billed, black-and-white wading birds**. Avocets have **upturned bills**; stilts have **straight bills**.

2 Pied Avocet *Recurvirostra avosetta*

Common resident. **Thin, upturned bill diagnostic.** Where the **adult has black plumage**, the immature has dark brown. Call a liquid 'kluut', several birds sometimes calling together. Flocks, varying from a few individuals to hundreds, occur in shallow waters of inland lakes, dams and pans (especially sewage ponds) and at coastal lagoons and estuaries. Feeds by wading, the immersed bill being swept from side to side while the bird walks slowly forward, or while swimming. Nomadic when not breeding and irregular in many regions. **43 cm** (Bontelsie)

3 Black-winged Stilt *Himantopus himantopus*

Common resident. **Black-and-white plumage** and **long red legs** are conspicuous both at rest and in flight. Adult may have a **dusky crown**, while immature is even duskier about the head. The call, often given in flight, is a loud 'kik-kik-kik-kik-kik' or 'kyik'. Individuals, pairs or flocks occur at inland pans, dams and vleis, especially sewage ponds, and coastal lagoons and estuaries. Wades in the shallows with the legs well immersed while feeding on the surface. **38 cm** (Rooipootelsie)

heavy, dagger-like bill

1

J

blue-grey legs

unique upturned bill

2

bold black-and-white pattern

pale blueish legs

straight bill

3

young birds show variable amount of dusky moulting on head and side of neck

exceptionally long red legs

J

THICK-KNEES

Lapwing-like birds with **large heads and eyes, long legs,** feet without a hind claw and **tawny coloration**. They normally walk with short, mincing steps. **Nocturnal and crepuscular,** they spend the daytime resting in a concealed location. The name 'Thick-knee' is misleading; the term refers to the thickened tibio-tarsal joints (see p. 25), which are, in fact, not knees, but a bird's equivalent of ankle joints.

1 Spotted Thick-Knee   *Burhinus capensis*
Common resident. Distinguished from (2) by **heavily spotted upperparts, no wing-bar** and **habitat preference**. Most vocal on moonlit nights, flying about restlessly and calling a shrill, eerie 'chwee-chwee, chwee-chwee, chwee, chwee, chwee, tiu-tiu-tiu…', trailing off at the end. Pairs frequent dry, rocky ground with short grass, open fields and open areas within woodland; frequently in little-developed urban areas. Rests by day under bushes or among rocks, running off with lowered head if disturbed. **44 cm** (Gewone Dikkop)

2 Water Thick-Knee   *Burhinus vermiculatus*
Common resident. Distinguished from (1) by **distinct grey wing-bar, edged black,** and **habitat preference**. Calls at night and at dusk, a piping, melancholy 'whee-wheeoo-wheeoo'. Occurs singly or in small groups on the banks of large rivers or lakes where there is fringing vegetation. Rests during the day in reeds or beneath overhanging bushes, becoming active at dusk. **40 cm** (Waterdikkop)

PRATINCOLES AND COURSERS

Pratincoles are migratory and nomadic birds with **very short legs** in relation to the length of their bodies. At rest or in their **elegant, often erratic flight they resemble terns**. They **feed mostly in the air,** in flocks. Their calls are of a 'kip-kip-kip…' nature. The related coursers are more lapwing-like with erect stance, but unlike plovers lack a hind toe; they are **terrestrial feeders**. Sexes are alike in both groups.

NEAR THREATENED

3 Collared Pratincole   *Glareola pratincola*
Locally common summer resident. Differs from (4) in **rufous underwing coverts** and **white-tipped secondaries**; see flight illustration. At rest, tail projects beyond wing-tips and **base of bill redder (less black)** than (4). Flocks occur on floodplains, estuaries, lakesides and farmlands. Feeding flocks rise in great, wheeling columns and perform remarkable aerial manoeuvres. When settling, habitually stands briefly with wings raised. **25 cm** (Rooivlerksprinkaanvoël)

NEAR THREATENED

4 Black-winged Pratincole   *Glareola nordmanni*
Locally common summer visitor. Seen mostly in non-breeding plumage, when it lacks the **black collar**. Differs from (3) in **entirely blackish underwings, less red on the gape** and slightly more extensive **yellow-buff coloration on the lower breast**. Flocks on floodlands, estuaries, lakesides and farmlands. Behaviour the same as (3). **25 cm** (Swartvlerksprinkaanvoël)

5 Rock Pratincole   *Glareola nuchalis*
Common, localised resident. Smaller than (3) and (4). Has **no throat-patch; outer tail-feathers are only slightly elongated. Narrow white collar** and **red legs** diagnostic. Flocks on large rivers and lakes, especially **near boulder-strewn rapids**. Perches on rocks protruding from the water and feeds by hawking. **18 cm** (Withalssprinkaanvoël)

spotted upperparts

1

grey wing-bar

2

usually near water

noticeable whitish eye-ring

more red at base of bill

Br

generally paler than (4)

N-Br

3

white-tipped secondaries

tail projects beyond wing-tips

rufous underwing (can be hard to discern)

4

wholly blackish underwings

N-Br

Br

less red

tail shorter than wing-tips

narrow white collar

red legs

short tail

5

1 **Bronze-winged Courser** *Rhinoptilus chalcopterus*

Uncommon visitor and resident. Larger than most other coursers; has **red legs** and **distinctive head markings**, these less clearly defined in immature; cf. also Crowned Lapwing (p. 150). Shows a **narrow, iridescent purple trailing edge to its outer wings** (difficult to see in the field). At night calls a shrill 'ji-ku-it' or a plaintive 'gro-raag', but like other coursers, not particularly vocal. A nocturnal species of well-wooded regions, especially favouring mopane woodland. Roosts by day beneath bushes and feeds at night in open areas and on roads. **25 cm** (Bronsvlerkdrawwertjie)

2 **Temminck's Courser** *Cursorius temminckii*

Fairly common resident. A **small, white-legged, rufous-capped courser**; cf. (3) and larger Crowned Lapwing (p. 150). Immature is speckled buff on upperparts and crown. May call a sharp 'err-err-err' in flight. Pairs and small groups occur on freshly burned or well-grazed grassland and airfields. Stands with erect stance, then runs rapidly forward before stooping briefly to feed; occasionally bobs its head and tail. Nomadic. **20 cm** (Trekdrawwertjie)

3 **Burchell's Courser** *Cursorius rufus*   N E

Uncommon near-endemic resident. Differs from (2) mainly in **blue-grey hindcrown** and the extent of its **white belly, which is bordered by a narrow black bar** (not broad black wedge). In flight shows diagnostic **white trailing edges to its wings**. Immature is mottled on upperparts. A quiet species; may call 'kok-kok-kwich'. Habitat and habits very similar to (2). Occurs in small groups in short grassland. Bobs its head and hindquarters more than (2) and jerks its body backwards and forwards or sideways. Nomadic. **23 cm** (Bloukopdrawwertjie)

4 **Double-banded Courser** *Rhinoptilus africanus*

Common resident. A distinctive, **pale courser** with **two black bands encircling the lower neck and upper breast**. Immature is similar. In flight reveals striking **rufous panels on its upperwings**. Normally silent but may call 'pee-wee' if put to flight; also calls 'chik-kee, chik-kee, chik-kee-kee-kee' while flying at night. Occurs in pairs or scattered groups in arid grassland or semi-desert and on fringes of dry pans and barren, stony flats. Active day and night and seemingly indifferent to hot conditions. Runs rather than flies. Nomadic. **22 cm** (Dubbelbanddrawwertjie)

5 **Three-banded Courser** *Rhinoptilus cinctus*

Uncommon visitor and resident. Darker than (4) with **bold head markings** and **bands spanning the upper breast** (not encircling the neck). **Yellow base to bill; yellow eye-ring and legs** also diagnostic. Immature has lower band poorly defined. Mainly nocturnal, and calls mostly at night, 'chick-a-chuck-a-chuck-a-chuck'. Occurs singly or in pairs in well-grassed woodland and thornveld of the drier regions. When approached it freezes, usually with its back to the observer. **28 cm** (Driebanddrawwertjie)

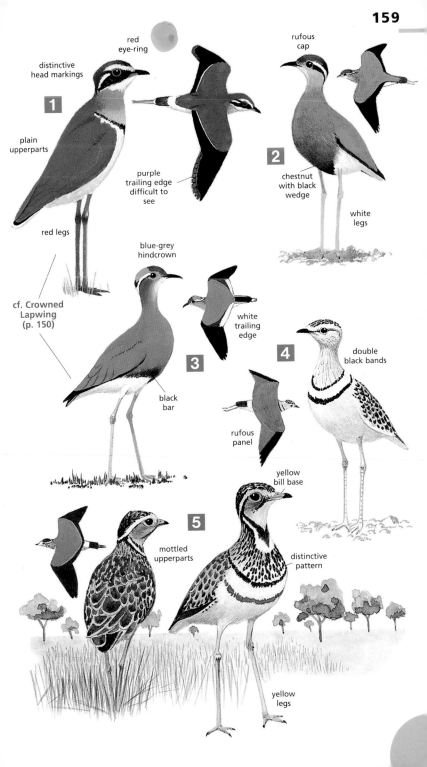

red
eye-ring

distinctive
head markings

1

plain
upperparts

purple
trailing edge
difficult to
see

red legs

cf. Crowned
Lapwing
(p. 150)

blue-grey
hindcrown

3

white
trailing edge

black
bar

rufous
panel

rufous
cap

2

chestnut
with black
wedge

white
legs

4

double
black bands

yellow
bill base

5

mottled
upperparts

distinctive
pattern

yellow
legs

BUSTARDS AND KORHAANS

Large, **long-legged, long-necked terrestrial birds**, cryptically coloured, with **short tails** and **feet having three forward-facing toes**. Most have elaborate courtship displays involving plumage transformations, flights or unusual calls. The smaller species are called korhaans locally.

VULNERABLE

1 Red-crested Korhaan   *Lophotus ruficrista*   N E

Common, near-endemic resident. Told from other small korhaans by **creamy-white 'V'-marks on upperparts**. Has **shorter legs** and **shorter neck** than Black-bellied Korhaan (p. 164). Female has **broad white band** across lower breast, reduced in male to **small white patch on sides of breast**. Very similar to (3), female of which has much brighter yellow legs. **Red crest** of courting male seldom seen and is not a field feature. Territorial call of male starts with a series of clicks increasing in speed and changing into a series of shrill, piercing whistles 'phee-phee-phee-phee…' repeated 10 or more times. Courting pairs perform a duet, a rapid 'wuk-wuk-wuk-wuk…' rising in volume and frequency to 'wuka-wuka-wuka-wuka…' before the male switches to the whistling call. In aerial display the male flies up steeply to about 20 m and then tumbles as though shot, almost to the ground. Occurs singly or in pairs in bushveld. **53 cm** (Boskorhaan)

2 White-bellied Bustard   *Eupodotis senegalensis*   E

Uncommon endemic resident. A small, distinctive bustard, **male with dark cap and throat, blue-grey front of neck** and **tawny hindneck**. Female is rather plain above, with **dull yellow legs** and **white belly and throat**. The call, heard morning and evening, is 'takwarat', repeated several times at decreasing volume; sometimes preceded by several 'throat-clearing' sounds: 'aaa-aaa-aaa-takwarat-takwarat-takwarat…'. If flushed calls 'kuk-pa-wow' as it flies off. Pairs and small parties occur in tall grassland, farmlands and, occasionally, thornveld. Taxonomic note: southern African populations are sometimes split as a separate species (Barrow's Korhaan, *Eupodotis barrowii*), as distinct from the White-bellied Bustard (*E. senegalensis*) of East Africa and the Sahel regions. **53 cm** (Noordelike Witpenskorhaan)

3 Southern Black Korhaan   *Afrotis afra*   E

Common endemic resident. On the ground indistinguishable from close relative (4), but in flight and seen from above, both sexes differ from (4) in having **entirely black primary wing feathers**. Male is unmistakable; female told from other female korhaans by **bright yellow legs** and **pink bill with a pale tip**, this feature also present in the immature. The male calls a raucous 'krra-a-a-aak wet-de-wet-de-wet-de…' in flight or from a slightly elevated position on the ground. It frequents Karoo scrub and coastal dunes. **53 cm** (Swartvlerkkorhaan)

4 White-quilled Bustard   *Afrotis afraoides*   E

Common endemic resident. On the ground difficult to distinguish from (3). In flight both sexes show **extensive white on their otherwise black primaries**. In all other respects, including voice, this species is identical to (3). It frequents dry, open grassland, arid scrublands and Kalahari sandveld. Males engage in raucous displays above their territories. **53 cm** (Witvlerkkorhaan)

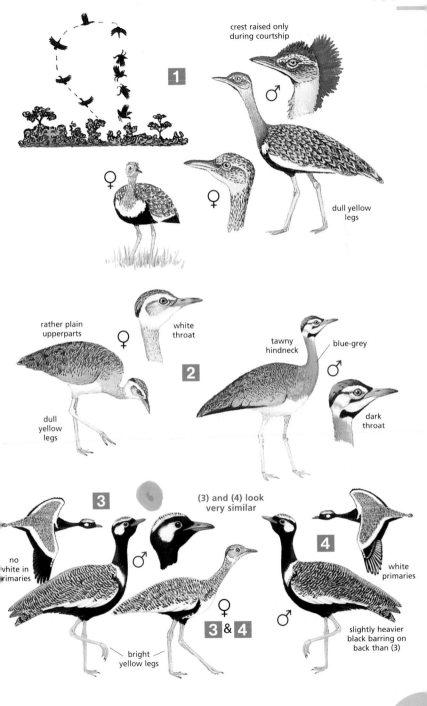

crest raised only
during courtship

1

♂

♀

♀

dull yellow
legs

rather plain
upperparts

♀

white
throat

2

tawny
hindneck

blue-grey

♂

dark
throat

dull
yellow
legs

3

(3) and (4) look
very similar

4

no
white in
rimaries

♂

white
primaries

♀

3 & 4

♂

bright
yellow legs

slightly heavier
black barring on
back than (3)

NEAR THREATENED

1 Blue Korhaan *Eupodotis caerulescens* E

Common endemic resident. The **only korhaan with entirely blue-grey neck and underparts**. Male calls mostly early morning 'kakow, kakow, kakow…', and several birds may call in unison. Flight call is a deep-throated 'knock-me-down…'. Pairs and small groups frequent highveld grassland and irrigated lands. Shy; crouches down and seemingly vanishes, even in very short vegetation. **50–58 cm** (Bloukorhaan)

2 Karoo Korhaan *Eupodotis vigorsii* E

Common endemic resident. Lacks the extensive head and neck markings of (3), the **black throat-patch** and **plain crown** distinguishing it from all other small korhaans. Sexes are alike. Calls in duet, loud frog-like sounds 'graag-uurg-og-og, graak-squark-kok-kok…'. Pairs or small parties occur in dry scrubland, semi-desert and arid thornveld, preferring stony ground with sparse vegetation. **56–60 cm** (Vaalkorhaan)

3 Rüppell's Korhaan *Eupodotis rueppellii* N E

Common resident, near-endemic to Namibia. Similar to (2), but has **more extensive head and neck markings** including a diagnostic **black line down the centre of its throat**. Sexes are similar. Calls in duet, a deep, resonant 'waaa-a-re-e, waaa-a-re-e…'; the first call by the male, the next three by the female, repeated in long sequences. Individuals also draw the head back and then thrust it forward, calling a deep 'augh'. Flight call is a rapid 'quark-quark-quark…'. Pairs frequent arid regions and stony desert plains in western Namibia. **56–60 cm** (Woestynkorhaan)

VULNERABLE

4 Ludwig's Bustard *Neotis ludwigii* N E

Fairly common near-endemic resident. Differs from (5) in **dark foreneck, unpatterned face, brown (not black) cap** and the limited area of white visible on the folded wing. The call, heard during courtship (Oct–Nov), is a deep-voiced 'klop… klop… klop'. When courting, the male fluffs out its plumage and inflates its neck, revealing **white underfeathers**, while calling at about 10-second intervals. Solitary or in small groups in semi-arid Karoo and arid Namib plains. **75–90 cm** (Ludwigpou)

NEAR THREATENED

a.k.a. Stanley♂

5 Denham's Bustard *Neotis denhami* N E

Uncommon near-endemic resident. Larger than (4), differing mainly in **ash-grey or whitish foreneck, black cap with white central parting** and **black-and-white wing coverts and secondaries**, which are visible as a large black-and-white patch on the folded wing. Breeding male has no grey on its neck. In courtship, the male fluffs its plumage, erects its fanned tail, revealing **white undertail coverts**, and inflates its neck. Normally silent, occurring in hilly grasslands of the eastern escarpment, eastern coastal regions and the Karoo. **86–110 cm** (Veldpou)

entirely blue-grey neck and underparts

plain face

black throat-patch

no black line

pied head pattern

black line down centre of throat

unpatterned face

rufous hindneck

dark foreneck

black cap with white central parting

much white in folded wing (variable)

black-and-white head pattern

variable white to ash-grey foreneck

NEAR THREATENED

1 **Black-bellied Korhaan** *Lissotis melanogaster*
Common resident. Characterised by **long legs** (proportionally longer than any other korhaan). Male in flight shows **white upperwings**. The **underwings are black** except for a **prominent white patch at the base of the primaries**. Male has entirely **black underparts, extending in a line up the front of the neck** to the chin. Female has **white underparts** (cf. female White-bellied Bustard, p. 160). Male calls while posturing as follows: the head and neck are withdrawn and wings drooped (a); the head and neck are then fully stretched upwards while the bird utters a dull 'waak' or 'phwoe' (b); the head is then lowered about halfway to the body and the bird utters a throaty grunt followed by a five-second pause; then it utters a sharp, whip-like sound 'ooor-whip'. During courtship the male performs an aerial display in which the white upperwings are strikingly presented. Found singly or in pairs in rank, moist grassland. **58–65 cm** (Langbeenkorhaan)

VULNERABLE

2 **Kori Bustard** *Ardeotis kori*
Common resident. Identified by **huge size** and **crested head**; only likely to be confused with Ludwig's and Denham's Bustards (p. 162). Sexes are alike, but male is about 20 per cent larger than female. Walks slowly with measured strides and flies reluctantly. In courtship the male calls a deep 'wum, wum, wum, wum, wummmmm'. Male also performs an elaborate courtship display: the throat-pouch is inflated and the frontal **neck-feathers splayed outwards revealing their white bases**; the head with raised crest is drawn back; the wings are drooped and the tail deflected upwards and forwards to the neck with the **white undertail coverts** splayed outwards conspicuously (see illustration of male in partial display). Occurs singly, in pairs or in groups in open woodland, bushveld and semi-arid grasslands in the Karoo and Namibia. **135 cm** (Gompou)

long, thin neck

white ear coverts

boldly patterned upperparts

♀

♂

black line down neck

no black

long legs

1

a

b

floppy crest

fine grey barring (no rufous on neck as in other large bustards)

2

1

huge size

displaying male

CRANES

Large, long-legged terrestrial birds, differing from storks in having **short bills** and being quite vocal. Like storks, they **fly with heads and necks outstretched**. They indulge in elaborate dancing displays with wings outstretched when courting, sometimes involving more than two birds. The South African populations of all three crane species have declined markedly in recent years. Whereas these cranes may be fairly common in some parts of southern Africa, their numbers have become very reduced in South Africa and all three species should be regarded as vulnerable.

VULNERABLE

1 **Blue Crane** *Anthropoides paradiseus* E
Uncommon endemic resident; vulnerable. Distinctive **blue-grey, long-legged bird** with bulbous head and **long wing-plumes** that look like a trailing tail. Immature lacks these plumes. The call is a loud, rattling, nasal 'kraaaarrk'. Occurs in pairs and flocks in the Cape wheatfields and the Karoo; in hilly grassland, moist valleys, farmlands and lakesides elsewhere. Prefers fairly high altitudes and is nomadic when not breeding. **105 cm** (Bloukraanvoël)

VULNERABLE

2 **Grey Crowned Crane** *Balearica regulorum*
Fairly common resident, but threatened. Unmistakable owing to **striking orange crest**. Immature has less-developed crest and wattles and looks browner. The call is a two-syllabled trumpeting, sounding like 'ma-hem'. Usually occurs in flocks in grassland, farmlands, near vleis and other marshy regions, both in highlands and at the coast. Roosts on offshore islands, in reed beds in river estuaries and in trees. Nomadic when not breeding. **105 cm** (Mahem)

VULNERABLE

3 **Wattled Crane** *Bugeranus carunculatus*
Uncommon resident; vulnerable. A **very large crane** with **distinctive wattles** hanging either side of the chin. Immature lacks wattles. Seldom vocal but can utter a loud, drawn-out, bell-like 'horuk'. Pairs and small groups are sparsely distributed in vleis, swamplands, fringes of large lakes and high-altitude grassland. Most frequent in northern wetlands of Botswana and central Mozambique. Often wades in shallow water while feeding. Wary and difficult to approach. **120 cm** (Lelkraanvoël)

white

blue-grey
neck

blue-grey

1

elongated
wing-plumes
(not tail)

white

2

dark grey

dark
face

white neck
visible from a
great distance

black

3

3

QUAILS, FRANCOLINS AND SPURFOWL

Terrestrial birds of mostly **gregarious habits** (quails excepted). Their crowing or cackling calls are useful identification features. Immatures resemble adults but are usually duller. Quails are **nomadic and irruptive**, whereas francolins are more sedentary. Cf. also buttonquails (p. 176).

1 Blue Quail *Excalfactoria adansonii* R

Rare summer visitor to eastern Zimbabwe and central Mozambique; occasionally further south in wet years. Male told by **dark overall coloration** and **large white throat-patch**, female from other female quails by smaller size and **lack of white eyebrow or throat-patch** (cf. female flufftails, p. 124–126). The call is a piping, three-note, descending whistle, the first note much louder than the others. Pairs or small parties occur in moist grassland and vleis. Sparsely distributed at all times, its occurrence infrequent. **15 cm** (Bloukwartel)

2 Common Quail *Coturnix coturnix*

Common resident and visitor. Told by **pale underparts in both sexes**; in flight difficult to tell from (3). The call is a penetrating 'whit-WHIttit, whit-WHIttit…' rendered as 'wet-my-lips', uttered day or night when breeding. If flushed calls 'pree-pree-pree'. Usually flushes with reluctance. Occurs in pairs in bushveld, grassland, pastures and cultivated fields. **18 cm** (Afrikaanse Kwartel)

3 Harlequin Quail *Coturnix delegorguei*

Uncommon to fairly common summer resident, a few all year. Male told by **bold black markings on white throat** and **chestnut underparts**. Female distinguished from female of (2) by **dark 'necklace' across throat extending to ear coverts**. The call is a loud 'wit, wit-wit, wit, wit-wit-it', similar in sound to (2) but more metallic. Pairs and small coveys occur in rank grass, especially in damp regions within grassland and bushveld. Most frequent in Zimbabwe and northern Botswana. Nomadic, sometimes irrupting in great numbers locally, then suddenly disappearing again. **18 cm** (Bontkwartel)

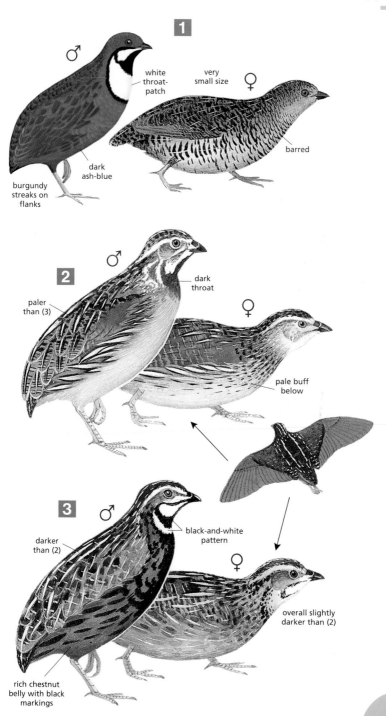

1 ♂
white throat-patch
very small size ♀
dark ash-blue
burgundy streaks on flanks
barred

2 ♂
dark throat
paler than (3)
♀
pale buff below

3 ♂
darker than (2)
black-and-white pattern
♀
overall slightly darker than (2)
rich chestnut belly with black markings

1 Coqui Francolin *Peliperdix coqui*

Common resident. A small species. Male has **tawny head and neck** and **barred underparts**. Female has **white throat bordered black** and **black eyebrow extending to the upper neck** (cf. Shelley's and Orange River Francolins, p. 174). The call is a piping 'ko-kwee, ko-kwee…' or 'be-quick, be-quick…' repeated continually. Males also utter a loud, high-pitched crowing 'kek, KEKekekekekekekekekek', the second note loudest and all others diminishing in volume. Habitually walks in a slow, stooped manner, as the female illustrated, especially when crossing roads and other open spaces; crouches motionless when alarmed. Pairs or small family groups frequent well-grassed bushveld and woodland. **28 cm** (Swempie)

2 Crested Francolin *Dendroperdix sephaena*

Common resident. Identified by **dark cap (the feathers of which are raised in alarm)** over a **prominent white eyebrow, red legs** and the habit of **holding the tail raised**. In flight, **black tail** is conspicuous. Race (a) is widespread. Race (b), previously known as Kirk's Francolin, is restricted to north of the Beira district and beyond the Zambezi. It differs in having **no dark blotching on the upper breast**; and having **streaked underparts** and **orange-yellow legs**. The call is a shrill 'kwerri-kwetchi, kwerri-kwetchi' sounding like 'beer and cognac, beer and cognac'. Pairs or small groups occur in bushveld, broad-leaved woodland, and thickets near rivers and forest fringes, mostly keeping within cover. **32 cm** (Bospatrys)

3 Red-billed Spurfowl *Pternistis adspersus* N E

Common, near-endemic resident. Identified by **red bill, yellow skin surrounding the eyes** and **finely barred underparts**; cf. Natal Spurfowl (p. 174). Has a very loud, harsh, crowing call, which increases to a frenzied cackling. Occurs in pairs and groups in Kalahari thornveld. Frequents low scrub and thickets, especially along rivers, but feeds on open ground. **30–38 cm** (Rooibekfisant)

4 Cape Spurfowl *Pternistis capensis* E

Common to abundant Cape endemic. A **large, dark francolin**, only the **underparts prominently streaked white**. Shows a **blackish tail** in flight. The call is a loud, high-pitched cackling 'kwek, kwek, kwek, kwekek-kwekek-kwekek-kwekek-kwekek-kwekek-kek-kek-kek…', the sound rising and then decreasing in volume and fading at the end. Occurs singly or in small coveys in fynbos, wooded kloofs and riverside scrub. **40–45 cm** (Kaapse Fisant)

tawny head
and neck with
dark crown

fine black
barring

♂

cf. Shelley's Francolin
(p. 174)

♀

1

small size and
horizontal posture
diagnostic

dark cap

often
raises tail

a

2

b

streaked

yellow
eye-ring

red bill

3

4

large size

1 Hartlaub's Spurfowl *Pternistis hartlaubi*

Fairly common, near-endemic resident. Differs from other spurfowls in small size. Male has **heavily streaked underparts** and **disproportionately large bill**. Female has generally **buff coloration**. Pairs call in a squeaky duet at sunrise and sunset 'eeha-weeha, eeha-ideo, eeha-weeha, eeha-ideo…'. Found in small parties on koppies and granite and sandstone outcrops. **25–30 cm** (Klipfisant)

2 Grey-winged Francolin *Scleroptila africana* E

Common endemic resident. **Predominantly grey**, the **throat well spotted with black**, and the **underparts closely barred black**, thus differing from all white-throated species (p. 174). Immature has more white about the throat and the barring of the underparts extends to the lower neck. The normal call is a squeaky 'kwe-kwe-kwe-kwe-skwekeeoo-skwekeeoo-skwekeeoo-keeoo-keeoo'. If flushed, groups rise steeply into the air with much noise. Occurs in coveys of five to 10 on grassy hillsides, montane grassland and coastal flats. **31–33 cm** (Bergpatrys)

3 Red-necked Spurfowl *Pternistis afer*

Common resident. At least six different plumage forms occur, but in all, the **bill, facial mask, throat and legs are red**. Morphs distributed as follows: (a) in Swaziland and northeastern South Africa; (b) from eastern Zimbabwe to Beira district; (c) (the smallest) in Kunene River region, Namibia; (d) in southeastern coastal areas. There are also other intermediate morphs. The call is a harsh crowing 'choorr, choorr, choorr, chwirr' fading at the end, or when flushed, 'choor-choor'. If pursued, takes refuge in trees. Small groups occur in valley bush, forest fringes, coastal bush and fallow agricultural lands. **32–44 cm** (Rooikeelfisant)

4 Swainson's Spurfowl *Pternistis swainsonii* N E

Common, near-endemic resident. The **only red-necked francolin with black legs and black bill**. Basic plumage colour **uniform**; cf. (3). Utters a harsh crowing 'krrraaak-krrraaak-krrraaak…' fading at the end. Male calls from a low branch or anthill. Occurs singly or in small coveys in bushveld, woodland and fallow agricultural lands, usually not far from water. **34–39 cm** (Bosveldfisant)

white eyebrow

long, decurved bill

♂

frequents rocky areas

♀

uniform buff

black-spotted throat

1

2

bare red throat

a

wholly red bill

b

be aware of regional variations

white streaks on black

3

c

black upper mandible

4

bare red throat

d

lacks distinctive patterning

rich red legs

black legs

1 Orange River Francolin *Scleroptila levaillantoides*

Common resident. Regionally variable. The **palest morph** (a) occurs in central and northern Botswana and, with more deep red spotting on the underparts, also in Namibia. Elsewhere is more **rufous about the head and underparts**, more liberally **spotted deep red** as (b) and (c). Distinguished from (3) by **red spotting of underparts extending up to the white throat** and **lack of a black-and-white speckled patch on upper breast**. Also similar to (2), but lacks blotchy black belly markings. The call is 'pirrie-perrie, pirrie-perrie, pirrie-perrie…', very similar to (2), but much faster. Occurs in coveys of about 12 in dry regions with sparse vegetation, flat, dry grassland and open woodland on sandy soils. **33–35 cm** (Kalaharipatrys)

2 Shelley's Francolin *Scleroptila shelleyi*

Uncommon to locally common resident. Differs from Grey-winged Francolin (p. 172) in **clear white throat with black surround, clear white stripe through the eye and ear coverts, bold, black blotches on its lower flanks**, and a large patch of **deep red blotches on the upper breast**, extending to the upper flanks. The call is a shrill, musical crowing sounding like 'I'll drink yer beer' repeated three or four times. Found in grassy woodland and grassland (montane grassland in eastern Zimbabwe), especially near rocky koppies. **33 cm** (Laeveldpatrys)

3 Red-winged Francolin *Scleroptila levaillantii*

Uncommon resident. Differs from (1) in **extensive ochre patch extending from the eye to the lower hindneck**, and **large patch of black-and-white speckling on the upper breast**. The call is a high-pitched 'cherp-cherp-cherp-cherp-chirreechoo-chirreechoo-chirreechoo…'. Favours grassland at all altitudes and grassy fynbos in the southern Cape. Usually in small coveys. **38–40 cm** (Rooivlerkpatrys)

4 Natal Spurfowl *Pternistis natalensis*

Common, near-endemic resident. Identified by entirely **black-and-white-barred underparts** (bolder bars than in Red-billed Spurfowl (p. 170)), **red legs** and **red bill with a yellow base**. The call is a harsh 'kwali, KWALI, kwali'; when alarmed utters a raucous cackling. Parties of six to 10 favour granite koppies, riverine forests, wooded valleys and thornveld, generally in rocky situations and seldom far from water. **30–38 cm** (Natalse Fisant)

5 Chukar Partridge *Alectoris chukar*

An introduced species; feral on Robben Island. Has **bold black barring on the flanks** plus a **black band encircling the foreparts** from forehead to upper breast. Has a cackling call. It occurs in coveys of five to 15 birds in alien *Acacia* on the island. **33 cm** (Asiatiese Patrys)

6 Indian Peafowl (Common Peacock) *Pavo cristatus*

(NOT ILLUSTRATED) Well known and unmistakable introduced species. A feral population exists on Robben Island. **120 cm** (Makpou)

a

1

b

white throat, black surround

c

no black blotches

regionally variable

2

white throat with black surround

blotchy black markings

much ochre on face

black-and-white speckling

3

4

no colourful eye-ring

red bill with yellow base

black-and-white barring

5

BUTTONQUAILS

Very small terrestrial birds, superficially similar to true quails but **lacking a hind toe**. Colour patterns are similar in both sexes, but **females are more richly coloured than males**. Immatures are like males, but their breasts are spotted. They flush reluctantly, usually at one's feet, then fly low for a short distance before settling again.

1 Kurrichane Buttonquail *Turnix sylvaticus*
Common resident. Told from (3) by **whitish sides to the head, cream-coloured eyes** and **heart-shaped spots on the sides of the neck and breast**. Female's call is a deep, resonant 'hoooo hoooo' made at two-second intervals. Occurs singly or in pairs in grassland with patches of tall grass, bush savanna, bushveld with good grass cover, and cultivated and fallow farmlands. **14–15 cm** (Bosveldkwarteltjie)

2 Hottentot Buttonquail *Turnix hottentottus* E
Uncommon, localised resident. Previously considered conspecific with (3). Very similar to (3) but overall **slightly paler; lacks black rump; legs and eyes yellow**. Noticeable **black spotting on the buff-coloured breast, sides of belly and flanks**. Female shows richer rufous coloration on breast than male, with brighter yellow legs. Occurs only in the Cape in fynbos biome and therefore range does not overlap with (3). Call a quick, deep 'whoo', repeated. **14–15 cm** (Kaapse Kwarteltjie)

ENDANGERED

3 Black-rumped Buttonquail *Turnix nanus* R
Uncommon resident and summer visitor. Told from (2) by **black rump** (most visible in flight). Overall darker with a **pale greyish eye**. **Sides of head and breast are more chestnut**, with **pale whitish scaling on sides of neck** (c.f. (1), which is very dark-spotted). **Rufous breast and whitish underparts**; black with white barring on sides of breast; no spotting on the flanks. Female similar to male but with deeper rufous coloration and less barring on underparts. Occurs sparsely from Eastern Cape to Kwa-Zulu Natal, Mozambique and Zimbabwe. Call similar to (2). **14–15 cm** (Swartrugkwarteltjie)

GUINEAFOWLS

Differ from pheasants, partridges, spurfowls and francolins in having **bare heads surmounted by casques or plumes**. Adults' **necks are unfeathered**.

4 Helmeted Guineafowl *Numida meleagris*
Very common resident. Told by **blue neck, red cap** and **horny casque on head**. Chick (a) is buffy-brown, striped darker; juvenile (b) predominantly brown, darker on upperparts, head-stripes remaining until casque starts growing; immature (c) resembles adult but has feathered neck, dark brown helmet and rudimentary casque. Normal adult call is a much-repeated 'ker-bek-ker-bek-ker-bek, krrrrrr…'; female also utters a continual piping 't-phueet-t-phueet-t-phueet…'. When not breeding, flocks are sometimes very large, occurring in grassland, bushveld and farmlands. Regularly goes to water in the evenings. **53–58 cm** (Gewone Tarentaal)

5 Crested Guineafowl *Guttera pucherani*
Locally common resident. Blacker than (4) with **characteristic black head-plumes**; further told by **unmarked black neck, pale outer secondaries** and **red eyes**. Immature is barred chestnut, buff and black on the upperparts. Has a rattling alarm call; when breeding, calls 'tick-tack, ticktack-tirr-tirr-tirr'. Flocks in lowland and riverine forests, lowveld broad-leaved woodland and thickets, coastal bush and dune forests. **50 cm** (Kuifkoptarentaal)

177

1 ♀

cream eye

chestnut brown rump

restricted rufous

heart-shaped spots

3 ♀

rich rufous

less extensive barring than male

pale greyish eye

♂

rufous breast, fine barring

black rump

2 ♂

yellow eye

paler overall than (3)

buff coloured, noticeable black spotting

unmistakable

4

b

c

a

5

red eye

unspotted black neck

bushy crest

blue-black base colour with fine white spots

OSTRICH

1 Common Ostrich *Struthio camelus*
Common resident. Well-known, **enormous, flightless bird**. Immature is like a small, scruffy female and is usually accompanied by adults. Male utters a lion-like roar. The **tail colour of adult males varies** according to region, from **whitish to grey or cinnamon-brown**. Wild ostriches occur in isolated pockets throughout southern Africa, especially in the large nature reserves, but interbreeding with domestic stock makes their genetic purity doubtful. Usually found in pairs or groups, sometimes with many young birds present. Inhabits woodland and wooded grassland in the east and thornveld or grassland in the more arid western regions. Height **1.8–2.8 m**; males usually taller than females. (Volstruis)

SECRETARYBIRD

NEAR THREATENED

2 Secretarybird *Sagittarius serpentarius*
Common resident. Large, **long-legged grey-and-black bird** with **long, loose black feathers projecting behind the head**. Adult has **orange face**; immature has yellow face. Normally silent but sometimes utters a frog-like croak. Usually occurs in pairs walking through grassland, bushveld or savanna at all altitudes. Sometimes runs a short distance with spread wings and may also soar to a great height. Roosts and breeds on top of thorn trees. **125–150 cm** (Sekretarisvoël)

largest and heaviest
living bird

tail colour
variable

males
black

♂

1

females
brown

♀

white

brightest red
when breeding

orange
face

long, floppy
plumes

2

could be mistaken
for Blue Crane
(p. 166)

black

long legs

VULTURES

Vultures are diurnal birds and, like other birds of prey (discussed on pp. 180–222) are characterised by **hooked bills suited to a mainly carnivorous diet**. Vultures are typified by their large size, heavy, hooked bills, **necks wholly or partially devoid of feathers** (the exception being the aberrant Bearded Vulture) and, for birds of prey, **relatively weak feet not suited to grasping prey**. Vultures feed on carrion, soar with ease during much of the day and bathe in ponds and rivers. They are **normally silent**, but hiss and squeal when squabbling over food.

NEAR THREATENED

1 **White-backed Vulture** *Gyps africanus*
Common resident. Adult difficult to distinguish from (2) unless **white back** is seen; smaller size not always apparent. At close range, the **dark (not honey-coloured) eye** is seen. Old birds become very pale. In flight and seen from below, **all flight feathers equally dark**. Immature lacks white rump but differs from immature of (2) in darker, less rufous plumage, **black (not pink) skin on neck** and lack of white collar feathers. A bushveld vulture, it normally outnumbers all others in this habitat and gathers regularly in considerable numbers at carrion sites. In good weather soars all day at a great height. Roosts and nests in trees; cf. (2). **90–98 cm** (Witrugaasvoël)

VULNERABLE

2 **Cape Vulture** *Gyps coprotheres*   E
Common endemic resident. Similar to (1), but larger. Adult is **very pale in colour** and may have an almost white back; at close range the **eye is honey-coloured**. In flight and seen from below, **darker outer primaries** contrast with **paler inner flight feathers**. Immature more rufous, warmer brown than immature of (1), the neck pink with white feathers at the base. The common vulture of the central regions and ranging widely when not breeding. Often perches on pylons. Frequents high cliffs when breeding (May–Oct); colonies then comprise dozens or hundreds of birds. Otherwise occurs singly or in groups anywhere, but rare in Zimbabwe and Mozambique. **105–115 cm** (Kransaasvoël)

NEAR THREATENED

3 **Rüppell's Vulture** *Gyps rueppellii*   R
Rare visitor or highly localised resident. Adult is similar to (2), but has **more white in the plumage**, giving it a **scaly appearance**. The **eye appears darker than (2), the bill yellowish**. The immature (not recorded in the subregion) is all-dark and may be difficult to tell from the young of (2). Adults have been seen in small numbers at Blouberg in the Limpopo Province. A common East African cliff-nesting vulture. **95–107 cm** (Rüppellaasvoël)

black outer
primaries contrast
with paler
secondaries

Underwing:
Cape Vulture

Underwing:
White-backed Vulture

white back hard to see when perched

dark eye

dark eye

1

dark underwing

dark eye

pale inner flight feathers

honey-coloured eye

blue neck

2

row of black spots along innner margin

yellowish bill

scaly upperparts

3

speckled body

1 Hooded Vulture *Necrosyrtes monachus*

Fairly common localised resident. A **small, slender-billed vulture** (cf. (2) and (3), which both have heavy bills). Rare Egyptian Vulture immature (p. 184) also has a slender bill but differs in having a well-feathered head. Adult's **white, downy feathers on the hindneck form a hood over the head**. Also told by **white ruff, 'pants' and legs**. See underwing flight patterns below. Immature is all-brown, including downy head and neck; only the face pink. Occurs in small numbers in protected game areas, the Okavango region and the Zambezi valley. Joins other vultures at carrion. Most frequently seen where mammalian predators occur. **70 cm** (Monnikaasvoël)

2 White-headed Vulture *Trigonoceps occipitalis*

Uncommon resident. Distinguished by large size, **white head, neck and underparts** (see below), **heavy red and blue bill** and **pink face and legs**. Female differs from male in having **white inner secondary wing feathers** visible both at rest and in flight. Immature much browner on underparts; head feathers tawny. At carrion, usually seen in pairs, greatly outnumbered by other vultures. **85 cm** (Witkopaasvoël)

3 Lappet-faced Vulture *Torgos tracheliotus*

Fairly common resident. A **huge, massive-billed** vulture. Adult has **crimson head and neck**, and **streaked underparts with white 'pants'**, which contrast with **dark body and underwings** in flight (see below). Immature has dark 'pants' and various amounts of white mottling on the mantle; the long feathers of its ruff can be raised to frame its head. Usually occurs in pairs in bushveld or, in the arid west, thornveld and desert. A powerfully built vulture that dominates all others at food sources. **115 cm** (Swartaasvoël)

Hooded Vulture from below

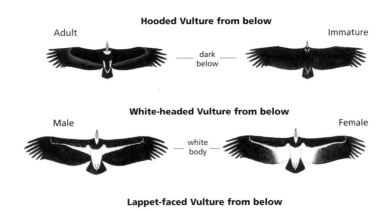

Adult   Immature

——— dark ——— below

White-headed Vulture from below

Male   Female

— white body

Lappet-faced Vulture from below

white crescents

Adult   Immature

white downy
feathers

downy
feathering

long, slender
bill

J

short
tail

1

white

♀

J

2

'peaked'
head shape

J

bare
crimson
skin

massive pale
yellowish bill

3

huge size

J

white
'pants'

1 **Egyptian Vulture** *Neophron percnopterus* R
Rare visitor. Immature can be confused with immature of Hooded Vulture (p. 182), but the **head is fully feathered**, not covered in woolly down. At all ages has a **distinctly diamond-shaped tail in flight**; cf. (2). Occurs singly or in pairs, especially in nature reserves or scavenging in rural areas, but very infrequent. **64–71 cm** (Egiptiese Aasvoël)

2 **Palm-nut Vulture** *Gypohierax angolensis* R
Rare visitor and localised resident. Adult and immature differ from (1) in **lack of loose feathers on the head, pink facial skin, heavier, more aquiline bill** and, in flight, **squarish (not diamond-shaped) tail**. Adult distinguished by **entirely white head, neck and body, black wing feathers and tail**; cf. African Fish-Eagle (p. 198). Occurs singly or in pairs most regularly in Mozambique and further south along the east coast; also in northern Botswana and northern Namibia. A vagrant to other scattered northerly points, particularly immature birds. At the coast, frequents stands of oil palms (on which it feeds and in which it breeds), forages on beaches and the shores of lagoons and pans, or catches its own fish. Spends long periods each day perched but, unlike other vultures, flies at any time regardless of thermals. **60 cm** (Witaasvoël)

3 **Bearded Vulture (Lammergeier)** *Gypaetus barbatus* R
Uncommon localised resident. Differs from all other vultures in **loosely feathered head and legs**, the **'beard'** visible in both adult and immature. Unlikely to be confused with any other bird of prey within its restricted range. In flight, **long, wedge-shaped tail** diagnostic. Occurs singly or in small numbers in the Drakensberg and Maluti mountains in the southeast, rarely further afield. Soars by day and roosts on inaccessible cliffs. South African population estimated at over 250 pairs. **110 cm** (Baardaasvoël)

J

long, plumy feathers

long, slender bill

exposed yellow facial skin

diamond-shaped tail

J

1

J

very white

short squarish tail

pink facial skin

J

broad wings (cf. African Fish-Eagle p. 198)

feathered face

J

2

dark head

rufous

long, wedge-shaped tail

J

black mask

'beard' difficult to see in the field

massive size

MILVUS KITES

Large, long-winged raptors with 'V'-shaped tails. They spend much of the day **flying in leisurely fashion at low altitude** while scanning the ground, their **tails constantly twisting** as they manoeuvre. They feed by scavenging and also catch various small animals.

1 **Yellow-billed Kite**   *Milvus parasitus*
Common summer visitor and resident. Sometimes considered to be merely a race of (2). Can be extremely difficult to distinguish from that species, especially in juvenile plumage. Mature adult distinguished from (2) by **yellow-based bill, brown (not pale greyish) head, dark brown (not pale) eyes** and **more deeply forked tail**. Immature has a black bill (only the cere is yellow) and a less deeply forked tail; often indistinguishable from juvenile (2) in the field, although sometimes shows more rufous coloration on underparts. While flying sometimes calls 'kleeeuw', ending with a trill. Occurs in a wide range of habitats, often in large aggregations at a food source, and mixes with (2). Breeds in southern Africa. **55 cm** (Geelbekkou)

2 **Black Kite**   *Milvus migrans*
Fairly common summer visitor in western regions, uncommon in the east. Distinguished from (1) with difficulty. Mature adult differs in **pale eyes, greyish head, black bill (only the cere is yellow)** and **less deeply forked tail**, which appears square when fanned, like immature of (1). Immature is paler below with brown blotches. More often seen in flocks than (1); especially large numbers gather at emergences of flying termites. Otherwise, behaviour as (1). A non-breeding migrant. **55 cm** (Swartwou)

SNAKE-EAGLES

Characterised by **unfeathered legs, heads with loose feathers** – giving a **round-headed appearance** – and **large yellow eyes**. They still-hunt by watching the ground from a perch, or hunt while flying.

3 **Western Banded Snake-Eagle**   *Circaetus cinerascens*   **R**
Uncommon, localised resident. A **small, robust, ash-brown eagle**, distinguished from (4) at all ages by the **single broad, dark tail-bar** (a second bar is mostly obscured by the undertail coverts) and by **indistinct barring on belly only**. Immature is variable, at first mainly white about the head and underparts. Occurs in riverine forests and floodplains, still-hunting from leafless branches in tall trees. **55 cm** (Enkelbandslangarend)

4 **Southern Banded Snake-Eagle**   **R**
Circaetus fasciolatus
Uncommon, localised resident. Distinguished from (3) at all ages by longer tail with a **broad subterminal band and two bars**. Adult also differs in **well-barred underparts from lower breast to vent**. Immature like that of (3) except for tail-bars. Occurs sparsely along the northeast coast and in Mozambique and eastern Zimbabwe. Frequents open areas near exotic plantations, and riverine and lowland forests. Still-hunts from a tree. **60 cm** (Dubbelbandslangarend)

NEAR THREATENED

J

yellow-based bill
with black tip

dark brown
eye

1

head and eyes become
progressively paler
with age

always
black tip

adult's tail
deeply forked

2

tail fork
shallower
than adult (1)

3

diagnostic
tail pattern

usually darker
below than
(4)

4

barred
tail

J

broad,
dark
tail-bar

J

tail barred
throughout

VULNERABLE

1 Bateleur *Terathopius ecaudatus*
Fairly common, localised resident. A distinctive, **bulky-looking black eagle** with **red facial skin and legs** and **tawny wing coverts**. Female has tawny secondaries. The **back is normally chestnut-brown**, less often creamy white as (a). **In flight appears almost tailless.** Wing-tips curl upward, long wings are tapered (broadest on middle secondaries); male has widest black trailing edge; see below. Immature has longer tail and progresses from uniformly dull brown with slaty face and legs (b) to brown mottling with purple face and legs (c); see also flight patterns below. In flight may call a loud 'schaaaaaaaw'; while perched often calls 'kau-kau-kau-ko-aaagh'. Sometimes makes wing-claps in the air. Normally flies at low altitude over bushveld and woodland, using little wing-flapping; **glides for long periods with a sideways rocking action as though balancing. 55–70 cm** (Berghaan)

2 Black-chested Snake-Eagle *Circaetus pectoralis*
Fairly common resident. Adult differs from larger Martial Eagle (p. 198) in **bare legs, unspotted underparts** and, in flight, **predominantly white (not dark) underwings** with **narrow black bars**. Immature starts as (a), then progresses to stage (b), the head gradually darkening, underparts becoming defined. Usually occurs singly in bushveld or grassland, occasionally perched, more often flying high and hovering; **the only eagle to hover regularly.** Snakes may be taken into the air, killed and eaten in flight. Nomadic. **63–68 cm** (Swartborsslangarend)

3 Brown Snake-Eagle *Circaetus cinereus*
Common resident. Large brown eagle identified by **whitish, unfeathered legs, large yellow eyes**, large head with forward-facing eyes and **erect stance**. In flight, **dark body and underwing coverts** contrast with **silvery-white flight feathers**. The tail has four clear, dark bands. Immature starts with similar plumage to adult but less dark (a), then progresses to mottled stage (b). At all ages the **downy under-feathers are white**, therefore even adult appears speckled when moulting. Solitary in any woodland or coastal grassland. Still-hunts conspicuously from a bare branch or pylon, killing and eating large snakes on the ground or in a tree. Occasionally hovers briefly. Nomadic. **71–76 cm** (Bruinslangarend)

Bateleur from below

Adult male; Adult female

Sub-adult male; Immature female

Black-chested Snake-Eagle from below

Adult

Immature

narrow
black bars

Brown Snake-Eagle from below

Adult

Immature

plain

Bateleurs can easily
be identified in flight
by their rocking
motion and short tail.

c

J

♀

female told from
male by broad,
pale secondaries

1

b

J

a

♂

b

J

yellow
eye

a

J

appears
tailless

cf. Martial Eagle
(p. 198)

2

unspotted
underparts

blotchy,
pale
chestnut

b

J

rounded head
with large
yellow, forward-
facing eyes

upright
posture

3

a

J

dark
overall

TRUE EAGLES

Distinguished from all other raptors by their **fully feathered legs**. Prey is killed either by impact or by crushing it in the **eagle's powerful talons**; flesh is torn by the well-hooked bill. Most eagles hunt while flying, **wheeling effortlessly in rising warm air**, and are seldom seen perched in fair weather.

1 Booted Eagle *Hieraaetus pennatus*
Fairly common resident and summer visitor. A small eagle of buzzard proportions. Occurs in two colour morphs: dark brown (a) and white or buffy (b), the latter most common. At rest, **buffy wing coverts** show as a broad bar on the folded wing; **white shoulder-patch** diagnostic. In flight, a translucent wedge shape is visible on the inner primaries. Upperwing pattern similar to *Milvus* kites (p. 186) with a **pale panel across the inner wing coverts**, but **tail not forked**. Immature similar to adult. Occurs mainly in the montane regions of western South Africa and Namibia; non-breeding visitors from the north range more widely in summer. **48–52 cm** (Dwergarend)

2 Wahlberg's Eagle *Hieraaetus wahlbergi*
Common summer resident (Aug–Mar). Occurs in several morphs; (a) probably most common. Dark-headed and white-headed individuals also occur: (d) and (e). In flight shows **fairly narrow parallel wings** and **longish square tail held mostly closed**; see below. Sometimes utters a whistling 'peeeeoo' in flight. A summer-breeding eagle and the most common brown eagle at that time of year. **55–60 cm** (Bruinarend)

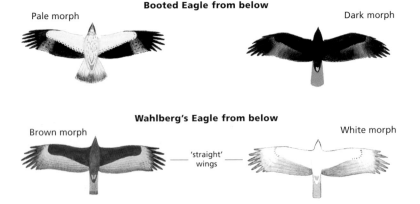

Booted Eagle from below

Pale morph

Dark morph

Wahlberg's Eagle from below

Brown morph

White morph

'straight' wings

pale panel across upperwing

white shoulder-patch

white crescent

a

1

buzzard-sized

b

b

unbarred, square tail

a

trailing edge of wing less rounded than Lesser Spotted Eagle (p. 192)

2

e

d

small crest

dark eye

a

b

c

e

b

longish square tail (looks rectangular when closed)

1 Lesser Spotted Eagle *Aquila pomarina*
Common summer visitor (Nov–Mar). Identified at rest by **narrowly feathered 'stovepipe' legs**, immature with **white spots on the folded wings**. In flight **appears broad-winged; tail fairly short and rounded**. From above immature shows translucent patches at the base of the primaries, thin white edges to the coverts and a white crescent at the base of the tail; cf. larger Steppe Eagle (p. 194). Usually in well-wooded regions of the Kruger National Park, Moremi Wildlife Reserve and Chobe National Park, where it often mixes with Steppe Eagle (p. 194). Flocks at termite emergences, groups often walking around on the ground to peck up termites. **65 cm** (Gevlekte Arend)

2 Greater Spotted Eagle *Aquila clanga* **V**
Rare vagrant, possibly overlooked. Like other brown eagles (pp. 190–194), can be difficult to identify. Overall **appears very dark**, with a compact shape and broad wings. Very similar to (1), but **gape extends to middle of eye only**, **upperwing more uniform** (lacking clearly contrasting paler brown coverts) and, from below, **coverts darker than flight feathers**. Further differs from (1) in **dark eyes, stronger bill, longer seventh primary** and **shorter tail**. From below, shows a variable **white carpal crescent** (or 'comma') at base of primaries. Tawny and Steppe eagles (p. 194) longer-winged and, at rest, lack tightly feathered tarsi and show elongated (not round) nostrils. Breeds in central Asia, wintering sparsely in the Middle East and northeast Africa (vagrant further south). Several unconfirmed records from southern Africa; possibly overlooked. **59–69 cm** (Groot Gevlekte Arend)

Lesser Spotted Eagle from below

Adult   Immature

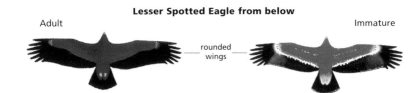

rounded wings

J

white crescent at base of tail

J

brown upperparts

variable spotting on wings

lighter brown upper wing coverts

1

yellowish eye

slender eagle, with short, rounded tail

J

2

uniformly dark with spotted upperparts

'stovepipe' legs

J

spots extend high on back

dark eye

more thickset than (1)

squarish tail longer than (1)

long, well-feathered legs

1 Long-crested Eagle *Lophaetus occipitalis*
Fairly common resident. **Long crest** on head and **wing pattern with bold white 'windows'** distinctive. **Legs may be white** (especially in males) or **black and white**. Sometimes calls in flight, a shrill 'weee-er' or 'peerr-wee' repeated. Usually occurs singly in forest fringes, exotic plantations (especially *Eucalyptus*) and wooded valleys; prefers hilly, moist conditions. Soars mostly in the mornings and frequently perches prominently at roadsides. **53–58 cm** (Langkuifarend)

2 Steppe Eagle *Aquila nipalensis*
Fairly common summer visitor. Can be difficult to distinguish from (1) and Lesser Spotted Eagle (p. 192). Adult is **darker and plainer** than the darkest of (3); its **prominent orange-yellow gape** extends back to a point level with the back of the eye (slightly shorter in race *A. n. orientalis*, but still larger than in (3)). A **buffy patch is often present on the hindcrown**. Immature very like (3) but has longer gape; in flight shows much white in the wings (see below; cf. (3) and Lesser Spotted Eagle (p. 192). Eats termites and is often seen consuming them on the ground, especially in the Kalahari. Also raids breeding colonies of queleas (pp. 442–444), feeding on eggs and nestlings. **75 cm** (Steppe-arend)

3 Tawny Eagle *Aquila rapax*
Fairly common resident. Adult either **tawny with or without dark brown mottling on the wings** (a) and (b), or **red-brown with dark mottling** (c). Immature may be gingery-brown or pale as (d); then very similar to immature of (2). At all ages the **gape does not extend beyond the centre of the eye**. In flight, the **barred tail appears plain**, little white in the wings and **none on the upper tail coverts**; see below. Most frequent in wooded game areas where it perches conspicuously on tree tops. **65–72 cm** (Roofarend)

VULNERABLE

Steppe Eagle from above

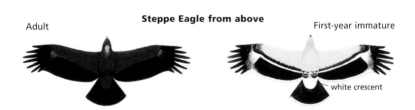

Adult

First-year immature

white crescent

Tawny Eagle from below

Adult (dark morph)

tail densely barred
(looks plain)

Immature (pale morph)

long crest

1

distinctive white 'windows'

J

pale band

nape often buffy

gape extends further back than mid-eye

2

J

2

faint barring on undertail

paler iris than (2)

a

gape extends only to middle of eye

b

usually paler than (2)

a

J d

3

c

1 Ayres's Hawk-Eagle *Hieraaetus ayresii*

R

Uncommon resident and summer visitor. A small, rapacious eagle with **white underparts either lightly spotted (a) or dark and heavily spotted (b)**. **Forehead may be white or dark**, the latter presenting as a cap extending to below the eyes. Leading edge of the wing often unspotted, showing as a **white shoulder-patch on the folded wing**. **Underwings heavily barred**. Immature much paler; see below. Frequents well-wooded regions, wooded hillsides and *Eucalyptus* plantations, occasionally even in rural suburbia. A summer visitor in the south of its range. **46–55 cm** (Kleinjagarend)

2 African Hawk-Eagle *Aquila spilogaster*

Fairly common resident. A medium-large eagle; female often more heavily spotted than male. Seen from below has **characteristic white 'windows' at the base of the primaries** and **broad terminal tail-band**. Immature is rufous on the head; underparts show varying amounts of dark streaking on the breast; cf. immature Black Sparrowhawk (p. 210), which has bare legs; see also below. The call is a flute-like 'klu-klu-klukluee'. Usually occurs in pairs in wooded savanna and well-wooded hillsides. Pairs soar conspicuously in the mornings. Otherwise, it perches within the canopy of a leafy tree for much of the day. **60–65 cm** (Grootjagarend)

3 African Crowned Eagle *Stephanoaetus coronatus*

Fairly common resident. Large and powerful, its **comparatively short wings** adapted to manoeuvring at speed through forest trees. Dark with **crested head** and **heavily barred or blotched underparts**; in flight **barred underwings and tail** and **rufous underwing coverts** diagnostic. Immature is **initially white on the head and underparts (a)**, becoming progressively spotted and blotched (b); see below, cf. immature Martial Eagle (p. 198). Pairs are very vocal within their territory. In display flight, calls 'cheeep chereep chereep…' speeding up when the bird dives. Pairs have territories in evergreen forests, forested kloofs, dense riparian forests with large trees and well-wooded hillsides. **80–90 cm** (Kroonarend)

**Ayres's Hawk-Eagle (immature)
from below**

**African Hawk-Eagle (immature)
from below**

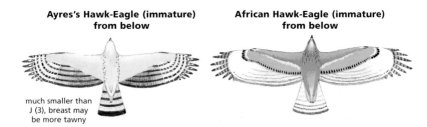

much smaller than
J (3), breast may
be more tawny

African Crowned Eagle (immature) from below

much larger than
J (1), may be more
pallid below

1

white edge

white shoulder-patch

short crest

a

b

J

heavily barred underwings

flanks heavily streaked

no distinctive crest

J

plain

2

flanks lack heavy streaking

terminal tail-band

pale head

J

a

rufous

3

crest

J

b

blotched underparts

massive talons

1 African Fish-Eagle *Haliaeetus vocifer*

Fairly common resident. Well known and distinctive. In flight, identified by combination of **broad wings** and **short, white tail** (cf. Palm-nut Vulture, p. 184). Very young, fledged birds ((a) and below) easily mistaken for other brown eagles or Western Osprey (p. 214), but pale demarcation line of **white upper breast** usually detectable. After one year, plumage pattern begins to resemble that of adult, although heavy brown streaks still remain on the white (b). The ringing, far-carrying call, in the air or while perched, is 'weee-ah, hyo-hyo-hyo', the male's voice more shrill than the female's. Usually occurs in pairs at inland waters and seashores in remoter regions. Conspicuous and noisy. **63–73 cm** (Visarend)

2 Martial Eagle *Polemaetus bellicosus*

Fairly common resident. Distinctive large, long-legged eagle, most similar to Black-chested Snake-Eagle (p. 188) but differing in **spotted underparts** and **fully feathered legs**; in flight by **dark (not whitish) underwings**. Immature differs from first-plumage African Crowned Eagle (p. 196) in **brownish or grey-blotched, not entirely white head**. Calls (rarely) a loud, ringing 'kloo-ee, kloo-ee...'. Occurs singly in bushveld, woodland and thornveld, but widespread; occasionally also found on open plains. Hunts while flying or from a hidden perch. **78–83 cm** (Breëkoparend)

VULNERABLE

3 Verreaux's Eagle *Aquila verreauxii*

Fairly common resident. **Large black eagle** with **white 'V'-mark on back**. In flight has characteristic **narrow-based wings with white flashes at the base of the primaries**. Immature **mottled brown** with **rufous crown and nape**, and **pale legs heavily marked with dark brown**. Usually silent, but utters a high-pitched scream near its nest. Pairs found in mountains, rocky hills and gorges, usually perched on rocks or flying at no great height. **84 cm** (Witkruisarend)

African Fish-Eagle (immature) from below

Martial Eagle (immature) from below

Verreaux's Eagle (immature) from below

cf. Western Osprey
(p. 214)

b

a

J

J

broad wings

white

1

short tail

dark brown
underwings

cf. Black-chested
Snake-Eagle
(p. 188)

crest

J

grey marks

black
spots

2

3

white 'V'

J

BUZZARDS

Large, soaring hawks about the size of a small eagle. They are robustly built with fairly **large, rounded heads, small aquiline bills, large ceres, unfeathered lower legs and moderately long and rounded wings**. Their tails appear rounded when spread.

1 Steppe Buzzard *Buteo buteo vulpinus*

Very common summer visitor. Adults **highly variable**. Occurs most commonly as (a) but dark morph (b) and russet morph (c) frequently seen; other variations also occur. Diagnostic feature common to all (except the very dark morph) is a **distinct pale zone across the breast**, which divides the **streaked or smudged upper breast** from the **banded underparts**. In flight, **spread tail appears pale cinnamon with a dark terminal band**. Immature has entirely streaked or blotched underparts, the eye paler. Much smaller than Brown Snake-Eagle (p. 188) and lacks that species' large yellow eyes. In flight sometimes calls 'kreeeeee', especially when two or more fly together. Commonly seen on roadside posts in summer, or circling slowly overhead. Northward-migrating flocks follow forested hills in early March. A non-breeding species; the vast majority only present in summer. **45–50 cm** (Bruinjakkalsvoël)

2 Forest Buzzard *Buteo trizonatus*   E

Uncommon endemic resident. Very similar to (1) and can be extremely difficult to tell apart. Somewhat smaller than (1); at all ages the underparts have **drop-shaped brown blotches (not horizontal bands)**, densest in adults, with clear regions across the lower breast and underbelly. In flight and seen from below, **wings appear whiter** than (1); tail has only indistinct terminal band (variable). Immature has little spotting on underparts. The call, uttered in flight, is 'keeeo-oo'. Usually occurs singly near montane plantations and forests or adjacent grassy plateaus, perching on the fringe of some open area. When disturbed flies easily through dense plantations. **45 cm** (Bosjakkalsvoël)

3 Long-legged Buzzard *Buteo rufinus*   V

Vagrant. The presence of this buzzard in southern Africa is controversial. It is a European species that normally migrates only as far as North Africa. Like the extremely similar (1), it is highly variable in colour, which complicates identification. Larger, **more bulky-bodied** than (1) with a **pale head**. Most common morph (a) in flight shows **dark underbelly and vent, broader, paler wings** with **dark carpal patches, white outer wing-panels** and a **plain tail**. Adult plumage can vary widely from very pale or honey-coloured (a) to very dark (b), although the latter is uncommon. **51–66 cm** (Langbeenjakkalsvoël)

plumage extremely variable

J

stocky with characteristic upright posture

1

b

dark eye

a

J

c

dark

banded

rufous

dark eye

pale

2

drop-shaped brown blotches on flanks

J

usually whiter below than (1)

typically bulkier and longer-winged than (1), with slower wing beats

often pale-headed

3

dark belly

b

a

1 European Honey-Buzzard *Pernis apivorus*

Fairly common summer visitor. Slightly larger than Common Buzzard (p. 200) but could be mistaken for it. Plumage very variable; (a) probably most common, while dark morph (b) and paler morphs occur. **Appears smaller-headed** than Common Buzzard, with **longer tail** and **yellow or orange (not brown) eyes**. In flight, head is kept well forward of the long wings; **underwings have dark carpal patches**, the **tail two dark central and one terminal band**. Immature lacks distinct tail-bands; has brown eyes. Prefers wooded country (including suburbia) and may walk about the ground in search of wasps' and bees' nests. **54–60 cm** (Wespedief)

2 Jackal Buzzard *Buteo rufofuscus*   E

Common endemic resident. **Chestnut breast and tail** distinctive. Flight pattern shows **rounded wings** and **wide, short chestnut tail**. Occasionally occurs with breast blotchy-black, even all-white; then distinguished from (3) by **dark (not white) underwing coverts**. Immature is pale rufous, often much paler than illustrated, and shows no tail-bands. The call is a jackal-like, high-pitched mewing 'kip-kweeeu, kweeeu, kweeeu' while flying. Occurs **in hilly or montane regions** and adjacent grassland. Often perches on roadside posts. **44–53 cm** (Rooiborsjakkalsvoël)

3 Augur Buzzard *Buteo augur*

Common resident. Adult distinctive with **reddish tail** and **almost entirely white underparts**. Female often has dark throat, otherwise size and proportions same as (2). Distinguished from the uncommon white-breasted morph of (2) by **white (not dark) underwing coverts**. In flight, female is told from Black-chested Snake-Eagle (p. 188) by reddish tail and **more rounded wings**. Immature similar to immature of (2) but lacks the rufous tail; underwing coverts are slightly buffy, the secondaries and tail have light barring. Voice similar to that of (2). Prefers well-wooded hill country with rocky outcrops. Distribution overlaps only marginally with that of (2). **44–53 cm** (Witborsjakkalsvoël)

Two pale-morph European Honey-Buzzards from below in fast-glide posture

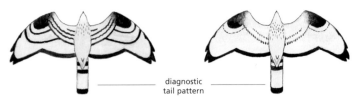

diagnostic
tail pattern

European Honey-Buzzard – rufous morph

dense, scaly feathers protect face from insect stings

yellow or orange eye

appears small-headed

a

1

brown eye

J

b

long tail

a

dark tail-bands

heavily barred underneath

J

2

dark underwing coverts

chestnut (very rarely white)

chestnut tail

♂

white below

♀

white underwing coverts

reddish tail

♂

3

small black crescent

1 Lizard Buzzard *Kaupifalco monogrammicus*
Fairly common resident. A **small, stocky grey hawk** resembling an *Accipiter* ((3) and pp. 206–210), but distinguished by **diagnostic white throat with vertical black streak** and **one (rarely two) bold white tail-band**. Immature more buffy above and below, throat-streak less clear. The call is a whistling 'klioo-klu-klu-klu', uttered regularly while perched; also a ringing 'peeeeo'. Occurs in broad-leaved woodland, mixed bushveld and well-treed farmlands. Often perches partially concealed in the canopy of a tree, but also conspicuously on telephone poles or dead trees. Nomadic. **35–37 cm** (Akkedisvalk)

2 Black-winged (Black-shouldered) Kite *Elanus caeruleus*
Common resident. A very common, distinctive small raptor with **pure white underparts, grey upperparts, black carpal patches** and **ruby-red eyes**. Graceful in flight; **wings appear whitish with black wingtips**; cf. much larger Pallid Harrier (p. 212). Immature similar but more buffy about the head and underparts. Normally silent, but may utter a weak 'weeet-weeet-weeet' when agitated, as well as scream like a Barn Owl (p. 246). Occurs singly or in pairs in grassland and lightly wooded country, including rural suburbia. Perches conspicuously on leafless trees, roadside posts or wires, often raising and lowering its tail while watching the ground. In flight may hover for periods of five to 20 seconds; frequently hunts at dusk. Roosts communally in reed beds or trees. Nomadic. **30 cm** (Blouvalk)

GOSHAWKS AND SPARROWHAWKS

True hawks, characterised by their secretive nature. They have slender bodies, **short, rounded wings, long tails, small, sharp bills** and **long, bare, often slender legs and toes**. They catch their prey (usually small birds) in a low, rapid aerial pursuit from the cover of a leafy tree. Females are larger than males.

3 Rufous-breasted Sparrowhawk *Accipiter rufiventris*
Fairly common, localised resident of the southern and eastern regions. **All-rufous, plain-bodied** sparrowhawk with **barred tail and underwing** and **very dark upperparts**. Could be mistaken for immature Ovambo Sparrowhawk (p. 206), but top of head and upperparts generally much darker. Occurs singly in stands of exotic trees and forest patches in montane grassland or fynbos. Often hunts over grassland by flying through cover, surprising small birds. **33–40 cm** (Rooiborssperwer)

vertical black gular streak

white tail-band

rather dumpy and less agile than *Accipiter* species ((3) and pp. 206–210)

1

ruby-red eye

black 'shoulders'

no black on upperwing (cf. Harriers pp. 210–212)

J

2

often repeatedly raises tail when perched

♂

uniform

3

♀ J

deep rufous

very dark upperwings

1 Little Sparrowhawk   *Accipiter minullus*

Fairly common resident. Adult identified by **very small size, yellow eyes, slender yellow legs** and, in flight, **two conspicuous white spots on upper tail**. Immature recognised by heavy spotting on the underparts. Call is a single-syllabled 'ki' rapidly repeated to sound like a small car's engine which is having trouble starting. Occurs singly in densely wooded situations, forest fringes, riverine forests, woodland, wooded valleys and stands of exotic trees. Secretive. **23–25 cm** (Kleinsperwer)

2 Shikra (Little Banded Goshawk)   *Accipiter badius*

Fairly common resident. Adult identified by **rufous-banded underparts that extend to the throat, red eyes** and, in flight, by **plain grey upperparts**, lacking any white on rump and upper tail. May sometimes show small white spots on the mantle. Immature differs from immature of (1) in eyes and legs being more orange-yellow, and broad reddish-brown streaks and banding on the underparts; and from immature of (3) in dark cap, lack of white rump, and different eye and leg colour. Call is a metallic, two-syllabled 'kli-vit' repeated, also a plaintive 'tee-uuu'. Occurs singly in a wide range of woodland types, even in semi-arid regions. Less secretive than other small *Accipiter* hawks, frequently perching in the open, even on posts. Feeds mainly on reptiles. **30–34 cm** (Gebande Sperwer)

3 Gabar Goshawk   *Micronisus gabar*

Fairly common resident. Normal adult (a) identified by **grey throat and breast, deep red eyes** and **red cere and legs**. In flight, told by **broad white rump patch**. Less common melanistic morph (b) has same colours of soft parts, but **lacks the white rump**. Immature is boldly blotched rufous all over head, neck and breast. **Eyes are yellow, cere and legs coral**. In flight shows white rump; cf. immature of (2). Call is a high-pitched, rapid piping 'pi-pi-pi-pi-pi…'. Occurs singly in open woodland, tree savanna and *Acacia*-dominated riparian bush. Hunts in low flight in more open country, otherwise from a perch within cover. **30–34 cm** (Witkruissperwer)

4 Ovambo Sparrowhawk   *Accipiter ovampensis*

Fairly common resident. Adult identified by **grey barring on underparts that extends to throat, yellow, orange or red cere** and **yellow or orange-red legs**. In flight shows **pale central tail-feather shafts; small white rump patch variable, often absent**. Immature either pale (a) or rufous (b), the rufous morph more common in Zimbabwe. Lightly marked on underparts; cere and legs are dull yellow or orange. A very rare melanistic morph occurs, similar to (3b). Call is a slowly repeated 'kiep, kiep, kiep…' rising in tone. Sparsely distributed in tall woodland or, on the highveld, in isolated stands of *Eucalyptus* or poplar (*Populus*), where it is the most common small *Accipiter*. **33–40 cm** (Ovambosperwer)

yellow eye

J

two white
tail-spots
and narrow
white rump

1

red eye

orange cere

plain grey
upperparts

2

J

no white
on tail
or rump

yellow-
orange
legs

deep
red eye

grey
throat

yellow eye

J

3

b

red cere

a

white
rump

red legs

barred
throat

brownish
eye

dark
mask

a

J

b

J

4

barred tail
conspicuous
in flight

yellow or
orange-red
legs

1 African Goshawk   *Accipiter tachiro*

Fairly common resident. A medium-sized goshawk (female much larger than male). Upperparts slate-grey in male, dark brown in female; **underparts barred rufous, finely in male, broadly in female. Eyes and legs are yellow** and the **cere is grey**. Immature browner above, the underparts well marked with black drop-shaped spots; cf. much smaller immature Little Sparrowhawk (p. 206). Territorial male displays prominently in the mornings by flying high with bouts of fast wing beats followed by glides while calling 'krit' at two- or three-second intervals. May also utter same call from cover while perched. Unobtrusive in montane, lowland and riparian forests, wooded valleys, exotic plantations and suburban fringes. Partially crepuscular. **36–40 cm** (Afrikaanse Sperwer)

2 Southern Pale Chanting Goshawk   N E

Melierax canorus

Common, near-endemic resident. **Large, pale-grey goshawk** with **coral-pink cere and legs**. Difficult to tell from (3) when perched, except for **slightly paler upperparts**, but in flight shows **much white on the inner upperwings and clear white rump**. Immature of this and (3) very similar. In breeding season, adults call loudly and melodiously while perched, especially at dawn 'kleeeeuw, kleeeeuw, kleeeeuw, klu-klu-klu-klu'. **Perches conspicuously with upright stance** on the top of a thornbush or on a roadside post. Also forages on the ground in search of small prey, peering under rocks and logs. **Seldom flies high**; usually moves with low swoops from perch to perch. Occurs in arid thornveld, Karoo and Kalahari sandveld. South of the Limpopo River its range is mostly west of (3). **53–63 cm** (Bleeksingvalk)

3 Dark Chanting Goshawk   *Melierax metabates*

Fairly common resident. Very similar to (2) but **slightly darker grey**. In flight, the **upperwings appear more uniformly grey, the rump finely barred (not pure white)**. Immature browner, the soft parts initially yellow, becoming orange or coral red while still in immature plumage. In breeding season, adults call from a perch for long periods 'phaleeoo-phwe-phwe-phwe-phwe…', the last sound often repeated up to 30 times. Frequents broad-leaved woodland and mixed bushveld; usually perches within the canopy on the top of a tree. South of the Limpopo River its range is mostly east of (2). **50–56 cm** (Donkersingvalk)

♂

grey cere

fine rufous bars

J

1

often located by distinctive call when displaying overhead

♀

broad rufous bars

more extensive black than (3)

white rump

white

pale grey appearance

2

more restricted black than (2)

darker grey than (2)

3

upright posture and long legs

dark grey appearance

J

1 Black Sparrowhawk *Accipiter melanoleucus*
Fairly common resident. **Large black-and-white hawk**, normally with **white or partially white underparts** (a), thighs and vent either speckled black and white or entirely black. **Eyes are orange or red, the cere and legs dull yellow**. Melanistic morph (b) only has **white throat** and some white feathers on the flanks. Immature buffy below streaked with dark brown (may be more streaked than shown); cf. immature African Hawk-Eagle (p. 196), which is larger and has fully feathered legs. Usually silent but may call 'weeeeeaa' or 'kew-kew-kew-kew-kew' near its nest. Occurs singly or in pairs in well-developed riverine forests, tall woodland or, more commonly, *Eucalyptus* plantations. Though retiring and difficult to see, frequently breeds near human habitations. **46–58 cm** (Swartsperwer)

HARRIERS AND MARSH-HARRIERS

Long-winged, long-tailed, long-legged hawks that inhabit grassland or marshes. **They usually fly low with leisurely, buoyant flight, head bent downwards and legs dangling slightly,** bouts of flapping alternating with glides and wings held in a shallow 'V'-shape above their bodies. They settle on the ground or perch on posts, less often in trees. Silent birds.

NEAR THREATENED

2 Black Harrier *Circus maurus* E
Fairly common endemic resident. Adult **appears entirely black** when settled, but in flight shows **striking white flight feathers, white rump** and **banded tail**. Sexes are alike. Immature has pale buff underparts and heavily spotted upper breast; in flight shows **white wing-flashes and white rump** like female and immature Pallid and Montagu's Harriers (p. 212). Occurs singly or in pairs over fynbos, Karoo, grassland and croplands, occasionally hovering briefly before dropping to the ground. **48–53 cm** (Witkruisvleivalk)

3 Western Marsh-Harrier *Circus aeruginosus*
Uncommon summer visitor. At rest, male told from African Marsh-Harrier (p. 212) by **paler head**; in flight by much **paler underwings** and **unbarred grey upperwings and tail**. Female much darker, almost black, with **pale crown, throat and leading edges to wings**. Juvenile similar to the female, but with browner coloration. Frequents marshlands and moist fields. **48–56 cm** (Europese Vleivalk)

cf. African Hawk-Eagle (p.196)

1

J

a

b

J

striking white
flight feathers

2

J

J

no
barring

♂

no barring

3

pale crown
and throat

♀

pale
leading
edge

1 African Marsh-Harrier *Circus ranivorus*

Common resident. Differs from uncommon Western Marsh-Harrier (p. 210) in **darker, more richly coloured underparts**, but old birds may become whiter about the head. Typically **more heavily barred on the underwings and tail** than that species; also more richly coloured on underparts than female of (2) or (3); tail less obviously barred above. Immature has **diagnostic pale breast-band**. Usually occurs singly, flying over marshland and reed beds, occasionally over cultivated fields. Rests on the ground, sometimes on a fence post. **44–49 cm** (Afrikaanse Vleivalk)

NEAR THREATENED

2 Pallid Harrier *Circus macrourus*

Uncommon summer visitor. Male differs from male of (3) in appearing **much whiter in the field, wing-tips with only narrow black sections. Plain pale grey above, totally white below**; cf. Black-winged Kite (p. 204). Female indistinguishable from female of (3) **unless white collar** is visible behind the **dark ear coverts; white rump** and clearly **banded tail** separate it from (1). Females and similar juveniles (often called 'ringtails' owing to their conspicuous white rumps) are often extremely difficult to distinguish from similar (3). Occurs singly, flying low over lowland and montane grassland, often near the edge of woodland. Nomadic. **44–48 cm** (Witborsvleivalk)

NEAR THREATENED

3 Montagu's Harrier *Circus pygargus*

Uncommon summer visitor. Male recognised by **darker grey coloration** than male of (2), this **extending over the head, throat and breast**. Rest of **underparts have brown streaks**. In flight differs from (2) in **entirely black wing-tips**, the **upperwings with additional black bars along the centre**, and **underwings with narrow black and rufous barring**. Altogether less white than (2). Female hardly distinguishable from female of (2) except for the **lack of white markings behind the ear coverts**. White rump and well-barred tail preclude confusion with (1). Females and similar juveniles (often called 'ringtails' owing to their conspicuous white rumps) are often extremely difficult to distinguish from similar (2). Occurs singly, flying low over grassland or savanna, frequently in same areas as (2). Nomadic. **40–47 cm** (Blouvleivalk)

heavily barred

1

J

J

J

barred tail

pale breast-band

♂

plain

♂

plain pale grey

white

2

narrow black section

♀

♀

white rump

banded tail

♂

narrow black and rufous barring

♂

black line

brown streaks

entirely black wing-tips

3

♀

HAWKS

A group of specialised hunters, larger than most Sparrowhawks and Goshawk. As with that group their lower legs are unfeathered, and the females larger than the males. Typically remain silent and, with the exception of the African Harrier Hawk, fairly secretive, often remaining perched for most of the day.

1 Bat Hawk *Macheiramphus alcinus*
Uncommon and sparsely distributed resident. A **dark-brown hawk** with **pale yellow eyes** and **white legs and feet**. At close range, **dark centre line on pale throat, two white spots on the back of the head** and **dark eyelids** diagnostic. In flight appears sharp-winged; the flight rapid. Immature has **white underparts with dark streaking on the breast, a dark patch on the lower breast** and a variable amount of white spotting on the underwings. When displaying, adult may call a high-pitched 'kik-kik-kik-kik-keee'. By day roosts well concealed in a leafy tree, emerging to hunt bats and small birds only at dusk and into the night or, in dull weather, also in the early morning. Frequents riparian forests, evergreen forests and other heavily wooded regions, including the edges of exotic plantations. **45 cm** (Vlermuisvalk)

2 Western Osprey *Pandion haliaetus*
Uncommon summer visitor. In waterside habitat most likely to be confused with immature African Fish-Eagle (p. 198). Slightly crested head, **masked appearance** and **white underparts** identify this large hawk at rest. **Breast-band often vestigial; strongest in immatures.** In flight appears large-winged and small-headed; **underwing has bold, dark carpal patch and dark central bar; tail is well banded.** Flies with wings bowed down, recalling a gull. Normally silent. Spends much of the day perched over or near water on a post, branch or rock. Hunts over water, flying slowly with shallow, loose wing beats, occasionally hovering briefly; plunge-dives when catching fish. Solitary at coastal bays, estuaries and lagoons or large inland waters. **55–63 cm** (Visvalk)

3 African Harrier-Hawk (Gymnogene) *Polyboroides typus*
Common resident. A large **grey hawk** with **black flight feathers** and **black tail with a bold white central band, bare yellow face** (flushes red when excited) and long, flexible **yellow legs**. In flight appears **broad-winged. White tail-band diagnostic; sometimes has dark carpal patches on the upperwings.** Immature initially dark brown, later light brown and more mottled. In flight may utter a high-pitched whistle 'su-eeee-oo', especially near its nest; otherwise silent. Clambers about trees and rocks, inserting its long legs into cavities in search of bats, lizards and other small creatures, and raids weaver, swift and woodpecker nests to eat the nestlings. Occurs in a wide range of habitats from montane forests and plantations to woodland, bushveld or thornveld at lower levels, especially riparian forests and wooded valleys. Becoming more common in well-wooded suburbs. **60–66 cm** (Kaalwangvalk)

long, pointed
bill

J

J

big, pale eyes and
white 'eyelids'

two white
spots on
back of head

dark
central
line

1

white legs
and feet

dark
carpal
patch

dark eye-
mask

2

dark
central
bar

speckled
breast-band
(variable)

cf. juvenile and immature
African Fish-Eagle (p. 198),
which occurs in same
habitat

face flushes red
when excited

head
proportionately
small

J

3

appears
'double-
jointed'

white
central
tail-band

J

J

broad grey-
and-black
wings

long
legs

barred tail

1 **African Cuckoo Hawk** *Aviceda cuculoides*
Uncommon resident. Recognised by its **short legs, crested grey head** –
the grey extending to neck and upper breast – and **boldly rufous-barred
underparts**. In flight appears harrier-like with **long wings and tail**. Flight
action is buoyant and leisurely, wing beats slow with spells of gliding
recalling a *Milvus* kite (p. 186). Immature also has crested head, its white
underparts with heart-shaped spots. Calls 'ticki-to-you' repeated slowly;
also a high 'peeeoo'. Spends much time perched on a conspicuous
vantage point but also makes occasional soaring flights. Usually
occurs singly near forest fringes, riparian forests, mixed woodland and
plantations. **40 cm** (Koekoekvalk)

FALCONS AND KESTRELS

Small raptors characterised by **pointed wings and, usually, prominent 'sideburns'**. Females
are larger than males. Falcons are aerial hunters, typically seizing smaller birds in a rapid
dive from above. Characteristic calls are high-pitched 'kek-kek-kek-kek' sounds, uttered
when agitated. Kestrels are small falcons that eat insects caught in the air with their feet,
or small mammals and reptiles caught on the ground. Their flight is more leisurely than
that of true falcons.

2 **Pygmy Falcon** *Polihierax semitorquatus*
Common resident. Identified by **very small size** and **entirely white
underparts**, the female with a **chestnut-brown mantle**. In flight, told by
speckled wings and **white rump**. When perched on roadside telephone
poles, can easily be mistaken for a shrike (pp. 410–414) owing to its small
size. A species of the dry west. Pairs usually seen perched on thorn trees
or baobabs, often close to the communal nests of the Sociable Weaver
(p. 446) or, less commonly, Red-billed Buffalo-Weaver (p. 444), with
which it lives in close association. **19,5 cm** (Dwergvalk)

3 **Taita Falcon** *Falco fasciinucha*   **R**
Uncommon, localised resident. A **stocky, short-tailed falcon** identified
by unmarked **rufous underparts** and **white chin and throat**. In flight,
rufous underwing coverts are visible. Haunts rocky gorges and cliffs.
Flies strongly and at speed, recalling a parrot (p. 232). May be seen
trying to catch swifts or bats in the evening. **28 cm** (Taitavalk)

NEAR THREATENED

4 **Sooty Falcon** *Falco concolor*   **R**
Rare summer visitor. Adult **all-grey** with **blackish face** and **pale yellow
cere and legs**, differing from Grey Kestrel (p. 220) in darker colour
and **long, pointed wings that extend beyond the tail** when perched.
Immature also **greyer than similar small falcons**, with grey spots on
creamy underparts, white hind-collar, no rufous coloration, broad dark
trailing edge to wings and dark subterminal band on tail. Occurs in
eastern coastal forests, bush and stands of large, broad-leaved trees,
being active mostly at dusk; otherwise perches most of the day. **31 cm**
(Roetvalk)

NEAR THREATENED

5 **Red-necked Falcon** *Falco chicquera*
Uncommon resident. Identified by **rusty crown and nape** and **well-barred
appearance**, except for **plain upper breast**. Immature has dark crown and
lightly barred underparts. Generally seen in palm savanna in the north
and east, and also among camelthorn trees in the west. Hunts other birds
in short sallies from a tree. Sometimes hunts in collaboration with the
Gabar Goshawk (p. 206) in the Kalahari. **30–36 cm** (Rooinekvalk)

rufous patch on nape ♂

♀ crested head

rufous bars

1

bold rufous bars

J

bold heart-shaped spots

♂

2

♀

tiny size

two rufous patches

short tail

white chin and throat

3

rufous underparts

stocky build

J

4

uniform grey, no barring

very long wings extend beyond tail

rust-coloured crown and nape

5

J

pale, unmarked upper breast

fine barring

NEAR THREATENED

1 **Peregrine Falcon** *Falco peregrinus*
Uncommon resident and summer visitor. Resident birds (a) have **closely barred underparts**; visiting birds (b) are **whiter, lightly spotted**; immatures lightly streaked. In flight appears **sharper-winged than (2)**, though less so than (3). Further distinguished from (2) by **broader 'sideburns', black (not rufous) crown**. Fast, purposeful flight action with rapid, shallow wing beats followed by a **brief glide**. Occurs anywhere, but usually seen perched near cliffs or skyscrapers when breeding. Sparsely distributed, but wide-ranging. **34–38 cm** (Swerfvalk)

NEAR THREATENED

2 **Lanner Falcon** *Falco biarmicus*
Fairly common resident. **Largest falcon in the region**, identified at all ages by **russet crown and pale-buff underparts**. Immature has heavily streaked underparts and paler crown. In flight appears **broader-winged than (1); tail is often spread**, with more leisurely flight action, deeper wing beats and **circling glides**. More often seen in flight than (1). Occurs in most habitats, often near cliffs in lightly wooded country. Also frequents buildings and Eucalyptus plantations. **40–50 cm** (Edelvalk)

NEAR THREATENED

3 **Eurasian Hobby** *Falco subbuteo*
Uncommon summer visitor. A **small falcon** identified by **heavily streaked body**, and **rufous thighs and undertail coverts**. Recalls a large swift in flight with **long pointed wings** and darkly marked underparts (see below and cf. Amur Falcon (p. 222)). Occurs singly or in small flocks in light woodland and suburbia. Hunts mostly as dusk, flying rapidly and with much agility, sometimes gliding. Preys on swallows, bats and termites. **30–35 cm** (Europese Boomvalk)

4 **Eleonora's Falcon** *Falco eleonorae*   **R**
Rare visitor from Mediterranean; migrates to Madagacar with occasional sightings in Zimbabwe and Mozambique. **Highly variable coloration between pale and dark morphs** (latter with darker belly). Pale morph has **pale chin and throat**. Juvenile shows creamy rufous throat. **Sooty underwings** and overall darker appearance idenwtify it from (1) and (3). Has a unique flight action with soft, slow wingbeats, but fast, dashing flight when hunting. **38 cm** (Eleonoravalk)

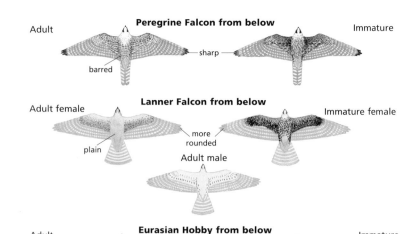

Peregrine Falcon from below
Adult — Immature
sharp
barred

Lanner Falcon from below
Adult female — Immature female
more rounded
plain
Adult male

Eurasian Hobby from below
Adult — Immature
very sharp

1
black crown
broad 'moustache'
a
a **J**
b
closely barred below

2
narrow 'moustache'
J
♂ russet crown
♀
pale buff or whitish underparts

3
J
heavy streaking
deep rufous 'trousers'
recalls a giant swift in flight

exceptionally long, narrow wings
J
J
heavily streaked
4
pale morph
long tail
deep, relaxed wing beats in cruising flight

1 **African Hobby** *Falco cuvierii* R

Rare summer visitor. The **most rufous falcon in the region**, differing from any rufous kestrel (p. 222) in its **dark upperparts** and behaviour. Could also be mistaken for Taita Falcon (p. 216), but **more slender**, with **longer wings and tail**, and **plain rufous (not whitish) throat**. Likely to be seen singly among scattered palm trees on Kalahari sand and in broad-leaved woodland (especially in the vicinity of tall palms or baobabs) elsewhere, but sparsely distributed and irregular over much of its range. Flight shape and behaviour similar to visiting Eurasian Hobby (p. 218). **28–30 cm** (Afrikaanse Boomvalk)

2 **Greater Kestrel** *Falco rupicoloides*

Common resident. At rest told from Rock or Lesser Kestrel (p. 222) by **entirely rufous plumage** with **blackish streaks, spots and bars all over**, and **whitish eyes**. In flight told by **white underwings**. Immature closely similar but has dark eyes. Occurs singly or in pairs in grassland or lightly wooded thornveld, especially in arid regions. Usually perches on top of a thorn tree or roadside post; sometimes hovers. **36 cm** (Grootrooivalk)

3 **Grey Kestrel** *Falco ardosiaceus* R

Rare, localised resident. An **all-grey kestrel** with **yellow soft parts**, differing from Sooty Falcon (p. 216) mainly in stockier build and **shorter wings that do not reach the end of the tail** when perched. Immature's plumage has a brown wash but otherwise resembles the adult. Resident in arid northwestern palm savanna and broad-leaved woodland. Usually perches on tree or post from where it makes short, rapid, low flights to another perch or across open, grassy areas. Flight always fast and direct, not typical of a kestrel. Occurs sparsely. **30–33 cm** (Donkergrysvalk)

4 **Dickinson's Kestrel** *Falco dickinsoni*

Uncommon, localised resident. Distinctive grey kestrel with **almost white head and neck, very pale rump** and **yellow soft parts**. **Tail is boldly barred with black**, unlike (4) (indistinct barring) and Sooty Falcon (p. 216) (plain, unbarred tail). Immature is slightly browner on its underparts. Occurs singly or in pairs in broad-leaved woodland, mixed bushveld and thornveld, especially among baobabs and palms in low-lying regions. Still-hunts from a tree perch, swooping to the ground to catch its prey. Capable of rapid flight but usually flies in a leisurely manner. **28–30 cm** (Dickensongrysvalk)

long tail

sharply pointed wings

1

completely rufous below

yellow legs

J

whitish eye

2

wing appears very white below

wholly grey

3

barred

short wings

indistinct bars

almost white head and neck

4

very pale rump

boldly barred tail

head paler than body

distinctly barred underparts

1 Rock Kestrel *Falco rupicolus*

Common resident. Female may or may not have grey head; sometimes like immature with **head the same colour as rest of plumage**, but **heavily streaked dark brown**. Differs from (2) mainly in **lack of contrast between upper- and underparts**, more robust shape, and behaviour. Occurs singly or in pairs (not flocks) in hilly country and grassland. Perches on roadside posts or flies 5–20 m above ground, frequently turning into wind and hovering. Cf. Black-winged Kite (p. 204), the only other small raptor that regularly hovers. Roosts on cliffs or in trees. **30–33 cm** (Kransvalk)

VULNERABLE

2 Lesser Kestrel *Falco naumanni*

Uncommon to locally common summer visitor. Male differs from (1) in **plain underwings, plain (not spotted) mantle** and **grey upperwing coverts**. Female differs from female and juvenile (1) in **more slender shape**, contrast between **paler underparts** and **darker upperparts**, and **brown (not grey) tail barred black**. Female occurs in flocks, often hundreds in grassland and Karoo, perching on roadside posts, pylons, wires or bushes, or wheeling in leisurely flight. Flocks roost in tall trees (usually *Eucalyptus*), often in country towns and sometimes in association with (3). Its numbers have declined dramatically in recent years. **28–30 cm** (Kleinrooivalk)

3 Amur Falcon *Falco amurensis*

Common summer visitor. A small, kestrel-like falcon; migrates to southern Africa from its breeding grounds in northern and eastern Asia, arriving in late spring and leaving by Apr–May. Female distinctive with **heavily spotted underparts** (including underwing coverts). Male very similar to male of (4), differing mainly in **white (not dark) underwing coverts**, the white often visible as a thin wedge on the underside of the folded wing even when perched. Immature greyer, less rufous than immature of (4). Occurs in grassland and farmlands in flocks, often large; frequently mixes with (2) or (4). Usually perches on power lines, roadside posts or fences, frequently taking flight for brief sorties before resettling. Roosts in tall trees and is most commonly seen in the eastern regions. **28–30 cm** (Oostelike Rooipootvalk)

NEAR THREATENED

4 Red-footed Falcon *Falco vespertinus*

Uncommon summer visitor. Female distinctive with **plain rufous underwing coverts and underparts** (streaked in juvenile). Male very similar to male of (3), differing mainly in **dark (not white) underwing coverts**. Immature more rufous than immature of (3). Occurs in flocks and often mixes with (3). Habitat and behaviour identical to (3) but distribution generally more westerly. **28–30 cm** (Westelike Rooipootvalk)

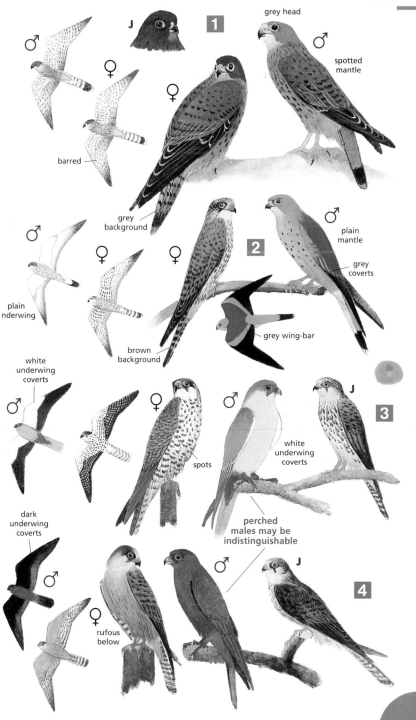

J

1

grey head

♂

spotted mantle

♀

♂

barred

grey background

♂

♀

♀

2

♂

plain mantle

grey coverts

plain underwing

grey wing-bar

brown background

white underwing coverts

♂

♀

spots

♂

white underwing coverts

J

3

dark underwing coverts

♂

♀

rufous below

♂

perched males may be indistinguishable

J

4

SANDGROUSE

Pigeon-like birds with cryptic coloration, males more boldly patterned than females. They have pointed wings and short bills and legs, with the front of the tarsus feathered to the toes. **Their walk is shuffling but their flight swift and powerful,** the birds often covering considerable distances daily to reach water where, at certain favoured pools, they gather in great flocks morning or evening. All inhabit arid western regions, the Double-banded Sandgrouse ranging more easterly.

1 Double-banded Sandgrouse *Pterocles bicinctus* N E
Common, near-endemic resident. Male distinguished by **black-and-white bars on forehead**, both sexes by **fine black barring on belly**. Calls 'chuck-chuck'; flocks come to drink after sunset calling 'Don't weep so Charlie'. Pairs or flocks widespread in bushveld and broad-leaved woodland, especially mopane woodland. **25 cm** (Dubbelbandsandpatrys)

2 Burchell's Sandgrouse *Pterocles burchelli* N E
Common, near-endemic resident. Both sexes told from other sandgrouse by **ochre colouring** and **heavy white spotting all over**. Male shows **grey about face, ear coverts and throat**; female has **yellowish face** and **ochre barring on belly**. If alarmed on the ground, utters a 'gug-gug-gug' sound but in flight calls 'chock-lit, chock-lit, chock-lit'. Normally occurs in pairs, but flocks at waterholes in Kalahari sandveld. Gathers to drink two or three hours after sunrise. **25 cm** (Gevlekte Sandpatrys)

3 Namaqua Sandgrouse *Pterocles namaqua* N E
Common, near-endemic resident. Best told from other sandgrouse by its **long, pointed tail**. Male also told by **plain cinnamon head and neck**, female by **densely streaked breast**. Flight call 'kelkiewyn'. Pairs or flocks occur in sandy or stony deserts, Kalahari, Karoo, thornveld and grassland. Most abundant in the Karoo and Namibia. Frequently mixes with (2) at waterholes, **drinking mainly in the mornings**, one or two hours after sunrise. **28 cm** (Kelkiewyn)

NEAR THREATENED

4 Yellow-throated Sandgrouse *Pterocles gutturalis*
Locally common resident and visitor. **Larger than other sandgrouse.** Male has **bold black gorget**; both sexes have **clear, pale yellow throats and ear coverts**, and **blackish bellies and underwings**. In flight calls a harsh 'tweet' or 'tweet-weet'; on arriving at a waterhole emits a hoarse 'golli, golli'. Mainly concentrated in northern Botswana, but range extends eastwards into Zimbabwe, southeast to as far as Rustenburg and westwards into northern Namibia. Drinks in the morning, sometimes also in the afternoon. **30 cm** (Geelkeelsandpatrys)

1 black-and-white forehead

barred (not streaked)

dark wings with white markings

finely barred black belly

2 grey face

overall ochre coloration

yellowish face

white spots

3 plain cinnamon head and neck

dense streaking on breast

long, pointed tail

4 rather plain, dark upperparts

black gorget

pale yellow throat and ear coverts

heavy streaking

blackish belly

PIGEONS AND DOVES

A well-known group of mostly **seed-eating, terrestrial** (except for the arboreal fruit-feeding pigeons) birds that build **flimsy stick platform nests in trees**. The distinction between pigeons and doves is ill-defined: larger species tend to be called pigeons, smaller ones doves. Immatures are dull versions of the adults. Many species become very common and tame near human habitation.

1 Mourning Collared Dove *Streptopelia decipiens*
Common resident. The only collared dove with a **totally grey head** and **yellow eye with red eye-ring**. The call is distinctive, a soft 'kur-kurr' repeated once or twice; also a soft, descending 'kur-r-r-r-r-r'. Occurs in mixed woodland adjacent to large rivers, as well as tropical woodland and mopane veld. Has a highly localised distribution, but is common where it occurs. **30 cm** (Rooioogtortelduif)

2 Red-eyed Dove *Streptopelia semitorquata*
Common resident. Differs from (1) in having **grey on top of the head only, red eye with a purple-pink eye-ring**, and a **deeper pink breast**. The call is 'coo-coo, coo-koo-cuk-coo', the accent on the fourth syllable, likened to 'I am, a RED-eyed dove'. Occurs in riverine forests, well-developed woodland, mixed bushveld, exotic plantations and suburbia. The largest of the ring-necked doves. **33–36 cm** (Grootringduif)

(Ring - necked ssp.)

3 Cape Turtle-Dove *Streptopelia capicola*
Very common, locally abundant resident. Coloration varies locally from **very pallid to quite sooty-grey**, but in all the **head is uniform** and **no eye-ring** is present. In flight, shows similar **white outer tail-feathers** to (4), but **mantle and wing coverts greyish** (not cinnamon). The call is a harsh 'work harder, work harder…' much repeated; also a snarling 'kerrr' on landing. One of the commonest, most widespread birds in the region, occurring in a wide range of habitats, frequently with (4). Also present in more arid regions. **28 cm** (Gewone Tortelduif)

4 Laughing Dove *Spilopelia senegalensis*
Very common, sometimes abundant resident. Has **no black collar**. **Pinkish head, cinnamon breast with black spots** and **rusty-coloured back** diagnostic. In flight shows **white outer tail feathers like** (3), but mantle is rusty or cinnamon-coloured. The call is a soft 'coo-coo-cuk-coo-coo' like someone laughing softly to themselves. Widespread in a variety of habitats, often with (3), yet unaccountably absent from some regions. Common in suburbia. **25 cm** (Rooiborsduifie)

5 European Turtle-Dove *Streptopelia turtur* [V]
Vagrant. About the same size as (3). Folded wings **dark chestnut mottled black**, crown and nape grey; no black collar but **black-and-white patches on either side of neck**. Shows **pinkish breast** and **white underbelly**. From below shows **dark underwings** and **black tail fringed white**. Breeds in Europe and North Africa and winters in the Sahelian zone. It is not always clear whether birds sighted in our region are genuine vagrants or escaped aviary birds. **27 cm** (Europese Tortelduif)

yellow eye and
red eye-ring

1

pale pink
head

red eye
with purple
eye-ring

pale
grey band

broad
collar

2

deep
pink

pale
grey band

pale head

black eye

narrow
collar

3

white outer
tail-feathers

no
collar

cinnamon with
black spots

blue

4

black-and-white
patch

5

orange eye
surrounded by
red skin

white outer
tail-feathers

chestnut
edges to
wings

pinkish
breast

1 Namaqua Dove   *Oena capensis*

Common resident. At all ages identified by **long tail**. Male also shows **black patch from forehead to breast** and **red bill with yellow tip**. In flight, combination of **brown flight feathers** and **long tail** diagnostic. The call is a seldom heard, explosive 'twoo-hoo'. Commonly seen in grassland, fallow fields, thornveld and eroded areas, particularly in dry regions. Perches on low bushes and fences; flies low at great speed. Nomadic; irregular visitor to southern and southeastern coastal areas. **27 cm** (Namakwaduifie)

2 Tambourine Dove   *Turtur tympanistria*

Fairly common resident. **White underparts** unique and conspicuous. Call 'coo, coo, cu-cu-du-du-du-du', very similar to that of (4), but speeds up and ends abruptly instead of tailing off. Occurs singly or in pairs in coastal bush and montane and riverine forests. Shy and elusive. Perches in a low position or feeds on the ground. Makes off at great speed when disturbed. **23 cm** (Witborsduifie)

3 Blue-spotted Wood-Dove   *Turtur afer*

Uncommon, localised resident. Very similar to (4) but upperparts browner, **wing-spots purple-blue** (when seen in good light) and **bill red with yellow tip**. In flight both species show **rufous wings** and **black back-bands**; probably indistinguishable unless settled. Call like that of (4) or (2) but more abruptly terminated, with less repeated notes at the end of the series. Occurs singly or in pairs on edges and in clearings of evergreen forests, in riverine forests and dense thickets. Occurs mostly in eastern Zimbabwe and the escarpment region of extreme northeast of South Africa. **22 cm** (Blouvlekduifie)

4 Emerald-spotted Wood-Dove   *Turtur chalcospilos*

Very common resident. Apart from **green wing-spots** (when seen in good light), differs from (3) in **all-dark, reddish bill** and **greyer upperparts**. Typical wood-dove flight pattern distinctive (see illustration) but not diagnostic. The well-known call is a soft, descending cooing 'du, du… du-du… du-du-dudu-du-du-du…' tailing off at the end. Occurs in woodland, bushveld, riparian forests and coastal bush. When flushed, rises abruptly and makes off at speed. **20 cm** (Groenvlekduifie)

5 Lemon Dove   *Columba larvata*

Fairly common resident. **Cinnamon-coloured body** with **darker bronze upperparts**; iridescent emerald sheen on upper back and wings. Red eye appears large on a distinctive **whitish face**. Coloration helps camouflage it with forest foliage, making it difficult to see. Very shy and secretive. Often only noticed when flushing noisily and unexpectedly from forest paths, flying off rapidly and dodging through the trees. Its presence is often revealed by its call, a soft, mournful 'hoo-oo' with rising tone on the second syllable. Pairs inhabit the interior of evergreen forests and plantations, feeding on the ground. **25–30 cm** (Kaneelduifie)

6 African Green-Pigeon   *Treron calvus*

Common resident. Told by **bright green coloration, yellow on wings** and **yellow leg feathers**, plus **red base to bill and red legs**. Call an explosive, high-pitched yet melodious bubbling, descending in pitch. Flocks frequent well-wooded regions, riverine forests and wooded hillsides where wild figs are fruiting. Difficult to locate from its habit of remaining still among the foliage, concealed by its cryptic coloration. When approaching closely, the flock explodes from the tree and flies off rapidly. **30 cm** (Papegaaiduif)

chestnut wing panels

♂

J

♀

diagnostic long tail

1

in flight, similar to wood-doves

2

♂ white eyebrow and forehead

♀

white underparts

rufous wing

3

red bill with yellow tip

colour of wing-spots difficult to judge in the shade

4

chestnut wing

all-dark, reddish bill

a touch greyer than (3)

5

whitish face

overall very bronze

6

predominantly green coloration

yellow 'leg-warmers'

1 Eastern Bronze-naped Pigeon

R

Columba delegorguei

Rare resident. A dark pigeon. Male told by **prominent white half-collar on hindneck**; **speckled in the immature** and **absent in the female**. The call is a quiet, mournful 'Coo-coo-coo-coo-coo-coo' descending in pitch. Sparsely distributed in coastal and eastern montane evergreen forests. Pairs and small flocks frequent forest canopies, where they feed on tree fruits, being most active early in the morning and late afternoon. Otherwise highly mobile between forests, searching for ripening fruits. **29 cm** (Withalsbosduif)

2 Speckled Pigeon *Columba guinea*

Very common resident. Told by **deep red, white-spotted upperparts, grey head and underparts** and **red facial mask**. Call is a loud and prolonged cooing 'cook, cook, cook, cook…' rising to a crescendo, then falling; also an enquiring 'VUkutu-whooo?' Flocks inhabit cliffs, mine shafts, road bridges, caves and buildings, often making lengthy daily flights to water or to feed in grain fields. **33 cm** (Kransduif)

3 Common Pigeon *Columba livia*

I

Common to abundant resident. An introduced species. Very well known and **highly variable in colour**. A wild-living domestic breed descended from the Rock Dove of North Africa and Europe. Main colour morphs shown, but many combinations also occur including pure white, white with dark head and dark grey with white head. Calls 'coo-roo-coo'. Mainly occurs in larger towns, where it is very tame. Dependent on human habitation but flocks may frequent cliffs, mine shafts and farmlands. **33 cm** (Tuinduif)

4 African Olive-Pigeon *Columba arquatrix*

Fairly common resident. **Yellow bill, eye-ring and feet** conspicuous, even in flight. Otherwise appears as a large, **dark pigeon** with **pale head**. Call is a deep bubbling 'crrooo, crooca, crooca, coooo'. Usually occurs in small flocks where trees are fruiting, even entering suburban gardens. In montane regions roosts in evergreen forests or exotic plantations, flying considerable distances daily to food sources. Often goes to roost early, sunning itself conspicuously on tree tops in late afternoon. **40 cm** (Geelbekbosduif)

1 white half-collar
(absent in female)

2 red mask

deep red upperparts
liberally spotted
with white

3 highly variable

pale head   yellow bill and eye-ring

4

speckled breast

dark overall

yellow feet

PARROTS AND LOVEBIRDS

A well-known group of gregarious birds with **hooked bills**. They **use their feet and bills to clamber about trees**. Parrots (including parakeets) **feed mainly in trees** on fruits and kernels, the latter obtained by cracking the hard pericarps. Lovebirds feed on seeds, grain, berries and flowers, frequently **foraging on the ground**. All are **highly social and utter shrill shrieks**.

1 Rose-ringed Parakeet *Psittacula krameri*

Fairly common, localised resident. An introduced Asian species. The only **long-tailed, apple-green parrot** in the region. Female has no neck-ring. Has established itself just north of Durban; occurs less frequently further north. Small flocks of (presumably) aviary escapees also occur in central Gauteng. **40 cm** (Ringnekparkiet)

2 Brown-headed Parrot *Poicephalus cryptoxanthus*

Common resident. A **green parrot** with **brown head** and **yellow eyes**; in flight shows an **apple-green back** and **yellow underwing coverts**. Immature is duller than adult. Small flocks occur in broad-leaved woodland, mixed bushveld and thornveld, feeding in large trees. **23 cm** (Bruinkoppapegaai)

3 Meyer's Parrot *Poicephalus meyeri*

Common resident. Differs from (2) in **entirely grey-brown upperparts, head and breast**. Has a **yellow bar on the forehead, yellow shoulders** and **some yellow on the underwing coverts**. In flight shows **blue-green back**. Immature has no yellow on forehead and very little on the shoulders. Pairs and small flocks occur in broad-leaved and riverine woodland. This species and (2) hybridise where their ranges overlap. **23 cm** (Bosveldpapegaai)

4 Rüppell's Parrot *Poicephalus rueppellii*   **N E**

Common, near-endemic resident. Differs from (3) in **grey head** and, in female, **blue back, belly and vent** and **yellow shoulders**. Male lacks blue back. Both sexes have **yellow underwing coverts**. Immature resembles female. Small flocks occur in arid woodland and thornveld. **23 cm** (Bloupenspapegaai)

a.k.a. Brown-necked

5 Cape Parrot *Poicephalus robustus*   **R E**

Uncommon resident. **Large, mostly green parrot** with **yellow-brown head and neck** and **orange-red forehead, shoulders and leg feathers**, these colours often absent or vestigial in immatures. In flight, shows pale-green back and rump. An evergreen forest species occurring in pairs and small flocks in a broken strip in the eastern interior. Small flocks often fly long distances daily to reach fruiting trees, returning at night to favoured forest roosts. Often located by call as it flies overhead. An endangered species. **35 cm** (Woudpapegaai)

ENDANGERED

6 Grey-headed Parrot *Poicephalus suahelicus*

Very uncommon, localised resident. Closely similar to the previous species but has a **silvery-grey (not yellow-brown) head and neck** and usually lacks the reddish forehead. Occurs in the north of the Kruger National Park (where it breeds in baobab trees), Zimbabwe, Mozambique and the Caprivi region of Botswana, extending beyond that to Tanzania. **35 cm** (Savannepapegaai)

1 ♂

neck-ring absent in female

dark upper mandible

2

green upperparts and wings

yellow underwing, but lacks colourful 'shoulder'

3

yellow bar (sometimes absent)

blue-green back

grey-brown above

yellow

long tail

head grey (not brown) and never shows yellow bar as (3)

4 ♀

silvery grey

6

orange-red patch (absent in female)

dull yellow bill

brown

5

red on leading edge of wing

large size

orange-red leg-feathers

VULNERABLE

1 Black-cheeked Lovebird *Agapornis nigrigenis*   **V**
Status uncertain; possible visitor from Zambia but probably locally extinct. The **dark face** distinguishes this lovebird. Old records exist for Victoria Falls and the Caprivi. It may still occur sparsely in those regions but no recent sightings recorded. Normally occurs in miombo woodland and river valleys. **13–14 cm** (Swartwangparkiet)

2 Rosy-faced Lovebird *Agapornis roseicollis*   **N E**
Locally common, near-endemic resident. Differs from (3) in **pale bill** and **bright blue back and rump** (not green); especially visible in flight. Occurs in flocks in dry woodland, tree-lined rocky gorges and along tree-lined watercourses in the arid west. **17–18 cm** (Rooiwangparkiet)

NEAR THREATENED

3 Lilian's Lovebird *Agapornis lilianae*   **R**
Locally common resident. Differs from (2) in **reddish bill** and **green (not bright blue) back and rump**. Flocks occur in thornveld and broad-leaved woodland in the Zambezi River valley. **17–18 cm** (Njassaparkiet)

TROGONS

Among the world's most colourful birds, trogons are found in Africa, America and Asia. They have **weak feet with two toes directed forwards and two backwards**. The skin of trogons is delicate and easily torn, while the feathers drop out easily if the bird is handled. In museum specimens, the **red breast-coloration** fades if exposed to light for long periods.

4 Narina Trogon *Apaloderma narina*
Fairly common resident. The only forest bird with **scarlet underparts** and **iridescent green upperparts**. The **bill is pale yellow**; the head shows **turquoise-blue skin patches when breeding**. Male inflates throat when calling. The immature resembles the female, but breast and shoulders lightly barred. In flight, the **long, square-ended tail** with striking white outer feathers is obvious. Difficult to locate in its forest habitat, since it often perches with its green back towards the observer. In the breeding season (Oct–Dec) it can be located by its call, a low 'hoot-hoot… hoot-hoot… hoot-hoot' repeated regularly and slowly. Usually occurs in pairs in evergreen forests or adjacent plantations (at high altitudes only in summer). Moves away from high-altitude haunts in winter; may then be encountered in lowland riverine forests and gardens. **29–34 cm** (Bosloerie)

combination of blackish or chocolate-brown face and red bill diagnostic

1

green

pink crown

2

pale bill

pronounced white eye-ring

3

bill mainly reddish

bright blue

green

pale yellow bill (brighter in female)

♂

orange-brown

♀

4

deep scarlet

♂

inflated throat when calling

white outer tail

long, square-ended tail conspicuous in flight

graduated tail

TURACOS AND ALLIES

Fruit-eating Afrotropical forest or bushveld birds with **crested heads, fairly long tails** and an agile springing action when jumping along branches. Turacos have **crimson primary feathers** that are strikingly revealed in flight. The grey species, which lack red wing feathers, are now known as 'Go-away-birds'.

1 **Grey Go-away-bird** *Corythaixoides concolor*
Common resident. **All-grey** with **pronounced head-crest**; sexes are alike. The well-known call is 'kweh-h-h' or 'go-way-y-y', the latter giving rise to its common name. Immature calls 'how, how…'. Pairs and small parties occur in mixed bushveld, woodland and well-wooded suburbia, usually in the upper stratum and invariably noisy. Flies with rather heavy wing movements, mostly below the tree tops. **47–50 cm** (Kwêvoël)

2 **Knysna Turaco** *Tauraco corythaix* [E]
Common, localised resident. At rest recognised by its **matt-green body** and **crested head with white markings. Upper tail and folded wings are an iridescent greenish blue; eye-rings and bill are red**. Within southern Africa, two long-crested species are recognised ((3) and (4)). Sexes alike; immatures duller. The normal call is a slow 'kerk-kerk-kerk-kawk-kawk-kawk-kawk'; a high-pitched 'kek-kek-kek-kek' alarm call is given as it flies away. Within its forest habitat, utters a hoarse 'breathing' sound 'hurr… hurr' when it detects the presence of human intruders. Usually occurs in pairs or family groups in montane mist-belt forests and evergreen forests in lowland and coastal regions. **47 cm** (Knysnaloerie)

3 **Livingstone's Turaco** *Tauraco livingstonii*
Locally common resident. Differs from (2) in having an **extended crest** (shorter than that of (4)); otherwise closely similar in most respects. Occurs in northern KwaZulu-Natal and further north into Mozambique and Zimbabwe. **40 cm** (Mosambiekloerie)

4 **Schalow's Turaco** *Tauraco schalowi* [R]
Locally common resident. Main difference between this and (3) is its **even longer crest, the tip of which tends to topple forward**. Occurs in riverine forests of the Victoria Falls region and the eastern Caprivi region. **40–42 cm**. (Langkuifloerie)

5 **Purple-crested Turaco** *Tauraco porphyreolophus*
Common resident. Told by its **dark-blue crest with a purple sheen, more blue on the folded wings and tail, ochre-washed breast** and **black bill**. The call is a long sequence of notes, starting quietly and rising to a crescendo 'kerkerkerkerker-kok-kok-kok-kok-kok-kok…', the last sound repeated about 20 times, becoming more deliberate and spaced out. Also utters a jumbled series of 'kokokok…' sounds. Pairs occur in coastal forests, riparian forests, bushveld and well-wooded valleys. **47 cm** (Bloukuifloerie)

6 **Ross's Turaco** *Musophaga rossae* [V]
Very rare vagrant from Central Africa. Recorded (and collected) in the Okavango Delta, northern Botswana. **50 cm** (Rooikuifloerie)

1

long, pointed crest

dark spots

2

rounded crest

red bill

matt green

3

completely grey

very long crest

4

crimson crest

dark blue crest with purple sheen

black bill

no white on face

5

ochre-washed breast

bright yellow shield, bill and eye-surround

6

crimson wings

deep purple overall

CUCKOOS

Cuckoos are **brood parasites, laying their eggs in the nests of other birds**, and the majority are absent from southern Africa during the period March–September. The related coucals are **larger, more robust** and **mainly sedentary birds** that build their own nests and rear young in the conventional manner.

1 Klaas's Cuckoo *Chrysococcyx klaas*

Common summer resident, some present all year. Male differs from (2) in having a **white mark behind the eye only** and **no white wing markings**; also **dark eyes**, **green bill** and **white outer tail-feathers**. Female differs from female of (3) in **white mark behind the eye** and finer, **darker barring below**. The call is a mournful 'hueet-jie' repeated five or six times. Usually occurs singly in a variety of wooded habitats including well-wooded suburbia. Parasitises a wide range of insectivorous passerine birds. **17 cm** (Meitjie)

2 Dideric Cuckoo *Chrysococcyx caprius*

Common summer resident. Both sexes differ from male of (1) in having **white marks before and behind the eyes, a white central stripe over the crown** and **multiple white marks on the wings**; also **red eyes** and a **black bill**. Female is more **coppery on the upperparts**. Immature has coral-red bill, blue eyes and spotted underparts; immature female mostly coppery above. Male calls a plaintive 'dee-dee-dee-deederik' from a tree top or in flight; female calls 'deea-deea-DEEA'. Usually occurs singly in a variety of wooded habitats, including reed beds and suburbia. Parasitises weavers, bishops and sparrows, and often seen while being chased off noisily by weavers. **18,5 cm** (Diederikkie)

3 African Emerald Cuckoo *Chrysococcyx cupreus*

Fairly common summer resident. Male identified by **yellow belly** and **lack of any white on the head**. Female distinguished from female of (1) by the **absence of a white mark behind the eye, much more bronze upperparts**, heavily barred underparts, **dark eyes** and **bluish bill and feet**. The call is a clear 'Pretty, Geor-gie'. Occurs in the upper stratum of forests and valley bush. Parasitises forest robins, warblers and flycatchers. **20 cm** (Mooimeisie)

4 Levaillant's Cuckoo *Clamator levaillantii*

Fairly common summer resident. Differs from the white morph of (5) in larger size and heavily **streaked throat and breast**. Sexes alike. The call is a flute-like 'peeeoo peeeoo…' six to eight times, followed by a rapid 'wherwherwher…' about 20 times. Occurs in pairs in woodland, riparian woodland and bushveld. Parasitises babblers (p. 348). **38–40 cm** (Gestreepte Nuwejaarsvoël)

5 Jacobin Cuckoo *Clamator jacobinus*

Common summer resident. Two colour morphs: (a) with **clear white underparts** and (b) **totally black except for white wing-bar**, which distinguishes it from Black Cuckoo, p. 242. Noisy and conspicuous, calling a shrill, flute-like 'kleeuw, pewp-pewp, kleeuw, pewp-pewp…'. Pairs occur in woodland, riparian forests, valley bush and bushveld. Parasitises bulbuls and other small birds. **33–34 cm** (Bontnuwejaarsvoël)

white patch behind eye

♂

1

plain wing

♀

fine barring

white in front of and behind eye

♂

white marks on wing

♀

coarse barring

2

coral-red bill

J

dark eye

♀

blueish bill and feet

3

♂

yellow belly

5

long tail

streaked

4

white wing-bar

crest (cf. Black Cuckoo p. 242)

b

a

clear white underparts

white wing-bar

1 Red-chested Cuckoo *Cuculus solitarius*

Common summer resident. Told from others on this page by **broad russet upper breast**. Recently fledged birds have the **entire head and upperparts dark charcoal-grey**, all feathers edged white. The well-known call of the male resembles the Afrikaans name 'Piet-my-vrou' or 'quid-pro-quo', loudly and frequently repeated; the female calls 'pik-pik-pik-pik'. Occurs in a variety of wooded habitats. Male calls from a high tree and often in flight when, in common with others on this page, it appears hawk-like. Parasitises mostly robins. Like other cuckoos, more often heard than seen. **28 cm** (Piet-my-vrou)

2 Common Cuckoo *Cuculus canorus*

Uncommon, non-breeding summer visitor. Female told from (1) by generally **much fainter russet collar** extending obscurely onto the nape and ear coverts. Male lacks russet colouring and is **almost indistinguishable from (3)**. Base of the bill only is normally greenish yellow, but sometimes like (3); see bill illustrations. **Undertail has white spots** (not white bars). Female occurs in rare brown morph as shown. A woodland species, silent in Africa (male's song on the Palearctic breeding grounds is the classic 'cu-koo' as immortalised in traditional 'cuckoo clocks'). **30–33 cm** (Europese Koekoek)

3 African Cuckoo *Cuculus gularis*

Fairly common summer resident. Scarcely differs from male of (2) but the **undertail is barred (not spotted)** while **the basal half of the bill is yellow and more conspicuous**; see bill illustrations. Told from (4) and (5) by larger size and **paler grey upperparts**. Immature well barred like that of (1) but with a **paler head**. Best identified by the male's call, a melancholy 'hoop-hoop' or 'coo-cuck' like African Hoopoe (p. 288); female utters a loud 'pik-pik-pik-pik'; cf. (1). Occurs in woodland and mixed bushveld. A known host is the Fork-tailed Drongo (p. 334). **32 cm** (Afrikaanse Koekoek)

4 Lesser Cuckoo *Cuculus poliocephalus* **V**

A rare, non-breeding visitor. Vagrants recorded in summer (Jan–Apr). Breeds in Asia and normally migrates as far south as Malawi and northern Mozambique. Difficult to distinguish from (2) and (3) apart from **smaller size, darker upperparts and head** and **broadly barred undertail coverts and lower flanks**. Distinguished from (5) by boldly barred (not plain) undertail. Probably silent in Africa, but on breeding grounds sings a 4–6 note song, which rises and then falls in pitch 'fi-fe-fu-fu' or 'fo-fo-fi-fe-fu'. Recorded in well-developed woodland and forest. **27 cm** (Kleinkoekoek)

5 Madagascar Cuckoo *Cuculus rochii* **R**

A rare, non-breeding visitor. Visits in winter (Apr–Sep); breeds in Madagascar and migrates to East Africa. The very similar (4) is a summer visitor; differs from that species in **plain, unmarked or indistinctly streaked undertail**. Usually silent in Africa, but on breeding grounds gives a deep song like (1), but with four syllables 'Piet-my-vrou-vrou'. **27 cm** (Madagaskarkoekoek)

6 Barred Long-tailed Cuckoo *Cercococcyx montanus* **R**

Rare summer visitor and resident. Told by **long tail** and **brown and tawny colouring**. Its call is distinctive, a much-repeated 'ree-reeoo...', rising to a crescendo and then fading. An elusive, localised species, recorded only in riparian and broad-leaved forests in eastern Zimbabwe and the Zambezi River valley. A suspected host is the African Broadbill (p. 306). **33 cm** (Langstertkoekoek)

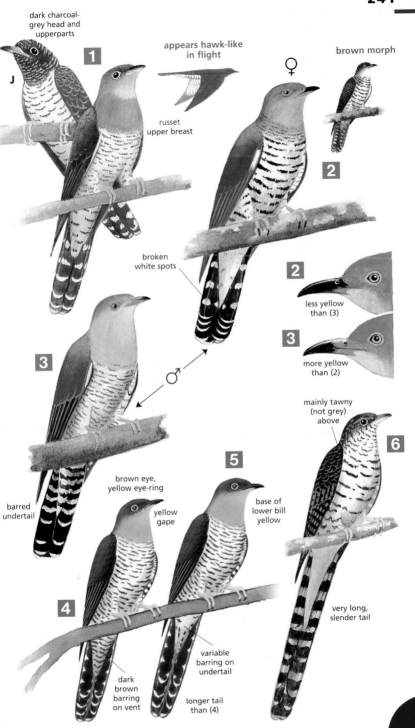

dark charcoal-grey head and upperparts

1

J

appears hawk-like in flight

♀

brown morph

russet upper breast

2

broken white spots

2

less yellow than (3)

3

more yellow than (2)

3

♂

mainly tawny (not grey) above

6

barred undertail

brown eye, yellow eye-ring

yellow gape

5

base of lower bill yellow

4

dark brown barring on vent

variable barring on undertail

longer tail than (4)

very long, slender tail

1 Great Spotted Cuckoo *Clamator glandarius*

Fairly common summer resident. A large cuckoo, distinguished by **crested grey head, white-spotted upperparts** and **creamy-white underparts**. Immature similar but the cap is black, crest less pronounced and the **primary feathers chestnut-brown**. The common call is a rasping, rapid 'keeow keeow keeow keeow…' repeated in phrases of about eight. Occurs in woodland and savanna. Parasitises crows and starlings. **38–40 cm** (Gevlekte Koekoek)

2 Thick-billed Cuckoo *Pachycoccyx audeberti* R

Uncommon summer resident. Adult told by **plain grey upperparts, entirely white underparts** and **heavy bill**. Immature has a white head dappled grey on the crown and **broad white edges to wing feathers**. Call is a loud 'pweee-peet, pweee-peet…' like a louder, more drawn-out version of Klaas's Cuckoo (p. 238), repeated several times. Usually solitary in any woodland; a restless, elusive species. Known to parasitise Retz's Helmet-Shrike (p. 420). **34 cm** (Dikbekkoekoek)

3 Black Cuckoo *Cuculus clamosus*

Common summer resident. **Entirely black**, but may show faint barring below (especially female). Immature more blackish brown. Male utters a much-repeated, monotonous call 'whoo whoo whee', rising on the last syllable, likened to 'I'm so sick'; female has an excitable-sounding 'wind-up' call 'yow-yow-yow-yow-yow-yow', reaching a crescendo and dying away. Occurs singly in any well-wooded region, including suburbia. Perches in one place for long periods when calling. Parasitises boubou shrikes, including the Crimson-breasted Shrike (p. 414). **30 cm** (Swartkoekoek)

COUCALS

Medium sized birds which are **notoriously secretive**, usually keeping to dense vegetation making them difficult to see. **Often the first give-away of their presence is their call.** They eat insects, small reptiles, amphibians and sometimes the **eggs and chicks of other birds**. Coucals breed in early summer, building their cup-shaped nests fairly low and well hidden in thick vegetation; some species' nests are completely covered over.

NEAR THREATENED

4 Black Coucal *Centropus grillii*

Uncommon summer resident. Breeding adult distinctive with **black underparts** and **chestnut wings**. Non-breeding adult similar to immature, but darker above. The call, with the bird in a hunched, head-lowered stance, starts with a low 'ooom ooom ooom', then, with the head lifted, the bird utters a bubbling 'pop pop'. When excited also calls 'kwik-kwik-kwik'. Occurs singly or in pairs in long, rank grass and associated bush thickets in marshes and flooded grassland. **32–37 cm** (Swartvleiloerie)

5 Green Malkoha *Ceuthmochares aereus*

Fairly common localised resident. **Large yellow bill** and **long green tail** diagnostic; immature similar. Has several loud calls, 'tik tik tik tiktiktik ker ker ker kerkerkerker…', speeding up towards the end, plus long-drawn-out sounds 'phooeeep, phooeeep, phooeeep…'. Occurs in thick vegetation in lowland and coastal forests. Shy and secretive. **33 cm** (Groenvleiloerie)

1 chestnut-brown primaries

J

crested grey head

yellowish wash

2 plain grey upperparts

J

spotted

yellow legs

no crest (cf. Jacobin Cuckoo, p. 238) **3**

indistinct barring visible in good light, especially on female

4

J

only local coucal with black underparts

5

diagnostic yellow 'banana' bill

grey-green

long, greenish tail and greenish wings

Note: The coucals on this page **cannot be safely identified by their** calls, which are nearly identical: a deep bubbling 'doo doo doo doo doo…' up to 20 times, descending then ascending, reminiscent of liquid pouring from a bottle. They also have harsh 'kurrr' alarm calls. Secretive, only occasionally perching conspicuously.

1 Senegal Coucal *Centropus senegalensis*
Common resident. Distinguished from (2) with difficulty, but is **smaller,** and has a **less heavy bill** and a **shorter tail with green iridescence.** Differs from (3) in having **unbarred upper tail coverts.** Immature is duller; upperparts barred black and upper tail coverts finely barred buff. Very similar to immature of (3), but their ranges are mutually exclusive. Occurs singly or in pairs in dense riparian vegetation, reed beds and thickets away from water. **41 cm** (Senegalvleiloerie)

2 Coppery-tailed Coucal *Centropus cupreicaudus*
Common resident. **Larger than (1) and (3)** with **heavier bill, darker mantle, purple-black cap** and **longer tail with a coppery sheen.** Upper tail coverts indistinctly barred buff. Immature has the **tips of wing feathers barred dark brown, tail-feathers barred tawny.** With experience can be told from other coucals by its deeper, richer call. Occurs in reed and papyrus beds, and riparian thickets in the Okavango Delta and Chobe River (northern Botswana) and the western Zambezi River (Zimbabwe). **44–50 cm** (Grootvleiloerie)

3 Burchell's Coucal *Centropus burchellii*   N E
Common, near-endemic resident. Adult slightly larger than (1) with **finely barred upper tail coverts,** otherwise closely similar. Their ranges do not overlap. Fledgling has a **small whitish eyebrow** (cf. (4)), fine whitish streaking on the head and dark barring on the upperparts; eyes blue-grey, not crimson. Occurs singly or in pairs in reeds, dense riparian and bushveld thickets, tall rank grass and well-wooded suburbia. Mostly secretive but will sometimes perch conspicuously. Spends much time running on the ground with a hunched back or clambering around in dense grass and shrubs. **44 cm** (Gewone Vleiloerie)

4 White-browed Coucal *Centropus superciliosus*
Common resident. Adult differs from (3) in having a **bold white eyebrow** and the **head and nape well streaked with white**; otherwise closely similar at all ages. Behaviour and habitat preferences similar to those of (3). **44 cm** (Gestreepte Vleiloerie)

1

no barring

green
iridescence

purple-black cap

heavy
bill

2

copper
iridescence

bold white
eyebrow

4

heavily
streaked
white

streaky
breast

whitish
eyebrow

3

young birds have
barred wings

finely
barred

J

OWLS

Nocturnal, erect-standing birds of prey characterised by **large, rounded heads, large forward-facing eyes** set in a flattened face and **feathered legs** (except for Pel's Fishing-Owl). Some have feather adornments on their heads that **resemble ears**, but they are not used for hearing. Immatures are usually darker and fluffier than adults.

1 **Marsh Owl** *Asio capensis*
Common to uncommon resident. Medium-sized, **dark-brown owl** with **small ear-tufts** (often not visible) and **dark eyes** set in a **buff face**. Shows **russet wings** in flight. When flying, sometimes calls 'kraak' like fabric being ripped. Occurs singly or in pairs in long grass on marshy ground, in vleis and near dams. Often active early mornings and late afternoons, flying low or perching on a fence post. When flushed from the grass during daytime often flies in circles over the intruder before resettling. **36 cm** (Vlei-uil)

2 **African Wood Owl** *Strix woodfordii*
Fairly common, localised resident. Told by yellow bill, lack of ear-tufts, large, pale, **spectacle-like eye-orbits** surrounding dark eyes and **barred underparts**. Immature has smaller eye-orbits and darker colouring. Male calls a rapid 'HU-hu, HU-hu-hu, hu-hu'; female replies with a higher-pitched 'whoo'. Pairs and family groups occur in forests, well-developed riverine forests and exotic plantations. During the day roosts in large trees close to the tree trunks. **30–36 cm** (Bosuil)

3 **Barn Owl** *Tyto alba*
Common resident. A **pale, slimly built owl** with **heart-shaped facial disc** and **whitish underparts**. Told from (4) by **paler upperparts**. The call is an eerie, wavering screech. Occurs singly or in pairs in a variety of habitats, roosting and breeding in large trees, caves, buildings and Hamerkop (p. 104) nests; common in suburbia. **30–33 cm** (Nonnetjie-uil)

VULNERABLE

4 **African Grass Owl** *Tyto capensis*
Uncommon resident. Closely similar to (3) but distinguished by **darker upperparts** and **different habitat**. More likely to be confused with (1), which occurs in the same habitat and also roosts on the ground. Distinguished from that species by **white (not buff) and heart-shaped facial disc** and **longer, narrower wings with less russet colouring**. Hisses when disturbed; also utters a husky screech resembling that of (3). Occurs singly or in pairs in moist grassland, roosting and breeding on the ground in dense, rank grass. When disturbed during the day usually flies directly away and resettles; cf. (1). **34–37 cm** (Grasuil)

buff face

dark eye

rich russet wings

small ear-tufts, often flattened

1

2

no ear-tufts

yellow bill

barring

whitish, heart-shaped facial disc

3

very pale overall

heart-shaped facial disc; cf. (1)

4

dark upperparts

no russet in outer wings as in (1)

1 African Scops Owl *Otus senegalensis*

Common resident. The **plumage resembles tree-bark**, the grey morph (a) being commoner than the brown (b). The **only very small owl with ear-tufts**. Calls mostly at night, sometimes by day, a soft 'prrrrp' repeated at about 10-second intervals. Occurs singly or in pairs in any woodland and mixed bushveld. By day perches in a tree, close to the trunk, where its cryptic colouring makes detection difficult. This camouflage is further enhanced by its habit of depressing its feathers to appear long and thin, raising its ear-tufts and half-closing its eyes, creating the illusion of a tree stump; see (a). **15–18 cm** (Skopsuil)

2 Southern White-faced Scops Owl *Ptilopsis granti*

Common resident. Largest of the small owls. Predominantly grey with **orange eyes**, a distinct **white facial disc with broad black outline, ear-tufts** and **fine black streaking on underparts**. The call, heard only at night, is an explosive, bubbling 'b-b-b-b-b-bhooo' repeated; at a distance only the 'bhooo' note is audible. Occurs singly or in pairs in woodland, riverine forests, mixed bushveld and thornveld, preferring drier regions with large trees. Moves into suburban areas in some years. **25–28 cm** (Witwanguil)

3 Pearl-spotted Owlet *Glaucidium perlatum*

Common resident. A **very small 'earless' owl**. Upperparts brown with small **white spots**; underparts white, streaked with brown and with pearl-like spots. Has **two black marks on its nape**, giving the impression of eyes. The call, often heard by day, is a long series of ascending notes 'tee-tee-tee-tee-tee-tee-tee-tee…' followed by a brief pause, then a series of descending notes 'teeew, teeew, tew, tew, tew, tew, tew…'. Occurs in any woodland, including mopane, mixed bushveld and riverine forests. Often seen by day. It is frequently mobbed by other small birds. A human whistled imitation of the call elicits the same response from small birds. **15–18 cm** (Witkoluil)

4 African Barred Owlet *Glaucidium capense*

Common resident. **Slightly larger and more dumpy than (3)**. Upperparts are finely barred; wings have a row of bold white spots reaching the shoulder, and underparts are white with brown spots arranged in rows. The call is an urgent 'kerrooo-kerrooo-krrooo-krrooo-krrooo-krrooo-krrooo…' or 'krrooo-trrooo, krrooo-trrooo…' repeated many times. Found mostly in well-developed riverine forests and large-tree woodland fringing lakes; also in mixed bushveld where it spends the day roosting in dense thickets. Less often seen by day than (3). **20 cm** (Gebande Uil)

like many owls, during the day it will lengthen its body to help camouflage itself, often resembling part of a tree trunk or branch

1

a

b

ear-tufts often held flat

tree-bark plumage

white face with broad black outline

2

orange eye

finely streaked

3

false 'eye-spots'

spotted

streaks

appears long-tailed

4

barred

appears dumpy, large-headed and short-tailed

1 Verreaux's Eagle-Owl   *Bubo lacteus*

Fairly common resident. A **large, uniformly grey owl**; immature is browner. Large size makes confusion unlikely with any other owls except *B. c. mackinderi* race of (2), from which told by **dark eyes** and **finely barred (not blotchy) underparts**; and, given a quick view, Pel's Fishing-Owl (p. 252), especially when roosting in tall riverine trees. Pink eyelids diagnostic but difficult to see in the field. Ear-tufts not always raised. Voice is a series of deep grunts 'hu-hu-hu, hu-hu'; female and young utter a long, drawn-out whistle that may be repeated all night. Occurs singly in large trees in bushveld and open savanna, especially along rivers and watercourses. **60–65 cm** (Reuse-ooruil)

2 Cape Eagle-Owl   *Bubo capensis*

Uncommon resident. A **large brownish owl** of **stocky proportions**. Easily confused with (3), but differs in **larger size, orange-yellow eyes** (orange in immature) and **heavily blotched underparts** with **bold barring**; feet and talons larger. Birds in Zimbabwe and Mozambique (*B. c. mackinderi*) are larger than the southern race (*B. c. capensis*). Calls 'HU-hu-hu' or 'HU-hu', with emphasis on the first syllable; alarm call 'wak-wak'. Pairs frequent valleys (in bush or grassland) with cliffs or rocks at the higher end, or grassland with rock outcrops and trees. Generally does not enter cities as (3) commonly does. **48–55 cm** (Kaapse Ooruil)

3 Spotted Eagle-Owl   *Bubo africanus*

Very common resident. A **fairly large grey-brown owl**, easily confused with (2). Differs in **smaller size, pale yellow eyes, lightly blotched underparts with fine barring** and smaller feet and talons. A rufous morph with orange-yellow eyes also occurs, though less commonly; this told from (2) by **fine barring on underparts**. Male calls 'hu-hooo', female 'hu-hu-hooo', the sound rising on the second syllable. Usually occurs in pairs in a wide range of habitats including bushveld and suburbia, where it perches on buildings and street lights or feeds on lawns at night. Large exotic trees and rocky hillsides are also much favoured. The most common large owl across the subregion. **43–50 cm** (Gevlekte Ooruil)

1

dark eye with pink eyelid

fine bars

2

orange-yellow eye

bold blotches

massive talons

orange-yellow eye

uncommon rufous morph

3

pale yellow eye

paler and greyer than (2)

fine barring

feet and talons smaller than (2)

VULNERABLE

1 **Pel's Fishing-Owl** *Scotopelia peli* R

Uncommon, localised resident. A **very large**, distinctive owl, differing from others in **dark eyes, cinnamon underparts** and **rufous-brown upperparts**. In repose, the **head has a flattish appearance** with the slightest suggestion of ear-tufts. When excited, the head feathers are fluffed out, giving the head a **rounded appearance**. Juvenile much paler than adult. Normal call is a deep, resonant 'oogh', the mate replying with a higher-pitched 'ooh'; also utters various other hoots, grunts and screeches. Pairs or single birds occur along large, slow-flowing and well-forested rivers. Strictly nocturnal; spends the day perched in the dense foliage of a large tree or creeper. When flushed, flies a short distance and resettles in another tree, from where it watches the intruder. Fishes in quiet pools or slow-running waters from a low perch, dropping feet first onto prey. **63–65 cm** (Visuil)

NIGHTJARS

Nocturnal, insectivorous birds with soft, cryptically coloured plumage, **short bills, wide gapes surrounded by stiff bristles, large eyes** and **short, weak legs**. They hawk insects at night, lying low by day. If approached, they may not flush until nearly trodden on; instead they close their eyes to narrow slits, thereby reducing the sun's reflection and so enhancing their camouflage. They **habitually settle on country roads at night**, their eyes reflecting in car headlights. All are so alike as to be **nearly indistinguishable**, but can be identified by **characteristic calls**. In the hand, they can be identified by wing and tail formulae (illustrated on pp. 256–257).

2 **Swamp Nightjar** *Caprimulgus natalensis* R

Uncommon, localised resident. In male, the **entire outer web of the outermost tail-feathers are white**; half the outer web of the second tail-feathers also white. Note wing-spot pattern on extended wing, as illustrated. In female, **wing and tail markings are buff-coloured**. Both males and females lack distinctive white or buff spots on the folded wing, and show a **dark face mask with a pale eyebrow**. From the ground calls a continuous 'chook-chook-chook-chook…' and a bubbling 'poi-poi-poi-poi-poi-poi…', both sequences less rapid than the call of the Square-tailed Nightjar (p. 254). Occurs mainly in grassy, swampy and waterside locations in the eastern coastal belt and the Zambezi–Okavango area. **23 cm** (Natalse Naguil)

1

cinnamon
underparts

unfeathered
legs

2

♂

dark face
mask and pale
eyebrow

full white outer
tail-feathers
(see p. 256)

no conspicuous
white spots on
folded wing

1 Pennant-winged Nightjar *Macrodipteryx vexillarius*

Fairly common summer resident. In breeding plumage, male with **long wing-pennants** unmistakable. These are lost soon after breeding, but male still identifiable by **bold white flash in outer wing**. Female **lacks any white in wings or tail** and appears large and nondescript on the ground. The call is a bat-like squeaking. Pairs occur in broad-leaved woodland and mixed bushveld, especially on hillsides in stony or sandy terrain. May be seen flying before nightfall, males sometimes gathering in loose aggregations to display. Roosts on the ground or a branch by day. **25–28 cm** (excluding male's wing-pennants). (Wimpelvlerknaguil)

2 Rufous-cheeked Nightjar *Caprimulgus rufigena*

Common summer resident. Identified by predominantly **pale grey coloration** and **pale-buff collar**; see p. 256 for full wing and tail formulae. Calls 'chwop, chwop, kewook-kwook' from ground or perch, and utters an even, sustained, purring sound like a small motor, with no variation (cf. (5)). Occurs in dry woodland (especially protea woodland), thornveld and sparsely vegetated Kalahari sandveld, often on stony or gravelly ground. Rests beneath trees during the day, but if flushed may temporarily settle in a tree. **23–24 cm** (Rooiwangnaguil)

3 European Nightjar *Caprimulgus europaeus*

Fairly common summer visitor. Identified by **large size** and **dark coloration** (some races paler); see p. 256 for full wing and tail formulae. Mostly silent in Africa but sometimes calls 'coo-ic' in flight and 'quick-quick-quick' from the ground. Occurs singly in woodland, riverine forests and plantations, preferring large trees. By day, roosts lengthwise on a horizontal branch; perches on branches more often than any resident nightjar. **25–28 cm** (Europese Naguil)

4 Fiery-necked Nightjar *Caprimulgus pectoralis*

Common resident. Has **extensive rufous coloration about the neck, head and upper breast**; see p. 257 for full wing and tail formulae. Has a characteristic descending, quavering call, resembling the words 'Good Lord, deliver us'. Occurs in any broad-leaved wooded region, often in well-wooded suburbia, and especially in stands of exotic trees. Roosts on the ground by day. **23–25 cm** (Afrikaanse Naguil)

5 Square-tailed Nightjar *Caprimulgus fossii*

Common resident. A **smallish, long-tailed nightjar** showing distinct **white spots on folded wing** and a **white line on back of wing** formed by white-tipped secondaries; also shows full **white (male) or buff (female) outer tail-feathers** recalling Swamp Nightjar (p. 252). No distinctive coloration apart from forewing and tail formulae; see p. 257. Utters a prolonged gurgling sound like an engine changing gears, becoming louder or quieter and increasing or decreasing in frequency; cf (2). Also calls 'whip-prrieoo'. Prefers open, sandy ground in woodland and savanna or near rivers and pans, plus coastal dunes. Roosts on the ground by day. **23–24 cm** (Laeveldnaguil)

6 Freckled Nightjar *Caprimulgus tristigma*

Common resident. Has **dark freckling overall** with few distinct markings, resembling weathered granite; see p. 257 for full wing and tail formulae. The call is a high-pitched 'wheeoo-wheeoo' or 'cow-cow', at a distance sounding like the yapping of a small dog. Occurs in woodland near rocky koppies, escarpments and granite outcrops. By day roosts on shaded rocks, even on flat roofs in country districts. **27–28 cm** (Donkernaguil)

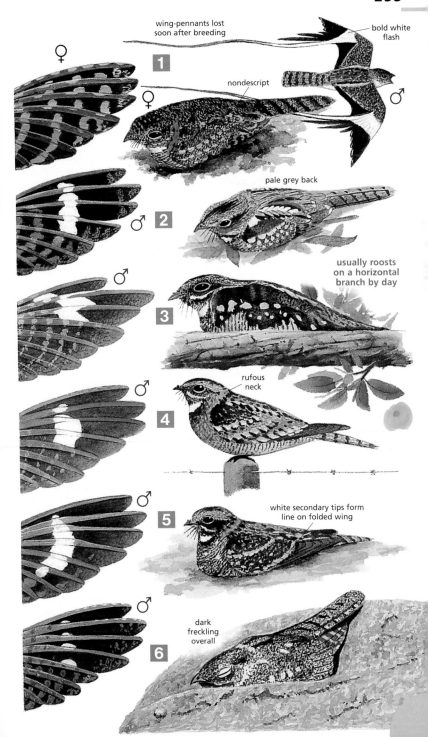

wing-pennants lost
soon after breeding

bold white
flash

♀

nondescript

♀

♂

1

pale grey back

♂

2

usually roosts
on a horizontal
branch by day

♂

3

♂

rufous
neck

4

♂

white secondary tips form
line on folded wing

5

♂

dark
freckling
overall

6

DIAGRAMMATIC ILLUSTRATIONS OF NIGHTJAR WINGS AND TAILS

These illustrations show the major wing-feathers and outer tail-feathers from above with the outer webs of each blackened for clarity. The position of the wing emarginations or

Swamp Nightjar

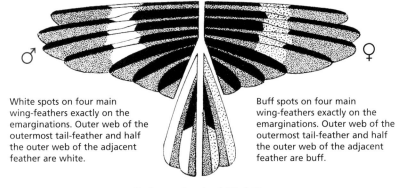

White spots on four main wing-feathers exactly on the emarginations. Outer web of the outermost tail-feather and half the outer web of the adjacent feather are white.

Buff spots on four main wing-feathers exactly on the emarginations. Outer web of the outermost tail-feather and half the outer web of the adjacent feather are buff.

Rufous-cheeked Nightjar

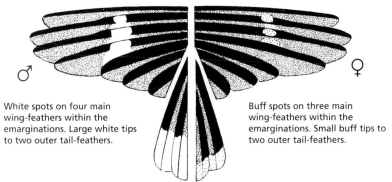

White spots on four main wing-feathers within the emarginations. Large white tips to two outer tail-feathers.

Buff spots on three main wing-feathers within the emarginations. Small buff tips to two outer tail-feathers.

European Nightjar

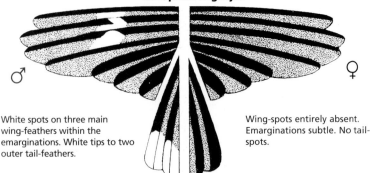

White spots on three main wing-feathers within the emarginations. White tips to two outer tail-feathers.

Wing-spots entirely absent. Emarginations subtle. No tail-spots.

'kinks' in relation to the wing-spots, the format and coloration of the wing-spots (if present) and the presence or absence of bold tail markings are diagnostic. The normal, irregular buff patterning present on nightjar feathers has been omitted. This diagram is intended to aid identification of nightjars in the hand.

Fiery-necked Nightjar

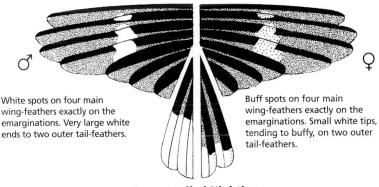

♂ White spots on four main wing-feathers exactly on the emarginations. Very large white ends to two outer tail-feathers.

♀ Buff spots on four main wing-feathers exactly on the emarginations. Small white tips, tending to buffy, on two outer tail-feathers.

Square-tailed Nightjar

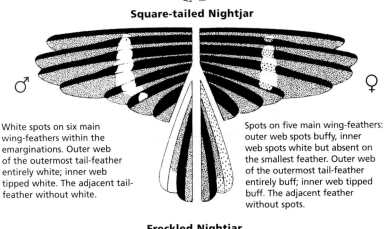

♂ White spots on six main wing-feathers within the emarginations. Outer web of the outermost tail-feather entirely white; inner web tipped white. The adjacent tail-feather without white.

♀ Spots on five main wing-feathers: outer web spots buffy, inner web spots white but absent on the smallest feather. Outer web of the outermost tail-feather entirely buff; inner web tipped buff. The adjacent feather without spots.

Freckled Nightjar

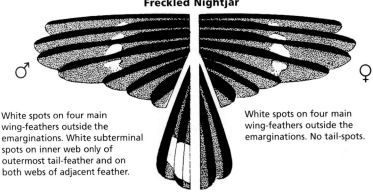

♂ White spots on four main wing-feathers outside the emarginations. White subterminal spots on inner web only of outermost tail-feather and on both webs of adjacent feather.

♀ White spots on four main wing-feathers outside the emarginations. No tail-spots.

SWALLOWS

Small, long-winged, **aerial-feeding** birds. Swallows have mostly **glossy-blue upperparts** (some with rufous caps) and **whitish, rufous or streaked underparts**; the blackish saw-wing swallows (p. 264) are an exception. Saw-wings have rough, saw-like leading edges to their primary feathers (not apparent in the field). In all species, immatures are duller than adults. They **build nests with mud pellets or burrow tunnels in banks or cliffs**; they **drink and bathe in flight by skimming the surface of still water**, and **perch to rest**. See comparison with swifts on pp. 268–269.

1 Red-breasted Swallow   *Cecropis semirufa*
Common summer resident. Identified by **large size, blue cap extending to below the eyes** and entirely **orange-chestnut underparts**. In flight differs from (2) in **buff (not white) underwing coverts** and **longer tail-shafts**. Immature duller above and much paler about the cheeks, chin and throat. Also, outer tail-feathers are shorter. Differs from (2) in having the dark cap extending below the eyes and onto the ear coverts. Adults utter a soft warbling and a strident trill. Pairs occur in summer near their nest sites: road culverts, low causeways (not over water) and aardvark holes in open savanna and grassland. Flight is low and slow with much leisurely gliding. **24 cm** (Rooiborsswael)

2 Mosque Swallow   *Cecropis senegalensis*
Fairly common, localised resident. Told from (1) by **white throat and upper breast**; in flight by **white underwing coverts** and **shorter tail-shafts**. Utters a nasal, tin-trumpet-like 'harrrp', occasionally a guttural chuckling. Pairs and small flocks occur over large-tree woodland, mostly near water. Usually flies at some height, with bursts of fluttering flight followed by a glide. Frequently skims across dams and pans or perches in trees. Constructs a mud nest in a cavity of a large tree, and often in the vicinity of nesting trees (especially baobabs). **23 cm** (Moskeeswael)

3 Greater Striped Swallow   *Cecropis cucullata*
Common summer resident. Identified by **chestnut cap, pale chestnut rump** and **lightly streaked underparts** that appear **almost white in flight**; cf. (4). The call, uttered in flight, is a soft 'chissik'; song is a pleasant trilling and warbling. Occurs in pairs when breeding; otherwise small flocks are found over open terrain, montane grassland, near culverts, rocky koppies and human habitation. Flies with much gliding and perches frequently on trees and wires. **20 cm** (Grootstreepswael)

4 Lesser Striped Swallow   *Cecropis abyssinica*
Common summer resident; some present all year. Differs from (3) in **more heavily streaked underparts**, appearing very dark in the field, and **orange cap extending over the ear coverts**. Flight call is a characteristic descending series of four notes 'eh-eh-eh-eh'. Pairs and small flocks occur near rivers, bridges, road culverts and buildings. Flies more actively than (3), with less gliding. Perches frequently in trees or on wires. **16 cm** (Kleinstreepswael)

large size

buff

blue cap extends below the eyes

longer tail-shafts than (2)

1

white

white cheeks

white

shorter tail-shafts than (1)

2

chestnut cap

pale cheeks

pale chestnut

narrow brown streaks on underparts

3

orange cheeks

dark chestnut

heavy black streaks on underparts

4

CRITICALLY ENDANGERED

1 Blue Swallow *Hirundo atrocaerulea* **R**

Rare, localised summer resident. Told by **entirely glossy-blue plumage** and **extended tail-shafts**, longest in males. Saw-wings (p. 264) are blacker and shorter-tailed. Has a wheezy, chittering call and a short, soft warbling song. Occurs singly or in small parties in the vicinity of small streams in eastern montane grassland. Constructs a mud nest against the wall of an aardvark burrow, old mine shaft or some other cavity in the ground. **20–25 cm** (Blouswael)

2 South African Cliff Swallow *Pterodelichon spilodera* **N E**

Common, near-endemic summer resident. It has a **square tail** (sometimes with slight notch) and shows **dark mottled chin and throat**. Similar to Barn Swallow (p. 262) but with more robust appearance, **pale rump** and **paler throat**. Immature browner and duller above. Has a three- or four-syllable call 'chor-chor-chor-choor'. Flocks frequent the vicinity of their **colonial breeding sites**: cliffs, water towers and other buildings in dry grassland regions. Often seen wheeling about large mud-nest colonies under road bridges along major highways; nests often taken over by other species such as Little Swift, Red-headed Finch and House Sparrow. **15 cm** (Familieswael)

3 White-throated Swallow *Hirundo albigularis*

Common summer resident; all year at low altitudes. Told from Barn Swallow (p. 262) by **clear white underparts with black breast-band**. Juvenile lacks **chestnut forehead-patch**. Utters a soft twittering and has a warbling song. Found in pairs near nesting sites under rock overhangs, bridges, culverts, outbuildings or other artificial structures near or over water. A particularly acrobatic and high-speed flier. **17 cm** (Witkeelswael)

4 Red-rumped Swallow *Cecropis daurica* **V**

Rare vagrant. Told from other red-rumped swallows (p. 258) by **lightly streaked or plain tawny underparts, chestnut band across nape** and **black vent**. Utters a hoarse 'chirp' and subdued twittering. Frequents hilly districts and mixes with other swallows when feeding. A wanderer from north of the subregion. **18 cm** (Rooinekswael)

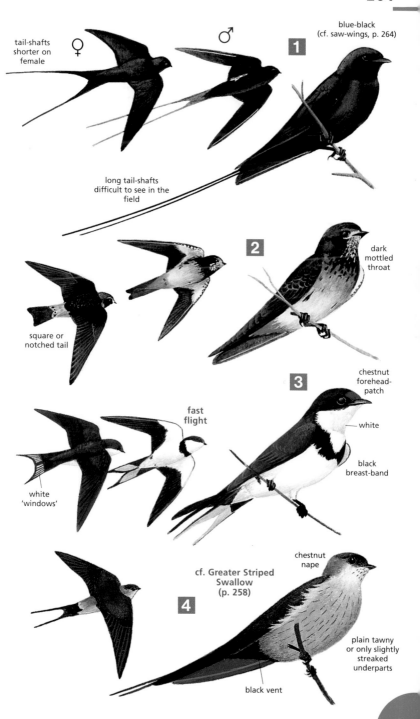

♀ tail-shafts shorter on female

♂

blue-black (cf. saw-wings, p. 264)

1

long tail-shafts difficult to see in the field

2

dark mottled throat

square or notched tail

3

chestnut forehead-patch

fast flight

white

white 'windows'

black breast-band

cf. Greater Striped Swallow (p. 258)

4

chestnut nape

plain tawny or only slightly streaked underparts

black vent

1 Barn Swallow *Hirundo rustica*

Abundant summer visitor. Told by **chestnut chin and throat** (looks all-dark at a distance). Moulting birds often **without chestnut chin** or **long tail-shafts** (Nov–Jan); immatures (common Oct–Dec) can show very pale throats; cf. Common House-Martin (p. 266) and Sand Martin (p. 264). Flocks utter a soft twittering sound, especially when settled. Most characteristic call is a soft 'wheet'; males give a short warbling sequence followed by a wheezy 'intake of breath'. Outnumbers all other swallows in summer, and mixes freely in flight with other swallows and with swifts over most habitats. Large flocks perch on telephone wires along roads and very large flocks gather to roost in reed beds. **18 cm** (Europese Swael)

2 Angola Swallow *Hirundo angolensis* ⬛V

Rare vagrant to the extreme northern Caprivi region. Closely similar to (1), but **chestnut chin colour extends to breast**; the **blackish breast-band is narrow, broken or indistinct**; and **rest of underparts dull ash-brown**. Outer tail-feathers only slightly elongated; may be confused with (1) with worn or moulting plumage. May utter a warbling song in flight with wings depressed and quivering. Habits otherwise much the same as (1). **15 cm** (Angolaswael)

3 Wire-tailed Swallow *Hirundo smithii*

Fairly common wetland resident. Told by **full orange cap, entirely white underparts** (except for narrow darker line on lower flanks) and **wire-like tail-shafts** (difficult to see when flying). The call is a twittering 'chirrik-weet' repeated from a perch and 'chit-chit' while flying. Pairs, sometimes small groups, are found near river bridges, dam walls, river gorges and buildings; seldom far from water. Perches on dead trees in water and on bridge rails; settles on the road surface of bridges and causeways. **13 cm** (Draadstertswael)

4 Pearl-breasted Swallow *Hirundo dimidiata*

Uncommon to fairly common resident and winter visitor. Identified by **entirely blue upperparts** (including head and rump), **entirely white underparts** and **lack of tail-shafts**. The call is a nasal, twittering 'chip-cheree-chip-chip'. Pairs frequent woodland and human settlements in summer; small flocks often found in vleis in winter. Mostly occurs in the drier regions. Sparsely distributed throughout its range and present only in summer in many regions, especially the south. **14 cm** (Pêrelborsswael)

5 Grey-rumped Swallow *Pseudhirundo griseopyga*

Locally common resident. **Grey-brown cap** and **pale grey rump** diagnostic, but cap not easily seen in flight. **Rump may appear almost white**; then told from Common House-Martin (p. 266) by more **deeply forked tail** and **slender appearance**. Utters a grating 'chaa' in flight. Usually occurs in flocks in grassland within woodland, vleis, coastal plains and grassy riverbanks. Nests in ground burrows and may be seen flying in and out of these. Often more common in the winter months. **14 cm** (Gryskruisswael)

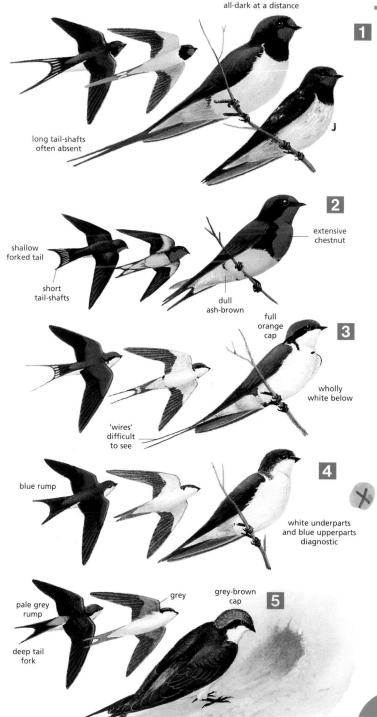

chestnut chin and throat look
all-dark at a distance

1

long tail-shafts
often absent

J

2

shallow
forked tail

extensive
chestnut

short
tail-shafts

dull
ash-brown

full
orange
cap

3

'wires'
difficult
to see

wholly
white below

blue rump

4

white underparts
and blue upperparts
diagnostic

grey

grey-brown
cap

5

pale grey
rump

deep tail
fork

1 Black Saw-wing *Psalidoprocne holomelaena*

Fairly common resident and local migrant. **All-black, fork-tailed swallow,** differing from (2) only in colour of underwing coverts. Could also be mistaken for Blue Swallow (p. 260). In flight differs from swifts in slower wing beats and steadier flight with much gliding. Pairs and small parties occur near eastern coastal forests and montane forest fringes of the mist-belt region, often near wooded rivers. It forages in low-level flight, mostly below the tree tops. **15 cm** (Swartsaagvlerkswael)

2 Eastern Saw-wing *Psalidoprocne orientalis*

Uncommon resident. Identical to (1) except for **white or greyish underwing coverts,** this feature also distinguishing it from any swift. Habits and habitat similar to those of (1). Gives a nasal, twittering song. **15 cm** (Tropiese Saagvlerkswael)

3 White-headed Saw-wing *Psalidoprocne albiceps* V

Rare vagrant from Angola and East Africa. The male is distinctive with its **white head** and **dark eye-stripe,** but the female has a **white chin only.** Immature entirely black and difficult to separate from (1). Frequents broad-leaved woodland. **12–15 cm** (Witkopsaagvlerkswael)

MARTINS

The name martin is loosely applied to certain **close relatives of swallows,** particularly species of the genus *Riparia* and their allies. Generally, with the exception of the House Martin, martins have **brown plumage** and **square tails,** and while some martins build typical swallow-type mud nests, most breed in holes in cliffs or banks.

4 Sand Martin *Riparia riparia*

Uncommon to locally common summer visitor. A **small martin** differing from the larger Banded Martin (p. 266) in smaller size, **all-dark underwings** and **lack of a white eyebrow.** Shape, size and general coloration make confusion more likely with Brown-throated Martin (p. 266), alongside which it often occurs in mixed flocks. Flocks usually occur near large inland waters or river estuaries and other eastern coastal localities, but small numbers or singletons may occur anywhere with flocks of other swallows. **12 cm** (Europese Oewerswael)

5 Mascarene Martin *Phedina borbonica* R

Uncommon winter visitor. In flight, differs from other martins in having **streaked underparts** (may be difficult to discern when flying high up) and **very dark upperparts;** cf. martins on p. 266. Small flocks occur occasionally over open woodland in Mozambique. An erratic visitor from Madagascar, recorded in the winter months. **13 cm** (Gestreepte Kransswael)

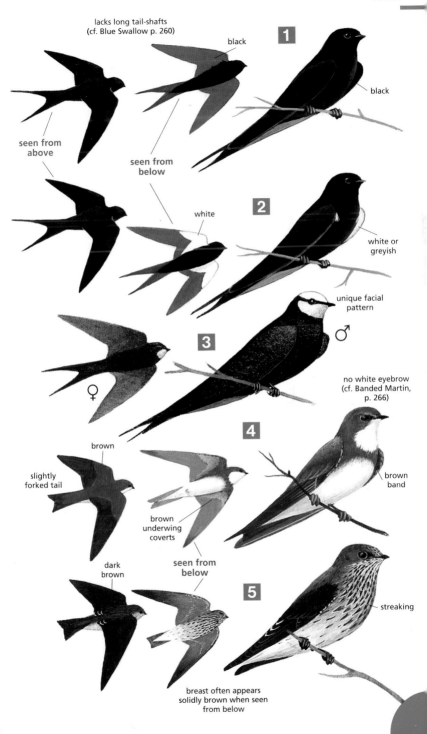

lacks long tail-shafts
(cf. Blue Swallow p. 260)

black

1

black

seen from
above

seen from
below

white

2

white or
greyish

unique facial
pattern

3

♂

♀

no white eyebrow
(cf. Banded Martin,
p. 266)

4

brown

slightly
forked tail

brown
band

brown
underwing
coverts

seen from
below

dark
brown

5

streaking

breast often appears
solidly brown when seen
from below

1 Common House Martin *Delichon urbicum*
Common summer visitor. The only martin with **blue upperparts, white rump** and **white underparts**. Immature (with off-white rump) told from Grey-rumped Swallow (p. 262) by **blue cap** (not grey-brown) and only **slightly forked tail**. The call is a single dry 'chirrup'. Flocks occur anywhere, often associating with Barn Swallows (p. 262), from which it can be told in the air by **smaller, more compact appearance, squarer tail** and **white rump**. Flocks habitually forage at high altitudes, but singletons often seen in mixed swallow flocks lower down. **14 cm** (Huisswael)

2 Brown-throated Martin *Riparia paludicola*
Locally common resident. A **small, almost entirely brown martin except for white belly**; see (a). Sometimes occurs with **entirely brown underparts** (b); then told from (4) by **lack of 'windows' in the tail** and **more slender appearance**. The call is a soft twittering. Flocks forage over rivers with sandy banks (in which it breeds), estuaries and other wetlands, roosting in reed beds when not breeding. **13 cm** (Afrikaanse Oewerswael)

3 Banded Martin *Riparia cincta*
Uncommon to locally common summer resident. Occurs all year in northern Botswana and KwaZulu-Natal coastal plains. A large, heavy-set martin differing from Sand Martin (p. 264) in **broad breast-band, white underwing coverts, white eyebrow** and **square tail**. Utters a melodious twittering while perched or flying. Small flocks or pairs forage over grassland, breeding in river banks and termite mounds. The flight is slow and leisurely, the birds alighting frequently on a branch or fence to rest. **17 cm** (Gebande Oewerswael)

4 Rock Martin *Ptyonoprogne fuligula*
Common resident. A stocky martin, told in flight by **broad wings** and **white 'windows' in fanned tail**. Utters a melodious twitter. Pairs and small flocks frequent rocky cliffs, bridges, dam walls and tall buildings, often associating with other swallows and swifts. Has adapted well to cities and towns, and often abundant around skyscrapers. The flight is slow, with much gliding, twisting and turning. **15 cm** (Kransswael)

J

juvenile has off-white or pale grey rump
(cf. Grey-rumped Swallow, p. 262)

blue cap

1

white
rump

uniformly
white below

2

brown

slightly
forked tail

a

b

short white
eyebrow

3

white

square
tail

broad brown
band

large and
robust

4

paler below
than dark
morph of (2)

distinctive
white 'windows'

usually near
cliffs or
buildings

IDENTIFYING CHARACTERISTICS
OF SWALLOWS AND MARTINS

- **Swallows** and **martins** can perch.

- **Swallows** and **martins** have wider, comparatively more rounded wings than swifts.

- **Swallows** are blue on their upperparts and white or orange, sometimes streaked or spotted, on their underparts.

- **Swallows** may have orange caps, foreheads or throats, and buff or orange rumps.

- **Martins** are brown, the underparts usually paler.

- The **Common House-Martin** is the exception, since it has the appearance of a swallow with a white rump.

- **Martins** have squarish tails, many with white 'windows' in them, visible when the tail is fanned.

- **Swallows** have forked tails, often with long streamers on the outer feathers.

- **Swallows** glide frequently between bouts of flapping flight.

IDENTIFYING CHARACTERISTICS OF SWIFTS

- **Swifts** cannot perch.

- The wings of a **swift** are slender and scimitar-like, and appear to sweep straight back from the body with little obvious bend at the carpal joint.

- **Swifts** are dark grey-brown, blackish or ash-brown, and mostly appear all-dark in flight.

- **Swifts** may have whitish throats and white rumps, but no bright colours.

- **Swifts** may have square or forked tails; in southern Africa only the **African Palm Swift** has tail streamers.

- Only the large **Alpine Swift** and the small **Böhm's Spinetail** have white on the belly.

- **Swifts** sometimes glide with their wings angled steeply upwards.

- Most **swifts** fly very rapidly with only brief gliding spells, and may flutter their wings briefly.

SWIFTS

All-dark birds, some with white markings. The sexes are alike, and immatures are similar to adults. They are **entirely aerial in habit**. They feed on airborne insects, **never intentionally settling on the ground or a perch**. They cling to vertical surfaces or scramble into crevices and their nests, which are glued into place with sticky saliva. Their calls are **high-pitched screams**. See pp. 268–269 for comparison with swallows and martins.

1 African Palm Swift *Cypsiurus parvus*

Common resident. The **most slender, longest-tailed swift**; entirely **grey-brown**. Usually occurs in flocks, flying rapidly around tall palm trees where they roost and nest, less commonly under bridges and eaves of buildings. May mix with other swifts when feeding, but slim build diagnostic. **15–16 cm** (Palmwindswael)

2 Bradfield's Swift *Apus bradfieldi*　　　　　　　**N E**

Common, near-endemic resident. Similar to Common and African Black Swifts (p. 272), but **body and underwing coverts paler**, contrasting with the **darker primaries and tail**. These features apparent when seen flying in company with all-dark swifts. Flocks occur in the dry west, especially in the montane regions of Namibia (in summer) and in rocky gorges of the western Orange River. At other times occurs singly or in small flocks away from mountains and gorges. **18 cm** (Muiskleurwindswael)

3 Little Swift *Apus affinis*

Very common resident. **Large white rump**, which extends over the sides of the body, and **square tail** distinguish this species from all but the Mottled Spinetail (p. 272). Differs from this species in **clear white throat**. **Wings less pointed** than those of other swifts. Often flies with wings angled steeply upwards, tail fanned. A noisy species, flocks making a high-pitched screaming in flight. During the day, feeds in flocks well away from its roost and regularly mixes with other swifts or swallows. Very common in towns, where it roosts and breeds under eaves and bridges, and on silos and tall buildings. **14 cm** (Kleinwindswael)

4 White-rumped Swift *Apus caffer*

Very common summer resident. Most easily confused with (5), but has a **slimmer build, more deeply forked tail** and **thin white 'half moon' on the rump** that does not extend over the sides of the body. Occurs in pairs or small, loose groups anywhere except the most arid regions; common in suburbia, frequently occupying swallows' nests attached to buildings. **15 cm** (Witkruiswindswael)

5 Horus Swift *Apus horus*

Uncommon resident and summer visitor. Differs from (4) in stouter appearance, **less deeply forked tail** and **large white rump patch** that extends to the sides of the body. Small flocks occur near riverbanks, sandbanks, quarries and cuttings, where they breed and roost in holes in the banks. Seen on the KwaZulu-Natal coast and in the Zambezi valley in winter. **17 cm** (Horuswindswael)

6 Alpine Swift *Tachymarptis melba*

Common resident and summer visitor. **Large size** and **white throat and belly** distinguish this from all other swifts. Seen mostly near high cliffs where it breeds and roosts, but also ranges far afield and at great height during the day. Flies with great power and speed, making an audible swishing sound. **22 cm** (Witpenswindswael)

grey-brown
(not black)

exceptionally slender body
and wings with long,
deeply forked tail

1

grey-brown,
not black

2

3

broad white
rump

square
tail

mottled

deeply forked
tail

thin white
'half moon'

4

6

5

broad white
rump patch

short, shallowly
forked tail

white belly
(variable)

thickset
appearance

large size

1 Scarce Swift *Schoutedenapus myoptilus* **R**
Rare, localised resident. Has no distinct markings. **A light-brown, fork-tailed swift,** chin slightly paler than rest of its underparts. In terms of shape and size, between (3) and African Palm Swift (p. 270). Groups and flocks occur near rocky mountains and hills of eastern Zimbabwe, usually above 1 200 m, where they breed and roost in fissures in inaccessible cliffs. **17 cm** (Skaarswindswael)

2 African Black Swift *Apus barbatus*
Common summer resident. **Fairly large, all-dark swift** closely similar to (3). Identification very difficult but, seen from above, has **marked contrast between paler inner secondaries and dark back and outer wings.** From below its tail appears more deeply forked than in (3). Flocks often seen flying in the vicinity of their roosts in mountain cliffs, especially in the late afternoon in summer. Unknown in Namibia, northwestern Cape and Botswana (except for the extreme southeast). **19 cm** (Swartwindswael)

3 Common Swift *Apus apus*
Common summer visitor. **All-blackish,** differing from (2) **in uniform upperparts** (no contrast between inner secondaries and body). From below, appears closely similar but **tail less deeply forked;** darker overall than Bradfield's Swift (p. 270). In flight, extremely difficult to separate from either Bradfield's Swift or (2), unless in optimum light conditions. Widespread occurrence in flocks (sometimes very big) Nov–Feb. Always seen flying, often following thunderstorms; no known roosts. **18 cm** (Europese Windswael)

4 Pallid Swift *Apus pallidus* **V**
Status uncertain. One specimen from Kuruman dated 1904 and one recent sight record on Cape west coast, with unconfirmed claims from elsewhere. A **pale swift** with **white throat** and **forked tail.** Separation from (3) problematic and requires exceptional views and optimum light conditions. Probably flies with flocks of other swifts and could be more regular than the few records suggest. **18 cm** (Bruinwindswael)

5 Mottled Swift *Tachymarptis aequatorialis*
Fairly common, localised resident. A **large, dark swift** with **mottled body** and **pale throat.** Flocks occur near rocky cliffs in montane and hilly regions of Zimbabwe, breeding and roosting there during summer, ranging more widely at other times. Flies with great power and speed, like related Alpine Swift (p. 270). **20 cm** (Bontwindswael)

6 Mottled Spinetail *Telecanthura ussheri*
Uncommon, localised resident. A **square-tailed, white-rumped swift** similar to Little Swift (p. 270), but with **pale (not white) and subtly mottled throat and upper breast** and **small white patches near the feet.** Projecting tail-feather shafts not an identifying feature in the field. Pairs and small parties frequent river valleys, broad-leaved woodland and forest fringes in the northeast. Normally breeds and roosts in tree cavities, especially baobab trees. **14 cm** (Gevlekte Stekelstert)

7 Böhm's Spinetail *Neafrapus boehmi*
Uncommon, localised resident. A small, distinctive swift with **white underparts, white rump** and **tailless appearance.** Pairs and small parties are found in dry, broad-leaved woodland with baobab trees, usually near rivers and lowland valley forests. Flight is fluttering, bat-like and erratic. Breeds and roosts in hollow baobab trees and holes in the ground. **10 cm** (Witpensstekelstert)

1
slender
light-brown
body

deeply
forked tail

2
plain all-
dark body

inner secondaries
paler, contrasting
with outer wing

3
plain all-
blackish body

inner secondaries
do not contrast
with rest of
upperwing

4
paler than (3)

5
mottled
appearance

large size

6
resembles
Little Swift
(p. 270)

7
broad-based
wings and
bat-like flight

appears
tailless

white
underparts

MOUSEBIRDS

Fruit-eating birds with **crested heads, soft, hair-like plumage** and **long, stiff tails**. They **usually occur in parties of about a dozen birds** that maintain contact by call. When feeding they clamber about, mouse-like, in bushes. Immatures resemble adults, but are duller and shorter-tailed.

1 Speckled Mousebird *Colius striatus*
Common resident. Identified by **dull-brown coloration and bill, black upper mandible, white lower mandible** and **black mask**. The call is a rasping 'zwit-wit'. Flocks, which fly in straggling groups, frequent dense bush, scrub, forest fringes and suburbia in the moister regions. **30–35 cm** (Gevlekte Muisvoël)

2 White-backed Mousebird *Colius colius*　　**E**
Common endemic resident. Identified by **pale grey upperparts, buff underparts, white back, maroon rump** (visible in flight only) and **whitish bill with black tip to upper mandible**. The call is 'zwee, wewit'. Occurs in flocks in thornveld, riverine bush and suburbia in the drier regions. **30–34 cm** (Witkruismuisvoël)

3 Red-faced Mousebird *Urocolius indicus*
Common resident. Identified by **red mask**. The call is a diagnostic descending whistle 'tree-ree-ree', frequently repeated and uttered in flight and at rest. Flocks, which fly in compact groups, occur in thornveld, riverine forests and especially suburbia, favouring the moister regions. **32–34 cm** (Rooiwangmuisvoël)

BEE-EATERS

Colourful, aerial-feeding birds with **long decurved bills**, many with **elongated tail-feathers** (absent in immatures). Most occur in flocks, catching flying insects while twisting and turning in graceful aerial manoeuvres or by hawking them from a perch in short aerial sallies, usually returning to the same perch to eat their prey. Immatures are dull versions of the adults. Sexes are alike.

4 White-throated Bee-eater *Merops albicollis*　　**V**
Rare vagrant. A **greenish bee-eater** told by its **prominent black-and-white head pattern**. It has the longest tail-streamers of all local bee-eaters. Flocks behave much as other colonial bee-eaters. Normally occurs in central and West Africa, extending southwards occasionally to northern Angola and eastern Tanzania. **20–32 cm** (Witkeelbyvreter)

5 Swallow-tailed Bee-eater *Merops hirundineus*
Common resident. A small, **fork-tailed bee-eater** told from Little Bee-eater (p. 276) by **bright blue collar** and **bluish underparts and tail**. Immature lacks the yellow and blue throat; underparts pale apple-green. The call is a soft 'kwit kwit'. Flocks occur in a variety of woodland habitats, being especially common in the regions of Kalahari sands. Hawks from a perch, often near pans and dry river beds. Nomadic when not breeding. **20–22 cm** (Swaelstertbyvreter)

black mask

black upper mandible;
white lower mandible

1

fine
barring

dark
feet

whitish bill,
tipped black

2

white
back

maroon
rump

red
mask

3

reddish
feet

pale
rump

unique facial
pattern

4

J

bright
blue
collar

blueish
belly

5

long tail-
streamers

forked, sky-
blue tail

1 Little Bee-eater *Merops pusillus*

Common resident. Identified by **small size, yellow throat, orange-buff underparts** and **squarish tail**. Immature lacks the black collar and has pale green underparts. The call is a quiet 'chip, chip, trree-trree-trree'. Occurs in pairs or groups near rivers and in open areas in any woodland or thornveld, usually hawking from some low branch or fence. **17 cm** (Kleinbyvreter)

2 Southern Carmine Bee-eater *Merops nubicoides*

Common summer resident and visitor. Adult **unmistakable**. Largest bee-eater in the region, with brilliant **carmine and blue plumage**. Immature has brown upperparts and **pale cinnamon underparts** with traces of pink. Individuals call a deep 'terk, terk'. Flocks occur near large rivers, marshes, in woodland and mixed bushveld, where they hawk from trees and from the ground. **33–38 cm** (Rooiborsbyvreter)

3 European Bee-eater *Merops apiaster*

Common resident and summer visitor. Identified by **gold-and-brown mantle, turquoise-blue forehead and underparts** and **yellow throat**. The call in flight is diagnostic, a clear, liquid 'quilp' or 'kwirry'. Occurs in flocks anywhere, often mixing with other bee-eaters or perching on roadside telephone wires. Flocks frequently fly at great height. **25–29 cm** (Europese Byvreter)

4 Rosy Bee-eater *Merops malimbicus* **V**

Rare vagrant. A single bird recorded at Cape Recife, Port Elizabeth, in Apr–May 2003. Identified by unique combination of **striking pink underparts** and **slate-grey upperparts**. Bold **white moustache stripe** borders **black facial mask**. The **short tail-streamers are dull crimson**. **Iris red or reddish brown** and **legs yellowish brown**. Juvenile lacks the tail-streamers and is generally duller, showing dusky pink underparts, a grey mask and a buffy moustache. Could only be confused with (2). Calls most similar to (3). Breeding colonies normally located on sandbanks or islands in wide rivers in central and West Africa. Breeds Apr–Jun, then migrates to rainforest, savanna and mangrove habitats. Hawks for insects (mainly flying ants, bees and wasps) from a perch, or forages in flight high above the rainforest canopy or low over open water expanses. **22–28 cm** (Pienkborsbyvreter)

1

tiny size

black collar

creamy orange

no streamers; short tail

2

blue crown

deep pink below

3

gold-and-brown mantle

yellow throat

turquoise-blue underparts

4

bold white moustache stripe

slate-grey upperparts

short tail-streamers

1 Böhm's Bee-eater *Merops boehmi* R

Uncommon, localised resident. Distinguished from the much larger (4) by **longer tail-streamers, rich russet cap** (not dull olive-brown) and **rich green coloration overall**. The call is a chirping 'swee' and a liquid trill. Small flocks occur near riverine forests, on the edges of dense thickets and in woodland clearings; sometimes hawks from a perch within the forest-fringe canopy. Restricted to extreme north of the subregion, particularly in Mozambique, but status uncertain. **21 cm** (Roeskopbyvreter)

2 White-fronted Bee-eater *Merops bullockoides*

Common resident. Identified by **white forehead and upper throat, red lower throat** and **dark blue vent**. The call is a querulous 'quirk' and other similar sounds. It occurs in flocks near rivers with mud banks, where it nests. **22–24 cm** (Rooikeelbyvreter)

3 Blue-cheeked Bee-eater *Merops persicus*

Uncommon to locally common summer visitor. Distinguished from (4) by **pale blue forehead, eyebrows and cheeks**, and **yellow-and-brown throat and upper breast**. Told from European Bee-eater (p. 276) by green (not gold-and-brown) mantle. A large bee-eater of generally **green appearance**. The short, liquid call is 'prruik' or 'prree-oo, prree-oo'. Usually occurs in small flocks near large rivers, dams, floodplains and coastal grassland, where it often hawks from a dead tree standing in water. **27–33 cm** (Blouwangbyvreter)

4 Olive (Madagascar) Bee-eater *Merops superciliosus* R

Uncommon summer visitor. Distinguished from (3) by **olive-brown cap, all-brown throat** and **uniformly pale green underparts**. Young or heavily worn birds difficult to distinguish from (3). Told from (1) by **large size, olive-brown (not russet) cap** and paler green underparts. The call is similar to that of (3). Usually occurs in small flocks in northwestern Namibia, the Victoria Falls and Chobe River region, the middle Zambezi valley and coastal Mozambique, but far-ranging and may temporarily occur elsewhere. **29–33 cm** (Olyfbyvreter)

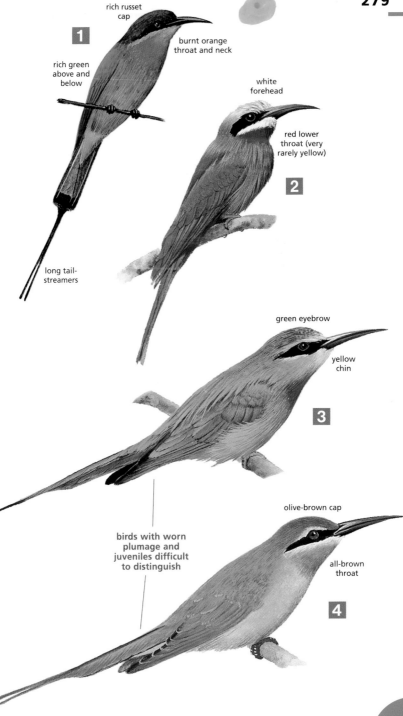

1

rich russet cap

burnt orange throat and neck

rich green above and below

long tail-streamers

2

white forehead

red lower throat (very rarely yellow)

3

green eyebrow

yellow chin

birds with worn plumage and juveniles difficult to distinguish

4

olive-brown cap

all-brown throat

KINGFISHERS

Fish- or insect-eating birds with **short legs** and **long, dagger-like bills**. The fish-eating species **plunge-dive for their food from a perch** or, in some cases, after hovering. Fish are beaten into immobility before being swallowed head-first. The insectivorous species hunt from a low branch, usually away from water, where they **watch for and seize insects on the ground**. They breed in holes in banks or trees. Immatures resemble adults but are duller.

1 **Giant Kingfisher** *Megaceryle maximus*
Common resident. **World's largest kingfisher**; much larger than (2). The **male shows a russet-brown breast** and the **female a belly of the same colour**. The call is a raucous 'kek-kek-kek-kek-kek', recalling a Hamerkop (p. 104). Occurs singly or in pairs near wooded rivers, wooded dams and coastal lagoons. Perches on a branch, bridge or wire, from where it watches the water; sometimes hovers briefly before plunge-diving. **43–46 cm** (Reuse Visvanger)

2 **Pied Kingfisher** *Ceryle rudis*
Common resident. A large kingfisher but smaller than (1). **Entirely black and white**, the sexes differing in their **breast-bands: double in the male, single in the female**. The call is a high-pitched twittering, often by two or more birds at the same time. Found in pairs or small family parties inland on rivers, lakes, streams, dams and at coastal lagoons, estuaries and shoreline rock pools. Habitually hovers over water while fishing, then plunge-dives to seize prey. **28–29 cm** (Bontvisvanger)

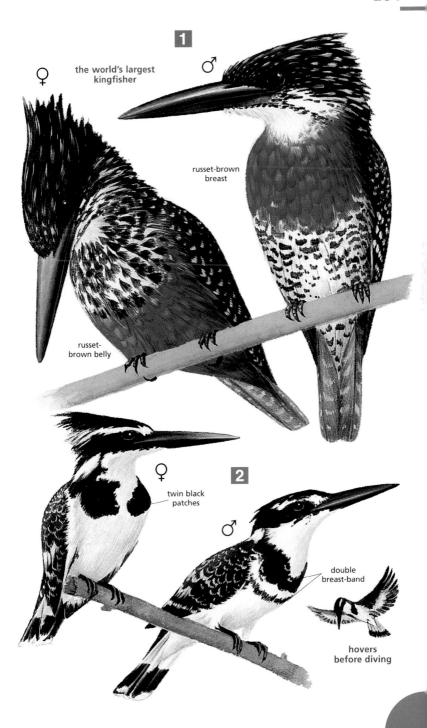

1

♀

the world's largest kingfisher

♂

russet-brown breast

russet-brown belly

♀

twin black patches

2

♂

double breast-band

hovers before diving

1 **Woodland Kingfisher** *Halcyon senegalensis*
Common summer resident. Differs from (3) in having a **red-and-black bill,
whiter head** and **black patch from bill to ear coverts**. Immature usually
has all-red bill, sometimes with a black tip; then told from (3) by eye-
stripe and **blue (not greyish) crown**. Male calls continuously after arrival
and until breeding is finished, a loud 'yimp-trrrrrrrrrrrrrrrrrrrrr', the
last part drawn out and descending. Present Oct–Apr, occasionally later, in
mixed bushveld and riverine or swamp-fringing woodland, singly or in
pairs. Catches insects on the ground by still-hunting from a perch. Pairs
greet each other with spread wings. **23–24 cm** (Bosveldvisvanger)

2 **Grey-headed Kingfisher** *Halcyon leucocephala*
Uncommon to locally common summer resident and visitor. Identified
by **grey head and mantle**, **chestnut belly** and **deep blue, almost
purple wings and tail**; cf. Brown-hooded Kingfisher (p. 284). Not very
vocal, the call a weak, descending 'chi-chi-chi-chi'. An insectivorous
kingfisher, found singly or in pairs in woodland or mixed bushveld
Sep–Apr. Occasionally catches fish. **20 cm** (Gryskopvisvanger)

VULNERABLE

3 **Mangrove Kingfisher** *Halcyon senegaloides* **R**
Uncommon resident. Differs from (1) in **completely red bill with bulging
base, black face mask not extending beyond eye** and **greyish crown
and mantle**. The call is a raucous 'tchit-tchoo, tcha-tcha-tcha-tch-tch-
tch', ending in a trill and performed with raised wings. Mainly during
summer, occurs singly or in pairs in mangroves at coastal estuaries in
the former Transkei region. During winter, occurs in KwaZulu-Natal
on major lowland rivers within 20 km of the coast. In South Africa
mainly restricted to coastal habitats and mangroves, but common in
inland woodlands in central Mozambique. Sparsely distributed on the
South African coast; more common in the Beira region. **23–24 cm**
(Manglietvisvanger)

pale whitish-blue head; cf. (3)

black extends behind eye

black lower mandible on most adults

1

J

summer visitor to woodland habitats

grey head (sometimes very pale)

2

no black behind eye

greyish crown; cf. (1)

chestnut belly

wholly red bill

3

deep blue (almost purple) wings and tail

1 Brown-hooded Kingfisher *Halcyon albiventris*

Common resident. Told from Grey-headed Kingfisher (p. 282) by larger size, **streaked brown head** and **streaked buffy breast and flanks**. Female has **brown (not black) wings and shoulders**. Told from (2) by **larger size, larger, heavier bill (wholly red, not red and black), less obvious black eye-stripes** and buffy underparts. The immature is duller. The call is a loud, descending 'kik-kik-kik-kik'. Usually occurs singly in mixed bushveld, woodland, riverine forests, suburban parks and gardens. Still-hunts for insects from a low branch – normally away from water – but will occasionally fish. **23–24 cm** (Bruinkopvisvanger)

2 Striped Kingfisher *Halcyon chelicuti*

Fairly common resident. A **small, sombrely coloured kingfisher**, distinguished from (1) by smaller size, **streaked head, two-coloured bill, bold black eye-stripe extending to the nape** and **white collar** encircling the neck. Male has darker underwings than female. The call is 'tirrrrrr, deeeoo-deeeoo-deeeoo'. Pairs call in a duet while performing a wing-opening display. Most often heard in the evening when several individuals may call from scattered points. Pairs occur in mixed bushveld and woodland, generally perched high on an outer branch far from water. **18–19 cm** (Gestreepte Visvanger)

3 African Pygmy Kingfisher *Ispidina picta*

Fairly common summer resident. Very similar to (5) but has **mauve wash on ear coverts**; and **blue crown** is the same colour as rest of upperparts (not turquoise) and does not reach the eyes, being bordered below by **orange eyebrow**. Has no territorial call but utters a hissing 'chip' or 'tseep' sound in flight. Occurs singly in a wide variety of wooded habitats from sea level to about 1 350 m, usually away from water. Still-hunts from a low perch, catching insects on the ground. Sparsely distributed. **13 cm** (Dwergvisvanger)

4 Half-collared Kingfisher *Alcedo semitorquata*

Uncommon resident. Larger than superficially similar (3) and (5). Identified by **black bill**, entirely **bright blue upperparts** and **cinnamon lower breast and belly**. Calls a shrill 'teep' or 'seek-seek'. Occurs singly on small, heavily wooded inland waters and well-wooded estuaries. A fish-eater, perching low down over the water. Sparse distribution. **20 cm** (Blouvisvanger)

NEAR THREATENED

5 Malachite Kingfisher *Alcedo cristata*

Common resident. Differs from (3) in **turquoise cap that reaches the eyes** and no mauve on the ear coverts. **Immature has a black bill** and duller plumage; cf. adult (4). Distinguished from (4) by smaller size, brighter orange underparts and orange (not blue) cheeks. When flushed, utters a shrill 'peep-peep'. Occurs singly on almost any water with fringing vegetation, perching low down on a reed, branch or rock. **14 cm** (Kuifkopvisvanger)

J

streaked
brown head

wholly
red bill

1

buffy
underparts

streaked
crown

distinctive black
eye-stripe and
white collar

black-and-red
bill

2

orange
eyebrow

mauve
wash

red bill

3

black bill

bright
blue

4

red bill

5

cinnamon lower
breast and belly
(paler than (5))

J

ROLLERS

Colourful, heavy-billed birds with **brilliant blue wing-feathers** and **harsh, croaking voices**. They spend much of the day still-hunting from a convenient perch, flying down to catch and eat large insects and other small prey on the ground. They breed in holes in trees (sometimes in holes in cliffs) and have active display flights, which involve **violent aerial manoeuvres** with much harsh calling.

1 Racket-tailed Roller *Coracias spatulatus*
Uncommon visitor and resident. Identified by **plain blue underparts** (pink further north in Africa) and **spatulate tips to the tail-shafts**; cf. (3) and (4). Immature lacks elongated tail-feathers and is more lilac on cheeks and sides of breast, but differs from immature of (4) in **deep blue primary wing coverts** (not greenish blue) and generally browner upperparts. Occurs singly or in pairs in well-developed, broad-leaved woodland. Unlike other rollers, often occurs in small parties and perches inconspicuously. Sparse and irregular south of the Limpopo River. **36 cm** (Knopsterttroupant)

2 Broad-billed Roller *Eurystomus glaucurus*
Fairly common summer resident. Told by **small size, cinnamon upperparts, purple underparts** and **yellow bill**. Immature is greenish blue below, with black streaks. Makes harsh croaking and cackling sounds. Occurs singly, in pairs or in scattered groups in mature riverine and palm forests and broad-leaved woodland; also found at the fringes of lowland forests. **27 cm** (Geelbektroupant)

3 Lilac-breasted Roller *Coracias caudatus*
Common resident. The only roller with **lilac throat and breast** and **blue belly, vent and undertail**. **Tail-shafts are straight**; often absent when moulting. Immature lacks tail-shafts and is duller, browner. Utters harsh rattling sounds and rolls in display. Occurs singly or in pairs in grassy regions within broad-leaved woodland and thornveld; often numerous in stunted mopane woodland. A common roadside bird in many areas, perching conspicuously on telephone wires and other exposed vantage points. **36 cm** (Gewone Troupant)

NEAR THREATENED

4 European Roller *Coracias garrulus*
Fairly common summer visitor. Differs from (1) and (3) in **lack of tail-shafts. Pale blue or greenish over entire head and underparts.** Rest of upperparts brown, but shows **electric-blue wings** in flight. Mostly silent in southern Africa but sometimes utters a harsh 'rack-kack, kacker'. Occurs singly – often many birds within sight of each other – in woodland, bushveld and grassland. Perches on power lines. **30–31 cm** (Europese Troupant)

5 Purple Roller *Coracias naevius*
Fairly common resident. A **large, heavily built roller** with a **square tail**. It has **olive-green upperparts, deep purple underparts heavily streaked with white** and a conspicuous **white eyebrow**. Immature is duller. Utters various harsh cackling and cawing sounds. In display makes a continuous 'ka-raa-ka-raa-ka-raa…' as it mounts upwards, while the wings appear to beat independently. Usually occurs singly in any woodland or thornveld. Perches fairly low down and is normally less active than other rollers. **36–40 cm** (Groottroupant)

generally browner upperparts

small

broad yellow bill

2

cinnamon above

purple below

1

no pink coloration on breast

turquoise hindcrown

3

lilac throat and breast

spatulate tips

long tail-shafts

no tail-shafts

4

wholly pale blue or greenish below

olive-green

5

deep purple with white streaks below

large and heavily built

WOOD HOOPOES

Glossy, dark blue-green birds with **long graduated tails, long decurved bills** and **short legs**. They clamber about on tree trunks and branches, **probing with their bills in search of insects**. They also investigate weaver and sparrow nests and may throw out eggs or small chicks while doing so. They nest in tree cavities. Flight patterns are diagnostic; see below.

1 **Violet Wood Hoopoe** *Phoeniculus damarensis* **R**

Fairly common, localised resident. Larger than (2) and **more violet-blue, even blackish, about the head and mantle**. Similar in all other respects to (2). May interbreed with Grant's Wood Hoopoe (*Phoeniculus granti*; sometimes considered a subspecies of *P. damarensis*) in northern Namibia. **40–42 cm** (Perskakelaar)

2 **Green Wood Hoopoe (Red-billed Wood Hoopoe)**
Phoeniculus purpureus

Common resident. Larger than (3) and with **red (not black) bill and feet**. Immature has a black bill, **less decurved** than that of (3). The call is a high-pitched cackle started by one and taken up by others to produce a hysterical cackling similar to but less mechanical-sounding than the babblers (p. 348). Occurs in parties of three to eight in woodland or well-wooded suburbia. Parties fly from tree to tree in straggling procession, settling low down and working their way upwards. **30–36 cm** (Rooibekkakelaar)

3 **Common Scimitarbill** *Rhinopomastus cyanomelas*

Fairly common woodland resident. Smaller than (1) and (2), **the bill more decurved and black**. Female and immature have **brownish throats and breasts**. During summer, calls 'pwep-pwep-pwep-pwep...' at half-second intervals. Solitary or in pairs in dry, well-developed, broad-leaved woodland and thornveld. Feeds in large trees, clambering about on the outer branches. Quieter, less conspicuous than (2). **24–28 cm** (Swartbekkakelaar)

HOOPOES

This family of distinctive birds occurs throughout sub-Saharan Africa, with a slightly duller, paler form found further north, into Europe and across the whole of Asia.

4 **African Hoopoe** *Upupa africana*

Common resident. The **crest is normally held down**, but raised briefly when the bird settles or when alarmed. Female and immature paler than male. Has an undulating, butterfly-like flight; **black-and-white wings** then conspicuous. Male shows **white flashes on inner wings** formed by white secondaries. In female, the **secondaries are barred with black**. The call is 'hoop-hoop, hoop-hoop-hoop' frequently repeated; also a harsh 'kwarrr' when alarmed. Fledglings call 'sweet, sweet'. Occurs singly or in pairs in any open woodland, bushveld, parks and gardens. Walks about probing the ground with its bill. Seasonal fluctuations occur in some regions. Breeds in existing cavities in trees, or any other protected hole in buildings, cliffs or even the ground. **27 cm** (Hoephoep)

violet-blue sheen

black bill

J

1

2

green iridescence

red bill

red feet

strongly decurved black bill

white spots on outer tail retrices

2

black feet

3

shorter tail than (1) and (2)

crest usually held closed

4

large white wing-patch on male; wings barred black and white on female

HORNBILLS

Insectivorous and frugivorous birds with **large, decurved bills, sometimes with a horny casque on the upper mandible**. Arboreal or terrestrial feeders, or both, they nest in holes in trees (among rocks in a few species) and, in most species, the female seals herself in during incubation. Their **flight is heavy and undulating with periods of gliding**.

1 Southern Yellow-billed Hornbill *Tockus leucomelas* N E
Common, near-endemic resident. **Large yellow bill** (with reddish base in immature) separates this from all other hornbills. The call is 'wurk, wurk, wurk, wurk, wurk, wurk, wukwukak, wukwukak…', the sound working up to a crescendo then fading away. Often two birds call simultaneously with a wing-opening, head-bowing display. Conspicuous in dry bushveld and savanna woodland. **48–60 cm** (Geelbekneushoringvoël)

2 Southern Red-billed Hornbill *Tockus erythrorhynchus*
Common resident. Identified by combination of **red bill** and **black-and-white chequered upperparts**; cf. (4), which has plain brown upperparts. Immature has a shorter bill and buff spots on upperparts. The call very difficult to distinguish from that of (1), but uttered more rapidly. Pairs and small flocks frequent dry bushveld, broad-leaved woodland (particularly mopane) and thornveld, preferring drier conditions than (1), but often mixing with that species. Forages mostly on open ground. **42–50 cm** (Rooibekneushoringvoël)

3 Damara Red-billed Hornbill *Tockus damarensis* N E
Fairly common, localised resident. Differs from (2) in having **dark (not yellow) eyes, white forehead and ear coverts**, and **more extensive facial skin**. Occurs in the Damaraland region of Namibia, especially around Windhoek. Habits and calls much as (2). **42–50 cm** (Damararooibekneushoringvoël)

4 Crowned Hornbill *Tockus alboterminatus*
Fairly common resident. Told by **casque on the red bill** and **entirely dark grey-brown upperparts**. Immature has a more orange bill and buff-tipped feathers on the upperparts. The call is a series of melancholy, piping whistles. Occurs in riverine forest fringes, the canopy and fringes of lowland and coastal forests and well-wooded valleys. Feeds in trees and roosts conspicuously on high, slender branches. **50–57 cm** (Gekroonde Neushoringvoël)

5 African Grey Hornbill *Tockus nasutus*
Common resident. Male's rather **small dark bill** diagnostic. Female's **smaller casque and upper mandible creamy**, the **bill-tip red**. Both sexes show a diagnostic **white eyebrow** and **pale feather edges on their wings**. Immature has a browner head and indistinct eyebrows. The call is a thin, piping, plaintive series of notes delivered with the bill pointing skywards 'phe, phephee, pheephee, pheeoo, phew, pheeoo-pheeooo…'. Pairs and, in winter, flocks of up to about 30, occur in dry, mixed bushveld, savanna and thornveld. Mainly arboreal. **43–48 cm** (Grysneushoringvoël)

yellow bill

1

yellow eye

red bill

black-and-white patterning

2

dark eye

whiter face than (2)

3

white outer tail

uniformly dark brown above

yellow bill base

4

reddish-orange bill with small casque

white tips

black tail

dark bill

creamy upper mandible

white eyebrow

♂ **5** ♀

grey-brown with pale feather edges

1 Monteiro's Hornbill *Tockus monteiri* N E

Fairly common, near-endemic resident. It differs from (2) in having **white spotting on the upperwing coverts** and **entirely white outer tail-feathers**. Also, when seen in flight, shows **entirely white secondary wing-feathers**, forming a pale panel. Female's **facial skin and eye-rings are blue**. The call when displaying is a hoarse 'tu-aack tu-aack', while its territorial call is 'kok kok kok kokok kokok kokok…' rising in volume. Usually seen singly or in pairs in rocky regions (where it breeds) and in dry woodland in northern Namibia, feeding mostly on the ground. **54–58 cm** (Monteironeushoringvoël)

2 Bradfield's Hornbill *Tockus bradfieldi* N E

Uncommon, near-endemic resident. Distinguished from (1) by **entirely brown wings** and its **outer tail-feathers having white tips only**; from the Crowned Hornbill (p. 290) by an **orange (not red) bill that lacks a casque**. The call is a series of piping whistles delivered with the bill pointing skywards. Found in a variety of habitats, but most common in broad-leaved and woodland on Kalahari sands in the dry northwestern regions. **50–57 cm** (Bradfieldneushoringvoël)

3 Silvery-cheeked Hornbill *Bycanistes brevis*

Uncommon, localised resident. Identified by **massive size, pied coloration** and **heavy yellow bill with large casque**. Likely to be confused only with (4), from which it differs in **blueish (not pink) facial skin**, limited **white area on lower belly only**, and mostly **black underwings**. A noisy species, the most common sound a loud braying or growling 'quark-quark-quark'. Occurs in pairs or flocks in forests and well-developed riverine forests where trees are fruiting; feeds in the canopy. The wings make an audible soughing in flight. **75–80 cm** (Kuifkopboskraai)

4 Trumpeter Hornbill *Bycanistes bucinator*

Common lowland resident. Distinguished from (3) by **smaller size, dusky (not yellow) bill, pink (not blueish) facial skin, white edges on underwings** and **more white on the underparts**. The characteristic call resembles the crying of a baby, a loud and far-carrying 'waaaa-aaa-aaa-aaa-aaaaaa' often uttered by several birds at once. Small flocks frequent well-developed riverine forests, lowland forests and moist woodland, feeding in the canopy of large fruiting trees. **58–65 cm** (Gewone Boskraai)

1
brown eye
streaky head
white spots on coverts
pale panel conspicuous in flight
white outer tail-feathers

2
paler brown above than Crowned Hornbill (p. 290)
orange bill
white tail-tips

3
blue facial skin
massive casque (smaller in female)
yellow bill
massive size
white restricted to lower belly

4
pink facial skin
♂
dusky bill
♀
broad white leading edge to wing
much white on underparts

1 **Southern Ground Hornbill** *Bucorvus leadbeateri*
Fairly common resident. A **turkey-sized black bird** with **bare red face and throat-pouch**. Female has a **blue central patch on the pouch**. In flight shows **white wing-feathers**. Immature has yellow facial skin and throat-pouch. The call is a deep booming, mostly heard at dawn 'oomph, oomph-oomph', frequently repeated. Usually occurs in groups of four to 10 in bushveld, woodland and montane grassland. Mainly terrestrial, walking slowly in loose array in search of food. Takes off in low flight only if disturbed or when going to roost in a tree. Numbers have decreased in recent years. **90 cm** (Bromvoël)

BARBETS AND TINKERBIRDS

Stout-billed, robust and often **colourful relatives of the woodpeckers**, with loud, characteristic calls. They feed on fruits and insects and **excavate nest-holes in trees**. The smaller species are called tinkerbirds from the likeness of their calls to the metallic sound of a hammer on an anvil. Immatures are duller than adults.

VULNERABLE

2 **Green Barbet** *Stactolaema olivacea* R
Fairly common, highly localised resident. Distinguished from Green Tinkerbird (p. 296) by larger size, **black cap** and **lime-yellow ear-patch**, but their ranges are mutually exclusive. The call is a monotonous 'quop-quop-quop-quop…'. **Found only in the Ongoye Forest** in KwaZulu-Natal and beyond the region's limits to the north. **17 cm** (Groenhoutkapper)

3 **Whyte's Barbet** *Stactolaema whytii*
Fairly common, localised resident. Identified by **brownish appearance, yellow forecrown** and **white wing feather edges**. Utters a soft 'coo' at about one-second intervals. Small parties of about four birds are found in broad-leaved woodland in the vicinity of fig trees, and in suburbia in Zimbabwe. **18 cm** (Geelbleshoutkapper)

4 **White-eared Barbet** *Stactolaema leucotis*
Common resident. Identified by **pied appearance, prominent white ear-stripe** and **white belly**. The common call is a loud 'trreee, trrree-trree-trree-trree-trree', which may be uttered by several birds simultaneously. Usually occurs in noisy, conspicuous groups of two to six in coastal and lowland forest canopies and fringes, riverine forests and moist woodland where fig trees are fruiting. **17 cm** (Witoorhoutkapper)

unmistakable

blue patch

♂

♀

1

J

facial skin yellow in young birds

2

lime-yellow ear-patch

black cap

3

yellow forecrown

white wing-feather edges

4

prominent white ear-stripe

white belly

1 Yellow-rumped Tinkerbird *Pogoniulus bilineatus*

Common resident. Similar in size and general appearance to the tinkerbirds on p. 298. Told by **black crown and back** and **white stripes on the sides of its head. Folded wing shows bold yellow feather edges.** In flight, its **yellow rump** is visible. The immature has yellow-tipped back-feathers. The call is 'poop poop poop poop poop', usually in a series of five or six notes. An active, noisy species. Occurs in coastal and montane forests (mostly below 1 000 m) and riverine forests. It frequents the canopy and midstratum singly or in pairs. **10 cm** (Swartblestinker)

2 Green Tinkerbird *Pogoniulus simplex*　🇻

Status unknown. A **small, dull-green bird** with **short, heavy bill, pale yellow edges to wing-feathers** and **golden rump**. Calls 'pop-op-op-op-op-op' in forest canopies. Recorded once south of Beira, but status in southern Africa unclear. Fairly common in coastal forests from northern Mozambique to Kenya. **10 cm** (Groentinker)

3 Acacia Pied Barbet *Tricholaema leucomelas*　N E

Common, near-endemic resident. Differs from Red-fronted Tinkerbird (p. 298) in larger size and **white underparts** (eastern race has yellow wash on flanks, no black streaks) and **black bib** of varying extent. Immature lacks the red forehead. The call is a loud nasal 'peh-peh…', less frequently a long series of hoopoe-like 'poop-poop…' calls. Occurs singly or in pairs in a wide range of dry woodland habitats. **17–18 cm** (Bonthoutkapper)

4 Black-collared Barbet *Lybius torquatus*

Common resident. **Bright red forehead, face and foreneck, broad black collar, golden edges to wing-feathers** and **heavy black bill with 'toothed' ridge.** Rarely, yellow replaces the red coloration; see illustration. Immature has red speckling on black. The call is a loud duet, starting with a whirring 'kerrr-kerrr-kerr' and then becoming 'too-puddely-too-puddely-too-puddely-too-puddely…' about eight times, accompanied by wing-quivering and bobbing. Also calls 'snaar'. Occurs in broad-leaved woodland, including well-wooded suburbia. **19–20 cm** (Rooikophoutkapper)

5 Crested Barbet *Trachyphonus vaillantii*

Common resident. Well-known barbet with characteristic **yellow-and-black plumage. Red scaling on the head** is variable and less profuse in females and immatures. The call is a distinctive trilling like a muffled alarm clock 'trrrrrr…', which sometimes continues for long periods. Call is louder, slower and of higher pitch when expressing agitation 'ke-ke-ke-ke-kek…'; female calls 'puta-puta-puta-puta…'. Found in well-wooded savanna, riverine forests and bushveld. Attracted to fruit in suburban gardens. **23 cm** (Kuifkophoutkapper)

black crown
(cf. tinkerbirds, p. 298)

white
stripes

1

yellow wing-
feather edges

yellow
rump

2

golden
rump

unmarked
face

red
forehead

3

black
bib

(eastern race) yellow wash
on flanks, no streaking

rarely, red
replaced by yellow

4

crest

'tooth'
on upper
mandible

black
collar

golden
wing-feather
edges

5

variable red
rump patch

1 Yellow-fronted Tinkerbird *Pogoniulus chrysoconus*

Common resident. Forehead **yellow** or, in the highveld, **orange**. **Pale-yellow underparts**; cf. (2). Immature has black forehead, sometimes with traces of yellow. The call is a monotonous 'phoo-phoo-phoo-phoo-phoo…' uttered for long periods on warm days. Also calls 'dit-dit-dit' rapidly. Occurs in a variety of woodland habitats, including riverine forests, mostly in the canopies of large trees. Greatly attracted to mistletoe-type parasites of the genera *Viscum* and *Loranthus* and may be abundant when these are plentiful. **12 cm** (Geelblestinker)

2 Red-fronted Tinkerbird *Pogoniulus pusillus*

Common resident. Differs from (1) in **red forehead** and **slightly yellower underparts**. Immature has black forehead or traces of red. The call is a monotonous 'purp-purp-purp-purp-purp…' repeated for long periods; also a high-pitched, rapid 'kew-kew-kew-kew…'. Inhabits coastal and lowland forests, well-wooded riverbanks and valleys, where it frequents tree canopies. Distribution overlaps with (1) only in Swaziland. **10,5 cm** (Rooiblestinker)

WOODPECKERS

Small, robust birds with **straight, pointed bills, stiff tails** and **zygodactylous feet** (the inner and outer toes are directed backward and the two central toes forward). They glean insects and their larvae from within crevices in trees and from beneath bark by **tapping with their bills** to loosen or chip the wood and inserting their long sticky tongues. While feeding, they use the tail as a prop. They normally occur in pairs and **excavate holes in trees for nesting**, these frequently being used in turn by other hole-nesting species. Many woodpeckers are very similar in appearance. They are **best identified by head and breast markings plus call**. The aberrant Ground Woodpecker is entirely terrestrial and nests in holes in banks.

3 Olive Woodpecker *Dendropicos griseocephalus*

Common resident. The only woodpecker in southern Africa with an **unmarked olive-green mantle**. The call is a shrill 'chee-wit, chee-wit, chee-wit…' or 'weer-dit weer-dit weerditdit', depending on locality. Pairs occur in lowland and montane forests and along adjacent forested streams. Feeds mostly in the mid- and upper strata amid moss- and lichen-encrusted branches. Pairs roost nightly in their nest-holes and, during inclement weather, will remain in the hole all day. **18–20 cm** (Gryskopspeg)

4 Ground Woodpecker *Geocolaptes olivaceus*   E

Common endemic resident. Easily recognised by large size, plain appearance and terrestrial habits. The only **red-breasted woodpecker** in southern Africa, but red coloration often less bold, less extensive than illustrated. Female lacks russet malar streak. Immature is duller than adult, underparts with little red. Has a loud, harsh call 'kee-urrr, kee-urrr, kee-urrr'. Found in hilly, rock-strewn grassland, mountain slopes and dry gullies. Feeds entirely on the ground among rocks, singly or in small parties, often perching on a prominent rock or roadside fence post. Nesting holes excavated in earth banks or erosion gulleys. **26 cm** (Grondspeg)

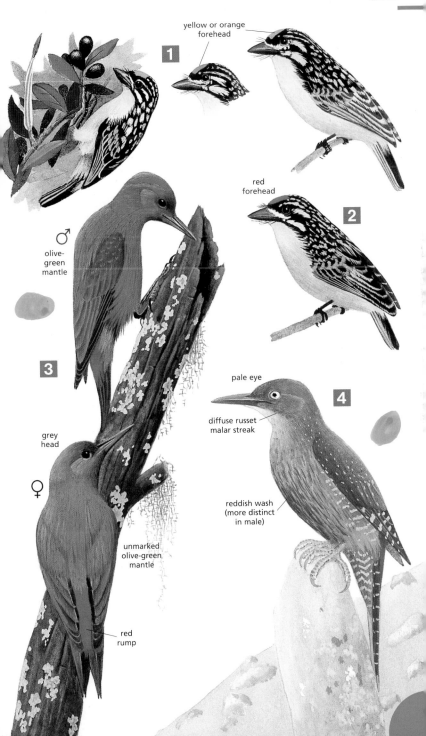

yellow or orange forehead

1

red forehead

2

♂ olive-green mantle

3

grey head

♀

unmarked olive-green mantle

red rump

pale eye

diffuse russet malar streak

4

reddish wash (more distinct in male)

1 Cardinal Woodpecker *Dendropicos fuscescens*

Common resident. Both sexes identified by **small size, streaked breast, black malar streak** and **brown forehead**; male with crimson crown, female with black crown. The call is a high-pitched, chittering 'ke-ke-ke-ke-ke-ke-kek'. Occurs in pairs in any broad-leaved woodland, thornveld or riverine bush, often in bird parties of the same species and frequently in quite small trees. Taps quietly. **14–16 cm** (Kardinaalspeg)

2 Golden-tailed Woodpecker *Campethera abingoni*

Common resident. Has **streaks on breast** but is larger than (1). Male has **red malar streak** and **entire crown is red with black spots**. Female has **black crown with white spots**, only the nape being red. The call is a distinctive, single nasal 'waaa'. Pairs occur in broad-leaved woodland, thornveld and bush fringing dry river beds. **20–23 cm** (Goudstertspeg)

3 Bennett's Woodpecker *Campethera bennettii*

Fairly common resident. A medium-sized woodpecker with **spotted underparts** (except in Namibia, where it is unspotted). Male identified by **entirely red crown and malar streak**, female by **brown facial and throat-patches**. The call is an excitable, high-pitched chattering, sometimes by two or three birds together 'whirrwhirrwhirrwhir-it-whir-it-whir-it-wrrrrrrrrr…', often accompanied by wing-flapping. Usually occurs in pairs or groups in broad-leaved woodland and thornveld, feeding mainly on the ground. **22–24 cm** (Bennettspeg)

4 Bearded Woodpecker *Dendropicos namaquus*

Common resident. A **large, long-billed** species with **barred underparts** and a **bold black malar streak and ear-patch**. Only the **top of male's crown is red**; female has a **black crown**. The call is a loud 'wickwickwick-wick-wick'. Male indulges in bouts of territorial drumming with its bill on a hollow branch, the drumming particularly loud and far-carrying 'trrrrrr-tap-tap-tap-tap-tap'. Solitary in any tall woodland and riverine forest, especially where there are plenty of tall, dead trees. **23–25 cm** (Baardspeg)

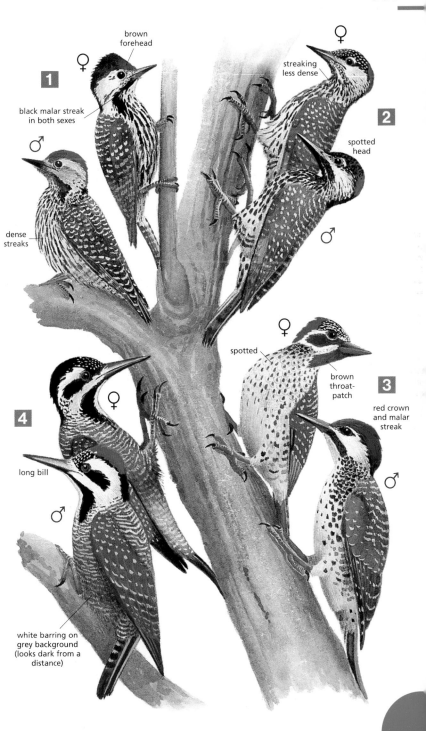

1 ♀ brown forehead

black malar streak in both sexes

♂ dense streaks

2 ♀ streaking less dense

spotted head

♂

3 ♀ spotted

brown throat-patch

red crown and malar streak

♂

4 ♀

long bill

♂

white barring on grey background (looks dark from a distance)

1 **Green-backed Woodpecker** *Campethera cailliautii*
Common, localised resident. Recognised by **small size** and **lack of a malar streak** in both sexes; cf. Cardinal Woodpecker (p. 300). The call is a 'hee' repeated about four times; similar to call of Golden-tailed Woodpecker (p. 300), but shriller, higher in pitch and shorter. Pairs are found in thick woodland and on the fringes of forests. Taps with a rapid action and feeds on ants. **16 cm** (Gevlekte Speg)

2 **Speckle-throated Woodpecker**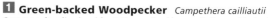
Campethera scriptoricauda
Uncommon, localised resident. Identified by **pale yellowish base to lower mandible**. Both sexes have a **finely speckled throat** and **reddish eyes**. Female differs from female Golden-tailed Woodpecker (p. 300) in **spotted (not streaked) breast**. Call closely resembles that of Bennett's Woodpecker (p. 300). In southern Africa, recorded only in woodland between Beira and the Zambezi River in Mozambique. **19 cm** (Tanzaniese Speg)

NEAR THREATENED

3 **Knysna Woodpecker** *Campethera notata* E
Fairly common, localised, endemic resident. Both sexes have **well-spotted underparts from chin to vent** (except in northeasterly distribution, where it is less spotted). Male's **forecrown and malar streak are red with heavy black spots**. Female has no distinct malar streak. The call is 'keeek', recalling that of Golden-tailed Woodpecker (p. 300), but higher in pitch and more sibilant. Pairs occur in coastal and valley bush, woodland and forest fringes. **20 cm** (Knysnaspeg)

WRYNECKS

Although related to woodpeckers, **wrynecks do not excavate nests** but use natural tree cavities or the disused nests of barbets and woodpeckers. They feed on ants and termites.

4 **Red-throated Wryneck** *Jynx ruficollis*
Common, localised resident. Identified by **rust-brown patch on throat and upper breast**, and **brown-speckled upperparts** with **blackish broken line from crown to mantle**. The call, frequently uttered, is a high-pitched 'kek-kek-kek-kek'. Occurs singly or in pairs in various types of woodland and in suburbia, often in wattle trees (Australian *Acacia* spp.). Creeps about branches like a woodpecker, perches like a passerine or hops about the ground with its tail raised. **18 cm** (Draaihals)

cf. similarly sized
Cardinal Woodpecker (p. 300)

1

♂ red

2

♀ base of lower mandible pale yellowish

finely speckled

reddish eye

♀ spotted throat and cheeks

♂ finely speckled throat

spotted back and underparts

3

♀ dense blotches

♂

intricately marked above with broken line down centre of head and mantle

4

rust-brown patch on throat and upper breast

HONEYGUIDES AND HONEYBIRDS

Small, inconspicuous birds that show **white outer tail-feathers in flight**. Some species have distinctive calls and regular call-sites; others have weak, sibilant calls, which are seldom heard. They are **mostly insectivorous**, but a few species have developed the habit of **leading people to wild bees' nests** (as suggested by their genus name, *Indicator*) by continually chattering and fluttering conspicuously in the desired direction. When the bees' nest is broken open, the honeyguide **feeds on the wax and grubs**. Like cuckoos, they build no nests but parasitise various other small birds. The smaller species of the genus *Prodotiscus* are now called honeybirds.

1 Pallid Honeyguide *Indicator meliphilus*

Uncommon, localised resident. Difficult to distinguish from (2), and much less common and widespread. Told by **stubby bill, greenish wash to head and upperparts**, lack of a dark malar stripe, **fine streaking on the throat and flanks** and **pale yellowish underparts**. Song of male superficially similar to that of (2): a long series of high-pitched whistles. Sparsely distributed on forest fringes, in degraded forest and in woodland, with records from eastern Zimbabwe and Mozambique. Known to parasitise the White-eared Barbet (p. 294) and Yellow-rumped Tinkerbird (p. 296). **13 cm** (Oostelike Heuningwyser)

2 Lesser Honeyguide *Indicator minor*

Common resident. Characterised by **thick bill** with a **pale patch at the base** and **yellow edges to the wing-feathers**. Told from (1) by duller appearance, **dull grey-brown (not greenish) head, dark grey malar stripe** and lack of any streaking on the underparts. Uses a regular call-site, from where it calls 'tzeeu… sheek, sheek, sheek…' repeated 30 to 40 times. Occurs singly in various wooded habitats, including suburbia. **15 cm** (Kleinheuningwyser)

3 Scaly-throated Honeyguide *Indicator variegatus*

Fairly common resident. Told by **streaky head** and **scaly breast**, usually with **yellow wash**. Utters a high-pitched 'foyt-foyt-foyt' or, from a call-site, a purring 'trrrrrrrr' (like Crested Barbet (p. 296) but rising at the end). A bird of forest fringes, riverine forests and valley bush; usually solitary. Has been known to guide to bees' nests, otherwise hawks insects like a flycatcher. **19 cm** (Gevlekte Heuningwyser)

4 Greater Honeyguide *Indicator indicator*

Common resident. In both sexes, **yellow shoulder-patch** is often vestigial or absent and the **dark throat of the male** incomplete; thus adults often appear as nondescript, bulbul-sized birds. However, **white outer tail-feathers** always present and **ear coverts have a distinctive pale patch**. Immature is distinctive with pink eye-surround and lemon-yellow underparts. Male calls frequently and for long periods in summer from a regularly used call-site 'vic-terrr, vic-terrr…', up to 11 times. Male performs a swooping display while making audible whirring sounds with its wings. Guides people to bees' nests, the call then a high-pitched chattering while the bird flutters in an agitated manner. Occurs singly in woodland, bushveld, exotic plantations and suburbia. **19–20 cm** (Grootheuningwyser)

1 greenish wash on head

fine streaking

fine streaking

2 dull grey-brown head

stubby bill

dark grey malar stripe

plain

3 scaly breast

4 J

wholly lemon-yellow below

white

4

♀

sometimes restricted spots or streaks on throat

♂ pallid pink bill

dark throat

yellow shoulder-patch not always visible

white outer tail (in all honeyguides)

1 Green-backed Honeybird *Prodotiscus zambesiae* R

Fairly common resident. Differs from (2) in **greener upperparts** with **yellow-edged flight feathers**. **Throat is dark, finely streaked with white.** May be confused with Pallid Honeyguide (p. 304), but has a much finer bill. The call is a harsh repetitive 'skee-aa' while in undulating display flight over trees. Found singly in broad-leaved woodland, usually in the canopy. Parasitises mostly white-eyes. **11,5 cm** (Dunbekheuningvoël)

2 Brown-backed Honeybird *Prodotiscus regulus*

Uncommon resident. Told from (1) by **brown (not greenish) upperparts** and **white throat**. A rather small, nondescript species. Usually seen only during high-speed aerial display flights: two birds chase each other around while uttering a high-pitched, insect-like 'tseet' note. Also has a thin, trilling call note 'tirrrrrrr…', lasting about four seconds. Often perches high in a tree and peers slowly from side to side while bobbing its head up and down prior to calling. Hawks insects from a tree perch, displaying the **white patches on the sides of the rump** and **brown-tipped, white outer tail-feathers**. Occurs singly in open bushveld, plantations and suburbia. **13 cm** (Skerpbekheuningvoël)

CREEPERS

Monospecific in Africa and India.

3 Spotted Creeper *Salpornis spilonotus* R

Uncommon, localised resident. Identified by **decurved bill, heavily spotted appearance** and behaviour. Calls a series of rapid, sibilant notes 'sweepy-swip-swip-swip-swip' repeated five or six times. Works its way to the top of a tree before flying down to the base of the next, keeping out of sight behind the tree trunk or branch. Occurs singly or in monogomous pairs in broad-leaved woodland (especially miombo). Builds small, well-camouflaged, cup-shaped nests. **15 cm** (Boomkruiper)

BROADBILLS

One species in sub-Saharan Africa, 13 species in Asia.

4 African Broadbill *Smithornis capensis* R

Uncommon resident. **Broad bill, dumpy appearance, black crown** and **heavily streaked underparts** diagnostic. Frequents forests, coastal bush and thickets, where it perches low down and hawks insects like a flycatcher. When displaying, flies in a circular path and reveals **white feathers on its back**; also gives a frog-like 'purrrr-rupp' call. **14 cm** (Breëbek)

NEAR THREATENED

PITTAS

Twenty-five species with a tropical distribution, of which one in southern Africa.

5 African Pitta *Pitta angolensis* R

Rare, summer-breeding intra-African migrant. An unmistakable, **colourful**, thrush-sized terrestrial bird with a **short tail**; sexes alike. Its call is a brief, frog-like 'quoip' as the bird flutters upwards a short distance. Normally occurs in moist areas in forests, thickets and riverine forests, where it scratches about the ground debris for grubs and other insects, often using its bill to move leaves. Flies into a tree when alarmed. Remarkably inconspicuous within its preferred habitat, where it moves in quick hops. Vagrants sometimes occur well south of its normal distribution. **23 cm** (Angolapitta)

1

greenish
upperparts

dark,
finely
streaked

brown
above

white
throat

2

white outer
tail-feathers
conspicuous
in flight

3

black crown

♂

bill appears
flattened
(if viewed from
above)

well
camouflaged;
difficult to
spot

4

♀

heavily
streaked

can raise
short crest

unmistakable

blue

short
tail

5

despite bright
colours, can be very
difficult to spot

LARKS

Small, **sombrely coloured terrestrial birds** with confusingly similar, nondescript plumage patterns consisting of **greyish speckled upperparts** and **pale underparts**, usually with some streaking or spotting on the breast. Many species show **regional plumage variations**, palest or greyest in the north or west. Immature birds resemble adults but are generally more speckled. They are **best identified by the male's call** as well as behaviour and habitat. Most species tend to run rather than fly away when approached; males of many species have **prolonged aerial display flights**.

NEAR THREATENED

1 Melodious Lark *Mirafra cheniana* E

Fairly common, endemic resident. Distinguished from (2) with difficulty, but unlikely to be confused, as distributions are mostly exclusive and habitats differ significantly. Shows a conspicuous **white or pale buff eyebrow, well-streaked upperparts**, rather **dark buffy underparts** and a **well-streaked breast-band**, contrasting with its **white throat**. The **bill is short and conical**. It utters a lively song, mostly in high flight, at which time **rufous wing-patches** are visible. Song continues for long periods and mimics the calls of other birds. It inhabits relatively dry grasslands dominated by rooigras (*Themeda triandra*), grassy Karoo and sweet or mixed grasslands and pastures. **12 cm** (Spotlewerik)

2 Monotonous Lark *Mirafra passerina* N E

Common, near-endemic resident. Told from (1) by the **lack of a distinct eyebrow**, generally **paler underparts** and **less clearly streaked breast** (variable). In many regions, arrives in the summer rains. Male immediately starts calling, a monotonous and oft-repeated 'corr-weeoooo' throughout the day and on moonlit nights. Calls from the ground or a small bush, or during parachuting display flight. When singing, **white throat** puffed up, head held forward and **small crest** raised. Occurs singly or in closely scattered groups, several males often calling at the same time, in dry, open, mixed woodland with bare and stony patches and variable grass cover. **14 cm** (Bosveldlewerik)

3 Rufous-naped Lark *Mirafra africana*

Common resident. Distinguished by **rather long, strong, slightly decurved bill, rufous crown** and **rufous wing-feather edges** (common to all larks in the genus *Mirafra*). Typically with much **rufous coloration above and below** (a) or, in paler western birds (b), with **white underparts faintly tinged buff** and **pale-edged feathers on the upperparts**. Male has an **erectile crest**, which is raised when singing; at other times crest not visible and then easily confused with other larks and pipits. The call is a melancholy 'tseep-tseeooo' repeated at about eight-second intervals. Also sings during aerial cruises, especially at dusk, when it imitates other birds. Usually occurs singly in open grassland, the male perching conspicuously on anthills, low bushes or posts when calling, frequently shuffling the wings and raising the crest. **18–19 cm** (Rooineklewerik)

4 Fawn-coloured Lark *Calendulauda africanoides* N E

Common resident. Best told by **reddish-fawn (a) to distinctly fawn (b) coloration of upperparts** (palest in the west) and **white underparts**. The **white eyebrow** is fairly distinctive; a **white stripe below the eye** is visible at close range. The song, given from the top of a small tree, is a rapid and urgent 'te-e-e-tee-ree-tee-ree-chee' with variations, recalling the song of a Cape Grassbird (p. 388); also sings during display flights. Feeds on open ground but flies to a tree perch if disturbed. Usually occurs singly (in pairs when breeding) in thornveld and the edges of woodland, predominantly on Kalahari sand, being most frequent in the dry west. Localised in the east. **16 cm** (Vaalbruinlewerik)

extended hovering display flight

1

boldly streaked above

bold white or pale buff eyebrow

short, conical bill

white throat contrasts with dark breast-band and buff belly

male raises small crest when singing

2

rather featureless face; sometimes with indistinct eyebrow

pale buff belly

singing male raises crest

crest not always 'up'

b

a

western birds paler

3

rather long, slightly decurved bill

chunky appearance

white underparts faintly tinged buff

white eyebrow and stripe below eye

a

b

4

reddish fawn above (variable)

faint markings

white or very pale buff below

horizontal posture

western birds paler

1 Sabota Lark *Calendulauda sabota* N E

Common, widespread, near-endemic resident. Variable plumage throughout its distribution, but **always well streaked above and on the breast**. Brownest and slender-billed in the east (a), becoming paler and thicker-billed in the west (b); bill thickest (c) in central Namibia. The **white eyebrow** is distinctive in all races; the **wings have no rufous edges** and the **outer tail-feathers are white to pale buff**. The song is high-pitched, melodious and variable, incorporating the song phrases of other birds. Uttered either from a tree perch or in hovering flight. Usually occurs singly in bushveld and woodland (especially mopane woodland) with sparse grass cover or stony ground. **15 cm** (Sabotalewerik)

2 Dune Lark *Calendulauda erythrochlamys* R E

Localised and uncommon endemic resident. Closely similar to (3), but ranges are mutually exclusive. It has **plain, dune-red upperparts, no clear facial markings** and **light spotting on the upper breast** only; throat, belly and flanks unmarked. The song has two to five 'chip chip...' lead-in notes and a long, uniform trill at the end. Occupies a very restricted range along the western dunes of the Namib desert between Lüderitz and Walvis Bay. Frequents sparsely vegetated Namib sand dunes, scrubland and coarse grass clumps in the dune valleys. **17 cm** (Duinlewerik)

NEAR THREATENED

3 Barlow's Lark *Calendulauda barlowi* R E

Fairly common, endemic resident. Similar to (2) but with stronger coloration and bolder markings, these varying according to location. Birds in the north of its range resemble (2), but **upperparts have dark feather centres, distinct facial markings** and **bolder breast streaking**. In the south, range overlaps with that of (4), from which it differs in unstreaked flanks. The song phrase follows the pattern of the other 'red-backed larks', but variable throughout its range. Occupies a range between the Koichab River east of Lüderitz and south to Port Nolloth. Occurs in association with *Euphorbia* scrub-vegetated dunes and sparse succulent Karoo vegetation. **19 cm** (Barlowlewerik)

4 Karoo Lark *Calendulauda albescens* E

Fairly common, endemic resident. The smallest of the 'red-backed larks'. Distinguished by **slender bill** and **breast streaking that extends onto the belly and especially onto the flanks**. Coloration of upperparts varies from pale grey-brown on the west coast to rich rufous-brown or red in the western interior. In all colour morphs, **upperparts are well streaked**. The song differs from that of (5) in being higher-pitched and shorter. Occurs in dense succulent Karoo scrub and strandveld; does not occur in areas lacking bushes. **17 cm** (Karoolewerik)

VULNERABLE

5 Red Lark *Calendulauda burra* E

Fairly common, endemic resident. The **largest** and most distinctive of the four 'red-backed larks'. It has a comparatively **long tail**, a **stubby, deep bill** and a heavy flight action. Coloration of **upperparts ranges from brick-red with no dark streaking** in northern and eastern dune regions to much **browner and variably streaked** in central and southern regions. All are **heavily blotched on the breast**, but with **plain bellies and flanks**. The song, repeated monotonously every two to five seconds, is a series of 'chip-chip-chip' lead-in notes followed by one or more low whistles and a slow, complex trill at the end. Occurs on well-vegetated red sand dunes in the north and east and on scrubby Karoo plains further south; seldom on stony ground. **19 cm** (Rooilewerik)

clear white eyebrow

a

boldly streaked above

boldly streaked

no rufous in wing

b

western birds have thicker bills

1

plain, dune-red upperparts

light spotting

2

c

geographical variations in streaking and colour of upperparts

slender bill

3

plain flanks

4

streaking extends onto belly and flanks

5

geographical variations in streaking and colour of upperparts

thick bill

broad, blotchy streaking

plain belly and flanks

1 Dusky Lark *Pinarocorys nigricans*

Uncommon, non-breeding summer visitor. **Dark coloration** and **bold markings of face and breast** resemble Groundscraper Thrush (p. 350), but **upperparts darker, bill more robust** and **legs white**. Like that species, flicks wings open while walking around. No distinctive call. Occurs in scattered flocks in low-altitude bushveld and broad-leaved woodland, foraging in open patches and occasionally perching in trees. Flies with sharply dipping flight. **19 cm** (Donkerlewerik)

2 Short-clawed Lark *Certhilauda chuana*   E

Uncommon endemic resident. Shape and posture similar to Buffy Pipit (p. 326) with **longish, slender and slightly decurved bill** and **long tail**. Long **eyebrow** gives it a capped appearance. **Upperparts well streaked** with no rufous on crown or wings, but **rusty colour on rump**. The call is a shrill 'phew-pheeoo-pheeoo, phew-pheeoo-pheeoo, pheeeeeoo, pheeeit…' with variations including several clear trills, usually uttered from the top of a bush. In display flight, rises and then drops steeply, calling a long, drawn-out 'foooeeee' much like the related long-billed larks (p. 316). Found in dry grassland with scattered bushes and *Acacia* savanna in the vicinity of Polokwane, as well as in southeastern Botswana and adjacent South Africa. **17–18 cm** (Kortkloulewerik)

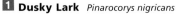

3 Flappet Lark *Mirafra rufocinnamomea*

Common resident. Similar to (4); best identified by territorial behaviour, different habitat and largely exclusive distribution. **Pallid northwestern race** *M. r. smithersi* (a) has shorter, stouter bill than **rufous eastern race** *M. r. pintoi* (b). Has a soft 'tuee-tui' call. Unobtrusive in non-breeding season. When breeding (early to late summer according to locality), male performs a high aerial cruise, making a thin, wispy call with bursts of clearly audible wing-claps, the sound a muffled 'purrit-purrit, purrit-purrit', like a ringing telephone. This is repeated after a pause; see illustration. Local variations occur in this flight pattern. Like other larks, may also ascend into wind to some height and then descend almost vertically before flying parallel to the ground prior to settling. Most common in open, stony, broad-leaved woodland, but locally also in hilly grassland, grassland fringing woodland and bushveld with grassy areas. **16 cm** (Laeveldklappertjie)

4 Eastern Clapper Lark *Mirafra fasciolata*   N E

Previously lumped with (5), but now considered a full species. Distribution replaces (3) in open grasslands. A medium-sized, rather dumpy lark with overall **rich rufous plumage** (conspicuous in flight), a **stubby bill** and **intricately patterned upperparts**. Difficult to distinguish from (5) unless display flight witnessed, but ranges barely overlap. May sing from the ground, but sings most strikingly when displaying. Mostly unobtrusive but when breeding (Oct–Feb), males display by flying steeply upwards, hovering briefly with audible wing-clapping, then dropping steeply while uttering a long, drawn-out 'fooeeeeee' which rises in pitch (opposite of Eastern Long-billed Lark, p. 316); see illustration. Also mimics the songs of other birds. Occurs singly or in pairs in open grassland. **16–17 cm** (Hoëveldklappertjie)

5 Cape Clapper Lark *Mirafra apiata*   E

Previously lumped with (4), but now considered a full species. The race *M. a. marjoriae* is sometimes considered a separate species (Agulhas Clapper Lark). Similar to (4), but darker overall: **upperparts and wings dark brown or greyish brown, with intricate barring patterns**. Best identified by display flight and song: audible wing-clapping faster than (4) and ascending whistle with greater change in pitch than (4). Birds in southern fynbos give two-note, descending songs. Inhabits fynbos, coastal scrub and Karoo plains. **15 cm** (Kaapse Klappertjie)

bold face pattern
(cf. Groundscraper Thrush, p. 350)

1

dark
upperparts

heavily
spotted
breast

**opens
wings while
foraging**

white
legs

capped
effect

rather long,
slender,
decurved bill

no
rufous

2

long
tail

a

3

b

intricate
pattern

appears dark
and rich rufous
on the ground

4

mottled

wings rich
rufous in
flight

dark brown or
greyish brown
upperparts

5

eastern birds
overall very red

noticeable
barring
pattern

**wide plumage
variations;
western birds
often paler**

'tooeeeeeee

1 Red-capped Lark *Calandrella cinerea*

Common resident. **Rufous crown and pectoral patches** diagnostic. Immature dark brown over entire upperparts, the breast well speckled blackish. The normal call is a brief 'cheep', 'chirrup' or 'cheeree'. Occurs in small to large flocks in short grass and especially dry pans, airstrips and dirt roads, walking rapidly or running, flying short distances then dropping down again. **15 cm** (Rooikoplewerik)

2 Spike-heeled Lark *Chersomanes albofasciata* N E

Common, near-endemic resident. Many races, the two colour extremes illustrated: northwestern (a) and southeastern (b). Characterised by erect stance, **long, slender, decurved bill** and **short tail with white terminal bar**. The **hind claw is long and straight**, but this is difficult to see in the field. Utters a rapid, mellow trill in flight. Occurs in small, loose parties in a wide range of habitats, from stony highveld grassland, Karoo scrubland to Kalahari dunes. Largely terrestrial in habits but perches briefly on low vegetation. **15–16 cm** (Vlaktelewerik)

3 Large-billed Lark *Galerida magnirostris* E

Common endemic resident. A **robust, heavily marked lark** with a fairly **short tail, heavy bill with a yellow base** and well-marked upperparts. The song is a short, musical 'chit-whitleooo-leooo' like a rusty gate being opened, with variations and repeated at brief intervals. Occurs in grassland, montane grassland, Karoo and wheat fields, being especially common on grassy roadside verges. Also common in high-altitude scrub in Lesotho. **18 cm** (Dikbeklewerik)

1

rufous crown

rufous pectoral patches

darkness of belly variable

a

2

long and slender, decurved bill

b

contrasting white throat

short tail, white terminal bar

eastern birds have rich rufous coloration below

long hind claw (spike-heel) difficult to see

heavy bill with yellow lower mandible

3

heavily marked

LONG-BILLED LARKS

Until recently considered to be a single, wide-ranging species, namely *Certhilauda curvirostris* (Long-billed Lark), but genetic, vocal and other evidence now supports the distinction of five separate species. Regional variations complicate identification, and vocalisations are confusingly similar: the **male's common call is a long, drawn-out 'cheeeeooo' that descends in pitch** (the opposite of the clapper larks, p. 312). The call is normally delivered while **plummeting downwards after a brief flight**. Best identified by distribution and subtle plumage differences.

1 Cape Long-billed Lark *Certhilauda curvirostris* E
Uncommon, localised resident. The largest and longest-billed of the *Certhilauda* species. Bill longest in males, some of which have **almost hoopoe-like, decurved bills**. Rather **pale, off-white below** and **heavily streaked**, with **markings extending down flanks**. Occurs sparingly in the Western Cape on coastal dunes from St Helena Bay to Langebaan. Occurs inland on Malmesbury shales south and east to Tygerberg and Gouda. It avoids mountain fynbos. **20–24 cm** (Weskuslangbeklewerik)

2 Karoo Long-billed Lark *Certhilauda subcoronata* E
Very common resident. Widespread, with considerable plumage variation across its extensive range. Normally **rich brown**, with contrasting **greyish nape** and reasonably **streaked breast, the streaking not continuing onto flanks** like (1) or (4). Prefers semi-arid dwarf shrublands of the Nama and succulent Karoo biomes, as well as southern Namibia. Prefers rocky or stony regions but is not confined to them. **18–22 cm** (Karoolangbeklewerik)

3 Benguela Long-billed Lark *Certhilauda benguelensis* R N E
Fairly common in the Namib and extending into southern Angola. Southern limit of range unclear; overlaps with very similar (2), from which it is distinguished with difficulty. Prefers arid and semi-arid grasslands and shrublands on rocky hills. **18–20 cm** (Kaokolangbeklewerik)

4 Agulhas Long-billed Lark *Certhilauda brevirostris* E
Very common resident. Within its small range, easily recognised by **heavily streaked appearance**, the **streaking extending down the flanks**. **Greyish brown** (not rich brown) above, and shorter-billed than (2). Restricted to the Agulhas plains from Bot River to George and extending up the Breede River valley. Occurs in stony wheat fields and pasture lands; also in succulent Karoo vegetation. Avoids mountain fynbos. **18–20 cm** (Overberglangbeklewerik)

NEAR THREATENED

5 Eastern Long-billed Lark *Certhilauda semitorquata* E
Uncommon, localised resident. The **smallest, dullest** and **least streaked** of the *Certhilauda* species. **Longish tail and bill** impart a pipit-like appearance. It occurs sparsely throughout its extensive range, preferring rocky slopes and ridges in grassland. **16–20 cm** (Grasveldlangbeklewerik)

1

long bill

grey-brown
above

heavy, dark
markings all
over

2

robust bill

rich brown
coloration

3

light chestnut
upperparts

overall paler
than (2)
(variable)

4

whitish with
dark streaking
on underparts

5

grey blotching
on breast

pale rufous

1 Rudd's Lark *Heteromirafra ruddi* R E

Uncommon, highly localised endemic resident. Told by **long legs, short, narrow tail, bulbous head** with **pale eye-stripes and central head-stripe**. Best seen in summer when male cruises about 15–35 m above ground alternately wing-flapping (noiselessly) and planing while calling 'pitchoo-cheree, pitchoo-cheree' rising on the last syllable. Does not mimic like other aerial-singing larks. Occurs singly in high-altitude grassland. A critically threatened species. **14–15 cm** (Drakensberglewerik)

CRITICALLY ENDANGERED

2 Botha's Lark *Spizocorys fringillaris* R E

Uncommon, localised endemic resident. Has a **conspicuous eye-stripe** and **dark, dappled upperparts**, much darker than any other small lark. Shows **streaked flanks, white or very pale belly** and **white outer tail-feathers**. On take-off calls 'chuck', often repeatedly, otherwise calls 'tcheree' several times in flight or while settled. Occurs in pairs or small parties in heavily grazed flats or upper slopes of high-altitude grassland and farmlands. Often associates with (3), but is undemonstrative and inconspicuous, with no aerial displays. **12 cm** (Vaalrivierlewerik)

ENDANGERED

3 Pink-billed Lark *Spizocorys conirostris* N E

Fairly common, near-endemic resident. A regionally variable, but **richly patterned**, finch-like lark with **straw-coloured outer tail-feathers**. Palest race (a) in the west, most rufous race (b) in the south and east; **short, conical, pink bill** in all races. The call is 'chiZIC' or 'twee twee twee'. Usually occurs in pairs or small parties in grassland, especially where grass is seeding; also burned and heavily grazed ground, and clumpy grasses on Kalahari sand. Can be difficult to see. **12 cm** (Pienkbeklewerik)

4 Sclater's Lark *Spizocorys sclateri* R E

Uncommon, localised endemic resident. Differs from (5) in richer colouring, bold facial markings including diagnostic **blackish mark below eye, more slender bill** and **lack of crest**. Some races paler than illustrated. The call, while feeding, is 'proo proo, turt turt, cheer cheer…'. Pairs, often flocks of six to 20, occur on arid plains, often in areas covered in flat stones and virtually devoid of plants. **13 cm** (Namakwalewerik)

NEAR THREATENED

5 Stark's Lark *Spizocorys starki* N E

Common to locally abundant, near-endemic resident. A **pale lark** with **small crest** giving its head a peaked appearance when raised. Crest and **distinct markings on the upperparts** distinguish it from (6). It has a melodious, rambling flight-display song 'prrt prrt troo chip chip pee-it…'. Occurs in arid grassland, sometimes in large flocks near pans in the dry season. When disturbed, flocks take off and fly in a wide arc before resettling. **13 cm** (Woestynlewerik)

6 Gray's Lark *Ammomanopsis grayi* R N E

Locally common, near-endemic resident. **Palest of the small larks, appearing almost white** in the field. Has **plain upperparts**, no white rump or crest and **short, pale, conical bill**. The alarm call is 'chee chee chee', while the song, heard in flight before dawn, is a high-pitched 'chee chee, sweet sweet…' series. Occurs in small parties in desert gravel plains near rock outcrops. When alarmed may remain motionless and unseen. If flushed, flies off low for a short distance before resettling. Nomadic within its range. **14 cm** (Namiblewerik)

head appears bulbous in the field

pale stripe down middle of crown

pinkish-grey bill

1

2

very short, thin tail

rather long legs

white or very pale below

outer tail-feathers white

streaking extends to flanks

a

3

regionally variable – western birds paler

bill looks heavy and slightly upturned

4

b

conical pink bill

white throat contrasts with rufous or buff belly

bold blackish mark below eye

outer tail-feathers straw-coloured

plain flanks

small crest raised in display

pale bill

5

pale, unmarked upperparts

6

upperparts straw-coloured ((6) is much creamier)

very pale below

very pale

SPARROW-LARKS

Small, sparrow-like larks with marked sexual plumage differences. Gregarious, usually **appearing in flocks even when breeding**. Sparrow-larks are nomadic with regional fluctuations influenced by rainfall and abundancy of food (seeds). Their habitat is mainly open grassland, scrubland and semi-arid areas.

1 Chestnut-backed Sparrow-Lark *Eremopterix leucotis*
Common to locally abundant resident. Both sexes differ from other sparrow-larks in having **chestnut wing coverts** and **grey underwings**. Female similar to females of (2) and (3), but has **thin whitish collar** and **dark belly spot**. Has a sharp, rattling call 'chip-chwep' and pretty song in fluttering flight. Flocks occur on open flats, airfields and cultivated lands, usually with low bushes nearby; typically on reddish soils. Makes off in low, irregular flight when disturbed, then suddenly resettles. **12–13 cm** (Rooiruglewerik)

2 Black-eared Sparrow-Lark *Eremopterix australis*   E
Common endemic resident. The male has **no white plumage**; the **upperparts of both sexes are rufous** while the **belly of the female lacks the black patch** of other female sparrow-larks. It calls 'cht cht cht' in flight. It occurs in sparse, dwarf shrublands and grasslands, mostly on red sands. **12–13 cm** (Swartoorlewerik)

3 Grey-backed Sparrow-Lark *Eremopterix verticalis*   N E
Very common, near-endemic resident. Both sexes are distinguished by **grey upperparts**. Male further differs from male of (1) in **small white cap**. Flocks make various shrill chirps while feeding. The flocks, often very large, occur in a wide variety of semi-arid to arid grasslands, gravel plains with scattered bushes or trees and dry pans. Typically on pale, calcrete soils. **12–13 cm** (Grysruglewerik)

1 ♂ ♀

whitish collar

chestnut

dark belly patch

chestnut

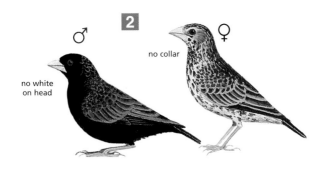

2 ♂ ♀

no collar

no white on head

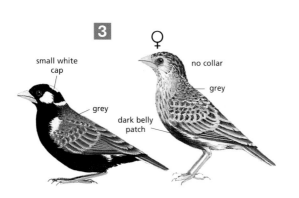

3 ♀

small white cap

grey

dark belly patch

no collar

grey

PIPITS, LONGCLAWS AND WAGTAILS

Small, insectivorous **terrestrial birds**, water-associated in wagtails. The sexes are alike or closely similar, all with **white or buff outer tail-feathers**. Pipits are among the most difficult birds to identify in the field. Reliable identification relies on careful observation of the **coloration of bare parts** (influenced by blood circulation), as well as proportions, calls, tail-wagging, behaviour and **subtle plumage differences**. Nevertheless, it is often impossible to confidently identify pipits to species level. Most pipits utter a 'chissik' or 'chip' call on take-off, their **flight low and dipping**. Longclaws are large, colourful pipits, while wagtails are mostly well known because of their **confiding and friendly behaviour**. Wagtails (and many pipits) have the habit of **continually bobbing their tails up and down**.

VULNERABLE

1 Short-tailed Pipit *Anthus brachyurus*

Uncommon resident. **Small size, short, narrow tail, dark upperparts** and **well-streaked chest** (on white or buff background) diagnostic. Occurs singly or in pairs, sparsely distributed in grassland but inconspicuous and elusive. Entirely terrestrial, never perching on bushes. It may utter a short song while perched on a mound 'cheeroo, trree tree trree trreeree, trree trree…'. This song is also uttered in wide circular display flight, performed mostly just before dawn. When disturbed, it flushes reluctantly and flies off directly, showing its **white outer tail-feathers**, the **wings appearing broad-based and triangular**. **12 cm** (Kortstertkoester)

2 Bushveld Pipit *Anthus caffer*

Fairly common resident. Differs from (3) in **smaller size, off-white throat, breast markings less distinct but forming stripes**, and more **rufous or golden coloration**. Face markings indistinct, except for pronounced **pale eye-ring**. From a tree-top perch calls 'skeer-trurp, skeer-trurp, skeer-trurp-skee-skee…'; from the ground or when flushed, calls 'tshweep'. Usually occurs singly. Sparsely distributed in rocky broad-leaved woodland or dry bushveld. If disturbed on the ground, makes off with erratic flight, then settles on a tree from where it may call. **13,5 cm** (Bosveldkoester)

3 Tree Pipit *Anthus trivialis*

Uncommon summer visitor. **Short, stubby bill with pink base, white throat, pale yellowish breast with tear-shaped spots** (becoming finer and more linear on the flanks) useful identifying characteristics, but best identified by behaviour. Flight call 'teez'; also has a canary-like song. Occurs singly or in pairs (in flocks when migrating) in woodland, parks and gardens, mostly in Zimbabwe and Mozambique. Forages on the ground with flexed legs, gently pumping tail. When disturbed takes refuge in a tree, where it walks confidently along the branches. **16 cm** (Boomkoester)

4 Red-throated Pipit *Anthus cervinus*   **V**

Vagrant. In breeding plumage, has **variable amount of brick-red on its throat** and even on the breast and eyebrow, traces of which may be visible in non-breeding plumage. Otherwise differs from similar (3) in **heavier breast-streaking** (not becoming finer on flanks), **pale lores**, much **thinner and more pointed bill with yellowish (not pink) base** and a **streaked rump**. Does not habitually perch in trees or wag its tail like (3). **Outer tail-feathers appear very white** in flight. Frequents marshes, estuaries, vleis and wet fields. Breeds in the Arctic; normally winters in East Africa. **14,5 cm** (Rooikeelkoester)

1

lacks clear facial markings

heavy streaking

white or dark-buff belly

2

rufous or golden; heavily marked

apart from eye-ring, lacks distinct facial markings

white

clear eyebrow

short, stubby bill

3

pale yellowish background

streaks thinner on flanks

continuous gentle tail pumping

thin pointed bill with yellowish base

N-Br

Br

4

contrasting streaky back and rump

breast and flanks heavily streaked

whitish feather edges

1 African Pipit *Anthus cinnamomeus*

Common resident. By far the most common and widespread pipit species, occurring in virtually any open grassland, including urban areas. Fairly easily identified by small size, **white (not buff) outer tail-feathers, yellow base to the bill, bold facial markings** and **boldly marked breast**. When disturbed, takes off with a diagnostic 'chissik' call and characteristic dipping flight. Male utters 'chree-chree-chree-chree' during each dip of its undulating display flight. Usually occurs singly or in pairs. **16 cm** (Gewone Koester)

2 Long-billed Pipit *Anthus similis*

Common resident. Significantly larger than (1), from which it further differs in **less distinct breast streaking** and **buff (not white) outer tail-feather edges**. The **base of the bill is yellow**, but bill length is not a field feature. The **upperparts are lightly streaked**, but may look plain from a distance, cf. Buffy Pipit (p. 326) and (1). May call for long periods from a rock, bush or fence, a clear metallic 'kilink' or 'chip, chreep, chroop, chreep, chip…'. Occurs singly on hillsides, especially stony regions with sparse vegetation, and in burned areas. Sometimes bobs tail gently in relaxed, shallow motions while foraging. **18 cm** (Nicholsonkoester)

3 Kimberley Pipit *Anthus pseudosimilis* E

Status unclear. Recently described (2002) as a separate species. Field identification problematic. Closer in size and shape to darker (2), but plumage most like (1). Shows **bold breast streaks or blotches, strong facial markings, broad creamy eyebrow, black malar stripe, yellowish base to bill, dark crown** and clearly **scalloped mantle**. Ear coverts sometimes **rufous** (especially in male). **Legs orange; outer tail-feathers buff or white**. In the field appears squat and lark-like, but long-legged. Gives single, clipped notes in flight at measured intervals. Song like (2), delivered either in low display flight or from a perch. Often crouches while feeding, and flicks tail more than (2), usually with deliberate downward motion. Occurs on sparsely vegetated plains in arid western regions, but distribution poorly documented. **18 cm** (Kimberleykoester)

4 Mountain Pipit *Anthus hoeschi*

Fairly common, localised summer resident. Resembles a large version of (1) but **upperparts darker, breast more boldly streaked, base of bill pink (not yellow), outer tail-feathers buff**. Call similar to that of (1) but deeper, slower. Occurs in montane grassland above 2 000 m in Lesotho and surroundings during summer; believed to overwinter in eastern Angola. **18 cm** (Bergkoester)

5 Wood Pipit *Anthus nyassae*

Fairly common, localised resident. Wooded habitat is first clue to this pipit's identity: it occurs only in miombo broad-leaved woodland, where it readily perches in trees if disturbed, otherwise forages on the ground in clearings. Closely similar to (2) but ranges not known to overlap. Also, it is **more slender, bill and tail slightly shorter** and **eyebrow whiter** and more pronounced. Song similar to (2), but higher-pitched and usually delivered from a tree. **18 cm** (Boskoester)

small size

distinct facial markings

yellow bill base

marked mantle

1

neat necklace of streaks

white outer tail-feathers

face not as boldly marked as (1)

mantle with weak markings (can look plain)

bill not always longer than other pipits

weak breast streaking

2

facial markings more striking and russety than (2)

overall paler than (2)

may appear taller and more slender than (2)

3

distinctive grey and brown streaks on back

4

pink lower mandible

breast heavily marked

pale underparts

pale buff feather edges

dark, streaked back

5

pale brown streaks

pale buff feather edges

1 Buffy Pipit *Anthus vaalensis*

Uncommon resident. **Mantle plain and unstreaked** like (2). **Malar streaks variable**, but usually not pronounced. **Breast streaking variable**, often indistinct, **edges of outer tail-feathers pale buff**, the **base of the bill pink**. In flight utters an occasional 'chissik' or single 'chik' call. Frequently bobs its tail in a deep, exaggerated motion, the whole rear half of the body moving up and down. Has the habit of running a short distance, then standing erect with breast thrown out. Occurs singly in short, open grassland and on bare ground dotted with anthills and low scrub. Where distribution overlaps with (2), identification can be problematic; typically frequents drier habitats than that species. **19 cm** (Vaalkoester)

2 Plain-backed Pipit *Anthus leucophrys*

Fairly common resident. Told by **indistinct breast markings** and **lack of distinct markings on the upperparts** like (1). Difficult to distinguish from that species, but not as lanky, with proportionally **shorter tail and legs**, a **yellow (not pink) base to its bill** and a **more pronounced pale eyebrow (variable)**. **Edges of outer tail-feathers are buff.** From the ground calls a sparrow-like 'jhreet-jhroot'. Occurs singly or in small flocks in moist grassland with short or burned grass; also fallow lands and hilly coastal regions. Bobs tail deeply, but motion not quite as exaggerated as (1), and typically only when standing still (not while foraging). **17 cm** (Donkerkoester)

DATA DEFICIENT

3 Long-tailed Pipit *Anthus longicaudatus*

Recently described; status uncertain and validity under investigation. A **large**, **plain-backed** pipit with **longish, broad and square-tipped tail** (outer tail-feathers buff), **shortish bill** (buffy at base of lower mandible), **long tarsus** and **short claws**. Head shows **prominent eyebrows and malar stripes**; the **upper breast only lightly spotted or smudged**. Best told by behaviour: it bobs its rear body and tail frequently and adopts a horizontal posture when feeding. Visits the Kimberley region during winter, but probably more widespread. **19 cm** (Langstertkoester)

4 African Rock Pipit *Anthus crenatus* E

Locally common endemic resident. Drab, indistinctly marked, appearing **almost plain-backed** (light mottling visible in good light). At close range **yellowish shoulder-patch and feather edges** visible, plus **faint streaking on breast**. Other features include prominent **creamy eyebrow and submoustachial streak**, offset by **dark moustachial and malar streaks**. Underparts often saturated with **dark buff colour**. Has a characteristic erect stance while calling from a low perch 'treee-terroooo, treee-terroooo', the last syllable descending; may call while hovering. Occurs singly or in pairs among rocks on grassy hillsides and montane grassland. **16 cm** (Klipkoester)

5 Striped Pipit *Anthus lineiventris*

Common resident. Distinguished by clearly **yellow-edged wing-feathers**, these more obvious than in (4), from which it also differs in **well-streaked underparts** on whitish background. **Face speckled**, lacking clearly delineated markings. Has a loud, whistling, thrush-like song unlike those of other pipits. Occurs singly or in pairs on well-wooded stony slopes, ridges, road cuttings and rocky banks of small rivers. When disturbed, flies to a tree, where it may perch lengthwise along a branch. **18 cm** (Gestreepte Koester)

1

pink lower mandible

unmarked sandy-brown

usually faint breast streaking

buff-coloured underparts

ong, heavy-ooking tail wagged in xaggerated motion

long legs

2

greyish brown, no distinct markings

yellow lower mandible

medium length legs

tail wagging not quite as pronounced as that of (1)

3

unmarked, dark grey-brown

short bill

lightly smudged breast

long tail frequently bobbed up and down

characteristic erect stance when calling

distinct creamy eyebrow

4

faint breast streaking

plain or subtly mottled brown back

yellowish shoulder-patches and feather edges

yellow edges

5

greyish speckled face

heavily marked

underparts heavily streaked

VULNERABLE

1 Yellow-breasted Pipit *Anthus chloris*   R E

Rare, localised endemic resident. **Yellow underparts** diagnostic, but difficult to see, as bird skulks in the grass. **White outer tail-feathers** and **streaked mantle** recall African Pipit (p. 324). **Non-breeding plumage lacks yellow** except for underwing coverts and sometimes small patch on belly; buffy-white below with light streaking on breast as illustrated. Male calls from grass tufts and in hovering flight, a rapid chipping 'chip chip chip chip…'. Occurs singly or in pairs in dense, high-altitude montane grassland, where it breeds in summer, moving to lower-altitude grassland in winter. Inconspicuous and secretive; lies close in the grass and flushes reluctantly, but flies far away if flushed. **16–18 cm** (Geelborskoester)

2 Golden Pipit *Tmetothylacus tenellus*   V

Very rare vagrant from northeast Africa. Much smaller than (3); **male's breast-band does not reach the base of the bill**. Male **appears rich yellow** at all times, including the wings and tail. **Female is buffy and has no breast-band**, but shows **yellow edges to tail-feathers**. In both sexes the visible **upper leg (tibia) is unfeathered**. A terrestrial species; frequents dry bushveld, occasionally perching on bushes. **15 cm** (Goudkoester)

3 Yellow-throated Longclaw *Macronyx croceus*

Common resident. Differs from Bokmakierie (p. 420) in **scalloped brown upperparts** and **pink-brown legs**; cf. that species. Distinguished from (5) by **yellow (not orange) throat**; like that species shows **broad white tail-tips** in flight. Utters a monotonous mewing from the top of a bush 'triooo, triooo, trroo-chit-chit, trroo-chit-chit-trroo-chit' and sings in flight. A terrestrial species. Occurs singly or in pairs in moist grassland with scattered trees. **20 cm** (Geelkeelkalkoentjie)

4 Fülleborn's Longclaw *Macronyx fuelleborni*   V

Similar to (3) but duller; **yellow about the body. Lacks any black streaking on the sides of the breast below the black gorget**. Makes a sparrow-like chirping and a whistling 'jee-o-wee' from the tops of bushes. Common in Angola and has been reported in the extreme north of Namibia (unconfirmed). Not yet positively recorded in the subregion, but probably an occasional visitor. **21 cm.** (Angolakalkoentjie)

5 Cape Longclaw *Macronyx capensis*   E

Common endemic resident. **Orange throat with black surround** is diagnostic of adult. Immature's throat may be same colour as underparts; then distinguished from (3) by **deeper yellow coloration and buff (not yellow) edges to wing-feathers**. Normal call is a mewing 'me-yew'; also a far-reaching whistle. Occurs singly or in pairs in grassland. Often momentarily stands upright on a grass tuft, stone or anthill. If disturbed, flies a short distance, uttering its characteristic call and showing off its **broad, white-tipped tail. 20 cm** (Oranjekeelkalkoentjie)

NEAR THREATENED

6 Rosy-throated Longclaw *Macronyx ameliae*

Uncommon resident. Adult male unmistakable. Female and immature **less pink, throat more buffy, black gorget vestigial**. The call is a squeaky 'teee-yoo tyip-tyip-tyip-TEE YOOOO'. Occurs singly or in pairs in marshy grassland. Less conspicuous than other longclaws. Lies low when approached, then makes off in erratic flight for a short distance; **white outer tail-feathers** (not white tips), **white wing-bars** and **dark back markings** can be seen before the bird settles and hides again. **20 cm** (Rooskeelkalkoentjie)

streaked mantle (like longclaws; unlike other pipits)

white outer tail

2

yellow wings

♂

black band does not extend to face

♀

1

N-Br

light streaking

unfeathered tibia

black gorget

cf. (3)

4

no black streaks on breast sides

white tail-tips visible in flight

3

dull yellow

5

rich orange

scalloped

no white wing-bar

tail shows clear white tips (conspicuous in flight)

♀ J

duller below

6

white along length of outer tail

black gorget

white wing-bar visible in flight

♂

1 Western Yellow Wagtail *Motacilla flava*

Locally common summer visitor. Many distinct races visit southern Africa; best identified by the differing head patterns that males acquire in late summer after completing their moult. Identification of non-breeding males and females almost impossible. At least five races have been recorded (some are sometimes considered separate species). Most common are *M. f. flava* (Blue-headed Wagtail; not illustrated), *M. f. lutea* (Yellow-headed Wagtail; (c)) and *M. f. thunbergi* (Grey-headed Wagtail; (a)). Less often encountered are *M. f. beema* (Sykes's Wagtail; (d)) and *M. f. feldegg* (Black-headed Wagtail; (b)). Overall distinguished from (2) by **shorter tail, olive-green (not grey) upperparts** including rump, and **entirely yellow underparts**. Non-breeding birds (especially females and immatures) much duller; **yellow coloration faint and restricted to lower belly**. Immature in first winter plumage can also be confused with (2); cf. that species. The call is 'tsee-ip'. Occurs singly in floodplains and moist grassland; often at sewage works or in cattle pens and feedlots. **18 cm** (Geelkwikkie)

2 Grey Wagtail *Motacilla cinerea* 　R

Rare summer visitor. Distinguished from (1) by **grey upperparts (not olive-green), dark shoulder-patch** and **white throat. Long tail is yellow at base** (above and below). **Yellow-and-white underparts with faint brownish smudges**; cf. (1). Unlike other wagtails, **legs pinkish** (not black). Call is a short, metallic 'tit' or 'tidit'. Walks about bobbing its long tail constantly, usually near fast-flowing water in wooded environments and in association with Mountain Wagtail (p. 332). **18 cm** (Gryskwikkie)

3 Citrine Wagtail *Motacilla citreola* 　V

Rare vagrant. Could only be confused with (1) and (2), but can be told from both by **white wing-bars** and **whitish (not bright yellow) vent**. In breeding plumage (during the southern winter) further differs from (1) in **longer tail, black hind-collar** and **grey (not olive-green) mantle**. Differs from (2) in **longer black (not pinkish) legs**. In non-breeding plumage, identified by **grey flanks, pale lores** and **eyebrow that extends down behind the ear coverts**; also, **dusky cheeks and crown, no black hind-collar** and **less yellow below**. A central European species, currently expanding its range westwards. The majority of the global population spends the non-breeding season in southeast Asia, but increasingly recorded in East Africa. A single bird was present at the Gamtoos River mouth in the Eastern Cape during the winter of 1998. Thought to be the result of 'misoriented migration'. **15,5–17 cm** (Sitrienkwikkie)

1 **N-Br**

olive-green
upperparts

b

a

c

d

variable
(females and
non-breeding males
much duller)

black legs

shortish
tail

J

2 ♂ **N-Br**

grey

yellow
rump

long tail

♂
Br

bright lemon-
yellow vent

♀ **N-Br**

pinkish legs

3 **Br** ♂

black hind-collar

grey (not
olive-green)

much white on
feather edges

N-Br ♂ ♀

whitish
vent

yellowish tinge to
breast feathers;
belly whitish

1 Mountain Wagtail   *Motacilla clara*

Fairly common, localised resident. Told by **very long tail** and mostly **grey-and-white coloration**; much paler than other wagtails. Calls 'chirrup' on taking flight; also sings 'ti-tuu-ui-tui-tui'. Pairs or small groups occur along fast-running forest rivers and streams in the eastern regions. Hops and flits from boulder to boulder with much tail-wagging. **19–20 cm** (Bergkwikkie)

2 Cape Wagtail   *Motacilla capensis*

Common resident. **Shorter-tailed** than Grey Wagtail (p. 330) and (1) and **greyer than other wagtails**. Northern races (b) have **breast-band absent or vestigial**. Call is a loud, cheerful 'tseep-eep' or 'tseeep'. Occurs singly or in pairs near water, in suburban gardens, cities and at sewage works. Walks about feeding on the ground, occasionally wagging its tail. If disturbed, will perch briefly on a tree, wall, fence or building. Tame and confiding. **18 cm** (Gewone Kwikkie)

3 African Pied Wagtail   *Motacilla aguimp*

Common resident. Told from other wagtails by striking **black-and-white plumage**; tail length as in (2). Female and juvenile have black areas of male replaced by dark brown or grey. Call is a loud 'tu-weee' and 'twee-twee-twee'. Occurs singly, in pairs or in family groups at lakes, dams, large rivers, sewage works, lagoons and estuaries. Habits much like (2) but enters suburbia only in the north of its distribution. **20 cm** (Bontkwikkie)

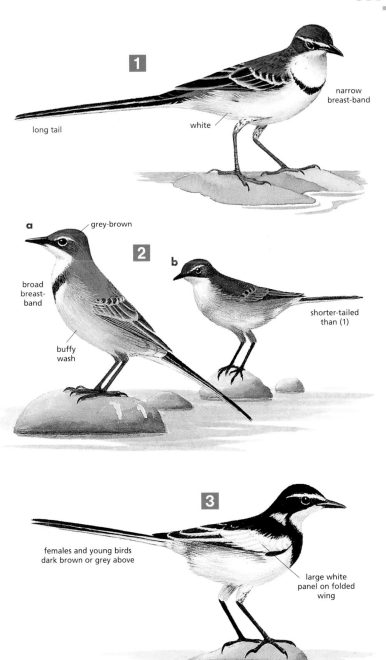

1
narrow breast-band
long tail
white

2
a grey-brown
broad breast-band
buffy wash
b
shorter-tailed than (1)

3
females and young birds dark brown or grey above
large white panel on folded wing

DRONGOS

Black insectivorous birds with **prominent rictal bristles**. They **hawk insects from a perch** in woodland and bushveld and are **pugnacious, habitually mobbing larger birds**, even pecking the heads of eagles. Species (2) and (3) belong in different family groups but are included on this plate for direct comparison with drongos, which they resemble. See also pp. 400–404 and p. 336.

1 Fork-tailed Drongo   *Dicrurus adsimilis*

Common resident. Differs from all similar black birds in **prominent forked tail, the outer feathers splayed outwards**; cf. (4), which has only a shallow fork in its tail. Other features are **deep ruby-red eye** and **powerful bill**. Sexes alike; immature as illustrated. Utters a variety of unmusical twanging notes interspersed with imitations of other bird calls, especially those of owls and other birds of prey. Occurs singly or in pairs in almost any non-forest habitat with trees. Noisy and aggressive. **25 cm** (Mikstertbyvanger)

2 Southern Black Flycatcher   *Melaenornis pammelaina*

(See p. 404 for full account.) The **tail shows a small indentation at the tip** (not a distinct fork, like (1)). Other tail-feathers are straight, not splayed like those of (1) and (4). **19–22 cm** (Swartvlieëvanger)

3 Black Cuckooshrike   *Campephaga flava*

(See p. 336 for full account.) Only the male is black, differing from similar black birds in having a **rounded tail** and prominent **orange-yellow gape**. Sometimes has a **yellow shoulder**. A quiet, arboreal species. **22 cm** (Swartkatakoeroe)

4 Square-tailed Drongo   *Dicrurus ludwigii*

Common, localised resident. Has **splayed outer tail-feathers** like (1) but with only a **shallow indentation**; also has **ruby-red eyes**. Calls are a loud 'cherit! cherit!' or 'cherit-wit-wit', plus other strident sounds and imitations of other bird calls. Occurs singly or in pairs in eastern evergreen forests, riparian forests and dense woodland, where it frequents the midstratum, hawking from a perch. Active, noisy and aggressive. **19 cm** (Kleinbyvanger)

ruby-red eye

strong, hooked bill

common and conspicuous in various habitats

J

1

tail splayed and deeply forked

J

2

dark brown iris

less robustly built than drongos

♂

3

orange-yellow gape

ruby-red eye

4

straight tail (not splayed)

square or shallowly notched tail

forages unobtrusively in canopy; does not pounce on prey from an exposed perch or hunt on the wing

rounded tail

tail splayed; shallowly forked or square-tipped

CUCKOOSHRIKES

A large family of slender, medium-sized birds with **sturdy bills**, neither related to Cuckoos nor Shrikes, despite some species having a superficial resemblance to both. They are found in pairs or small, loose groups in the larger trees of forest fringes, riparian forest and woodland. They **feed on insects (caterpillars in particular) and, occasionally, fruit.**

1 White-breasted Cuckooshrike *Coracina pectoralis*

Uncommon resident. Adults with **soft-grey upperparts** and contrasting **white underparts**. Throat grey in male, white in female. Immature like female but with white barring on upperparts; grey spotting below. In flight, **broad, square-ended tail** obvious. The call is a softly whistled 'duid duid' by the male, and a trilling 'che-e-e-e-e' by the female. Usually occurs singly in large trees in riparian forests and broad-leaved woodland. A lethargic species, moving from branch to branch with long hops, peering closely at leaves in search of insects or making short aerial sallies. Sparsely distributed. **27 cm** (Witborskatakoeroe)

2 Grey Cuckooshrike *Coracina caesia*

Uncommon, localised resident. **All-grey coloration** diagnostic; **female lacks the black lores**. Immature has white-tipped feathers, giving a freckled appearance. In flight, **broad, square-ended tail** obvious. The call is a quiet, high-pitched 'peeeeeooooo', usually while perched; also utters a variety of chittering and trilling sounds while feeding. Occurs singly or in pairs in eastern evergreen forests, riparian forests and forested valleys, where it frequents tree canopies. **27 cm** (Bloukatakoeroe)

3 Black Cuckooshrike *Campephaga flava*

Uncommon summer resident. See p. 334 for comparison of male with other similar black birds. About half of South African male birds show the **yellow shoulder** (a); in Zimbabwe and Botswana most males lack this (b). Female is strikingly different, **cuckoo-like** as illustrated. Immature like female, young males with increasing areas of black. The call, not often heard, is a soft, high-pitched trill 'trrrrrrrr…'. Pairs occur sparsely in a variety of wooded habitats, thornveld, mixed bushveld, broad-leaved woodland and coastal bush. Unobtrusive unless calling, frequenting the midstratum. Often joins bird parties. **22 cm** (Swartkatakoeroe)

1

grey plumage and large size impart dove-like appearance; looks large-headed with conspicuous dark eye

♀

♂

2

broad, square-ended tail conspicuous in flight and when perched

♂ **J**

3

orange gape (and inside of mouth)

♂ **a**

♂ **b**

variable yellow shoulder-patch on some males

heavy, rounded tail

♀

heavily barred (cf. female cuckoos p. 238–242)

yellow edges

bright yellow panel

CROWS

Large, mainly glossy black birds, and the largest members of the passerines. They are often seen in **large flocks**. They are **omnivorous and opportunistic**, with a diet ranging from seeds and fruits to the flesh of young, weakened or dead animals. Sexes are alike and immatures are similar to adults. All have **loud cawing calls**.

1 Pied Crow *Corvus albus*

Common and widespread resident. Distinguished by **white breast and collar**. The call is a loud 'kwaak'. A bold species usually found in association with human settlements, where it gleans food scraps, especially haunting refuse dumps, school playing fields, highways and farmlands. Usually in loose flocks or large communal roosts. **46–52 cm** (Witborskraai)

2 Cape Crow *Corvus capensis*

Common and widespread resident. **Entirely glossy black.** The call is a high-pitched 'kraaa'. Single birds, pairs or flocks frequent farmlands and open country. Generally less common than (1). Habitually perches and nests on pylons and tolerates more arid regions than (1). **48–53 cm** (Swartkraai)

3 White-necked Raven *Corvus albicollis*

Common, localised resident. Has a **white nape only**, otherwise **black** with a **very heavy, white-tipped bill**. In flight appears **broad-winged**, with a **short tail**. The call is a falsetto 'kraak', although deeper notes are sometimes uttered. Normally occurs in montane regions but wanders far in search of food. A bold species and a great scavenger, often feeding on carrion. Individuals usually forage alone but many may gather at food sources. **50–54 cm** (Withalskraai)

4 House Crow *Corvus splendens*   I

Common, localised resident. An introduced species. **Lacks any white plumage**. Smaller than (2) and with **grey nape, mantle and breast**. Voice a shrill 'kwaa, kwaa'. Strictly commensal with humans, occurring in Maputo, Inhaca Island, Durban, East London and Cape Town. **43 cm** (Huiskraai)

ORIOLES

Medium-sized family of birds, with **brightly coloured, predominantly yellow plumage and longish pink bills**. Their diet is omnivorous, but consists primarily of insects and fruit; they feed mostly in the canopies of large trees. Their **call is clear and liquid-sounding**.

5 Green-headed Oriole *Oriolus chlorocephalus*   R

Rare, localised resident. Distinguished from other orioles by **green upperparts (including head and throat)** and **yellow collar and underparts**. Sexes alike; immature is duller yellow below, the head a paler green. Call is very similar to African Black-headed Oriole (p. 340). In southern Africa, occurs only in the montane forests of Mount Gorongosa in central Mozambique, where it is locally common. **24 cm** (Groenkopwielewaal)

1

white breast
and collar

2

no
white

3

white
nape

massive bill
with white tip

broad
wings

short,
rounded tail

**very raptor-like
in flight**

4

grey

grey

green head may look
dark in forest interior

yellow collar isolates
head from green
mantle

5

1 Eurasian Golden Oriole *Oriolus oriolus*

Fairly common to uncommon summer visitor. Male differs from male of (2) in having **black wings** and **less extensive black mask**. Female resembles immature illustrated. The seldom-heard call is a ringing 'weela-weeoo', plus a churring alarm note common to all orioles. Occurs singly in broad-leaved woodland, mixed bushveld, riverine forests and various other well-wooded habitats – including exotic trees. Infrequent over much of the interior, females and immatures outnumbering males at all times. **24 cm** (Europese Wielewaal)

2 African Golden Oriole *Oriolus auratus*

Uncommon summer resident. Male is the **yellowest of all orioles** with a **distinct black line through the eye to the ear coverts**, this line also being present in immature. Female less bright than male, **upperparts greener, underparts paler**. The calls are liquid whistles 'wee-er-er-wul' or 'fee-yoo-fee-yoo-fee-yoo', longer than the calls of (3). Occurs in any well-developed woodland or riverine forest. **24 cm** (Afrikaanse Wielewaal)

3 Black-headed Oriole *Oriolus larvatus*

Common resident. Distinguished by **black head** and **pink bill**; cf. masked-weavers (p. 452), which are smaller with black bills. Sexes are alike; immature as illustrated. The usual call is a **loud, liquid 'pheeoo'** but it also utters a 'churr' alarm call. Singly or in pairs in moist, well-developed woodland or mixed bushveld, riverine forests and exotic trees. A noisy, conspicuous species. It is absent from the dry central and western regions. **25 cm** (Swartkopwielewaal)

mask does not extend markedly behind eye

♂

black wings

1

J

green tones

whitish

yellow tail tips

black mask extends behind eye

♂

yellow

2

black extends behind eye

J

yellow tones

yellowish

wholly yellow tail

black head

yellowish mantle

pink bill

3

J

green with dense streaking

BULBULS AND ALLIES

Frugivorous and insectivorous birds with **clear, whistling calls**. They frequent evergreen bush and forests. Sexes are alike, and immatures are duller.

1 Bush Blackcap *Lioptilus nigricapillus* R E

Uncommon endemic resident. Distinguished by **black cap** and **pink or orange bill and legs**. The song is a lively jumble of notes similar to Dark-capped Bulbul (p. 344) but more liquid and varied. Occurs singly or in pairs in **forest-fringing scrub at high altitudes**, especially on the slopes of the Drakensberg escarpment. Keeps mainly within cover and is not easily seen. **17 cm** (Rooibektiptol)

NEAR THREATENED

2 Sombre Greenbul *Andropadus importunus*

Common resident. Southern morph (a) is **plain olive-green**; northern morph (b), in lower Zambezi valley and beyond, is **much yellower, upperparts greener**. Eye colour diagnostic: **creamy-white** in adults of both colour morphs, greyish in immatures. Heard more often than seen. Usually calls a strident 'Willie!'; in the breeding season followed by a babbling trill. In southern coastal bush, call is often shortened to 'peeeit', usually answered by others of the same species. When agitated, this call becomes 'peeet peeet peeet…' in rapid succession. Usually occurs singly in forest fringes and adjacent thickets, riverine forests and well-wooded valleys; especially common in coastal bush. Not particularly secretive, but cryptic coloration makes it difficult to see. **19–24 cm** (Gewone willie)

3 Eastern Nicator *Nicator gularis*

Uncommon resident. Very similar in appearance to Western Nicator (*N. chloris*) found further north and west, which is slightly larger in size. Identified by **heavy, shrike-like bill** and **yellow-spotted wing-feathers**, the spots smaller in immatures. The call is a series of mellow trills and warbles rising to a climax and then restarting at low volume; call a loud 'chuck' when alarmed. Occurs singly in dense coastal, riverine and forest-fringe thickets or in the midstratum of riverine forests and mixed bushveld. Secretive and easily overlooked if not calling. Sparsely distributed. **23 cm** (Geelvleknikator)

4 Yellow-bellied Greenbul *Chlorocichla flaviventris*

Fairly common resident. **Olive-green upperparts** and **bright-yellow underparts** (including underwings), plus **reddish eyes with conspicuous white eyelids**. Immature similar, but crown the same colour as back. Noisy at times, the call is a loud, nasal 'pur, pur, pur, pur, peh, peh, peh, peh, peh…', often several birds at once. Occurs singly or in pairs in well-developed riverine forests, coastal and lowland forests, and thickets on moist, rocky hillsides. Spends much time foraging on the ground or in the midstratum. **20–23 cm** (Geelborswillie)

5 Terrestrial Brownbul *Phyllastrephus terrestris*

Common resident. A **very drab brown bird**, apart from the **white throat** and **reddish eyes**. Underparts barely paler than the upperparts; at close range a **yellowish gape** is discernible. Immature has redder wing-feather edges. **Usually in parties of six or more, individuals maintaining contact by quietly chuckling or murmuring**. Frequents dense riverside and hillside thickets, and dense undergrowth in forests and bushveld, **scratching noisily about in debris** and seldom ascending above the lower stratum. Easily overlooked unless heard. **21–22 cm** (Boskrapper)

creamy-white eye

plain olive-green overall

a

2

salmon-pink bill

black cap

1

grey

salmon-pink feet

creamy-white eye

b

yellowish below

yellow-spotted wing-feathers

powerful hooked bill

yellow tail tip

3

reddish eye with white 'eyelids'

4

yellow below

5

contrasting white throat

1 Dark-capped Bulbul *Pycnonotus tricolor*

Very common resident. **Dark, crested head, dark eye** and **yellow vent** identify this well-known species. Has several cheerful calls such as a short phrase sounding like 'Wake-up, Gregory' and a much-repeated 'chit, chit, chit…'. Gregarious, inhabiting most **moist eastern and northern regions** with bush and trees, especially riverine forests, but not evergreen forests. Abundant in **suburban gardens**. Noisy and tame; often one of the first species to sound the alarm when a predator is spotted. **20–22 cm** (Swartoogtiptol)

2 African Red-eyed Bulbul *Pycnonotus nigricans* N E

Very common, near-endemic resident. Differs from (1) mainly in **red eye-ring**. Has a variety of cheerful, chattering calls similar to (1); very alike in most other ways. Frequents **drier western regions**, usually associating with human habitation and bush along watercourses. Occasionally hybridises with (1) and (3), with the offspring showing characteristics intermediate between these species. **19–21 cm** (Rooioogtiptol)

3 Cape Bulbul *Pycnonotus capensis* E

Common endemic resident. Differs from (1) and (2) in **white eye-ring** and **browner appearance of head**. Has similar cheerful calls, including a liquid 'piet-piet-patata'. A lively, conspicuous species frequenting scrub, wooded watercourses and exotic coastal bush in the western and southern Cape. **19–21 cm** (Kaapse Tiptol)

4 Yellow-streaked Greenbul *Phyllastrephus flavostriatus*

Fairly common, localised resident. Told from (5) by **larger size, darker head, dark eye** with **white eye-ring** and **rather long, prominent bill. Yellow streaks of underparts** difficult to see in the field. Has various strident call notes 'chur, chur, chi-cheee…'. Small groups occur in the midstratum of evergreen forests and adjacent bush. Clambers about moss-covered tree trunks, branches and creepers, often hanging head downwards. Frequently flicks open one wing at a time. Tame and conspicuous, often in mixed bird parties. **18–21 cm** (Geelstreepboskruiper)

5 Tiny Greenbul *Phyllastrephus debilis*

Fairly common, localised resident. Much **smaller than (4); head and eye paler; bill paler and shorter.** Immature has greenish head and face. Has a loud, warbling song of explosive quality, a sibilant, ventriloquial call rising in pitch, and a gurgling alarm note. Frequents evergreen forests and fringing secondary growth. Warbler-like in behaviour, feeding in the upper and lower strata. Restricted distribution in northern Mozambique. **14 cm** (Kleinboskruiper)

6 Stripe-cheeked Greenbul *Andropadus milanjensis*

Fairly common, localised resident. **Distinctly green** with **dark-grey cap** and **white streaks on ear coverts. Underparts much greener** than Yellow-bellied Greenbul (p. 342). Mostly silent but has various harsh calls 'chuck, churr, chuck, churr-churr-trrrr…', made while sidling along a branch in small hops. Feeds at the edges of evergreen forests, dense lowland forest scrub, thickets and, sometimes, in broad-leaved woodland. Restricted distribution in eastern Zimbabwe and across the border into western Mozambique. **19–21 cm** (Streepwangwillie)

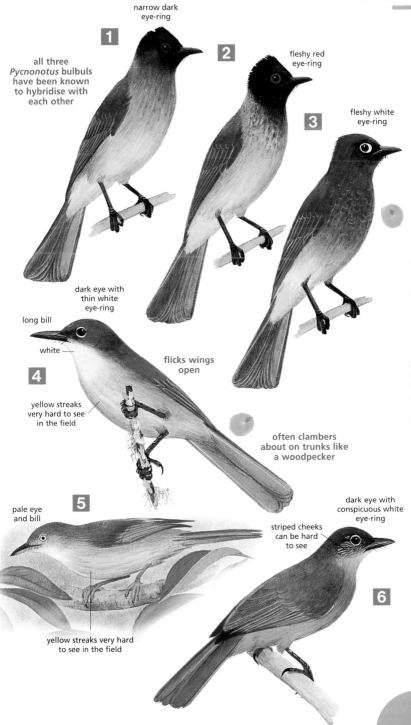

narrow dark
eye-ring

1

2

all three
Pycnonotus bulbuls
have been known
to hybridise with
each other

fleshy red
eye-ring

fleshy white
eye-ring

3

dark eye with
thin white
eye-ring

long bill

white

4

yellow streaks
very hard to see
in the field

flicks wings
open

often clambers
about on trunks like
a woodpecker

pale eye
and bill

5

dark eye with
conspicuous white
eye-ring

striped cheeks
can be hard
to see

6

yellow streaks very hard
to see in the field

TITS

Small insectivorous, arboreal birds with short stout bills, the **nostrils obscured by bristles**. They habitually forage in the tree canopies **in bird parties, clambering about the branches in agile fashion** and frequently **feeding in inverted positions**. They have rasping calls.

1 Southern Black Tit *Parus niger*

Common resident. Male distinguished from (2) by **heavier bill** and **more white on the vent and undertail**. Northern races may show more or less white on folded wings than illustrated. Female as illustrated or darker on underparts; immature similar. The calls are harsh and rasping, a rapid 'twiddy-zeet-zeet-zeet' or 'zeu-zeu-zeu-twit'. Pairs or groups occur in a wide variety of wooded habitats. **16 cm** (Gewone Swartmees)

2 Carp's Black Tit *Parus carpi* N E

Common, localised, near-endemic resident. In limited zone where distribution overlaps with (1), identification problematic. Slightly smaller than (1), the **vent and undertail with either small traces of white or none**, the **bill smaller** and **more white in the wing**. Female and immature are duller. Calls and habits like (1). Occurs in mopane and *Acacia* savanna in northern Namibia. **14 cm** (Ovamboswartmees)

3 Grey Tit *Parus afer* E

Common, endemic resident. Similar to (4) but ranges largely exclusive; distinguished by habitat preference where ranges overlap. Told from (4) by **grey-brown (not blue-grey) mantle and back, more tawny appearance** and **shorter tail**. Sexes are alike; immature similar. The call can be likened to 'Piet-jou-jou'. Pairs or small groups occur in Karoo scrub, dry thornveld, rocky hills and gorges; also open scrub in Lesotho highlands. A restless species, frequenting smaller trees and bushes and spending much time on the ground. **13 cm** (Piet-tjou-tjou-grysmees)

4 Ashy Tit *Parus cinerascens* N E

Common, near-endemic resident. Identified by **blue-grey mantle, back and underparts**; of generally greyer appearance than either (3) or (5). Sexes are alike; immature duller. Most often located by its lively bubbling and grating calls. Occurs singly or in pairs in thornveld and mixed bushveld, frequently in bird parties. **14 cm** (Acaciagrysmees)

5 Miombo Tit *Parus griseiventris*

Common resident. Distinguished from (4) by **white underparts (not grey)** and **broader white regions on sides of head**. Pairs, usually in bird parties, are found in the broad-leaved miombo woodland of Zimbabwe. **14 cm** (Miombogrysmees)

6 Rufous-bellied Tit *Parus rufiventris* R

Uncommon, localised resident. The western race *P. r. diligens* (a) with **black head, cream-coloured eyes** and **rufous underparts** distinctive (the underparts paler when not breeding). The pale eastern race *P. r. pallidiventris* (Cinnamon-breasted Tit) (b) occurs only in the Zimbabwe–Mozambique border regions; shows **dark brown eyes** and **pale cinnamon underparts**. Immature is duller, with brown eyes, the wing-feathers edged yellowish. Calls 'chik-wee' and a rasping 'chrrr'. Pairs and small groups frequent **well-developed miombo woodland**, feeding mostly in bird parties in the upper stratum. **15 cm** (Rooipensmees)

♂

restricted white in wings (variable)

♀

1

white barring

2

extensive white in wings (variable)

black

grey-brown mantle

3

shorter tail than (4) and (5)

tawny wash

blue-grey mantle

4

dark brown eye

b

6

a

cream-coloured eye

blue-grey wash

white outer tail

5

pale grey mantle

pale grey outer tail

white wash

BABBLERS

Insectivorous, **thrush-like terrestrial birds of gregarious habits** and with **distinctive babbling calls**. Sexes are alike.

1 Arrow-marked Babbler *Turdoides jardineii*

Common resident. Told by call and **whitish, arrow-like streaks above and below**; cf. (4), which has scale-like markings and a white rump. Immature lacks the arrow marks but is usually seen with adults. The call is an excitable whirring started by one bird and taken up by all the others until it resembles hysterical giggling. The basic sound is 'scurr-scurr-scurr…', more mechanical than the Green Wood Hoopoe (p. 288). Occurs in parties of six to 10 birds within thickets in woodland, mixed bushveld, wooded hillsides, plus suburbia in Zimbabwe. Usually in the lower stratum, calling frequently. **23–25 cm** (Pylvlekkatlagter)

2 Southern Pied Babbler *Turdoides bicolor* `E`

Common, endemic resident. **Entirely white** except for **black wings and tail**. Immature is initially olive-brown, becoming white gradually. The call is a high-pitched babbling, one bird commencing 'skerr-skerr-skerr-kikikikikikerrkerrkerr…' and all others joining in; shriller than (1). Parties of up to 12 birds frequent dry thornveld and woodland. **26 cm** (Witkatlagter)

3 Bare-cheeked Babbler *Turdoides gymnogenys* `R`

Fairly common resident. Adult resembles immature of (2) except for **bare black skin under eye**. Differs from adult of (2) in this and in being less white, **upperparts and sides of neck brown or cinnamon**. Groups utter a typical babbler cackling, a high-pitched 'kurrkurrkurrkurrkurr…'. Found in arid mopane woodland in northwestern Namibia, frequenting dry watercourses and hillsides with trees. **24 cm** (Kaalwangkatlagter)

4 Hartlaub's Babbler *Turdoides hartlaubii*

Common, localised resident. Differs from (1) mainly in diagnostic **white rump**, the head and breast with all **feathers pale-edged, giving a scaly appearance; underbelly and vent also white**. Immature has a paler throat. The call is a noisy, high-pitched babbling 'kwekwekwekwekwekwekwe…' similar to (5). Parties occur in riverine woodland, and reed beds and papyrus beds on floodplains of the Zambezi–Okavango–Kunene River system. **26 cm** (Witkruiskatlagter)

5 Black-faced Babbler *Turdoides melanops* `N E`

Uncommon, localised, near-endemic resident. **Black mask** and **distinctive yellow eyes** diagnostic. The call is a high-pitched 'papapapapapapa…' by several birds. Small parties occur in broad-leaved woodland and *Acacia* thickets in northern Namibia and northwest Botswana. Unlike other babblers is shy and secretive, keeping to thick cover. **28 cm** (Swartwangkatlagter)

1 reddish-orange eye

whitish arrowheads

orange-red eye

2 black wings

cinnamon or brown sides to neck

yellow eye

3 dark brown wings

white rump and belly

scaly appearance

reddish eye

4

yellow eye

black lores

often more secretive than other babblers

5 indistinct scalloping

no white on vent and belly

THRUSHES, CHATS AND ROBINS

Largely terrestrial, insectivorous or frugivorous birds that sing from trees, some robins rating as among our finest songsters. The sexes are alike unless otherwise stated, while immatures usually have the **feathers of the upperparts pale-edged, the underparts spotted**.

1 **Groundscraper Thrush** *Psophocichla litsitsirupa*
Common resident. Differs from (2) in erect stance, absence of white wing-spots and habitat preference. In flight shows **chestnut wings**. Differs from Dusky Lark (p. 312) in **grey-brown (not dark brown) upperparts**. Calls 'lip-sitsirupa' (hence its scientific name) and sings a brisk, melodious song, the phrases continually varied. Occurs singly in open woodland, mixed bushveld, cattle kraals and rural suburbia. Runs briskly and stands upright, flicking one or both wings open momentarily. **22 cm** (Gevlekte Lyster)

ENDANGERED

2 **Spotted Ground-Thrush** *Zothera guttata* **R**
Fairly common, localised resident. Differs from (1) in **bold white wing-spots**. Has a clear, flute-like song, the accent always on the first syllable 'TCHEEooo-che-chichoo, TREEoo-tretrree…'. Found singly or in pairs in the **lower stratum of evergreen forests** of the eastern seaboard; a winter visitor to upland KwaZulu-Natal forests. **23 cm** (Natallyster)

NEAR THREATENED

3 **Orange Ground-Thrush** *Zothera gurneyi*
Uncommon, localised resident. Told by **dark bill, rich orange throat, breast and flanks** and **bold white wing-bars**. Immature has darker mottled underparts. Sings mostly at dawn and at last light, a variety of whistled phrases with clear notes and complicated trills. Occurs singly or in pairs in mist-belt evergreen forests. Seldom seen; secretive. **23 cm** (Oranjelyster)

4 **Kurrichane Thrush** *Turdus libonyanus*
Common resident. Differs from (3) and (5) in distinct **black-and-white throat markings** and **white eyebrows (no white wing-bars)**; immature as illustrated. Calls a loud 'peet-peeoo' at dusk and has a mellow, complicated song with trills and warbles in short outbursts. Found mostly singly in a variety of wooded habitats, including rural suburbia. **22 cm** (Rooibeklyster)

5 **Olive Thrush** *Turdus olivaceus*
Common resident. Similar to recently split (6), from which told by **more orange underparts, speckled throat, dark wedge on culmen, brown eye-ring** and **white vent**. From the ground calls a thin 'wheet'; from a tree during summer has a variety of loud, pleasant songs. Display behaviour similar to that of (6). Occurs singly or in pairs in both high- and low-altitude evergreen forests and riverine woodland. Generally more secretive and less common than (6). **24 cm** (Olyflyster)

6 **Karoo Thrush** *Turdus smithi* **E**
Common endemic resident. Previously regarded as a race of (5), but is **much duller. Throat-spotting absent or vestigial, underparts drab grey-brown (with only under-belly orange), vent greyish** (occasionally white); **bill and legs orange-yellow**, and **eye-ring orange** (not brown). Common in the Karoo and very common in highveld regions, where it frequents parks and gardens. Males display with drooping wings and splayed tail dragging on the ground. **24 cm** (Geelbeklyster)

1
grey-brown upperparts
flicks wings open while foraging
heavily spotted below
occurs in open woodland

2
rust-brown above
white wing-spots
occurs in forest interior

orange bill
obvious, densely streaked malar stripe
white vent and belly

white eye-ring
conspicuous white wing-bars

3

4
J
heavily spotted below (as in all young thrushes)

brown eye-ring
speckled throat
extensive orange
vent usually white

5

orange eye-ring
plain orange-yellow bill
plain or indistinctly mottled
vent usually greyish
orange restricted to lower belly

6

1 **Short-toed Rock-Thrush** *Monticola brevipes*   N·E·

Fairly common, near-endemic resident. In western regions male distinguished by **whitish crown**, but in its eastern distribution male **lacks the pale crown**, being of the race *M. b. pretoriae* (sometimes considered a separate species: Pretoria Rock-Thrush). Then difficult to distinguish from (4) except for **greyer upperparts (sometimes with darker mottling)**, proportionally **longer bill** and **whiter wing-feather edges**. Female told from female of (4) by **paler upperparts and throat**. Distribution and habitat distinguish it from (3). Sings a sweet song phrase incorporating imitations. Occurs singly or in pairs in arid regions, frequenting bush-covered rocky hills and rocky ridges. Often perches on roadside telephone wires in Namibia. **18 cm** (Korttoonkliplyster)

2 **Miombo Rock-Thrush** *Monticola angolensis*

Common, localised resident. Male distinguished by **grey head** with **spotted crown**, female by **white throat** and **dark, speckled malar streak**. Immature like female but throat more speckled, only the chin white. The song is 'pe-pe-per-pee-pew, per-per, pee-pew…'. Pairs occur in broad-leaved woodland (especially miombo). Not necessarily associated with rocky habitats. **18 cm** (Angolaklipyster)

3 **Sentinel Rock-Thrush** *Monticola explorator*   E

Common, localised endemic resident. Male differs from other male rock-thrushes in the **blue-grey of the head extending to the mantle and onto the breast**. Female likewise shows **more extensive mottled area on breast**. Has a lively, melodious song beginning 'chu-chu-chu-chee-chree, chee-chroo-chi-chi-chee-troo-tree…', followed by a sequence of warbles, trills and chattering phrases. Female utters a shorter, harsher version of the initial sequence. Alarm call is a rapid, descending 'tre-e-e-e-e-e'. Pairs frequent rocky uplands and montane grasslands in summer; in winter they move to lower levels and then favour Karoo vegetation, fynbos and grassland. Perches prominently with erect stance. **21 cm** (Langtoonklipyster)

4 **Cape Rock-Thrush** *Monticola rupestris*   E

Common endemic resident. **Larger and more bulky than other rock-thrushes**, both sexes **more richly coloured**. Immature more spotted than adult. The song is a soft 'checheroo' followed immediately by a loud 'cheewoo-chirri-cheewoo-tiriri', often repeated. Pairs frequent montane slopes, rocky, bush-covered hillsides at all altitudes, and rocky gorges. **21 cm** (Kaapse Kliplyster)

M. b. pretoriae

blue head

♀

1

pale throat

♂

2

dark, speckled malar streaks

♀

♂

both sexes heavily mottled above

♀

3

extensive mottling

♂

extensive blue-grey

♀

4

♂

rich orange upper breast

1 Cape Rockjumper *Chaetops frenatus*

Common, localised endemic resident. Range does not overlap with that of (2). Unmistakable, with **bold white malar stripe** contrasting with **black throat** and **red rump and underparts**. From close range, the **red eye** is diagnostic. Male more richly rufous than male of (2); female has less black about the head and dull rufous underparts. The call is a rapid whistle 'pee-pee-pee-pee-pee…'. Pairs and small parties occur on rocky mountain slopes within the fynbos biome. Hops and runs from rock to rock in a lively manner, or flies from one outcrop to another, raising and spreading its tail after landing to expose **broad white tail-tips**. **25 cm** (Kaapse Berglyster)

2 Drakensberg Rockjumper *Chaetops aurantius*

Common, localised endemic resident. Both sexes are **paler than (1)** but are identical in all other ways. Pairs or small parties occur in the mountains of Lesotho and surroundings in boulder-strewn grasslands, mainly above 2 000 m; range is north of (1). Best located by piercing whistled calls, very similar to (1). Often appears unexpectedly behind boulders, just to vanish again and reappear some way off. **21 cm** (Oranjeborsberglyster)

3 Mocking Cliff Chat *Thamnolaea cinnamomeiventris*

Common resident. Sexes differ as illustrated; immature like female. Differs from (1) in **plain upperparts**. The male is **black above** with **chestnut belly and vent** and **white shoulder-bar**. The female has **dark ash-grey plumage above, deep rufous underparts** and no white markings. Has various mellow calls and an attractive song, mostly involving imitations of other birds. A cheerful, lively bird that habitually raises its tail. Pairs occur in various rocky habitats with bushes, especially where the fig tree *Ficus ingens* is present. Often becomes tame near country dwellings. **20–23 cm** (Dassievoël)

4 Boulder Chat *Pinarornis plumosus*

Fairly common, near-endemic, localised resident. **Sooty black** except for **white in the wings and tail**; immature similar. Utters a monotonous squeaking 'ink, ink, wink, wink' like an unoiled wheel, plus a clear whistle with the bill held vertically. Lively and agile, raising its tail when landing. Pairs frequent the well-wooded lower slopes of hills with rounded, granite boulders, occasionally in similar habitat at higher levels. Is most numerous in the Matobo National Park of southern Zimbabwe. Sparsely distributed in most regions and often difficult to locate. Singletons have been recorded in northern South Africa; possibly overlooked there, as much suitable habitat exists. **23–27 cm** (Swartberglyster)

ranges do not overlap

1

♂

♀

white-tipped tail

♂

♀

2

often raises tail

3

♀

white shoulder-bar

chestnut underparts

deep rufous underparts

sooty black overall

4

white flashes

white-tipped tail

1 Arnot's Chat *Pentholaea arnotti*

a.k.a. White headed Black-Chat

Fairly common resident. Resembles (3) but **male has a white cap** (not grey); **female has a white throat**. Utters a shrill song containing a musical 'feeee' ascending and descending in pitch. Pairs or small parties occur beneath trees, hopping about on the trunks and on the ground. Only in broad-leaved woodland with well-developed trees in flat country, especially mopane woodland. **18 cm** (Bontpiek)

2 Ant-eating Chat *Myrmecocichla formicivora* **E**

Common endemic resident. Entirely **dull brown. Male usually has white shoulder-patch** (sometimes obscured by wing-feathers); female lacks shoulder-patch and is **paler brown. Both sexes show white wing-feathers, most conspicuous during brief, fluttering flights.** Call is a sharp 'peek'. A terrestrial species. Often perches with **erect stance** on termite mounds, bushes or fences in short grassland. **Often in parties near nesting burrows (especially Aardvark burrows). 18 cm** (Swartpiek)

3 Mountain Wheatear *Oenanthe monticola* **N E**

Fairly common near-endemic resident. **Male variable**, usually as (a) or (b); in Namibia may have **white underparts from lower breast to vent** as (c). **Female rather nondescript; best identified by white rump and outer tail-feathers (conspicuous in flight).** Immature resembles female. Similar to (1) but occurs in totally different habitat: **boulder-strewn slopes, grassland with rocks or anthills**, and **farmyards. Especially common in new townhouse developments in peri-urban areas.** One of earliest songsters (often starting to sing just after midnight); also sings late in the day, mainly Sep–Jan, the song a loud jumble of flute-like notes. May fly upwards a short distance, then drop down and fly low to another perch. Occurs singly or in small groups, perching conspicuously on rocks, anthills and, in suburbia, roofs. **17–20 cm** (Bergwagter)

1 ♀ extensive white throat

wings striking in flight

no white on tail or rump

white cap

♂

2 striking white windows in wings ♂

♂ white shoulder-patch

♀ no white on rump or tail

stocky build

c ♂ males extremely variable

3 a ♂

♀

white rump and outer tail-feathers

b ♂

1 **Capped Wheatear**   *Oenanthe pileata*
Common, localised resident. Adult has **broad black breast-band** and **white eyebrow**. Immature lacks breast-band and eyebrow barely discernible; often mistaken for rare Palearctic vagrant species. Sings from some low prominence or while fluttering straight up into the air, the song variable with imitations of other birds, even mechanical sounds. Walks about with much wing-flicking and tail-jerking. Loose groups occur on bare ground, short grassland near dams, airfields, well-grazed farmlands and burned areas. Nomadic, appearing in large numbers in burned areas but disappearing when grass height makes terrestrial foraging difficult. **18 cm** (Hoëveldskaapwagter)

2 **Pied Wheatear**   *Oenanthe pleschanka* $\boxed{\text{V}}$
Vagrant. The male in breeding plumage is distinctive, but is most likely to be seen in non-breeding plumage. Female confusingly similar to female (4) except for **duller brown upperparts, dusky throat** (which might suggest juvenile (1)) and **upper tail pattern**. Has a 'zack' call note. Prefers stony scrublands, and cultivated and fallow lands. Breeds in the Palearctic, and spends the non-breeding season in northeastern Africa; vagrant further south. One record from KwaZulu-Natal. **15 cm** (Bontskaapwagter)

3 **Isabelline Wheatear**   *Oenanthe isabellina* $\boxed{\text{V}}$
Extremely rare (recorded over 30 years ago in Chobe) visitor from Asia, some populations overwintering in central sub-Saharan Africa. Told from a non-breeding (4) only with difficulty unless the diagnostic **upper tail pattern** can be seen. The **terminal half of the tail is black**, and there is **less extensive white on the rump**. Other features are **longish legs**, the **black alula** and an erect posture. Favours dry grasslands and scrub-bush. **16,5 cm** (Isabellaskaapwagter)

4 **Northern Wheatear**   *Oenanthe oenanthe* $\boxed{\text{V}}$
Very rare summer vagrant. In southern Africa, occurs in non-breeding plumage. Has a characteristic wheatear bowing action with tail raised high, at which time the **T-shaped tail pattern** can be seen; cf. (3), from which it can only be distinguished with difficulty. The common call is 'chack-chack'. Occurs singly in Kalahari grassland and similar dry terrain with sparse grass cover. **16 cm** (Europese Skaapwagter)

white
eyebrow

1

broad black
breast-band

black forms
inverted
'V'-shape

J

immature has
speckled breast

♀
very
similar to
(3), but
darker

N-Br ♂

2

dusky,
blotchy
throat

♂
Br

much
white

3

white

♂

Br

black
alula
feathers

broad black
band

4

buff

plain

extensive white at base of
tail (black forms distinctive
inverted 'T'-pattern)

1 Sickle-winged Chat *Cercomela sinuata* E

Locally common endemic resident. Most resembles (2) but is more slightly built, **wing-feathers more distinctly edged rufous, legs longer** and **eye-wattle more accentuated. Tail dark with buff outer edges**; only **upper tail coverts rufous.** Immature spotted but tail pattern as adult. Frequently flicks wings open when perched. Occurs on open ground with short, scrubby vegetation, including fallow croplands and road verges. Gives a soft 'chak' or double 'chak-chak' but less vocal than (2). **15 cm** (Vlaktespekvreter)

2 Familiar Chat *Cercomela familiaris*

Common resident. A tame, rather nondescript small chat. Best recognised by its habit of repeatedly flicking its wings when landing or when hopping on the ground (like some other chats and Spotted Flycatcher, p. 402), in combination with its **striking rufous or orange rump and tail panels.** Very similar to (1), but **edges of wing-feathers buffy** and less obvious, **tail pattern different, less contrast between upperparts and underparts** and **legs shorter.** More dependent on rocky ground than (1), but also occurs around stone walls and outbuildings on farms. Southern and eastern races (a) darkest and largest; Namibian race (b) palest and smallest. **Tail deep rufous with dark central feathers and subterminal band.** Immature told from immature of (1) only by tail pattern. Frequently utters a characteristic 'feeu... chak-chak' and less often sings a soft, warbling song. **15 cm** (Gewone Spekvreter)

3 Tractrac Chat *Cercomela tractrac* N E

Common, near-endemic resident. Smaller and plumper than (1), (2) or (4). Dark southern race (a) has **upper tail coverts very pale buff, almost white**; pale Namibian race (b) has **pure white on tail** (like a wheatear, p. 358). Gives a dry, scratchy 'char-charr' call; also musical rolling and chattering. Occurs in flat, arid plains, spending much time on the ground, where it runs swiftly. **14–15 cm** (Woestynspekvreter)

4 Karoo Chat *Cercomela schlegelii* N E

Common near-endemic resident. Larger, more robust and elongated than (1) to (3). Southern and eastern races (a) darkest with **grey rump** and **white on outer tail-feathers extending to tip of tail**; smallest, palest Namibian race (b) has **white on outer tail-feathers and upper tail coverts**, plus **beige rump**; cf. also Mountain Wheatear (p. 356). Has a rattling call 'tirr-tit-tat'. Frequents succulent Karoo scrub and perches on tall scrub, fences and telephone wires. **15–18 cm** (Karoospekvreter)

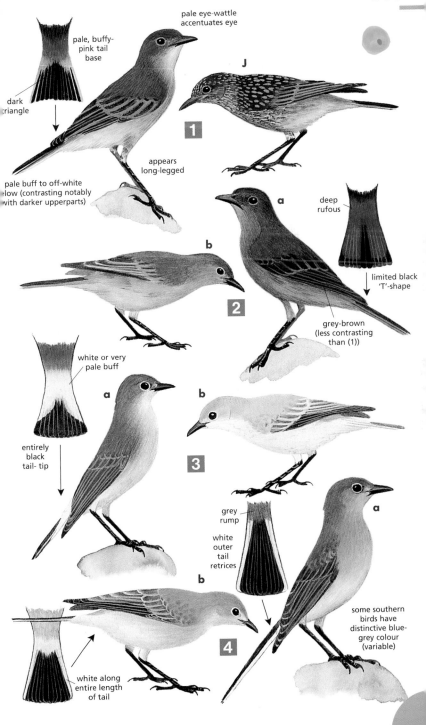

pale eye-wattle accentuates eye

pale, buffy-pink tail base

dark triangle

J

1

appears long-legged

pale buff to off-white below (contrasting notably with darker upperparts)

a

deep rufous

b

limited black 'T'-shape

grey-brown (less contrasting than (1))

2

white or very pale buff

a

b

entirely black tail-tip

3

grey rump

white outer tail retrices

a

b

4

white along entire length of tail

some southern birds have distinctive blue-grey colour (variable)

1 Whinchat *Saxicola rubetra*

Very rare summer vagrant. Non-breeding male resembles female; this plumage most likely in southern Africa. Differs from (2) in slimmer build, **bold white or buff eyebrows** and **heavily streaked upperparts**. Further differs in **streaked (not white) rump, white patches at the base of its tail-feathers** and **white primary coverts** (shows as a white spot on folded wing). Habits much like (2), perching low down in open scrublands. **13–14 cm** (Europese Bontrokkie)

2 African Stonechat *Saxicola torquatus*

Common resident. At rest, male is striking and unmistakable. In flight, female is identified by **white wing-patches**. Both sexes identified by **white rump**; cf. (1). Immature like adult but more speckled and may show indistinct buff eyebrow. Utters a grating 'tsak, tsak' like two marbles being struck together; usually preceded by a short, sharp whistle. Also has a short, shrill, warbling song. Usually found in pairs in a wide variety of open grassland habitats: near marshes, vleis, dams, streams and roadsides, perching on low shrubs or fences, from where it watches the ground for insects. Seasonal in some regions, moving to lower or higher altitudes. **14 cm** (Gewone Bontrokkie)

3 Buff-streaked Chat *Campicoloides bifasciata* E

Common endemic resident. Identified by **striking plumage patterns** and lively, demonstrative behaviour. Has a loud and pleasant song with snatches of mimicry, song phrases usually starting with two rapid clicking notes: 'chit, chit, leleoo-chit, cherr-wee-oo, too-weelie, too-weeoo…'. Pairs inhabit rocky or stony hills and montane regions in sour grasslands. Tame, flitting from rock to rock with much flicking of tail and wings. **15–17 cm** (Bergklipwagter)

4 Common Redstart *Phoenicurus phoenicurus* V

A robin-like bird with **rufous tail in both sexes**. Male in breeding plumage (recorded in southern Africa) is distinctive with **grey upperparts, white eyebrow, black mask and throat** and **rufous breast**. Female much duller: except for rufous tail has **pale sandy-grey upperparts** and **whitish underparts** (could be confused with related Familiar Chat, p. 360). Exhibits diagnostic tail-vibrating or tail-shivering behaviour. Calls 'hwee-tuc-tuc' and frequents a range of lightly wooded habitats. Breeds in Europe; winters in Africa. One record from North West Province. **14 cm** (Europese Rooistert)

5 Herero Chat *Namibornis herero* N E

Uncommon, near-endemic resident. Unlikely to be confused with any other within its restricted distribution. Easily identified by combination of **dark ear coverts, finely streaked breast** and **orange outer tail-feathers**. Silent except when breeding, then utters a subdued 'ji-ju-jjiu' contact call, a mellow warbling song in jumbled, short phrases and a 'churrr' alarm note. Hunts from a low perch, occasionally flying down to seize insects on the ground. Found on hillsides, at the foot of hills and near dry watercourses in the arid Namib escarpment areas. Most plentiful at Groot Spitzkop, near Usakos. **17 cm** (Hererospekvreter)

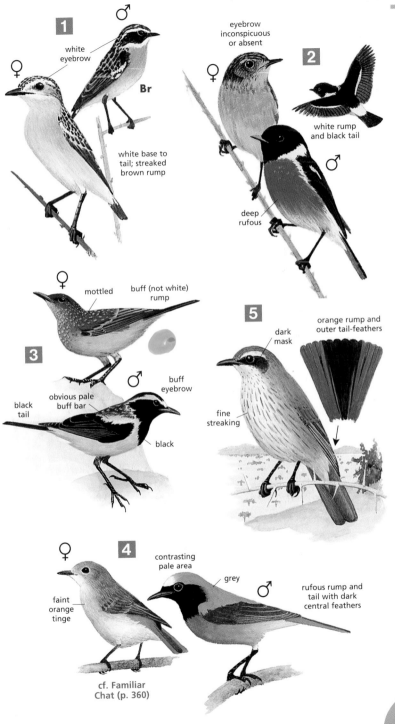

1 ♂ ♀
white eyebrow
Br
white base to tail; streaked brown rump

2 ♀ ♂
eyebrow inconspicuous or absent
white rump and black tail
deep rufous

3 ♀ ♂
mottled
buff (not white) rump
obvious pale buff bar
black tail
buff eyebrow
black

5
dark mask
orange rump and outer tail-feathers
fine streaking

4 ♀ ♂
contrasting pale area
grey
faint orange tinge
rufous rump and tail with dark central feathers
cf. Familiar Chat (p. 360)

1 White-chested Alethe *Pseudalethe fuelleborni* R
Rare, localised resident. **Clear white eyebrows** and lack of white eyebrows and **robust appearance** distinguish this species from robins. Sings a lively 'fweer-her-heee-her-hee-her'. A shy, retiring species. Inhabits the lower stratum of lowland forests north of Beira, as well as montane forests in the Gorongosa region of Mozambique. **18–20 cm** (Witborswoudlyster)

2 Cape Robin-Chat *Cossypha caffra*
Common resident. Distinguished by **white eyebrows, orange upper breast** and **greyish underparts**. Like all robin-chats, shows **orange tail-feathers and back** in flight. Immature has a pale orange breast spotted with black. Has a pleasant and continuing song, each passage starting on the same note and with the phrase 'Jan-Frederik' often repeated (hence Afrikaans name). Jerks its tail up when alarmed, and utters a low, growling 'wur-da-wur'. Occurs in the fringes of forests at all levels (montane forests in eastern Zimbabwe), in riverine bush, patches of bush and rock on heath-covered hillsides – especially at the base of cliffs – and, in many regions, commonly in gardens. A winter visitor to eastern coastal districts. **18 cm** (Gewone Janfrederik)

3 White-throated Robin-Chat *Cossypha humeralis* E
Common endemic resident. Distinguished by **white breast and wing-bar**. Immature is well spotted like all young robin-chats. In the early morning calls repeatedly 'swee-swer, swee-swer...'; cf. Red-capped Robin-Chat (p. 368). The call note is a quiet 'tseep... tseep... tseep...'. Also has a beautiful song that incorporates much mimicry. Occurs singly or in pairs in thickets in dry, mixed bushveld, in riverine forests and at the foot of rocky, bush-covered hills and termitaria. Frequents gardens in some regions. **16–18 cm** (Witkeeljanfrederik)

4 White-browed Robin-Chat *Cossypha heuglini*
Common, localised resident. Told from other white-browed robin-chats by **entirely deep orange underparts** plus **black cap and mask** offset by **bold white eyebrow**. Immature similar but spotted. Considered by some as the best songster in Africa. The song consists of various melodious phrases repeated, starting quietly then working up to a crescendo 'pip-pip-uree, pip-pip-uree...' or 'don't-you-do-it, don't-you-do-it...' or 'tirrootirree, tirrootirree...' each phrase repeated up to about 16 times. Sings mostly at dawn and dusk, often two birds together. Inhabits dense thickets in riverine forests and at the base of densely wooded hills and termitaria. A garden bird in some Zimbabwe towns. **19–20 cm** (Heuglinjanfrederik)

5 White-throated Robin *Irania gutturalis* V
Rare vagrant. Thrush-like with a **long black bill** and **dark tail**, which is often raised. Male unmistakable with **lead-grey upperparts, partly black face, white eyebrow** and **white throat-patch**, offset by **orange-brown underparts** and **white vent**. Female and immature duller, with **grey-brown upperparts, pale-buff forehead, whitish throat, conspicuous white eye-ring** and **orange-washed flanks**. Could be confused with a female rock-thrush (p. 352) or Familiar Chat (p. 360), but lacks any orange in the tail. Song is a very rapid, excited warbling. Usual call is a wagtail-like disyllabic 'chi-chet'. Forages on the ground, where normally rather shy and skulking. On central Asian breeding grounds, frequents bushy ravines and thickets in dry areas. Spends the non-breeding season (Oct–Mar) in northeastern Africa. Recorded once near Williston in the Northern Cape in Jul 2006. **16–18 cm** (Irania)

1

no white eyebrow

difficult to see in the forest understorey

rich orange-brown mantle, wings and tail

white

2

brownish grey

greyish flanks contrast with orange throat and vent

3

blueish grey

crisp white

white wing-bar

4

bold white eyebrow

wholly deep orange below

5

contrasting white eyebrow and throat-patch

♂

lead-grey

white eye-ring

♀

duller coloration

dark tail, often raised

NEAR THREATENED

VULNERABLE

1 East Coast Akalat *Sheppardia gunningi*   Ⓡ
Uncommon, localised resident. Differs from other robins in **entirely brown upperparts extending to below eye-level**, and in **orange breast** with **whitish belly and vent**. **Eyebrows grey** with a **small, barely visible white 'star' on the lores** immediately in front of the eyes. The song is loud, rapid and arresting, 'tirripeepoo-tirripeepoo-tirripeepoo, tirritee-tirritee-tirritee...'. A **small** robin of Mozambique lowland forests from the Beira region northwards. Keeps mostly to the lower stratum, feeding on the ground. Shy and little known. **14 cm** (Gunningjanfrederik)

2 Swynnerton's Robin *Swynnertonia swynnertoni*
Fairly common, localised resident. Identified by **white breast-band with black border**. Frequently utters a quiet, sibilant 'si-see-see' (like a distant Rufous-naped Lark, p. 308) and has a stuttering, drawn-out call note 'trrr-e-e-e-e-e-e'. A small, tame robin of montane forests in eastern Zimbabwe. Frequents the lower stratum, hopping about in a lively manner with much wing- and tail-flicking. **14 cm** (Bandkeeljanfrederik)

3 White-starred Robin *Pogonocichla stellata*
Common resident. Told by **entirely grey head, greenish upperparts** and **orange-yellow underparts**. **White 'stars' before eyes and on central breast** evident only when the bird is excited or alarmed. Immature fledges with typical spotted appearance of young robins; later attains lemon-yellow underparts for one year (see illustration). The call in coastal areas is a piping 'too-twee' frequently repeated, in montane areas a repeated 'pee, du-du WHEEE...', the accent on the last syllable, which has a whip-like quality. Also has a subdued, piping song. Occurs in the lower stratum of coastal and montane evergreen forests. A quiet, lively species but not secretive. **15–17 cm** (Witkoljanfrederik)

4 Chorister Robin-Chat *Cossypha dichroa*   Ⓔ
Common endemic resident. A fairly large robin with **black hood (no white eyebrow)** and **clear orange underparts**; immature well spotted. The contact call is a monotonous 'toy, toy, toy...' repeated for long periods, the song a variety of beautiful, mellow phrases incorporating imitations of other bird calls. Very vocal Oct–Jan. A species of montane evergreen forests, inhabiting the midstratum. Often absent from montane forests Apr–Sep, but present in coastal forests at this time. **20 cm** (Lawaaimakerjanfrederik)

white 'star' on lores best seen when singing

1

entirely brown above

whitish belly and vent

2

white breast-band can be hard to see

orange

J

3

greenish mantle

white 'stars' in front of eye and on central breast only visible when displaying

black hood

4

J

4

orange underparts contrast strongly with dark upperparts

all juvenile robin-chats are heavily spotted below but are recognisable by their orange tail with blackish central tail-feathers

1 Red-capped Robin-Chat *Cossypha natalensis*
Common resident. **Entirely orange from above the eyes and sides of head to undertail; no white eyebrow.** Immature has pale spotting on the upperparts, dark spotting below. Has a monotonous double call note 'trrree-trrirr, trrree-trrirr, trrree-trrirr...' continued for long periods. The song is composed of various melodious phrases (remarkably similar to human whistling) and imitations of other bird calls; easily mistaken for the song of the Chorister Robin-Chat (p. 366). Occurs singly or in pairs in thickets within coastal bush, forests, riverine forests and valley bush. Raises its tail frequently. Keeps mostly within dense cover in the lower and midstrata but feeds in the open late in the day. **18–20 cm** (Nataljanfrederik)

2 White-browed Scrub Robin *Erythropygia leucophrys*
Common resident. A **small, brownish robin** with **white wing markings** and a **well-streaked breast**. In the Okavango Delta the breast has an **orange wash** but is unstreaked; cf. (3). In flight it reveals **orange rump and upper tail coverts**, while the **fanned tail shows white tips**. Immature has mottled upperparts. Sings for long periods on warm days; often the first species to start singing in the morning. Various loud phrases repeated almost without pause 'pirit-pirit-tertwee-pirit-pirit-tertwee-chee-chee-chu-it-chu-it...'. Alarm call is a drawn-out 'churrrr', also given before settling down to roost for the night. Occurs in mixed bushveld, thornveld and woodland, especially within thickets formed by low bushes and long grass. Sings from an exposed bush-top perch; otherwise secretive in the lower stratum. **15 cm** (Gestreepte Wipstert)

3 Bearded Scrub Robin *Erythropygia quadrivirgata*
Fairly common resident. Identified by **bold face pattern**, including **white eyebrows bordered by black lines**, plus **white throat with black malar streak**. **Breast and flanks are a dull creamy orange**, colour extending to the rump. Immature more mottled. The song is loud and clear, a series of pleasant phrases repeated three or four times with short pauses 'pee-pee-pee, terr-treee, chiroo-chiroo-chiroo, witchoo-witchoo-witchoo, pee-pee-pee, chu-it, chu-it, chu-it...', some phrases rising in volume; also imitates other bird calls. Usually occurs singly in broad-leaved and riverine woodland. Largely terrestrial unless singing. **16–18 cm** (Baardwipstert)

4 Brown Scrub Robin *Erythropygia signata* ☐ E
Uncommon endemic resident. A brown forest robin with **white eyebrows and wing markings** and **whitish underparts**. Immature is spotted and scaled, otherwise similar. The song, rendered at dawn and last light, is a high-pitched series of melancholy phrases, always beginning on a single or double high note 'treetroo-tretretre...'; the call is a sibilant 'zit-zeeeet'. Inhabits the interiors of mist-belt evergreen forests and dense riparian or coastal bush at lower altitudes, always within the lower and middle strata. Difficult to see in its habitat, but may become tame in coastal holiday resorts on the KwaZulu-Natal coast. **18 cm** (Bruinwipstert)

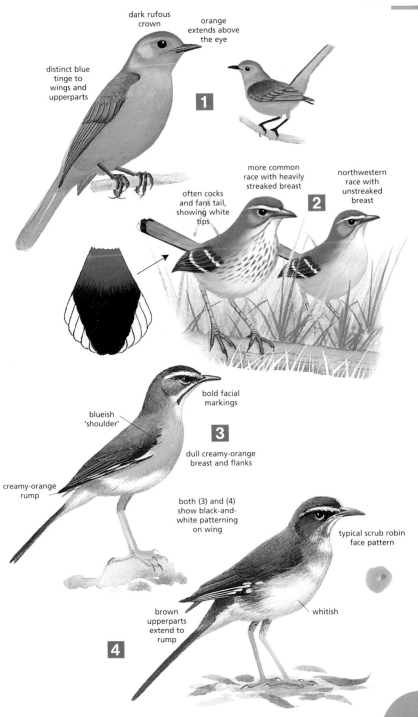

dark rufous crown

orange extends above the eye

distinct blue tinge to wings and upperparts

1

more common race with heavily streaked breast

northwestern race with unstreaked breast

often cocks and fans tail, showing white tips

2

bold facial markings

blueish 'shoulder'

3

dull creamy-orange breast and flanks

creamy-orange rump

both (3) and (4) show black-and-white patterning on wing

typical scrub robin face pattern

whitish

brown upperparts extend to rump

4

1 Karoo Scrub Robin *Erythropygia coryphoeus* **E**

Common endemic resident. **White eyebrows and throat** with **dark malar streak** and **white tail-tips** identify this otherwise **sombrely coloured** robin. Immature has buff-barred upperparts and dark-mottled underparts. Song composed of short, choppy phrases 'pheeoo, tirrit-tirrit, chuck, chuck, sweeoo, chuck…'. Alarm call is a penetrating, metallic 'zzzz'. Frequents Karoo veld, feeding on the ground amidst scrub. Conspicuous and noisy. **17 cm** (Slangverklikker)

2 Kalahari Scrub Robin *Erythropygia paena* **N E**

Common, near-endemic resident. Much **paler, sandier-looking** than (1). Conspicuous **rufous tail has black subterminal band and white tips** (cf. White-browed Scrub Robin, p. 368). Immature has lightly spotted underparts. Often perches on a bush calling 'twee' intermittently for long periods. The song is a high-pitched sequence of repeated phrases, 'seeoo-seeoo, tweetoo-tweetoo-tweetoo, seetoo-seetoo, trititritritri…'. Occurs singly or in pairs in **Kalahari thornveld** and fallow farmland, particularly in arid western regions. Feeds on open ground and sings from a tree top, but enters thorn thickets when alarmed. **16–17 cm** (Kalahariwipstert)

3 Rufous-tailed Palm-Thrush *Cichladusa ruficauda* **R**

Uncommon, localised resident. Identified by **rufous upperparts, reddish eye** and **plain buff underparts** with **long rufous tail**; cf. (4), which also has a rufous tail. Ranges of two species are mutually exclusive. Has a rich, melodious song heard mostly at dawn and dusk, pairs often singing in duet. Occurs in association with *Borassus* and oil palms on the Kunene River and northwards. Little known in southern Africa. **17 cm** (Rooistertmôrelyster)

4 Collared Palm-Thrush *Cichladusa arquata*

Common, localised resident. Differs from (3) mainly in **black-bordered throat-patch** (often broken or incomplete), **grey nape, duller mantle** and **straw-coloured eyes**, but has similar **long rufous tail**. Immature is mottled below; black throat-border vestigial. Has a melodious, liquid song heard mostly mornings and evenings. Normally lively and conspicuous but more secretive when breeding. Spends much time foraging on the ground. When perched on a branch, droops its wings and raises and lowers its tail continuously. Pairs and small parties in palm savanna with *Borassus* and *Hyphaene* palms, being especially numerous in the Victoria Falls and Gorongosa regions. **19 cm** (Palmmôrelyster)

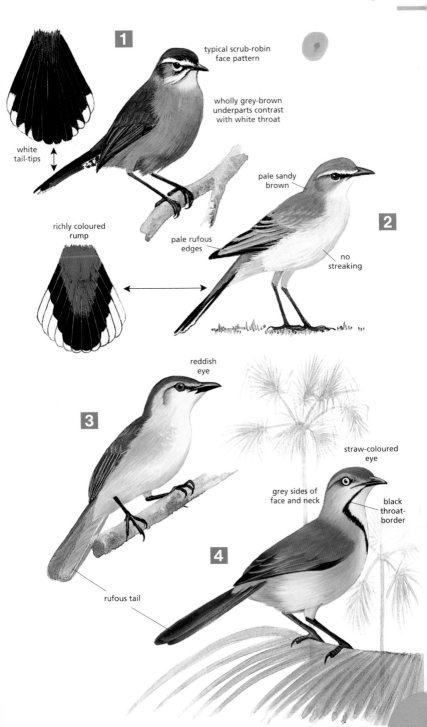

1

typical scrub-robin
face pattern

wholly grey-brown
underparts contrast
with white throat

white
tail-tips

richly coloured
rump

pale sandy
brown

pale rufous
edges

no
streaking

2

reddish
eye

3

straw-coloured
eye

grey sides of
face and neck

black
throat-
border

4

rufous tail

WARBLERS AND ALLIES

Small, insectivorous birds of mostly sombre colouring. Many have **attractive warbling songs** and short calls that aid identification to the practised ear, but sound confusingly similar to the inexperienced. Several species visit southern Africa from Europe during summer. Sexes are alike.

1 Willow Warbler *Phylloscopus trochilus*
Common summer visitor. Variable; occurs in much paler morph and also with brown upperparts and white underparts. Identified by **distinct eyebrows** and **notched tail-tip. Small, with a fine bill and weak legs.** While feeding calls a querulous, quiet 'foo-wee'. Sings, usually in the mornings, especially upon arrival and before departure to breeding grounds, a descending jumble of notes 'tee-tee-tee-tee-tu-tu-tu-twee-twee-sweet-sweet-sweet-sweet'. Occurs singly in almost any bush habitat, including suburbia. Busily works its way through the canopy and midstratum, inspecting leaves for insects. Occasionally darts out to hawk a flying insect or hover momentarily at the canopy edge. **12 cm** (Hofsanger)

2 Icterine Warbler *Hippolais icterina*
Fairly common summer visitor. Larger than (1); usually **more yellow** with clearly **yellow-edged wing coverts, sharply sloping forehead, orange lower mandible** to broad-based bill and **unnotched tail-tip**. Sings a repetitive jumble of warbled notes, some pleasant, others harsh and nasal. Solitary; prefers *Acacia* thornveld. Hops about while feeding in tree canopies, often singing. Sparsely distributed. **14–15 cm** (Spotsanger)

3 Garden Warbler *Sylvia borin*
Fairly common summer visitor. A plain-coloured warbler **without distinctive markings. Bill rather stubby, eyes large and dark** and **body plump**. Usually located by song, a quiet, monotonous warbling uttered from the depths of a bush. Song usually louder and more insistent upon arrival and before northward departure. Solitary in dense bush or thickets, especially along watercourses and in parks and gardens. May emerge from dense canopies to visit fruiting shrubs in more open situations. **15 cm** (Tuinsanger)

4 Eurasian Blackcap *Sylvia atricapilla* 　🅁
A small warbler easily identified by **male's black cap** and **female's rusty cap** (cf. Neddicky, p. 392). Calls 'tuc-tuc' or 'churr' and has a subdued warbling song, very similar to that of the closely related (3). Frequents mixed woodland, forest edges and gardens, particularly in mountainous regions. Breeds in Europe, winters in Africa. **14 cm** (Swartkroonsanger)

5 Thrush Nightingale *Luscinia luscinia* 　🅁
Rare to locally common summer visitor. Nondescript, secretive and best located by song. **Tail and wing-feather margins rich rufous, underparts whitish** with **mottled breast**. The song is a rich melody of variable notes, some sweet, some harsh. Solitary in dense thickets, often in riverine bush. Returns to the same thicket from mid-December to January, departing Mar–Apr each year. **16–18 cm** (Lysternagtegaal)

6 Olive-tree Warbler *Hippolais olivetorum*
Uncommon, localised summer visitor. A large greyish warbler with **white eyebrows** not extending behind eye, **sharply sloping forehead, large two-coloured bill** and **pale outer edges to wing-feathers (when fresh) and tail-tip**. Song louder and deeper than most warblers, a grating jumble of notes with sharp 'tch-tch' sounds interspersed; similar to that of Great Reed-Warbler (p. 378). Solitary in dense thickets in *Acacia* thornveld, feeding and singing from within the foliage. **16–18 cm** (Olyfboomsanger)

1

il often
ows slight
notch

distinctive
long
eyebrow

square-
ended tail

fresh plumage
shows pale
windows in
wings

dark form

short
eyebrow

pale lores

fine
bill

2

broad-based
bill with orange
lower mandible

sloping
forehead

3

touch of
blue-grey on neck

pale form

blue-grey
legs

short, rather
stubby bill

rusty cap

diagnostic
black cap

♀

♂

4

large
eye

cf. Neddicky
(p. 392)

5

mottled
(variable)

rich rufous tone
to rump and tail

whitish
underparts

eyebrow does not
extend behind eye

6

strong bill with
pale base

very long primary
projection

off-white or
pale greyish

long blackish
tail

pale wing panel
in fresh plumage
(mostly late
summer)

strong
feet

1 Common Whitethroat *Sylvia communis*

Uncommon summer visitor. Identified by **bright white throat** contrasting with **pale buff breast, whitish eye-ring, prominent rufous wing-feather edges** and **white outer tail-feathers**. The crown feathers are frequently raised, giving the head a peaked appearance. Has sharp 'tacc-tacc' and grating 'ksssh' calls, a conversational 'wheet, wheet-whit-whit-whit' and a brisk, scratchy warble. A restless, lively species found in dry scrub thickets and thornveld; Nov–Mar. **15 cm** (Witkeelsanger)

2 River Warbler *Locustella fluviatilis* R

Rare midsummer visitor. Very rarely seen unless singing, thus unlikely to be confused with any other species. Told by **pale-tipped, buffy undertail coverts**, which extend down two thirds of the graduated tail and create a characteristic cigar shape. Also shows a **mottled throat** (variable), **chocolate-brown upperparts** and **indistinct facial markings**. Utters an intermittent, cricket-like 'zer zer zer zer…'. Alarm call is a piercing 'whit' like Green-winged Pytilia (p. 460). Exceptionally secretive in dense shrubs and thickets, usually near water. Creeps about near or on the ground, but sings from an elevated position. When alarmed, drops to the ground and runs away. **13 cm** (Sprinkaansanger)

3 Barratt's Warbler *Bradypterus barratti* E

Fairly common endemic resident. A highly secretive species usually located only by its remarkably loud song. Very similar to (2) except for **narrower, more profuse breast markings** (extending onto flanks in southern races), **large, rounded tail** and **darker legs**. Call is a soft 'tuc' or 'trrr' as it creeps about. In early summer, sings a diagnostic accelerating 'chree, chree, chooree-ree-ree-ree-ree-ree'. Frequents patches of dense bush, tangled scrub and bracken in montane forest fringes. Highly secretive. **15–16 cm** (Ruigtesanger)

4 Knysna Warbler *Bradypterus sylvaticus* R E

Fairly common, localised endemic resident. Differs from (3) in **duskier underparts** and **lack of clear breast markings**. Has a high-pitched, staccato song uttered with increasing speed and ending with a trill 'tsip-tsip-tsip-tsip-tsiptsiptsiptsiptrrrrrrrrrrrrrrr'. Remains concealed in the dense foliage of forest fringes and wooded kloofs, but lively and active; feeds in both the mid- and lower strata. **14–15 cm** (Knysnaruigtesanger)

VULNERABLE

5 Victorin's Warbler *Cryptillas victorini* E

Common, localised endemic resident. Best identified by **orange-yellow eyes** in combination with **grey ear coverts** and **orange tones to underparts**. In the brief song the notes go up and down with increasing rapidity: 'mississippippippippi'. Occurs in dense montane fynbos and scrub on rain-exposed slopes, in rocky kloofs and alongside mountain streams. Emerges from cover to sing from a low bush. **16 cm** (Rooiborsruigtesanger)

6 Fan-tailed Grassbird (Broad-tailed Warbler)
Schoenicola brevirostris

Uncommon resident. Recognised by **voluminous black tail with buff-tipped feathers**. Male utters a weak, metallic 'trreep, trreep, trreep' call from a perch or in a low display flight; female a harsh 'chick' and 'zink, zink, zink' repeated rapidly and regularly. Frequents tall grass, reeds and tangled vegetation near streams and vleis. Remains mostly within the vegetation, but sometimes perches conspicuously in a vertical position. If flushed makes off with conspicuous bobbing flight, then drops down and runs off; seldom flushes a second time. **17 cm** (Breëstertsanger)

NEAR THREATENED

often raises
crown feathers

conspicuous rufous
edges to wing-
feathers

1

greyish crown
contrasts with
pure white throat

2

indistinct facial
markings

chocolate
brown

dark mottling
(variable)

white
tips

graduated
tail

3

profuse
breast
markings

very long
rounded tail

paler than
(4)

tail shorter
than (3)

4

subtle
mottling

underparts only
slightly paler than
upperparts

orange-yellow eye

grey ear
coverts

5

orange tones
to underparts

flat
forehead

6

exceptionally broad
black tail with narrow
buff feather edges

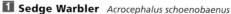

1 Sedge Warbler *Acrocephalus schoenobaenus*
Fairly common summer visitor. Recognised by **boldly streaked upperparts and crown**, and **conspicuous buff eyebrows**. Feeding call is a quiet 'tick, tick…'; alarm call a harsh, rasping 'churrr'. Has a loud, hurried, scratchy song with little repetition, chattering interspersed with sweet passages. Solitary in dense riverside vegetation, marsh fringes and sewage settlement pans. Creeps about at low level over the water, often in sparser vegetation than other warblers. **13 cm** (Europese Vleisanger)

2 African Reed Warbler *Acrocephalus baeticatus*
Common summer resident; occasional in winter. No distinctive eyebrow. **Underparts predominantly white, legs purple-brown.** Utters a sharp 'tik' while creeping about in thick cover, plus a harsh, racket-like 'churrr' when alarmed. Song is a slow, monotonous warbling 'chuck-chuck-weee-chirruc-churr-werr-weee-weee-chirruc…' for long periods when breeding; cf. (5). Usually occurs in reeds or other dense herbage near swamps; occasionally away from water in tall grass, bushes and suburbia. Remains well hidden but moves about constantly. The most numerous of the reed bed warblers on this page. **13 cm** (Kleinrietsanger)

3 Lesser Swamp Warbler *Acrocephalus gracilirostris*
Common resident. Has a **distinct white eyebrow** and **dark brown legs**. The rich, melodious song is 'chiroo-chrooo, tiririririri', slowly at first, then fast. Always found over fresh water in reeds, bulrushes or other waterside herbage. Bolder and more inquisitive than other species on this page. **15–17 cm** (Kaapse Rietsanger)

4 Little Rush Warbler *Bradypterus baboecala*
Common resident. Told by **dark upperparts, broad and rounded tail, definite eye-stripe** plus **faint markings on the upper breast**. Call is a loud, accelerating, distinctive 'cruk, cruk, cruk, cruk-cruk-cruk-crukcrukcrukcruk', like a stick drawn across a railing, followed by wing-snapping. Occurs singly or in pairs in dense vegetation over water. Secretive, mostly in the lower stratum. **17 cm** (Kaapse Vleisanger)

5 Marsh Warbler *Acrocephalus palustris*
Common, widespread summer visitor. **Eyebrows indistinct, underparts (except throat) lightly washed yellow-buff, upperparts (including rump) uniformly olive-brown.** Cf. (6), from which it **cannot be reliably distinguished in the field**. Utters a frequent 'tuc' and a rasping 'tsssh' while creeping about in cover, and has a pleasant, varied warbling song that includes much mimicry. Found **away from water** in dense bracken-briar patches, riparian thickets, parks and gardens, from where it sings almost continuously from Dec–Mar. Highly secretive. **12 cm** (Europese Rietsanger)

6 Eurasian Reed Warbler *Acrocephalus scirpaceus*
Rare summer visitor. Very few records for southern Africa. Accurate identification relies on measurements of the relative lengths of flight feathers. Song virtually indistinguishable from that of (2). Usually found in waterside vegetation. **13 cm** (Hermanrietsanger)

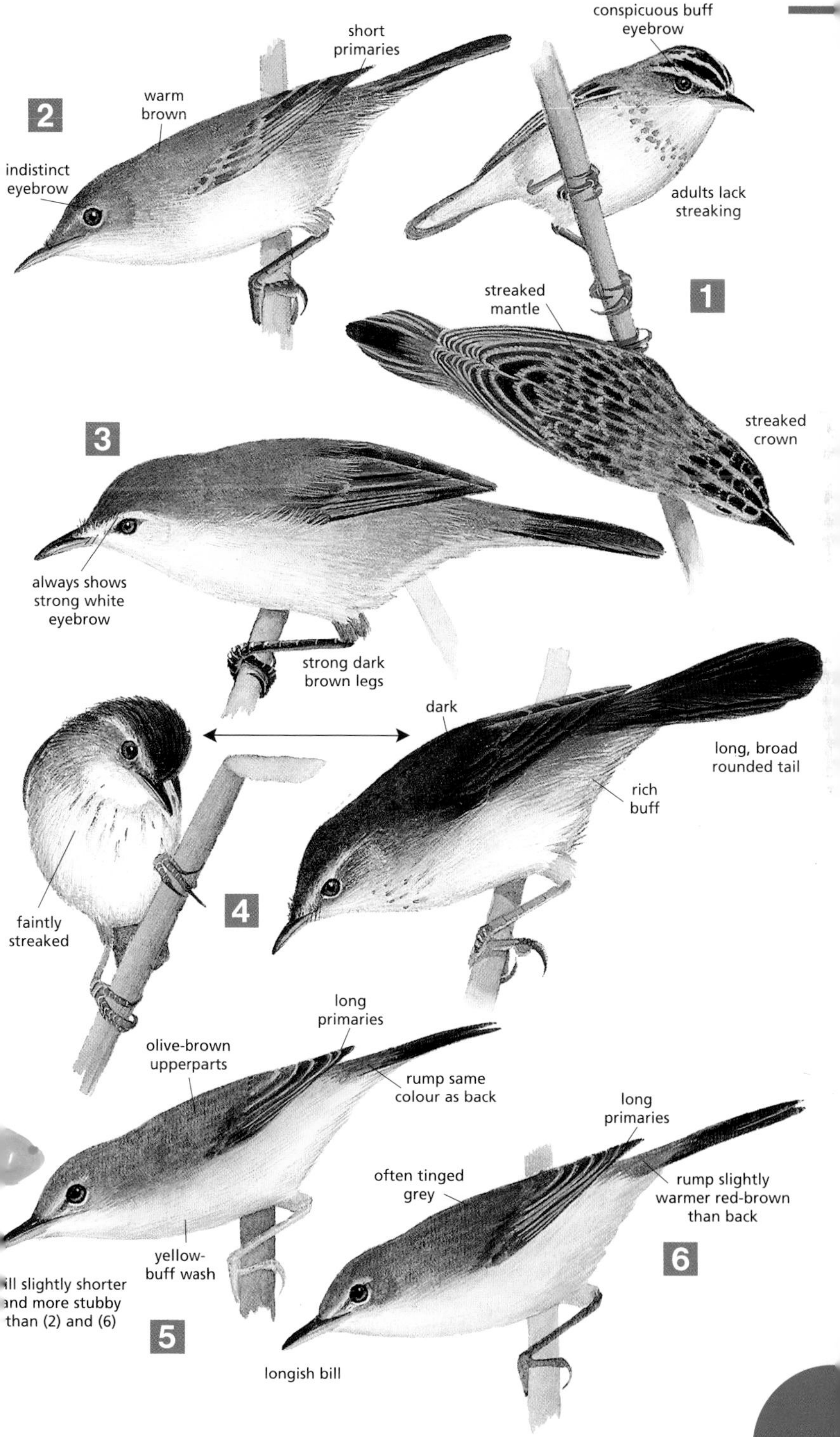

2
short primaries
warm brown
indistinct eyebrow

conspicuous buff eyebrow
adults lack streaking
1
streaked mantle
streaked crown

3
always shows strong white eyebrow
strong dark brown legs

dark
long, broad rounded tail
rich buff

faintly streaked
4

olive-brown upperparts
long primaries
rump same colour as back

often tinged grey
long primaries
rump slightly warmer red-brown than back
6

ill slightly shorter and more stubby than (2) and (6)
yellow-buff wash
5
longish bill

1 Greater Swamp Warbler *Acrocephalus rufescens* **R**
Fairly common, highly localised resident. A **large, dark warbler** with **prominent slender bill** and **dark legs; no eyebrow**. Has a rich, short song recalling that of Lesser Swamp-Warbler (p. 376), but deeper and more guttural in tone 'cheruckle, truptruptruptruptrup, weeweeweewee'. Heard more often than seen. Secretive in permanent papyrus and, less frequently, reed beds of the Okavango–Linyanti–Chobe region of northern Botswana. **18 cm** (Rooibruinrietsanger)

ENDANGERED

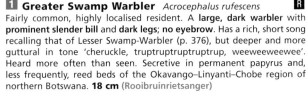

2 Basra Reed Warbler *Acrocephalus griseldis* **V**
Rare summer visitor. In size intermediate between African Reed-Warbler (p. 376) and (3). **Narrow, pointed and long bill** gives this species a long-faced appearance, further accentuated by its **dark eye-stripe** and **white eyebrow**. **Legs greyer**, and overall colder and darker in coloration compared to (3). Gives a slow, guttural song with slurred, nasal notes from thickets in moist, riverine woodland; sings throughout the heat of the day. Little known but possibly overlooked. Most records in Feb. **15 cm** (Basrarietsanger)

3 Great Reed Warbler *Acrocephalus arundinaceus*
Fairly common summer visitor. Best told by **very large size** (for a warbler), **powerful bill** and characteristic song: a slow, harsh warble of alternating low croaking and high squeaking 'gurk-gurk, twee-twee, gurk-gurk, trrit-trrit, gackle, kurra-kurra…'. Sings throughout the heat of the day. Solitary in reed beds, thickets or dense bush in suburbia. Less secretive and more inquisitive than most reed warblers, occasionally perching conspicuously, its movements heavy. **19 cm** (Grootrietsanger)

4 Dark-capped Yellow Warbler *Iduna natalensis*
Fairly common resident. Differs from the yellow weavers (p. 450), which are often found in the same habitat, in more **slender bill** and **longer tail**. Female is duller yellow; immature orange-yellow, the wing edges, rump and tail more buff. Cf. also Icterine Warbler (p. 372), which has blue-grey (not blackish) legs and frequents drier habitats. The song is 'trrp-trrp-chiri-chiri-chiri-chiri', rendered quickly and frequently repeated. Occurs singly or in pairs near water in reeds or other tall, rank cover, or away from water in bracken-briar patches of highveld valleys and forest fringes. Present in lower-lying localities during winter. Its habits are typical of the reed-warblers: secretive, but ascends some vertical stem occasionally to perch conspicuously, especially when singing. **14–15 cm** (Geelsanger)

eyebrow indistinct or absent

1

very long, narrow and pointed bill creates long-faced appearance

grey wash

sharp white eyebrow

2

dark eye-stripe

rather cold grey-brown

off-white

greyish legs

blackish legs

powerful bill

diffuse buff eyebrow

3

large body

warm brown

slender bill

olive-green

strong grey-brown legs

4

bright yellow (duller on female)

blackish legs

cf. Icterine Warbler (p. 372)

1 Bar-throated Apalis *Apalis thoracica*
Common resident. **Highly variable**; most common morphs illustrated, all males. Yellowest morph (a) occurs in northern South Africa; brown-capped morph (b) in Zimbabwe; morph with grey upperparts (c) in the southwest. Subtler variations also occur. In female, the **black throat-band** is usually narrower, sometimes entirely lacking. Told from (2) by **pale yellow eye, white outer tail-feathers** plus **darker upperparts**. Has a loud, distinctive call, 'pilly-pilly-pilly…'; pairs also sing in duet, the female's call being much faster than the male's. Occurs in pairs and frequently in bird parties in heavily wooded kloofs, streams, hillsides and forests. **12–13 cm** (Bandkeelkleinjantjie)

NEAR THREATENED

2 Rudd's Apalis *Apalis ruddi* `N E`
Locally common, near-endemic resident. Differs from (1) in **dark eye**, predominantly **yellow-and-green (not white) undertail**, more **yellow-green upperparts** and **buff wash to underparts**, especially throat. The call is a fast, loud 'trititritritritritritrit…' by one bird, the other calling at the same time (but out of phase) 'punk-punk-punk…'. Usually seen in pairs in coastal bush and dune forests, especially in dense thickets overgrown with creepers. Not secretive. **10,5–12 cm** (Ruddkleinjantjie)

3 Chirinda Apalis *Apalis chirindensis* `R E`
Uncommon, localised endemic resident. More **uniformly grey** than (5); cf. also co-occuring White-tailed Crested Flycatcher (p. 408). The call is a series of 'whit' notes with a whiplash quality. Occurs in highland forests and dense woodland where it frequents open, sunny patches rather than the gloomy interior. Often joins mixed bird parties. **13,5 cm** (Gryskleinjantjie)

4 Yellow-breasted Apalis *Apalis flavida*
Common resident. Easily identified by combination of **grey head, reddish-orange eye, yellow breast** and **green upperparts**. Amount of grey on head varies: most extensive (a) in northern Namibia and northern Botswana; least extensive (b) in Mozambique, elsewhere variable between these extremes. Tail length also varies. In all races **black central breast-bar may be absent or vestigial**. The normal call is a buzzy 'skee-skee-skee-chizZICK-chizZICK', to which the mate replies 'krik-krik-krik'. Usually occurs in pairs in a variety of bushveld habitats, riverine bush and forest fringes. **10–12,5 cm** (Geelborskleinjantjie)

5 Black-headed Apalis *Apalis melanocephala*
Common, localised resident. Distinguished from (3) by contrasting **dark upperparts** and **whitish underparts**. The call is a fast, slightly sibilant 'pee-pee-pee-pee…' repeated 20–30 times, often answered by another bird. Occurs in lowland forests, dense woodland, thick riverine bush and coastal scrub, often in the tree canopies. Fairly common in lowland Mozambique; marginal in eastern Zimbabwe. **14 cm** (Swartkopkleinjantjie)

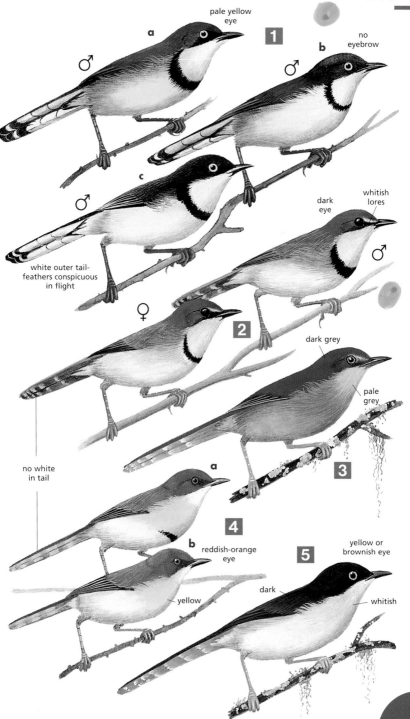

pale yellow eye

a

♂

1

b

no eyebrow

♂

c

♂

white outer tail-feathers conspicuous in flight

dark eye

whitish lores

♂

♀

2

dark grey

pale grey

3

no white in tail

a

4

b reddish-orange eye

yellow

5

yellow or brownish eye

dark

whitish

1 Long-billed Crombec *Sylvietta rufescens*

Common resident. **Tailless appearance** makes confusion possible only with (2) and (3), but beware of other small warblers that have lost their tails. Most similar to (2), but has **distinct eyebrow, dusky eye-stripe, paler coloration about face and ear coverts** and **more prominent bill**. Age differences negligible. The song is a loud, urgent-sounding 'tree-cheer, tree-cheer, tree-cheer…'. Call a short, dry trill. Usually occurs in pairs in bushveld and woodland, often in bird parties. Feeds among branches and tree trunks, clambering acrobatically about all levels of the vegetation. **10–12 cm** (Bosveldstompstert)

2 Red-faced Crombec *Sylvietta whytii*

Fairly common resident. Differs from (1) in **lack of distinct eye-stripe**; has a **more rufous face and ear coverts** and **shorter bill**. The call is a twittering 'si-si-si-see'; also a sharp 'tip', uttered so frequently as to become a long, rattling trill. Occurs in broad-leaved woodland (especially Miombo), feeding mainly among the small branches and outer twigs of trees. **10–11 cm** (Rooiwangstompstert)

3 Red-capped Crombec *Sylvietta ruficapilla*   R

Very rare in our subregion; exact status uncertain. Identified by **chestnut ear coverts and upper breast** (crown may lack chestnut entirely); **upperparts and underparts washed pale lemon**. Immature undescribed. The call is a loud 'richi-chichi-chichir' repeated about six times. Behaviour similar to other crombecs, but feeds in tree canopies. One record west of Victoria Falls. **11 cm** (Rooikroonstompstert)

4 Layard's Warbler *Sylvia layardi*   E

Uncommon endemic resident. Told from (5) by **white undertail coverts**; otherwise distinguished by **pale yellow eye** and **spotted throat**. Immature has brownish upperparts; throat less clearly spotted. Utters several clear song phrases, each interspersed with rattling notes, 'chiroo-chirroo-chirroo, trrrrr, chirree-chirree-chirree, trrrrr…'. Creeps about actively within dense cover, then darts to the next bush in quick, jerky flight. Occurs in fynbos and in both desert and mountain scrub throughout the more arid western regions, as well as in the Lesotho highlands. **15 cm** (Grysjeriktik)

5 Chestnut-vented Warbler (Tit-Babbler)   N E
Sylvia subcaerulea

Common, near-endemic resident. Easily identified by **pale eye** and **heavily spotted throat**. Told from (4) by **chestnut vent**. Immature resembles adult. Calls frequently, a variety of clear, ringing, quickly rendered notes, typically 'cheriktiktik' or 'chuu-ti chuu-ti chuu-chuu'. Also an accomplished mimic of other bird calls. Occurs in thickets in any woodland, mixed bushveld or thornveld. Habits very similar to those of (4). One of the standard members of bird parties in bushveld and Kalahari environments, but does not occur in the Lowveld. **15 cm** (Bosveldtjeriktik)

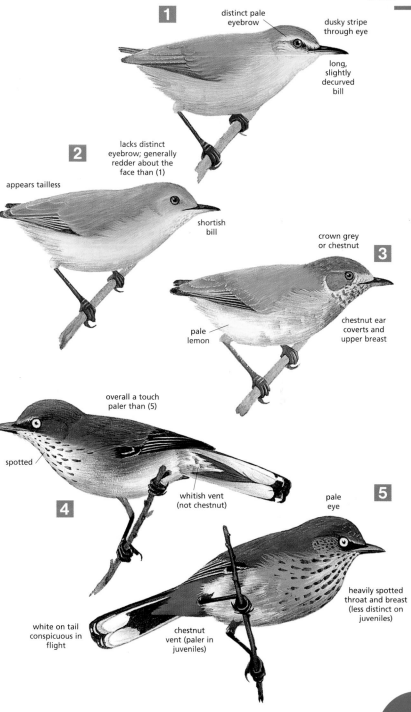

1

distinct pale eyebrow

dusky stripe through eye

long, slightly decurved bill

2

lacks distinct eyebrow; generally redder about the face than (1)

appears tailless

shortish bill

crown grey or chestnut

3

pale lemon

chestnut ear coverts and upper breast

overall a touch paler than (5)

spotted

whitish vent (not chestnut)

pale eye

4

5

white on tail conspicuous in flight

chestnut vent (paler in juveniles)

heavily spotted throat and breast (less distinct on juveniles)

1 Cape Penduline Tit *Anthoscopus minutus* N E

Common near-endemic resident. Distinguished by **very small size, black forehead** and **yellow underparts**; immature similar. Some western birds are greyer above than illustrated. Utters a sibilant 'swee-swee-swee-swee, tree-tree-tree'. Usually in groups of two to eight in dry *Acacia* woodland, thickets and fynbos. Feeds in the outer canopies of trees, flitting one after the other from tree to tree, constantly on the move. Most common in dry regions, but easily overlooked owing to tiny size and inconspicuous calls. **9–10 cm** (Kaapse Kapokvoël)

2 Grey Penduline Tit *Anthoscopus caroli*

Common resident. One of the **smallest birds in the region**. Underparts more buff than (1), **throat and breast pale grey** and forehead buffy; immature similar. Western and some northern races are **olive-green or yellow-green above**, more yellowish on belly. The call is 'chikchikZEE, chikchikZEE, chikchikZEE…'. Occurs in small groups in moist broad-leaved woodland; feeds mainly in the tree tops. **8–9 cm** (Gryskapokvoël)

3 Burnt-necked Eremomela *Eremomela usticollis*

Common resident. Distinguished by **brown throat-bar** (if present), otherwise best told from other similar species by **pale yellow-buff underparts** and **pale eye with brown surround**. The call is a rapid, high-pitched whistled series 'teeup-ti-ti-ti-ti-ti-ti-ti…', followed by a short trill. Occurs in groups of two to five in *Acacia* woodland, feeding in the tree canopies. **12 cm** (Bruinkeelbossanger)

4 Yellow-bellied Eremomela *Eremomela icteropygialis*

Common resident. Differs from white-eyes (p. 442) in lacking a white eye-ring and having **grey (not green) upperparts** and a **dark eye-stripe**. Western birds generally paler; central birds have a fulvous wash to the breast. Has a lively song 'chirri-chee-chee-choo' or 'How are you two' superficially similar to that of the Long-billed Crombec (p. 382). Occurs singly or in pairs in mixed bushveld or in arid regions and scrub, feeding in the outer and lower branches of bushes. **9–10 cm** (Geelpensbossanger)

5 Green-capped Eremomela *Eremomela scotops*

Uncommon resident. Identified by **greyish lores** and **yellow eye surrounded by a red ring**. Northwestern birds are whiter on lower abdomen and vent. Has various calls, a twittering 'nyum-nyum-nyum' or a repeated, monotonous 'tip-tip-tip…', plus a liquid song. Found in the leafy canopies of woodland and riverine forests, often in small groups that chase about restlessly in the upper branches while feeding. In bird parties in winter. **12 cm** (Donkerwangbossanger)

6 Yellow-throated Woodland-Warbler
Phylloscopus ruficapilla

Common resident. Differs from other small yellow warblers and white-eyes (p. 442) in **chestnut cap and eye-stripe** and habitat preference. In southern birds, yellow extends onto flanks and belly; in northern birds yellow confined mainly to throat. Immature has a greenish wash to the breast. Usually located by plaintive 'tieuu' call repeated for long periods, plus a high-pitched whistled song 'tirritee tirritee tirritee' or 'sip sip sip sip pilly pilly pilly'. A bird of evergreen forests and forested kloofs, where it forages in the canopy and midstratum. Related to Willow Warbler (p. 372). **11 cm** (Geelkeelsanger)

black-and-white speckles

1

yellow (variable)

buff

tiny size

2

buff (variable)

blueish grey

pale eye

blueish grey

3

not always present

pale yellow-buff

grey

4

yellow (regionally variable)

green face

greyish green

5

red eye-ring and yellow eye

yellow eyebrow

chestnut cap and eye-stripe

yellow vent

cf. white-eyes (p. 442)

6

1 Barred Wren-Warbler *Calamonastes fasciolatus*   N-E

Common, near-endemic resident. **Less white, less clearly barred on the underparts** than (2); **duller about the breast in non-breeding plumage.** Easily overlooked, and best located by its mournful call 'brreeet-brreeet-brreeet-brreeet…' uttered in bursts of three to five for long periods. Occurs in thornveld and broad-leaved woodland, usually in pairs. Secretive, creeps about in thickets, gradually working its way to the top before flitting to the next thicket. Its tail is held raised when alarmed. **13–15 cm** (Gebande Sanger)

2 Miombo Wren-Warbler *Calamonastes stierlingi*

Common resident. **Whiter,** more **boldly barred below** than (1); **tail shorter, bill blacker.** Has a far-carrying, much-repeated call 'birribit-birribit-birribit-birribit' or 'bullybeef-bullybeef-bullybeef'. Found within thickets in mixed bushveld and broad-leaved woodland, but may ascend to the tree canopy if disturbed. Very secretive, often creeping about with tail raised. **11,5–13 cm** (Stierlingsanger)

aka Kopje Warbler

3 Cinnamon-breasted Warbler *Euryptila subcinnamomea*   E

Fairly common, localised endemic resident. **Blackish tail** and **cinnamon forehead, breast and tail coverts** diagnostic. The call is a long, plaintive whistle 'eeeeeeee…', lasting about one and a half seconds, like a person whistling to attract someone's attention. Found on rock- and bush-strewn hills in arid regions. Hops about rocks with great agility, tail usually raised. Secretive and easily overlooked. **13–14 cm** (Kaneelborssanger)

4 Green-backed Camaroptera *Camaroptera brachyura*

Common resident. A dull, noisy inhabitant of the shady understorey. **Upperparts entirely dark olive-green** (has grey crown in central and southern Mozambique); closely similar to (5). Utters a goat-like bleating 'bzeeeb' and, in the breeding season, a loud territorial call 'chirrup, chirrup, chirrup…' continued for long periods. Occurs singly or in pairs in evergreen forest fringes, moist, well-wooded lowland valleys, and riverine and coastal bush. Mostly secretive in the lower stratum except when male ascends to a higher level to call. **12 cm** (Groenrugkwêkwêvoël)

5 Grey-backed Camaroptera *Camaroptera brevicaudata*

Common resident. In non-breeding plumage, some races have a **white to deep cream-buff upper breast,** not grey. Differs from (4) in **grey (not olive-green) upperparts;** immature does have green upperparts. Voice as (4). Occurs singly or in pairs in dry thickets in thornveld, woodland and especially bush-covered termitaria. **Shortish tail** often held cocked. Replaces the previous species in northern and western localities. **12 cm** (Grysrugkwêkwêvoël)

aka Yellow-rumped…

6 Karoo Eremomela *Eremomela gregalis*   E

Uncommon, localised endemic resident. Distribution does not overlap with (5); differs in having **pale yellow eyes,** a **smaller bill, pale yellow undertail coverts** and **black legs.** Calls a continuous, high-pitched 'peewip peewip peewip…'. Contact call a sharp 'twink'. Feeding groups call continuously 'ti-ti-ti-ti…'. Small groups occur in Karoo scrub. **12 cm** (Groenbossanger)

tail often cocked

1

2

dark brown or greyish eye

Br

pale reddish eye

N-Br

neat dark barring on white background

brown barring on buffy background

3

cinnamon outer tail coverts

grey face

cinnamon

tail often cocked

dark olive-green

4

grey-brown

N-Br

5

grey

Br

yellow undertail coverts

pale yellow eye

black legs

6

white or pale greyish

1 **Moustached Grass Warbler** *Melocichla mentalis*
Uncommon, localised resident. Told from (2) by **plain upperparts and underparts, rounded tail** and **rufous forehead, not crown**. The song is 'tip, tip, twiddle-iddle-see', the first two sounds slow, the rest fast. Occurs in short, rank grass, bracken and scattered bushes in marshy ground near streams. Very similar in behaviour to (2). Remains mostly concealed within vegetation. **19 cm** (Breëstertgrasvoël)

2 **Cape Grassbird** *Sphenoeacus afer*   E
Common endemic resident. Differs from (1) in **heavily marked upperparts, streaked underparts** (except race (b) of eastern regions) and generally **rusty coloration**; from cisticolas in **larger size, black malar streaks** and **long, rufous tail with tapering, straggly feathers**. Has a distinctive burst of song 'chirp-chirp-chirp does it tickle yooou', plus a cat-like mewing like Cape Longclaw (p. 328). Frequents the long grass and bracken of hillsides and open streams away from hills. Occasionally perches prominently on some tall grass or weed; otherwise skulks within the vegetation. **19–23 cm** (Grasvoël)

aka Damara Rockjumper

3 **Rockrunner** *Achaetops pycnopygius*   N E
Common, localised near-endemic resident. Differs from other grass-warblers within its limited distribution in **heavily streaked head and mantle, bold facial markings, rufous belly** and habit of keeping its tail raised high. Song is a warbling 'tip-tip-tootle-titootle-tootle-too' heard early mornings and evenings. A shy but lively bird of grassy rock- and bush-strewn hillsides and dry watercourses in Namibia. **17 cm** (Rotsvoël)

CISTICOLAS

Small, closely similar, **brown grass-warblers**. There are often subtle differences between sexes and breeding and non-breeding plumages; tail lengths differ also. They are **best identified by song, habitat preference and behaviour**, as plumage differences are difficult to identify in the field. Territorial behaviour common to the very small 'cloud' cisticolas (this page and overleaf) is an **aerial cruise accompanied by continuous singing** by the males. They rise high into the air with rapidly whirring wings, often out of sight, and then cruise about singing, while some species make audible wing-snaps. The descent is a near-vertical plunge, but they check just above the grass and fly level briefly before dropping down. In some species the descent is accompanied by wing-snaps.

4 **Pale-crowned Cisticola** *Cisticola cinnamomeus*
Uncommon, localised resident. Male in summer identified by **pale crown** and **dark loral spot**; both sexes otherwise indistinguishable from Cloud and Wing-snapping Cisticolas (p. 390). Immature has bright yellow underparts. The song in flight is a quiet and very high-pitched, continually repeated 'siep-siep-siep…', sometimes varied every few seconds by scarcely audible notes 'twee-twee-twee-ti-ti-ti-ti-ti-ti-ti-ti-tsee-tsee…'. This may be repeated rapidly during the descent, which occurs without wing-snaps. Occurs in grassland in damp localities in both lowland and highland regions. **9–11 cm** (Bleekkopklopkloppie)

cf. Fan-tailed
Grassbird (p. 374)

1

rusty cap

a

heavily marked

black malar streak

plain brown; unstreaked

conspicuous black malar streak

b

2

heavily streaked head and mantle

3

dark spots

rufous

broad, dark tail with rounded tip

long, straggly tail

unstreaked pale crown

♂ **Br**

dark lores

♀ **Br**

female and non-br male virtually indistinguishable from other small, short-tailed cisticolas (p. 390)

4

1 Zitting Cisticola *Cisticola juncidis*

Common resident. Female resembles non-breeding male. More **richly coloured** than other small cisticolas. Conspicuous only in summer, when male cruises at a height of about 10–50 m with **dipping flight, calling 'zit zit zit zit...'** at each dip at about half-second intervals. The call may also be made while perched on a grass stem. **Does not snap its wings.** Found in grassland, often near marshes or vleis, and on fallow lands and waste ground. **10–12 cm** (Landeryklopkloppie)

2 Desert Cisticola *Cisticola aridulus*

Common resident. Sexes closely similar. **Paler** and **more slender** than other small cisticolas. In summer, male utters a repetitive, high-pitched 'zink zink zink zink...' while **cruising low over grassland**, climbing and dropping with **wing-snaps and irregular dashes**; also calls 'tuc tuc tuc tuc weee'. Occurs in more arid grassland than (1), especially short grass, old burned areas and fallow lands; seldom in moist regions. **10–12 cm** (Woestynklopkloppie)

3 Cloud Cisticola *Cisticola textrix*   N E

Common, near-endemic resident. Female resembles male. In the Western Cape, both sexes may have **clear or heavily spotted underparts**. In summer, male rises high into the air, **usually out of sight**, and cruises about, uttering a wispy 'see-see-see-see-chick-chick-chick' repeated at two- or three-second intervals. Song superficially similar to that of (4), but much faster. **When descending makes an almost vertical plunge,** calling a rapid 'chick-chick-chick-chick...'. **Does not snap its wings** when descending. Occurs in short grassland at most levels, but not montane grassland. **10 cm** (Gevlekte Klopkloppie)

4 Wing-snapping Cisticola *Cisticola ayresii*

Common resident. In summer, male cruises high in the sky, **usually out of sight**, calling a wispy, high-pitched 'soo-see-see-see...' at about three-second intervals while flying into wind. Song similar to that of (3), but with slower notes. This is followed by **10 or more volleys of wing-snaps while flying downwind, before plummeting to earth** while calling a rapid 'ticka-ticka-ticka...'; accompanied by **violent wing-snapping** and terminal swooping and swerving. Occurs in high-altitude short, dry grassland and near vleis; does not perch conspicuously. **9–11 cm** (Kleinste Klopkloppie)

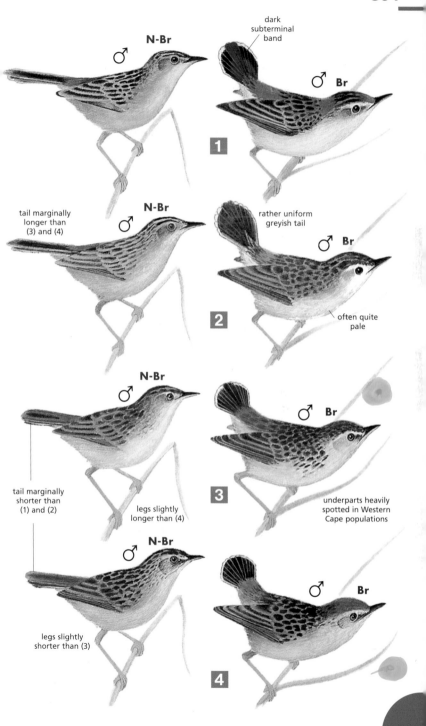

N-Br ♂

dark subterminal band

♂ **Br**

1

tail marginally longer than (3) and (4)

N-Br ♂

rather uniform greyish tail

♂ **Br**

often quite pale

2

N-Br ♂

♂ **Br**

tail marginally shorter than (1) and (2)

legs slightly longer than (4)

underparts heavily spotted in Western Cape populations

3

N-Br ♂

legs slightly shorter than (3)

♂ **Br**

4

1 Short-winged Cisticola *Cisticola brachypterus* [R]

Uncommon, localised resident. **Dark brown cap** the same colour as rest of the **unmarked upperparts**; sexes are alike. Immature is more yellow-washed; eyes grey. In the breeding season, male sings from the **top of a dead tree**, a wispy, descending series of notes 'seee see-see-see…'. Also has a high aerial display and plunge-dives like Cloud Cisticola (p. 390). Occurs in broad-leaved woodland, where it forages below the canopy or in the grass. Occurs mostly in palm savanna in Mozambique, just entering eastern Zimbabwe. **10–11 cm** (Kortvlerktinktinkie)

aka Piping …

2 Neddicky *Cisticola fulvicapilla*

Common resident. Sexes are alike; immature dull. **Plain-backed** like (1) but **larger and longer-tailed**, the cap rufous. Closer in size to the 'cloud' cisticolas on pp. 388–390, but with longer tail and plain mantle. Southern and eastern races (a) have **blue-grey underparts** and a pure, whistled song 'fee-fee-fee-fee…'. Northern races (b) are **browner below** and utter a more scratchy 'chirri-chirri-chirri…'. In the rainy season sings for long periods from an exposed high perch. The alarm call is a rapid tinkling by several birds 'ticki-ticki-ticki-ticki-ticki' (sounds like a fingernail drawn across the teeth of a comb) while flitting from bush to bush. Occurs in pairs and family parties, frequenting the lower stratum: (a) in montane and fynbos regions, (b) in grassy woodlands and thornveld thickets. **10–11 cm** (Neddikkie)

3 Chirping Cisticola *Cisticola pipiens* [R]

Fairly common, localised resident. Non-breeding plumage illustrated. Breeding plumage **less rufous about the face, lores and underparts**, the **tail shorter**; cf. Rufous-winged Cisticola (p. 394). The song, in late summer, is four twanging notes repeated 'trrrit-trrrit-trree-trreeeeee…'. Occurs in the northern Botswana wetlands, inhabiting reeds and papyrus in water, or shoreline bushes and grass. In display flight the tail is fanned and flirted from side to side as though loose. **12,5–15 cm** (Piepende Tinktinkie)

4 Singing Cisticola *Cisticola cantans* [R]

Uncommon, localised resident. The only plain-backed cisticola with conspicuous **reddish primary feathers**, these and the crown contrasting with **grey-brown upperparts** when breeding (summer); cf. also Red-winged Warbler (p. 400). Brighter in winter: **upperparts washed rufous** with **faint, darker blotches**; **eyebrow then distinct** and **tail longer**. Immature is duller, sulphured yellow on the breast and belly. The call is a loud 'jhu-jee' or 'wheech-oo'; also 'cheer cheer cheer', reminiscent of Rattling Cisticola (p. 394). Secretive in rank undergrowth and bracken-briar patches near forest fringes in eastern Zimbabwe and adjacent Mozambique. **12–14 cm** (Singende Tinktinkie)

aka Red-headed …

5 Grey-backed Cisticola *Cisticola subruficapilla* [N E]

Common, near-endemic resident. Southern race (a) has **grey back** with **black streaking extending to forehead, ear coverts and upper breast**. Northwestern race (b) has **upperparts less obviously grey, streaks finer and fainter**, and the sub-loral spot absent. Immature is rustier; yellow-orange about the face, eyes grey, bill yellower and legs paler. The breeding song is a hurried, high-pitched jumble of descending notes 'weesisee-chizzarizzaree-chichioo…'; at other times calls 'prouee, tweep, tweep'. Alarm note is a piping 'tee-tee-tee…'. Songs and calls very similar to those of Wailing Cisticola (p. 394). A lively species found in coastal fynbos, scrub and grass on estuarine flats, montane foothills, Karoo and semi-desert western regions. **12–13 cm** (Grysrugtinktinkie)

Br **1**
not rufous

dark brown unmarked upperparts

whitish

2 **a**
rufous cap

blue-grey

plain dark brown

b
washed pale dusky brown

N-Br **3**
buff

cf. Luapula Cisticola (p. 394)

long brown tail

5 **a**
streaked upper breast

grey back with black streaking

b
faint streaking

4 **Br**
grey-brown upperparts

reddish panel

N-Br
rufous crown

washed rufous

1 Rufous-winged Cisticola *Cisticola galactotes* N E

Common, near-endemic resident. Best identified by habitat, behaviour and call. Associated mostly with large waterways, marshes and swamps; also cane fields near water along the east coast. When breeding, male calls a loud, rasping 'zreeee' or 'rraaare', often interspersed with various chirps 'chit-chit-chit...' or 'trrrp-trrrp-trrrp...'. When alarmed, calls a loud, deliberate 'prrrit-prrrit-prrrit'. Similar to (2) with **dark-streaked mantle** and **rufous crown**, but replaces that species at lower altitudes and in tropical areas. **12–13 cm** (Swartrugtinktinkie)

2 Luapula Cisticola *Cisticola luapula* R

NOT ILLUSTRATED. Common resident. Previously considered a subspecies of (1). In southern Africa, restricted to the swamps and waterways of the Okavango Delta and Caprivi region of northern Namibia; thus unlikely to be confused with (1). However, cf. co-occurring and very similar Chirping Cisticola (p. 392). Generally **brighter, paler** and **less brown** than that species, and has a **shorter tail** and more **distinctly marked mantle**. Best distinguished by habitat of tangled growth and reeds at water's edge, avoiding papyrus beds over open water; and call, similar to that of (1). **12–13 cm** (Luapulatinktinkie)

3 Levaillant's Cisticola *Cisticola tinniens*

Common resident. Superficially similar to (1) in having a **black back** and **rufous crown**, but confusion is unlikely since there is very little overlap in the ranges of the two species. Common pond and streamside cisticola frequenting waterside sedges and the edges of reed beds; seldom enters reed beds. Very rarely also found in tall, dry grassland away from water. Perches conspicuously and sings 'chi-chi-chirrrueee', the first two notes almost inaudible, the final phrase loud; also has a plaintive 'dzwee, dzwee, dzwee' alarm call. **12,5 cm** (Vleitinktinkie)

4 Rattling Cisticola *Cisticola chiniana*

Very common resident. A **robust cisticola** with few distinguishing features; seasonal differences slight. Best told by habitat, behaviour and song. Male's characteristic song, with slight locality differences, is 'chi chi chi ch-r-r-r-r-r', the last syllable with a distinct rattle. When alarmed calls a continuing 'cheer, cheer, cheer...'. The common bushveld cisticola that can be heard, and seen, singing for much of the year from the top of a bush. Also occurs in thornveld and coastal bush. Forages low down in tangled grass and bush. **14–16 cm** (Bosveldtinktinkie)

5 Tinkling Cisticola *Cisticola rufilatus*

Fairly common, localised resident. Has distinct **reddish head markings, white eyebrow** and **long, orange-brown tail**. The male's song is a leisurely series of high, bell-like notes 'to-wee, to-wee, to-wee...' repeated six to eight times; alarm call a high-pitched series of bubbling 'dididididi' notes. Occurs in dry, small-tree savanna with rank grass and scrub. In the western part of its range, particularly attracted to broad-leaved woodland on sandy soil. Shy and retiring. **13–14 cm** (Rooitinktinkie)

6 Wailing Cisticola *Cisticola lais*

Common resident. The **head is well marked** throughout the year; **lores and ear coverts dusky. Plumage redder and tail longer when not breeding**. Immature has strongly sulphured underparts. Characteristic call is a piercing wailing note 'hweeeeeet' or 'to-weee-yeh' increasing in volume. Also gives a bubbling trill like Grey-backed Cisticola (p. 392). Occurs on well-grassed hillsides and mountain slopes, often in patches of scrub. **13–14 cm** (Huiltinktinkie)

bright rufous crown

heavily streaked black back

3

1

a

rufous wing panel

b

1

4

best identified by voice

J

brown tail

prominent whitish eyebrow

most juvenile cisticolas show a yellow wash on their underparts

N-Br

reddish cap and nape

Br

N-Br

streaked

Br

6

5

long orange-brown tail

aka Rock- loving ...

1 Lazy Cisticola *Cisticola aberrans*

Common, localised resident. Appears **plain-backed**; non-breeding plumage (Apr–Oct) generally **warmer rufous on upperparts, underparts more strongly suffused with ochre**; tail length constant. Immature is more rusty-coloured. The song is a series of fairly loud metallic notes 'tu-hwee-tu-hwee-tu-hwee…' reaching a crescendo; alarm call a loud 'breeerp' or 'tu-hweeee', usually uttered with the longish tail cocked vertically. Frequents hillsides with bushes, rocks and long grass, often in the dense vegetation near the foot of a hill close to a stream; also forest-fringe scrub. Hops about on rocks and flirts its tail upwards like a prinia (p. 398). **14–16 cm** (Luitinktinkie)

2 Red-faced Cisticola *Cisticola erythrops*

Common resident. A **plain-backed** cisticola. Crown the same colour as rest of upperparts in all seasons: **greyish when breeding** (Dec–Mar), **more rufous at other times. Lores, eyebrows and ear coverts washed reddish**, most strongly when not breeding. The call, loud and arresting, is 'wink-wink-WINK' getting louder with successive notes, or a series of eight to 10 notes, 'weep, weep, weep…' rising to a crescendo. Inhabits waterside vegetation near rivers, dams and swamps, or away from water in damp situations. Secretive, but presence given away by frequent and loud calls. **12–13 cm** (Rooiwangtinktinkie)

3 Croaking Cisticola *Cisticola natalensis*

Common resident. A **large, heavy-bodied, thick-billed** cisticola with **well-streaked upperparts** and **without rufous crown**. Seasonal differences as illustrated. Female smaller than male; immature like non-breeding adult but bright sulphur below. Breeding male cruises a few metres above the ground with a loose wing action, uttering a harsh 'cru-cru-cru-cru…'; also calls from a low bush, a harsh 'chee-fro' or 'chip-munk'. Alarm call is a frog-like 'tee-yrrr'. Frequents rank grassland with scattered bushes, or grassy clearings in bushveld. Very active and conspicuous when breeding (Nov–Mar); unobtrusive at other times. Often feeds on the ground. **13–17 cm** (Groottinktinkie)

1 dull-rufous crown

plain or very faintly mottled

long tail often cocked

cf. Neddicky (p. 392)

2 Br

N-Br

J

2

plain

no rufous

N-Br

stout bill

3

Br

longer tail in non-breeding plumage

large size and bulky shape

♀

short tail when breeding

PRINIAS

Small warblers with **long tails frequently held in a near-vertical position**. Sexes are alike. Calls consist of a **single repetitive note** and are often closely similar.

1 **Black-chested Prinia** *Prinia flavicans*

Common, near-endemic resident. Distinctive in breeding plumage (summer) with **yellow or white underparts**. At other times the **black breast-band** is either absent or vestigial and the **underparts pale sulphurous-yellow**. The call is a loud, much-repeated 'chip-chip chip...'; also an occasional 'zrrrrt-zrrrrt-zrrrrt'; more scratchy and buzzy than that of widely overlapping (2). Pairs and small family parties occur in dry thornveld, scrub, rank grass and suburbia. **13–15 cm** (Swartbandlangstertjie)

2 **Tawny-flanked Prinia** *Prinia subflava*

Common resident. Told by **clear white underparts, tawny flanks** and **red-brown wing edges**. When disturbed utters a characteristic weeping sound 'sbeeeee-sbeeeee...'. The normal call is a loud, continuous 'przzt-ptzzt-przzt...' or 'trit-trit-trit...', the actual sound variable, but sharper and more pure than other prinias' calls. Noisy and conspicuous, usually in parties of four to six in riverine vegetation and suburban gardens, preferring moister situations than (1). **10–15 cm** (Bruinsylangstertjie)

3 **Roberts's Warbler** *Oreophilais robertsi*

Uncommon, localised endemic resident. A **dusky, prinia-like bird lacking any distinctive markings**. Utters occasional outbursts of noisy chattering 'cha cha cha cha...'. Usually found in small groups in dense scrub and bracken-briar patches, or in bush among rocks and near forests in the eastern highlands of Zimbabwe. Cf. also co-occurring Chirinda Apalis (p. 380). **14 cm** (Woudlangstertjie)

4 **Karoo Prinia** *Prinia maculosa*

Very common endemic resident. Told by **well-spotted breast and flanks, pale yellow underparts** and **pale brown eyes**. The voice is a chirping 'tweet-tweet-tweet' and a churring alarm call: cf (5). Its general actions and behaviour much like other prinias. Occurs in small family parties in dense, matted scrub and fynbos within the Karoo – from the southern Drakensberg to southern Namibia. Easily located by its call from within dense habitat. **14 cm** (Karoolangstertjie)

5 **Drakensberg Prinia** *Prinia hypoxantha*

Fairly common endemic resident. Closely similar to (4) in all ways except coloration, its **underparts being a rich saffron-yellow** while its **upper breast is only lightly spotted**. Its call is identical to that of (4). Occurs in small family groups in rank growth in vleis, matted river scrub and forest-edge thickets northwards along the Drakensberg escarpment from about East London to the Soutpansberg. Shares its habitat with (2). **14 cm** (Drakensberglangstertjie)

6 **Namaqua Warbler** *Phragmacia substriata*

Fairly common endemic resident. Differs from (4) in **white underparts** with **more rufous flanks** and vent plus **more rufous upperparts**. The call is an explosive 'chit-churrr'; also calls 'che-kee-kee', the song a rapid series of 'tik-tik-tik-tik...' notes. Often found in small family groups. More secretive than other prinias and rapid in movements. Occurs in *Acacia* scrub in dry Karoo river gullies and in reed beds along watercourses and near dams. **14 cm** (Namakwalangstertjie)

N-Br

no rufous in wing

pale sulphurous-yellow

1

Br

black band

red-brown wing edges

white

tawny flanks

2

pale eye

very dark above

grey

3

4

grey-brown tone

well-spotted breast and flanks

pale yellow underparts

rufous tone

plain

lightly spotted rich saffron-yellow

5

fine streaking

6

1 Rufous-eared Warbler *Malcorus pectoralis*   **E**
Common endemic resident. A **prinia-like** bird with variable **black breast-band** and **rufous ear-patches**, these being paler in female. Has a loud, penetrating call 'tee tee tee tee' plus a quiet 'chit'. Occurs in low, sparse scrub where pairs or small parties spend much time on the ground, often preferring to run rather than fly. The **long, thin tail** is characteristically held upright. **14–16 cm** (Rooioorlangstertjie)

2 Red-winged Warbler *Heliolais erythropterus*   **R**
Uncommon resident. Seasonal plumage differences as illustrated. At all times the **red-brown wings** and **yellow-brown eyes** are conspicuous and distinguish this species from other small warblers; cf. also Singing Cisticola (p. 392). Calls frequently, a squeaky 'pseep-pseep-pseep'; also utters a high-pitched 'chirrr'. An active, restless bird that occurs in well-grassed woodland, especially where long grass touches low branches. **13,5 cm** (Rooivlerksanger)

3 Southern Hyliota *Hyliota australis*
Uncommon resident. Male told from (4) by **dull, purple-black upperparts** and **limited white wing markings**, these **not extending onto the tertials**; **underparts marginally paler**. Female told by **dark brownish (not dark grey) upperparts**. Immature resembles female but is lighter brown. Has a two-syllabled chippering whistle and a trilling warble. A highly mobile, active leaf-gleaner found mostly in the upper canopy of broad-leaved woodland, often in bird parties. **14 cm** (Mashonahyliota)

4 Yellow-bellied Hyliota *Hyliota flavigaster*   **R**
Rare resident. Very similar to more common (3) and often mistaken for that species. Given a good view, male can be told by **glossy blue-black upperparts** and **white wing-feather edges extending to the tertials**; female by **dark grey (not dark brownish) coloration above**. Immature has finely barred upperparts and pale feather edges. Calls and habits are very similar to those of (3). Occurs sparsely in miombo woodland in Mozambique. **14 cm** (Geelborshyliota)

FLYCATCHERS

Small, insectivorous birds with **prominent bristles protruding from the base of their bills**. Many of the soberly coloured species **catch insects on the ground** or in flight after watching from a low perch; others, especially the colourful and ornate species, are leaf-gleaners, but also **hawk insects in short aerial sallies**.

5 Collared Flycatcher *Ficedula albicollis*   **R**
Rare summer visitor. Male in breeding plumage told from other pied flycatchers, especially Fiscal Flycatcher (p. 404), by **smaller size, white forehead and collar** and **small bill**. Non-breeding male, normally seen in southern Africa, resembles female and **lacks the collar**. Female told by **more extensive white on wings, duskier breast** and small bill. The call is a sharp 'whit-whit'. Perches on some low branch from where it hunts insects; usually solitary. Recorded mostly in miombo woodland in Zimbabwe; vagrant further south, where it may occur in any wooded habitat. **13 cm** (Withalsvlieëvanger)

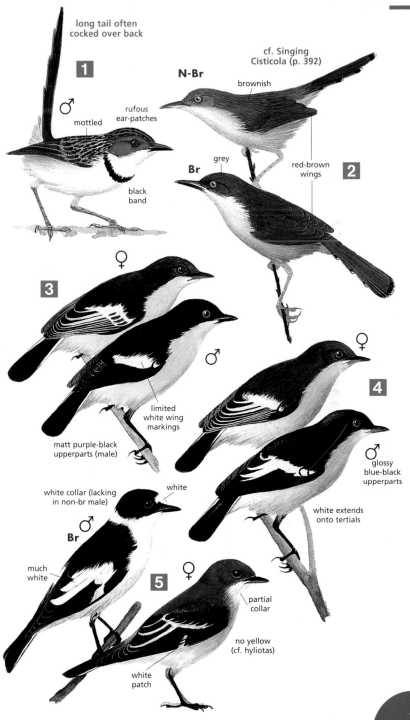

long tail often cocked over back

1

♂

mottled

rufous ear-patches

black band

N-Br

cf. Singing Cisticola (p. 392)

brownish

Br

grey

red-brown wings

2

3

♀

♂

limited white wing markings

matt purple-black upperparts (male)

♀

4

♂ glossy blue-black upperparts

white extends onto tertials

white collar (lacking in non-br male)

white

Br ♂

much white

5

♀

partial collar

no yellow (cf. hyliotas)

white patch

1 Spotted Flycatcher *Muscicapa striata*

Common summer visitor. Distinguished from (2) by **slimmer, less dumpy shape** plus **streaked crown and underparts**. Sometimes utters a thin, sibilant, two-syllabled 'tzee-chick' while flicking its wings; also a sibilant 'tssssssss'. Solitary in any open woodland, mixed bushveld and well-wooded suburbia. Perches on a low branch beneath a tree, from where it hawks insects or catches them on the ground, frequently returning to the same perch and flicking its wings after landing. **14–15 cm** (Europese Vlieëvanger)

2 African Dusky Flycatcher *Muscicapa adusta*

Common, localised resident. **More dumpy than (1)**, the **underparts duskier with faint smudges** (not streaks). Immature is like adult. Utters a thin, sibilant 'zeeet' and a characteristic 'tsi-ri-rt'. Occurs singly or in pairs in forest fringes, riverine forests and broad-leaved woodland in moister regions. Behaviour much like (1) but frequents the more lush coastal and montane mist-belt regions. **12–13 cm** (Donkervlieëvanger)

3 Pale Flycatcher *Bradornis pallidus*

Uncommon resident. A **dull, featureless bird, the underparts scarcely paler than the upperparts**; cf. Chat Flycatcher (p. 404). Immature has upperparts with buff-edged feathers; streaked below. Mostly silent. Usually found in pairs or small parties in broad-leaved woodland or mixed bushveld (not thornveld). Perches on a low branch from where it watches the ground for insects. Sparsely distributed throughout its range. **15–17 cm** (Muiskleurvlieëvanger)

4 Grey Tit-Flycatcher *Myioparus plumbeus*

Uncommon resident. Differs from (5) mainly in behaviour and **white outer tail-feathers**. Immature is like adult. The call is a loud, cheerful 'teee-reee', the second syllable lower than the first, like a distant ringing telephone. At close quarters, also a trilling 'wir-ri-rit'. Occurs singly or in pairs in broad-leaved woodland, mixed bushveld and riverine forests. Calls frequently and fans its tail while raising and lowering it, constantly moving through the midstratum; cf. habits of (5). Often joins bird parties. **14 cm** (Waaierstertvlieëvanger)

5 Ashy Flycatcher *Muscicapa caerulescens*

Fairly common resident. **Blue-grey coloration** makes this species confusable only with (4), from which it differs in behaviour and **lack of any white in tail**. Immature has spotted upperparts and mottled underparts. Calls a short descending phrase 'tsip-tsip-tsip-tsip-tse-tslipip' but is mostly silent. Occurs in pairs in coastal bush, riverine forests, forest fringes and broad-leaved woodland. Perches in the midstratum and watches the ground for insects or catches them in mid-air, often returning to the same perch. A quiet, inconspicuous species. **14–15 cm** (Blougrysvlieëvanger)

6 Fairy Flycatcher *Stenostira scita* E

Common endemic resident. **Very small grey-and-black bird** with **conspicuous white wing-bar and outer tail-feathers**. The **pink central belly** is inconspicuous in the field. Immature has brownish rather than grey plumage. The call is a short, sibilant trill 'kisskisskisskiss'. The short musical song usually descends in pitch. Flits about actively, feeding within bushes or the outer canopy of trees within the Karoo biome, frequently bobbing and fanning its tail. In the south often occurs near rivers; moves north in winter where it frequents woodland, montane scrub, plantations and suburbia in Gauteng. **12 cm** (Feevlieëvanger)

1

elongated shape

streaked crown

notably long wings (long-distance migrant)

streaked

rather pale

flicks wings open when landing

2

plain or very faintly streaked

often shows short white eyebrow

dumpy shape

smudged

dusky

3

overall comparatively featureless

4

tail often fanned and raised, showing white edges

overall greyish head

J

5

white eyebrow, white eye-ring and black lores

no white in tail

6

cf. batises (p. 406)

long tail

white outer tail-feathers

faint pink wash

1 Chat Flycatcher *Bradornis infuscatus*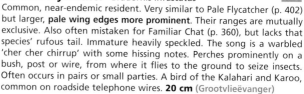

Common, near-endemic resident. Very similar to Pale Flycatcher (p. 402) but larger, **pale wing edges more prominent**. Their ranges are mutually exclusive. Also often mistaken for Familiar Chat (p. 360), but lacks that species' rufous tail. Immature heavily speckled. The song is a warbled 'cher cher chirrup' with some hissing notes. Perches prominently on a bush, post or wire, from where it flies to the ground to seize insects. Often occurs in pairs or small parties. A bird of the Kalahari and Karoo, common on roadside telephone wires. **20 cm** (Grootvlieëvanger)

2 Marico Flycatcher *Bradornis mariquensis* N E

Common, near-endemic resident. Differs from similar flycatchers in **white underparts contrasting strongly with brown upperparts**. Immature is spotted whitish above, streaked dark on white below – this streaking heavier than in immature of (1). Call is a soft, sparrow-like 'chew-week'. Frequents *Acacia* thornveld. Perches prominently on the outer branch of a bush, from where it watches the ground for insects, occasionally hawking them in the air. **18 cm** (Maricovlieëvanger)

3 Black-and-white Flycatcher *Bias musicus* R

Rare resident. Sexes markedly different. Both have **crested heads, heavy bills, prominent rictal bristles, yellow eyes** and **short yellow legs**. Utters sharp whistling notes 'tchi-kik-you' or 'we-chip! we-chip!' and sings 'wit-tu-wit-tu-tu-tu', the notes first ascending then descending in pitch. Pairs or parties occur in the tops of tall trees in forest fringes and bushveld in central Mozambique. Has the habit of circling around a tree in slow flight with rapid wing beats. **16 cm** (Witpensvlieëvanger)

4 Fiscal Flycatcher *Sigelus silens* E

Common endemic resident. Differs from Common Fiscal (p. 412) in **less robust bill** and prominent **white 'windows' in the tail**; the white wing-bar extends only halfway along the folded wing, not to the shoulder. Female's plumage is duller grey-brown (not black, as in male). Has a sibilant, rather weak song 'swee-swee-ur' and other similar sounds, often in prolonged sequence. Usually occurs in pairs in bush country, grassy Karoo, fynbos and suburbia. Perches prominently on a branch or post and flies to the ground to seize insects. **17–20 cm** (Fiskaalvlieëvanger)

5 Southern Black Flycatcher *Melaenornis pammelaina*

(ILLUSTRATED ON P. 335) Common resident. The tail shows a small indentation at the tip (not a distinct fork), the outer tail-feathers being straight, not splayed. Delicate insectivorous bill; eye has a dark-brown iris. Sexes are alike; immature as illustrated. Not very vocal, uttering various low sibilant sounds 'swee' or 'swee-ur'. Singly or in pairs in any woodland, thornveld or bushveld. Catches insects on the ground, flying down from a perch in typical flycatcher fashion. Often occurs alongside (1) but, by contrast, is quiet. **19–22 cm** (Swartvlieëvanger)

large size diagnostic
(cf. Familiar Chat, p. 360)

2

1

J

white

J

conspicuous
pale wing
edges

crest

yellow
eye

♂

rufous

♀

cf. batises
(p. 406)

3

short
yellow legs

♂

no white on
'shoulder'

4

♀

duller grey-brown
above than male

bill not
hooked

medium
length
tail

J

cf. Common
Fiscal (p. 412)

white 'windows'
striking in flight

BATISES AND SMALL FLYCATCHERS

Small **leaf-gleaning flycatchers** of similar appearance, characterised by **grey caps and upperparts, black masks, black or rufous breast-bands** and **varying amounts of rufous coloration** elsewhere. Immatures are dull versions of the adults. They are often found in bird parties. When alarmed they fly about with whirring wings.

1 Pririt Batis *Batis pririt*   N E
Common, near-endemic resident. Most resembles (5), but their ranges are almost mutually exclusive. The **males are difficult to tell apart**; the female has a diagnostic **pale buff throat and breast**. Further told from (5) by call: a long, descending sequence of notes 'peep-peep-peep-peep… choo-choo-choo-choo…' up to about 100 times. Pairs occur in **dry western thornveld**, often along watercourses. **12 cm** (Priritbosbontrokkie)

NEAR THREATENED

2 Woodwards' Batis *Batis fratrum*   N E
Fairly common, near-endemic resident. **Male lacks black breast-band** and resembles female; confusion with (1) is unlikely as their distributions are widely separated. The contact call by either sex is 'phoee-phoee-phoee'; male also calls 'chuririri, chuririri, chuririri…'. A species of coastal bush, forests and riverine forests, preferring dense undergrowth and **usually remaining in the lower stratum**. **11–12 cm** (Woodwardbosbontrokkie)

3 Pale Batis *Batis soror*
Common resident. Like a **small version** of (5), and sometimes regarded as a race of that species, but in both sexes the **markings of the underparts are less clearly defined with narrower breast-bands**. Male generally more **speckled on the back and flanks**. The call is a long, monotonous series of notes 'tiroo, tiroo, tiroo, whit, whit, whit, phep, phep…'. Habits like (5), but occurs only in Mozambique from Inhambane northwards, and in extreme eastern Zimbabwe. **10 cm** (Mosambiekbosbontrokkie)

4 Cape Batis *Batis capensis*   E
Common endemic resident. The **most heavily marked batis**. Male has a **very broad black breast-band** and **rufous flanks; female rich rufous breast-band, throat and flanks**. Both have **rufous on wing coverts; eyes yellow** when not breeding. Has a grinding 'prrritt, prrritt, prrritt' alarm note; other calls variable: a monotonous 'keep, keep, keep…', a grating 'WEE-warrawarra' and a soft 'foo-foo-foo-foo…'. Occurs in pairs and small parties in forests, forested kloofs, fynbos, succulent scrub and well-wooded suburban gardens; in the north confined to montane forests. **12–13 cm** (Kaapse Bosbontrokkie)

5 Chinspot Batis *Batis molitor*   E
Very common resident. Male **lacks any rufous coloration**. Very similar to (1) and (2) but their ranges are almost mutually exclusive. Female has a **clearly defined, rich rufous chin-spot and breast-band**, but **white flanks**. Has several calls, the most characteristic a descending series of three notes 'choi-choi-choi', sounding like 'three blind mice'. Also calls 'chi-chirr' or 'chee-chir-chir'; one of the first species to be heard at dawn. Occurs in pairs in mixed bushveld and woodland, always in drier country than (4). Often joins bird parties, feeding in the mid- and lower strata. **12–13 cm** (Witliesbosbontrokkie)

1

♀

pale buff throat and breast

♂

narrow white eyebrow

♀

rufous panel

pale orange wash

♂

2

absence of black breast-band

3

♀

narrow breast-band

speckled

♂

long, narrow white eyebrow

narrow black breast-band

spotted flanks

eye orange when breeding

♀

rufous chin-spot

5

♀

rufous wing coverts

♂

♂

4

very broad black breast-band

rufous flanks

wide breast-band

♂

1 Blue-mantled Crested Flycatcher
Trochocercus cyanomelas
Fairly common resident. Both sexes differ from (5) in **white wing-bars** and **whiter underparts**. Male has **black throat and breast**; mottled in female. Crest length varies regionally. Usually first detected by call, a rasping 'zwee-zwer' uttered frequently, virtually identical to that of (2). Male also sings a high-pitched 'kwew-ew-ew-ew' (like a bush-shrike, p. 418) followed by four clicks. A lively, active little bird, usually in pairs in the mid- and higher strata of dense coastal bush, coastal forests and montane forests near streams. **17–18 cm** (Bloukuifvlieëvanger)

2 African Paradise-Flycatcher *Terpsiphone viridis*
Common summer resident, present all year in the east and northeast. Unmistakable with **orange-brown upperparts, blue eye-wattle and bill** and, in male, **ribbon-like central tail feathers**. Some females have slightly elongated tails. The call, a sharp 'zwee-zwer', is virtually identical to that of (1); the song is a lively trill 'wee-te-tiddly, wit-wit'. A highly active and vociferous little bird found among large trees along rivers, forest fringes, well-wooded hills and suburbia. Male **41 cm**; Female **23 cm** (Paradysvlieëvanger)

3 Livingstone's Flycatcher *Erythrocercus livingstonei* R
Uncommon, localised resident. Colour combination distinctive; most prominent feature is **orange tail with black subterminal band formed by dark dots on the tail-feathers**. Immatures and adults of northern races have the head the same colour as the back. Has a sharp 'chip-chip' or 'zert' call, plus a sunbird-like 'tweet' in flight. Also gives an occasional outburst of warbling song and makes snapping sounds with its bill. Found in bird parties in thickets and large trees in riverine forests; also on the edges of woodland clearings. A highly agile, restless little bird, constantly flitting from branch to branch or sidling down branches with fanned tail moving. **12 cm** (Rooistertvlieëvanger)

4 Black-throated Wattle-eye *Platysteira peltata*
Uncommon resident. **Female has all-black breast, male has narrow breast-band only**; both have **red eye-wattles**. Immature male lacks breast-band. Has a guttural 'chak-chak' call, a weak, tinkling song 'er-er-fea-er-er-fee-fea' and a louder 'tree-tree-tree, che-chreet-che-chreet-che-chreet...'. Pairs live in the lower stratum of riverine and coastal thickets. **18 cm** (Beloogbosbontrokkie)

NEAR THREATENED

5 White-tailed Crested Flycatcher *Elminia albonotata* R
Fairly common, localised resident. Most resembles (1) but is **smaller and greyer**, with **duskier underparts** and **no white wing-bar or crest**. The call is a rapid 'chrrit-tit-tit'. Highly active and agile in forest canopies and trees bordering forests. Fans its tail frequently (thus revealing the **white outer tail-feathers**) while working its way up and down branches. **14–15 cm** (Witstertvlieëvanger)

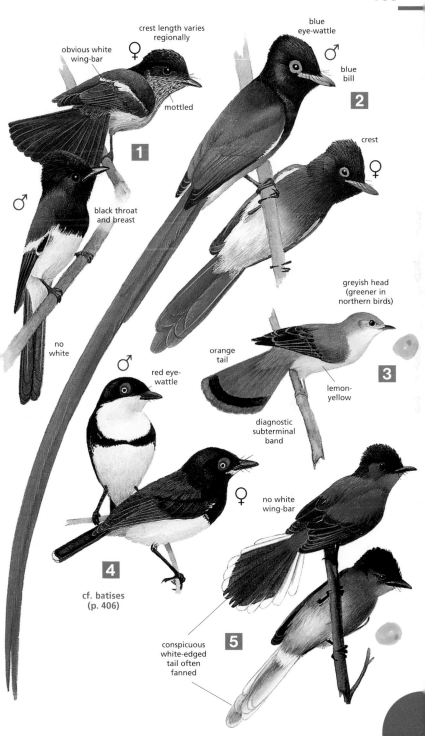

crest length varies
regionally

obvious white
wing-bar

♀

mottled

blue
eye-wattle

♂

blue
bill

2

crest

♀

1

♂

black throat
and breast

greyish head
(greener in
northern birds)

no
white

orange
tail

lemon-
yellow

3

♂

red eye-
wattle

diagnostic
subterminal
band

♀

no white
wing-bar

4

cf. batises
(p. 406)

conspicuous
white-edged
tail often
fanned

5

SHRIKES

Insectivorous or partially carnivorous birds with stout, hooked or slightly hooked bills. They are sometimes known as 'butcher birds' (genus *Lanius* means 'butcher') because of their habit of sometimes **impaling insects or small animals on a thorn or fence wire**, returning later to eat. Habitat preference is for open woodland, where they will still-hunt from a perch.

1 Magpie Shrike *Urolestes melanoleucus*
Common resident. A distinctive, **long-tailed pied** bird. Female may show **white on the flanks** and have a **shorter tail**. Immature is bronze-brown with a grey rump. From a distance could be mistaken for a widowbird (p. 458) or even a whydah (p. 472). The call is 'prooit-preeoo, prooit-preeoo-preeoo', the first sound descending, the second ascending. Small groups of three to 10 birds occur in thornveld and mixed bushveld, preferring lightly wooded, well-grassed regions where they hunt from a perch on a bush. **40–50 cm** (Langstertlaksman)

2 Red-backed Shrike *Lanius collurio*
Common summer visitor. Sexes differ as illustrated. Female differs from immature Common Fiscal (p. 412) in **more rufous upperparts** and **lack of white wing-bars**. Rarely, male occurs with white wing-bars, then resembles Souza's Shrike (p. 414) but differs in **more rufous unbarred mantle** and **clearer grey cap**. Mostly silent; sometimes utters a harsh 'chak, chak' when alarmed or a soft scratchy song easily mistaken for that of a warbler (pp. 372–400). Solitary in a variety of wooded habitats, preferring mixed bushveld and thornveld; most common in the central Kalahari. Perches conspicuously on a low branch and still-hunts. Arrives late Oct–Nov, departs early Apr. **18 cm** (Rooiruglaksman)

3 Southern White-crowned Shrike
Eurocephalus anguitimens
Common, near-endemic resident. Distinguished by **large size, bulky shape, white crown** and **black mask**. Sexes are alike. Has a fluttering, almost hawk-like flight. Utters a curious 'kwep, kwep' sound. Occurs singly or in small, scattered groups in mixed bushveld, thornveld and broad-leaved woodland. Perches conspicuously on a branch or roadside telephone wire, from where it still-hunts. **23–5 cm** (Kremetartlaksman)

4 Lesser Grey Shrike *Lanius minor*
Fairly common summer visitor. The **full black mask** (a) is absent in first-year birds; then appears as (b). Most likely to be mistaken for male of (2) but is larger, lacks the rufous mantle, has **less white at the tail** base and has a **white wing-bar** (conspicuous in flight). Sexes are alike. Normally silent. Solitary in thornveld and mixed bushveld, preferring more open habitat than (2). Still-hunts from a branch, pole or telephone wire. Arrives late Oct–Nov, departs early Apr. **20–22 cm** (Gryslaksman)

cf. Long-tailed
Widowbird (p. 458)

1

unmistakeable

2 ♀

vermiculated

♂

bright
rufous

white tail
base

white crown

extensive
black mask

3

a

black

grey

4

tinged pinkish
below in fresh
plumage

b

1 **Common Fiscal** *Lanius collaris*

Very common resident. A **heavy-bodied, heavy-billed, long-tailed, pied** bird with **white wing-bar extending to the shoulder**; cf. Fiscal Flycatcher (p. 404), which has thinner bill and wing-bar that does not reach the shoulder. **Female has rufous flanks** (often difficult to see). Western race *L. c. subcoronatus* (Latakoo Fiscal) (a) has a variable **white eyebrow**; variations between eastern and western extremes also occur. Immature is ash-brown above; greyish brown below with fine barring. Call is a harsh 'gercha, gercha…' or 'skiza, skiza…'; also a rambling song incorporating sweet notes and the characteristic 'gercha' sound. Perches conspicuously on a branch, post or wire, flying to the ground occasionally to seize insects and other small prey. Occurs singly or in pairs in lightly wooded country and suburbia. **23 cm** (Fiskaallaksman)

2 **Brubru** *Nilaus afer*

Fairly common resident. **Small pied bird** with **rich rufous flanks** in both sexes. Female is **dark brown above**. Immature is similar but has streaked breast. Male utters a drawn-out, far-carrying whistle 'trrioooo', like a telephone, the female replying with a softer, wheezy 'wheee'. An active, restless species of open woodlands. Usually occurs in pairs, which call continuously while working their way through the midstratum. **15 cm** (Bontroklaksman)

3 **Black-backed Puffback** *Dryoscopus cubla*

Common resident. **Small pied bird** with **crimson, orange or yellow eyes**. Female has a **white forehead and eyebrow**; both sexes have **distinctive wing-barring**. When excited, male erects its back feathers to form a puff (see illustration). May fly from tree to tree like this while calling sharply 'chick-weeu, chick-weeu…'; this call also uttered less frequently while feeding. Flies in a heavy manner, the wings making a distinct purring sound. Pairs, often in bird parties, occur in woodland, riverine bush and evergreen forest fringes in the canopies of large trees. **18 cm** (Sneeubal)

4 **White-tailed Shrike** *Lanioturdus torquatus* N E

Fairly common, localised, near-endemic resident. **Small black, white and grey bird** with a **very short tail** and **long legs**. Has a loud, clear 'huo-huo-huo' call similar to African Black-headed Oriole (p. 340), plus various querulous churrs, croaks and scolding notes. An active, restless species of striking appearance. Found in pairs or small groups (flocks of up to 20 in winter) in thornveld and mixed woodland in Namibia, **spending much time hopping about on the ground** with characteristic bouncing gait. **15 cm** (Kortstertlaksman)

cf. batises
(p. 406)

cf. Fiscal
Flycatcher (p. 404)

1

♀

bold white
eyebrow

rich
rufous

powerful,
hooked bill

♀

♂

white
'Y'

2

white
flecks

♂

white
edge

female
has rufous
flanks

long tail

crimson,
orange or
yellow eye ♀

white
eyebrow

♂

a

black
head

3

white
spots

♂

short white tail
with dark centre

4

pale
eye

grey

long
legs

narrow
black band

'puffback' only
visible during
display

cf. Pririt Batis (p. 406)

1 Souza's Shrike *Lanius souzae* **R**

Rare resident. Told from Red-backed Shrike (p. 410) by **dull brown wings and tail, bold white wing-bar reaching the shoulder** and **dusky underparts,** only the **throat being white. Tail-feathers very narrow.** Female has tawny flanks and immature is narrowly barred blackish on underparts. Has a low, scraping call note. Perches on some low branch, from where it flies down occasionally to seize insects on the ground. Occurs singly or in pairs in broad-leaved woodland in Kalahari sand. More secretive and far less conspicuous than other *Lanius* shrikes. **17–18 cm** (Souzalaksman)

BOUBOUS

Boubous are a group of striking, often brightly coloured Bushshrikes, with heavy shrike-like bills. Usually rather secretive, mostly preferring dense vegetation. Their distinctive calls, often sung in duet, are likely to be the first indication of their presence. Largely insectivorous, although some species will eat fruit and small reptiles.

2 Southern Boubou *Laniarius ferrugineus* **E**

Common endemic resident. **Cinnamon coloration of belly** sometimes extends in **pale wash to throat,** but is always richer towards belly and vent. **White wing-bar** appears narrow or wide depending on feather arrangement. Southeastern females are dark brown above, not black. Calls in duet: first bird utters 'ko-ko', replied to by 'kweet' or 'boo-boo', replied to by 'whee-oo' or a liquid-sounding 'phooweeol', replied to by 'hueee' or 'churrr'. Many variations of these basic calls occur, the pleasing melody and loudness of the calls quickly drawing even non-birders' attention. Fairly secretive, pairs remaining concealed in dense bush, usually in the lower stratum. **23 cm** (Suidelike Waterfiskaal)

3 Swamp Boubou *Laniarius bicolor*   *aka Swamp···*

Fairly common resident. Differs from (2) and (4) in **underparts being white, no pinkish tinge** even to feather bases. Similar to Common Fiscal (p. 412), but habits different. Call is less musical than other boubous, a short whistle replied to by a harsh 'kick-ick'. Also less secretive than other boubous; will perch openly while calling. Pairs occur in papyrus, riverine woodland and thickets in the Okavango–Linyanti–Chobe region of northern Botswana. **22–23 cm** (Moeraswaterfiskaal)

4 Tropical Boubou *Laniarius aethiopicus*

Fairly common resident. Differs from other boubous in **entire underparts being lightly washed pinkish,** with **less cinnamon on flanks and vent.** Calls a remarkable series of duets, the two calls uttered in such perfect time they sound like one: normally three liquid, bell-like notes answered by 'hueee'. Variations occur and some calls indistinguishable from those of (2). Pairs frequent dense vegetation in broad-leaved woodland, dense lowveld bushveld and riverine thickets. Replaces (2) in northern areas, but co-occurs with (3) in Botswana. **21 cm** (Tropiese Waterfiskaal)

5 Crimson-breasted Shrike *Laniarius atrococcineus* **N E**

Common, near-endemic resident. Distinctive because of **entirely scarlet underparts;** occurs **rarely with bright yellow underparts.** Otherwise identical to other boubous. Very young birds are ash-grey below, finely barred black. Calls in duet, both birds often calling almost simultaneously, a sharply delivered 'qui-quip-chiri'. Pairs occur mostly in thornveld, frequenting the lower stratum. Most common in arid western regions. **22–23 cm** (Rooiborslaksman)

1

black mask

white wing-bar sometimes less obvious in the field

unmarked dusky flanks

long, narrow brown tail

2

distinct cinnamon wash

3

wholly white below

4

no orange on flanks or undertail coverts

light pinkish wash

5

rare yellow morph

bright scarlet

TCHAGRAS

Heavy-billed, similarly coloured bushshrikes that **feed on or near the ground**, creeping about in the lower stratum of their preferred habitat and moving from bush to bush in **low, rather heavy flight**. They often reveal their presence by distinctive calls.

1 Anchieta's (Marsh) Tchagra *Bocagia anchietae* R

Uncommon, localised resident. Male told from other tchagras by **black cap extending to below eyes** and **very rufous body**; female has a **conspicuous white eyebrow**. Immature has a brownish cap and horn-coloured bill. The call resembles the words 'today or tomorrow' uttered slowly. In courtship sings a shrill song while mounting steeply upwards on rapidly fluttering wings. Frequents tall grass and reeds in swamps or low bushes adjacent to damp regions. Restricted to low-lying eastern Zimbabwe and Mozambique. **18 cm** (Vleitjagra)

2 Southern Tchagra *Tchagra tchagra* E

Common to fairly common endemic resident. Larger than (3), differing from it and (4) in **reddish-brown crown grading into olive-brown mantle, back and central tail-feathers.** Black line separating brown crown from pale eyebrow inconspicuous or absent. Also **greyer below than other tchagras.** Immature is duller, with buffy wing coverts and fulvous-grey underparts. The call is a loud rattling sound followed by a rapid 'chchchch…', ending with 'tew-a-tew'. Also has a loud whistle. Occurs singly or in pairs in dense thickets in coastal bush, thorny tangles and valley bush; less common in the north. A reluctant flier but performs an aerial display like (3). **21 cm** (Grysborstjagra)

3 Brown-crowned Tchagra *Tchagra australis*

Common resident. Smaller than (2) and (4), **less rufous, more buff-brown.** Grey-brown central crown separated from conspicuous black line. **Pale buff below.** The flight pattern is very similar to that of (4). Immature is like adult but duller. The alarm note is a guttural 'churr'. In summer, the male displays by flying steeply upwards to above tree height, then planing down with quivering wings while calling 'tui-tui-tui-tui-tui…' in a descending cadence. A thornveld species which spends much time in thickets or on the ground under bushes. If disturbed, hops onto some low branch before hopping or flying into cover. Usually seen singly. **19 cm** (Rooivlerktjagra)

4 Black-crowned Tchagra *Tchagra senegalus*

Common resident. Told from (2) and (3) by **black crown.** Immature has a blackish-brown crown and horn-coloured bill. Has a 'krok-krok-krokrakror' alarm note and a loud, ponderous and rather flat-sounding whistled series 'cheer-tcharee, trichi cheer-tcharoo, cheeroo, cheeroo'. Pairs also duet with a variety of grating, churring and whistling calls. Occurs singly or in pairs in thornveld, woodland, coastal bush and plantations, where it frequents the lower stratum. **21–23 cm** (Swartkroontjagra)

female has broad white eyebrow

rufous mantle

1

black line below crown inconspicuous or absent

brown crown grades into olive-brown mantle

distinct grey wash

2

contrasting paler grey hindneck

grey-brown crown bordered below by black line

3

pale buffy tinge

black crown

4

grey tinge

BUSH-SHRIKES

Colourful shrikes with **olive-green and grey upperparts** and **yellow or orange-yellow underparts**. Most inhabit dense bush, making them difficult to see, **continuously hopping from branch to branch**. Their diet is mainly insects, although some will eat fruit or small animals. All have distinctive calls, which aids identification.

1 Olive Bush-Shrike *Chlorophoneus olivaceus*   N E

Common, near-endemic resident. Two morphs: (a) with **cinnamon breast** (intensity variable), male with **white eyebrow**; (b) with **entirely olive-green upperparts** and **yellow underparts** in both sexes (cf. (3) and (4)). In both morphs, the **black mask does not reach the base of the bill**; cf. (4). Immature as illustrated. Calls include about six notes of varying pitch, sometimes preceded by a single higher note, 'phwee-phwee-phwee-phwee-phwee-phwee' or 'tew-tew-tew-tew-tew' or 'tee-toy-toy-toy-toy'; also a descending cadence 'CHE-che-che-che-che-che' and a warbling trill. Pairs occur in coastal and montane forest thickets, montane scrub, dense bush and plantations. In bush habitats, it feeds on insects and fruit in the lower stratum, in forests in the mid- and lower strata. Secretive at all times. **17 cm** (Olyfboslaksman)

aka Four-colored

2 Gorgeous Bush-Shrike *Chlorophoneus viridis*

Fairly common resident. Male distinguished by **scarlet throat** and **black gorget**; female similar but black gorget much reduced. Immature shown in first plumage. The call is a liquid, ventriloquial and rapidly delivered 'kong-kong-koit'. Pairs occur in dense coastal and valley bush, lowland forest fringes, riverine forests and mixed bushveld. Secretive, frequenting the lower stratum in search of insects. **20 cm** (Konkoit)

aka Sulphur-breasted...

3 Orange-breasted Bush-Shrike

Chlorophoneus sulfureopectus

Common resident. Male distinguished by **yellow forehead, eyebrow and underparts**, with **only the breast orange**, this much reduced in female. Immature shown in first plumage. Calls a musical, much-repeated 'poo-poo-poo-pooooo' or 'pipit-eeez, pipit-eeez…'. Pairs occur in mixed bushveld, thornveld and valley bush, plus riverine and coastal thickets, usually in the midstratum. Not secretive but often difficult to locate. **18–19 cm** (Oranjeborsboslaksman)

4 Black-fronted Bush-Shrike *Chlorophoneus nigrifrons*   R

Uncommon, localised resident. Male identified by **black forehead and facial mask (no eyebrow) that extends to the base of the bill**, plus **extensive orange wash from throat to belly**. Female's underparts less orange than male's, distinguished from female of (1b) by **grey head and mantle**. Normal call is a repetitive 'oo-poo', sounding like 'doh-me' in the tonic sol-fa scale. Pairs occur mainly in montane forests in the eastern regions. Feeds on insects in the upper and midstrata and joins bird parties in winter. **19 cm** (Swartoogboslaksman)

grey, lacks black eye-mask ♀

a cinnamon morph

white eyebrow ♂

black mask does not reach bill

1

olive-green

olive-green morph **b**

♀

♂

1

J

barred

J

2

♂

black tail

orange vent

scarlet

black gorget

J

3

♂

yellow

female is less orange

♀ grey

4

♂

black

yellow with slight orange tinge

orange

1 Bokmakierie *Telophorus zeylonus* **N E**

Common, near-endemic resident. Distinguished from Yellow-throated Longclaw (p. 328) by **grey-and-green upperparts** and **stronger bill**. In flight shows much **yellow on tail-tip**. Immature lacks the black gorget. The calls are duets and are variable: 'bok-makiri', 'kok-o-vik', 'bok-bok-chit', 'wit, wit-wit' or 'pirrapee-pirrapoo', each sequence repeated at about three-second intervals. Pairs occur in a wide range of habitats from montane foothills to the coast, in bush patches in grassland or on rocky hillsides and in semi-arid regions in the west; common in suburbia in most regions. Feeds on the ground. **23 cm** (Bokmakierie)

2 Grey-headed Bush-Shrike *Malaconotus blanchoti*

Fairly common resident. Identified by **large size, very heavy bill** and **white patch in front of yellow eye**. Immature has a horn-coloured bill. The most characteristic call is a haunting, drawn-out 'hooooooooooop'; also utters a 'clip-clip…' sound. Occurs singly or in pairs in coastal and lowland forests, riverine forests, mixed bushveld and thornveld. Usually feeds in the mid- and lower strata. A ferocious predator, preying on insects, reptiles, bats and even other birds. **25–27 cm** (Spookvoël)

HELMET-SHRIKES

Characterised by **intense sociability**; usually groups of six to 12 birds of all ages feed and roost together, and share nest-building and chick-feeding. They are nomadic unless breeding. They **move from tree to tree continuously** and maintain a noisy chattering comprised of harsh whirring and grating sounds plus bill-snapping. Sexes are alike.

3 Chestnut-fronted Helmet-Shrike *Prionops scopifrons* **R**

Uncommon resident. Distinguished by **grey underparts, chestnut forehead, white lores and chin, yellowish eye** plus **blueish eye-wattle**. Immature has dusky forehead. Occurs in lowland forests and adjacent woodland of the Rusitu–Haroni region of Zimbabwe and in Mozambique, where it frequents tree canopies. **19 cm** (Stekelkophelmlaksman)

4 Retz's Helmet-Shrike *Prionops retzii*

Fairly common resident. **Entirely black** except for **white vent and tail-tips. Legs, bill, eye and eye-wattle red.** Immature is browner. Parties occur in broad-leaved woodland or well-developed riverine forests where they frequent tree canopies, sometimes in company with (5). **22 cm** (Swarthelmlaksman)

aka white…

5 White-crested Helmet-Shrike *Prionops plumatus*

Common resident. Identified by **pied plumage, yellow eye plus eye-wattle** and **yellow legs**. Flight appears slow and laborious like that of a butterfly; this accentuates the **striking black-and-white wing markings**. Immature has a browner crown. Parties occur in broad-leaved and mixed woodland, frequenting the mid- and lower strata. Nomadic, sometimes appearing in apparently unsuitable habitat and even suburbia, especially during droughts. **20 cm** (Withelmlaksman)

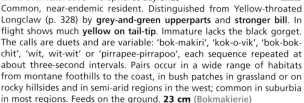

yellow
eyebrow

grey head
and nape

1

J

yellow throat
and black gorget

plain
green

white
patch

2

yellow
eye

massive
ooked bill

tail tipped
broadly yellow

cf. Yellow-throated
Longclaw (p. 328)

large
size

chestnut
bristles

3

red eye and
eye-wattle

black

blueish
ye-wattle

grey

black

pale-grey
bristles

yellow eye and
eye-wattle

5

4

yellow legs

STARLINGS

A well-known family of frugivorous and insectivorous birds with **strong, slightly decurved bills** and **strong legs**. Many species form flocks, especially when roosting. Their calls are mainly various unmusical squeaks and squawks. Several species have **adapted to town life** and two have been introduced from other countries. Unless otherwise stated, the immatures resemble adults.

1 Wattled Starling *Creatophora cinerea*
Common resident. A **pale starling**, male particularly so when breeding, at which time the head may be ornamented with **yellow-and-black skin plus wattles** (b); or have only the wattles (c). Female and non-breeding male (a) appear drab, but can be told by diagnostic **white rump** in flight. The call is a rasping, squeaky sound. Highly gregarious in dry grassland or open bushveld, often associating with cattle. Flocks feed on the ground. When breeding they build hundreds of nests colonially in thorn bushes; highly nomadic when not breeding. **21 cm** (Lelspreeu)

2 Red-winged Starling *Onychognathus morio*
Common resident. Told from (3) by larger size, entirely **red-brown flight feathers** and **sexual plumage differences**. The **eye is dark**. Has a variety of pleasant, loud whistles, the most frequent being a drawn-out 'spreeooo'. Pairs and flocks (large at communal roosts) frequent cliffs, caves or buildings where they roost and breed, dispersing daily to seek fruits and berries. **27–28 cm** (Rooivlerkspreeu)

3 Pale-winged Starling *Onychognathus nabouroup*   N E
Common, near-endemic resident. Told from (2) by **orange eyes** and **whitish wing-feathers tinged orange only on the leading edge**. Wing may look red when folded, but the **outer half of the wing appears entirely pale in flight**; cf. Red-billed Buffalo-Weaver (p. 444). Has similar melodious whistles to (2). Flocks occur in **rocky localities in arid regions** in the west and southwest. **26 cm** (Bleekvlerkspreeu)

(Spreo)   aka African Pied

4 Pied Starling *Lamprotornis bicolor*   E
Common endemic resident. A **long-legged, dark-brown starling** with **purple-green iridescence to the plumage** and **white vent and belly**. The **pale yellow eye** and prominent **orange gape** are good diagnostic features. Juvenile has a dark eye. Call is a soft 'squeer' and similar melancholy whistles. Occurs in flocks in grassveld and Karoo, where colonies breed in burrows in dry dongas and riverbeds. A common roadside bird in many regions. **25–27 cm** (Witgatspreeu)

white rump

variable

female has blue-grey head ♀

dark eye

♂

b

♂ **Br**

N-Br

a

red-brown wings conspicuous in flight

2

c

♂

Br

orange eye

3

whitish wing panels

pale yellow eye (dark in juveniles)

orange gape

4

white

1 Common Starling *Sturnus vulgaris*

Common introduced resident. At a distance **looks blackish; longer-billed, shorter-tailed and stockier** than Black-bellied Starling (p. 426). Sexes similar when not breeding (winter). Immature mouse-brown with whitish throat. In flight **appears sharp-winged** (cf. Wattled Starling, p. 422). Call is a grating 'tcheerr'; also a rambling song of throaty warbles, 'chirrup' notes and creaking whistles. Walks with a quick, jerky action, occasionally runs or hops, and feeds mostly on the ground. Often in flocks, especially when roosting. Occurs in various man-made habitats, including suburbia, playing fields and farms. **20–22 cm** (Europese Spreeu)

2 Rosy Starling *Pastor roseus*

Rare vagrant from Europe and Asia; overwinters further south. Breeding adult male striking with **pink and glossy black plumage**, with a **shaggy, drooping crest. Female paler;** less glossy black plumage and shorter crest. In non-breeding plumage (seen in southern Africa), pink plumage is duller; black feathers show **buff-coloured edges** (giving a scalloped appearance); and bill is **dull yellowish** with **dusky tip and culmen.** Immature sandy brown, similar to juvenile (1); also cf. Wattled Starling (p. 422). Song a mixed warbling. Calls short and harsh. Recorded only in Botswana, in the company of Wattled Starlings. Highly gregarious, found in the company of other starlings of the same and different species. Forages on open ground, often in stony, semi-arid areas. **19–22 cm** (Roosspreeu)

3 Common Myna *Acridotheres tristis*

Very common or abundant resident. In flight, **large white wing-patches** conspicuous. **Bright yellow legs** and **yellow facial skin and bill. Nape plumes long with greenish iridescence.** Immature has duller facial skin. Has a variety of chattering calls, clucking sounds, squeaks and melodious phrases; imitates human speech and other sounds in captivity. Struts about, in pairs or small flocks, gathering in large, noisy flocks to roost. Commensal with humans, their success directly related. Scavenges in urban habitats and associates with cattle and wild ungulates. **25 cm** (Indiese Spreeu)

4 Violet-backed Starling *Cinnyricinclus leucogaster*

Fairly common summer resident. Male unmistakable; female differs from spotted thrushes (p. 350) in **stockier build, shorter bill** with **yellow gape, yellow eyes** and lack of black markings on ear coverts. Immature like female; eyes darker. The call is a short series of pleasant, slurred notes. Arboreal and frugivorous; occurs in broad-leaved woodland. In pairs when breeding, otherwise in nomadic flocks of mostly one sex. Resident in the extreme northwest. **18–19 cm** (Witborsspreeu)

5 Meves's Starling *Lamprotornis mevesii*

Common resident. Differs from other glossy starlings in combination of **dark eyes** and **long, graduated and pointed tail**; might be mistaken for a wood hoopoe given a brief view. Could only be confused with shorter-tailed and much heavier-bodied (6). Immature similar, duller. Groups utter a chattering 'trrreer-eeear…'. Usually in small flocks in well-developed woodland (especially mopane) with open ground. **30–34 cm** (Langstertglansspreeu)

6 Burchell's Starling *Lamprotornis australis*

Common, near-endemic resident. The **largest glossy starling,** differing from most others in **dark eyes;** from (5) in **dark ear-patch, bulky appearance** and **shorter, rounded tail.** Immature duller, brownish below. The call is a squeaky 'churrik-urr, churrick-urrik-kerr…'. Occurs in pairs, small parties or large flocks in savanna woodland. Feeds on the ground, preferring heavily grazed areas. **30–34 cm** (Grootglansspreeu)

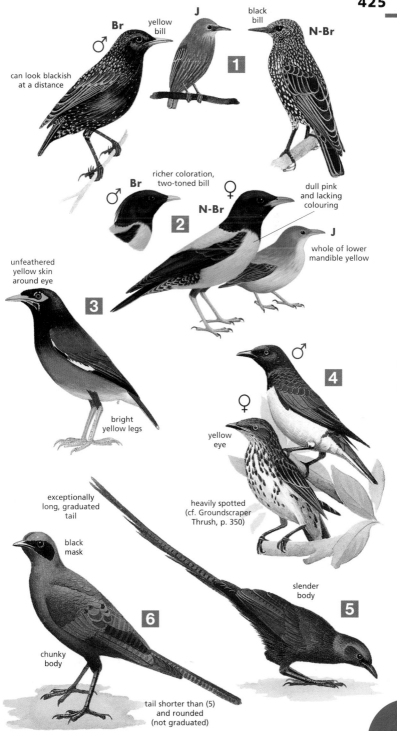

Br ♂ yellow bill

J

black bill **N-Br**

can look blackish at a distance

1

richer coloration, two-toned bill

Br ♂ ♀

N-Br

dull pink and lacking colouring

J

whole of lower mandible yellow

2

unfeathered yellow skin around eye

3

bright yellow legs

♂

4

♀

yellow eye

heavily spotted (cf. Groundscraper Thrush, p. 350)

exceptionally long, graduated tail

black mask

6

chunky body

slender body

5

tail shorter than (5) and rounded (not graduated)

1 Black-bellied Starling *Notophilia corruscus*
Common resident. **Dullest of the glossy starlings, appearing black at a distance**; female and immature duller than male. **Eye colour orange-yellow to red** in adult, dark grey in immature. Flocks utter various pleasant warbling notes while feeding. Breeding pairs make a garbled series of mellow trills interspersed with harsher notes. Nomadic when not breeding. Frequents moister, more shady habitats than other starlings, occurring in coastal towns, forests and bush, extending inland to riparian and lowland woodland in the north. In Zimbabwe occurs in summer only in the Rusitu–Haroni region. **20–21 cm** (Swartpensglansspreeu)

2 Greater Blue-eared Starling *Lamprotornis chalybaeus*
Common resident. One of three short-tailed and closely similar glossy starlings; cf. (3) and (5). Differs from (5) in **blackish ear-patch** and **royal-blue belly and flanks**. Difficult to distinguish from (3), but differs in **larger size, blue (not magenta) flanks** and **two variable rows of black spots on the wing coverts**. Immature is duller, underparts sooty, eye grey. The call is 'sque-eear, sque-eear-eeear', recalling White-fronted Bee-Eater (p. 278). Found in pairs when breeding, otherwise in large flocks in woodland and bushveld. In the Kruger National Park lives commensally with humans at rest camps during winter. **21–23 cm** (Groot-blouoorglansspreeu)

3 Miombo Blue-eared Starling *Lamprotornis elisabeth*
Common resident. Smaller than (2), **flanks more magenta**, the **upper row of wing covert spots usually obscured**; otherwise closely similar. Immature with diagnostic chestnut underparts; frequently flocks with adults. The song is a variety of pleasant notes 'chirp-chirrup-treerroo-chirp-trooo'; on take-off and in flight calls 'wirri-girri'. Occurs in broad-leaved woodland (especially miombo woodland) and bushveld, usually in flocks when not breeding. **20 cm** (Klein-blouoorglansspreeu)

4 Sharp-tailed Starling *Lamprotornis acuticaudus*   R
Fairly common, localised resident. Identified by **wedge-shaped tail**. General coloration like (5) but has **black ear-patch, blue flanks** and **red (male) or orange (female) eyes**. Immature has grey underparts, the feathers tipped buff. Calls 'wirri wirri' in flight. Occurs in deciduous woodland of the northeast. **26 cm** (Spitsstertglansspreeu)

5 Cape Starling *Lamprotornis nitens*   N E
Common, near-endemic resident. Differs from (2) and (3) in **lack of dark ear-patch, underparts uniformly blue-green**. In poor light appears blue overall, even blackish; in good light is peacock-blue or green. Immature is drabber with much dull, blackish feathering. Song is a pleasant 'trrr-treer-treer-cheer...'. By far the most common glossy starling in the region. Pairs or flocks occur in thornveld, mixed woodland and suburbia. Particularly common at camps in the southern Kruger National Park in winter. Also in arid western regions, extending into the Namib Desert within riverine bush. **23–25 cm** (Kleinglansspreeu)

1

can appear all-black
in shade

matt
black

2

broad blackish
eye-stripe and
ear-patch

royal blue
belly and
flanks

J

3

narrow blackish
eye-stripe and
ear-patch

slender
bill

red or
orange eye

black
ear-patch

magenta
flanks

4

lacks dark
ear-patch

5

graduated,
wedge-shaped tail

predominantly
blue-green below

SUGARBIRDS

Related to starlings and characterised by **long, graduated tails, decurved bills** and brown plumage with **yellow vents**. They feed on insects and nectar.

1 Cape Sugarbird *Promerops cafer* E

Common endemic resident. Female told from (2) by **shorter tail, pronounced malar streak, less rufous breast** and **lack of rufous cap**. The song is a series of jumbled metallic, grating and churring notes. When breeding (winter), male calls conspicuously from a perch or flies about in undulating flight, wing clapping with tail held high. Pairs occur in the southern and southwestern Cape on coastal mountain slopes and flats where proteas are flowering, moving about between seasons. Male **37–44 cm**; Female **24–29 cm** (Kaapse Suikervoël)

2 Gurney's Sugarbird *Promerops gurneyi* E

Locally common endemic resident. Told from (1) by lack of a dark malar streak, **more rufous breast** and **rufous cap**. The call is three or four ascending notes, the last one repeated several times. Occurs on eastern mountain slopes where proteas or aloes are flowering. Somewhat nomadic unless breeding (summer). **25–29 cm** (Rooiborssuikervoël)

OXPECKERS

Considered distant relatives of starlings and endemic to sub-Saharan Africa. They have very sharp claws for **clinging to large mammals**. They **use their bills to comb the animal's fur** for ticks and bloodsucking flies. Their diet also includes the blood and mucus of host animals; they will keep pecking at a wound to encourage blood flow. Oxpeckers' presence may reduce the time spent grooming by mammalian hosts by as much as a third. Their **tails are used as props** in woodpecker fashion as they clamber all over their hosts.

3 Yellow-billed Oxpecker *Buphagus africanus*

Fairly common, localised resident. Differs from (4) in **heavy yellow bill with red tip, pale rump and upper tail coverts** and **longer tail**. Immature has a dusky brown bill and is generally duller. Utters a hissing 'kuss, kuss' sound, higher-pitched than that of (4). Flocks are normally seen in association with buffalo, rhinoceros, domestic cattle and donkeys. **22 cm** (Geelbekrenostervoël)

4 Red-billed Oxpecker *Buphagus erythrorhynchus*

Common resident. Differs from (3) in **entirely red bill** and **large yellow eye-wattle**; **does not have a pale rump**. Immature has blackish bill and yellow gape; general appearance duller. Utters a hissing 'churr' and a 'tzik, tzik' sound; most noisy when flying high overhead. Normally seen in association with giraffe or antelope in game reserves; in remote rural areas on domestic cattle. In the evenings, flocks gather to roost in dead trees standing in water. **20–22 cm** (Rooibekrenostervoël)

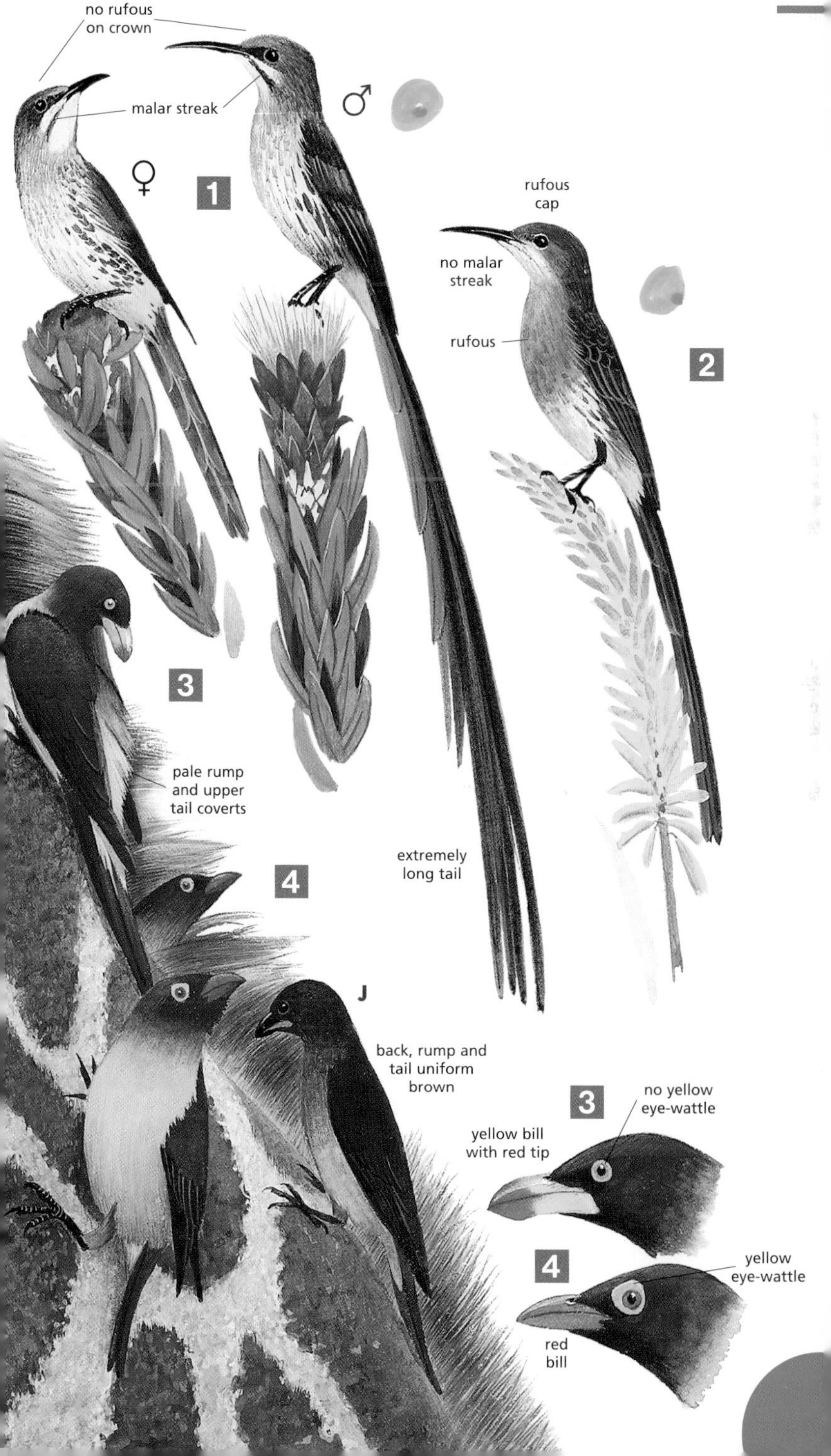

no rufous
on crown

malar streak

♀

♂

1

rufous
cap

no malar
streak

rufous

2

3

pale rump
and upper
tail coverts

4

extremely
long tail

J

back, rump and
tail uniform
brown

3   no yellow
eye-wattle

yellow bill
with red tip

4   yellow
eye-wattle

red
bill

SUNBIRDS

Small, insectivorous and nectar-drinking birds with **decurved bills** adapted to flower-probing. Males have **iridescent plumage** and **yellow, orange or red tufts** on the sides of the breast (pectoral tufts) that are displayed in excitement. Some males undergo an annual eclipse when they adopt drab, non-breeding plumage resembling the normal plumage of the female. **Immatures are like females, often with a dark throat**. Their flight is swift and erratic, males spending much time chasing females and other males. They gather in numbers when favoured nectar-rich plants are in blossom.

1 **Malachite Sunbird** *Nectarinia famosa*
Common resident. Breeding male is **entirely iridescent green** except for **blue-black wings and tail**. Non-breeding male is **yellow below, variably speckled overall with green feathers**. Female told by **large size** and **long bill**. The call is 'chew-chew-chew, chi-chi-chi-chiew... chit-chit-chit...' with variations in speed and sequence; also a rapid warbling song. Usually found in groups on fynbos-covered hillsides (including suburbia in coastal regions), Karoo hills and montane foothills. Male frequently calls from a high vantage point and is aggressive towards other males. Male **25 cm**; Female **15 cm** (Jangroentjie)

2 **Copper Sunbird** *Cinnyris cupreus*
Uncommon, localised resident. Male differs from (3) in **much smaller size** and **lack of elongated central tail-feathers**. Female differs in **clear, pale yellow underparts** except for some speckling on the throat and upper breast. Has a harsh 'chit-chat' call and a high-pitched 'cher, cher, cher...' alarm note, plus a soft warbling song. Pairs occur in a variety of habitats including woodland fringes, montane forest fringes, the edges of marshlands and suburbia. Sometimes roosts in large groups. **12 cm** (Kopersuikerbekkie)

3 **Bronzy Sunbird** *Nectarinia kilimensis*
Common, localised resident. A large sunbird of similar proportions to (1); differs from that species in **more decurved bill** and **black (male) or streaked (female) belly**. Male told from (2) by **long tail-shafts**; female by **streaked underparts**. Call is a shrill 'chee-oo, chee-oo' or 'pee-view, pee-view'. Pairs occur in montane grassland, montane forest fringes and woodland in eastern Zimbabwe and Mozambique. Male **21 cm**; Female **14 cm** (Bronssuikerbekkie)

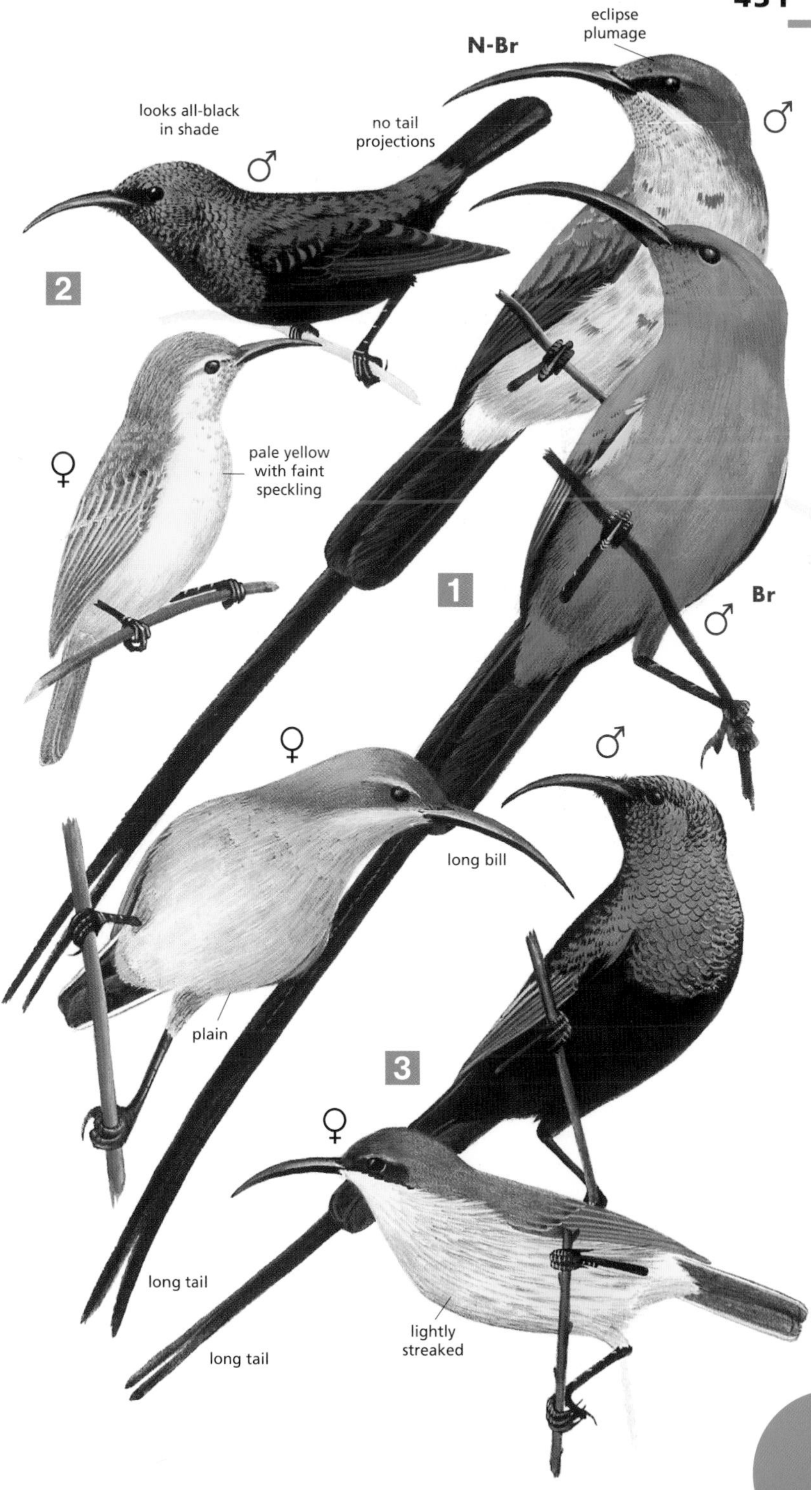

looks all-black in shade ♂

no tail projections

N-Br

eclipse plumage

♂

2

♀

pale yellow with faint speckling

1

Br

♂

♀

♂

long bill

3

♀

long tail

long tail

lightly streaked

NEAR THREATENED

1 **Neergaard's Sunbird** *Cinnyris neergaardi*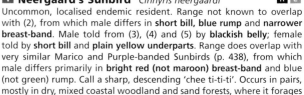
Uncommon, localised endemic resident. Range not known to overlap with (2), from which male differs in **short bill, blue rump** and **narrower breast-band**. Male told from (3), (4) and (5) by **blackish belly**; female told by **short bill** and **plain yellow underparts**. Range does overlap with very similar Marico and Purple-banded Sunbirds (p. 438), from which male differs primarily in **bright red (not maroon) breast-band** and blue (not green) rump. Call a sharp, descending 'chee ti-ti-ti'. Occurs in pairs, mostly in dry, mixed coastal woodland and sand forests, where it forages on the canopy edge. **10 cm** (Bloukruissuikerbekkie)

2 **Shelley's Sunbird** *Cinnyris shelleyi*
Rare, highly localised resident. Male most similar to (1), but ranges mutually exclusive. Differs from (3), (4) and (5) in **blackish belly**; female in **pale yellow underparts** and **streaked breast**. Cf. also Marico and Purple-banded Sunbirds (p. 438), which have maroon (not bright red) breast-bands. The call is a rapidly repeated 'didi-didi', the song a nasal 'chibbee-cheeu-cheeu'. Individuals occur sparsely in the Mana Pools region of the Zambezi River, upriver from Victoria Falls at Kazungula and in the Caprivi Strip. **12,5 cm** (Swartpenssuikerbekkie)

3 **Southern Double-collared Sunbird**
Cinnyris chalybeus
Common endemic resident. Male distinguished from male of (1) and (2) by **longer bill** and **greyish (not black) belly**, from (4) by **blue rump** (and non-overlapping ranges) and from (5) by **shorter bill** and **narrower breast-band**. Female differs from (1) and (2) in **greyer, less yellow underparts**, but distinguishable from (4) and (5) by bill length only. Calls a harsh 'zzik-zzik' and a soft, abrupt 'swik, swik'; also has a high-pitched, swizzling song. Pairs occur in a variety of habitats from forest fringes to Karoo; a common garden species in many regions where suitable flowering plants are present. **12,5 cm** (Klein-rooibandsuikerbekkie)

4 **Miombo Double-collared Sunbird** *Cinnyris manoensis*
Common resident of the Zimbabwean plateau. Male differs from male of (3) only in **grey upper rump** (blue restricted to upper tail coverts only) and **paler belly**; females indistinguishable. However, ranges are not known to overlap. Voice and behaviour like (3). Pairs occur in miombo and other broad-leaved woodland, montane forest fringes and suburbia. **13 cm** (Miombo-rooibandsuikerbekkie)

5 **Greater Double-collared Sunbird** *Cinnyris afer*
Common endemic resident. Distinguished from (3) and (4) by **larger size** and **longer bill**; male by **broad red breast-band**. Song is a loud, scratchy jumble of rapidly warbled notes frequently repeated. Pairs and small groups occur in coastal and montane forests plus coastal and valley bush, frequenting the fringes and canopies, depending on the availability of nectar-bearing flowers. **14 cm** (Groot-rooibandsuikerbekkie)

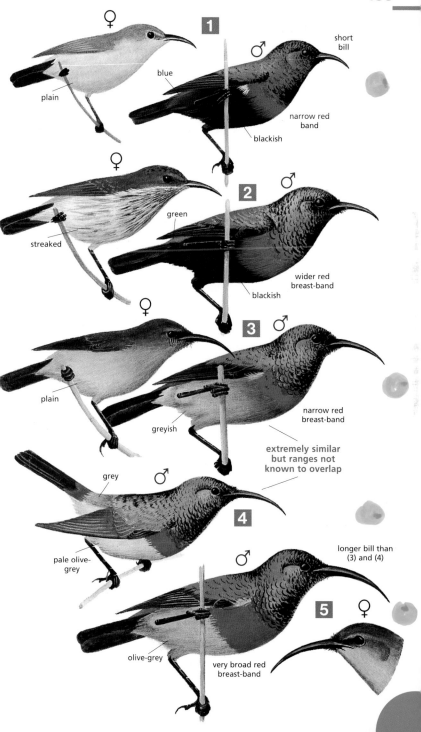

1

plain

♀

blue

short bill

narrow red band

blackish

♂

2

♀

green

streaked

blackish

♂

wider red breast-band

3

♀

plain

greyish

♂

narrow red breast-band

extremely similar but ranges not known to overlap

grey

♂

pale olive-grey

4

longer bill than (3) and (4)

olive-grey

♂

very broad red breast-band

5

♀

1 White-bellied Sunbird   *Cinnyris talatala*
Common resident. Male unique in having an **iridescent blue-green head, mantle, throat and breast** plus **white underparts**; cf. Dusky Sunbird (p. 440). Female very similar to female Dusky Sunbird, but underparts less clear white. Immature male may have **pale yellow underparts** and **blue throat-patch**; can then be mistaken for the smaller Plain-backed Sunbird (p. 440) in eastern regions, where their ranges overlap. The male has a loud, distinctive song, 'chu-ee, chu-ee, chuee-trrrrrr' or 'ta-la, ta-la, ta-la, trrrr' (hence scientific name), repeated frequently. Pairs occur in mixed bushveld and any woodland; particularly common in suburbia. Male is conspicuous by its habit of singing for long periods from a prominent perch. **11,5 cm** (Witpenssuikerbekkie)

2 Collared Sunbird   *Hedydipna collaris*
Common resident. A **tiny, short-billed and short-tailed sunbird**. Both sexes told from Plain-backed Sunbird (p. 440) by **iridescent green upperparts** and **rich yellow underparts**; male by **all-green head and throat** with **blue-and-purple collar**. Male told from (3) by short bill and **narrow collar**. Song is a weak, cricket-like 'chirrreee, chirreee, chirreee' or a brisk 'tseep, t-t-t-t'. Pairs frequent the fringes of forests, riverine forests, and coastal and valley bush, especially where there are flowering creepers. Often joins bird parties. **10 cm** (Kortbeksuikerbekkie)

3 Variable Sunbird   *Cinnyris venustus*
Fairly common resident. **Larger and longer-billed** than (2), male **more blue-green on the upperparts** and with a **broad purple breast-band**. Female differs from double-collared sunbird females (p. 432) in **whiter breast and throat**. Calls are 'tsiu-tse-tse' and an occasional trill, the song a rippling burst of twittering notes. Occurs on the fringes of forests, in riverine forests and patches of hillside bush, always preferring the lower scrubby vegetation and bracken-briar patches. **11 cm** (Geelpenssuikerbekkie)

♀

iridescent
blue-green

♂

whitish
underparts

white
belly

J

1

♀

iridescent
green

glossy,
metallic green

♂

very short
bill

short
tail

2

small
size

narrow blue-
and-purple
band

bright
yellow

♂

3

broad
purple
band

brown

long,
slender
bill

longer tail
than (2)

♀

dull yellow
wash

1 **Scarlet-chested Sunbird** *Chalcomitra senegalensis*
Common resident. Male resembles only the male of (2), but the **large red breast-patch** is diagnostic. Female told by the **heavy dark markings of the underparts**. Utters a high-pitched chattering sound and a much-repeated 'cheep, chip, chop' from a prominent perch. Pairs occur in a variety of habitats including bushveld, woodland, riverine forests and suburbia, where they are attracted to flowering creepers. A noisy, conspicuous species. Replaces (2) in northerly and low-lying localities, but ranges overlap extensively in certain areas. **13–15 cm** (Rooiborssuikerbekkie)

2 **Amethyst Sunbird** *Chalcomitra amethystina*
Common resident. Male lacks the scarlet breast of (1), appearing **all-black**, but at close range and in good light the **iridescent green cap** plus **violet throat, shoulder and rump patches** can be seen. Female is identified by **large size, creamy underparts** and **dusky throat** with **pale-yellow moustachial streak**. The call, often given in flight, is 'tschiek' or 'zit'; also utters a stuttering 'chichichichi'. The male utters a pleasant, subdued warbling song for long periods while concealed in foliage. Occurs singly or in pairs in woodland, forest and riverine forest fringes, less often in bushveld; frequently in suburbia. Lively and conspicuous. **15 cm** (Swartsuikerbekkie)

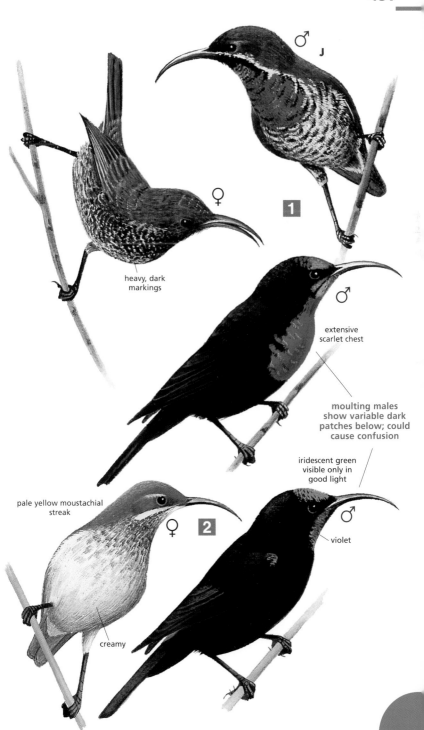

♂ J

♀

heavy, dark markings

1

extensive scarlet chest

moulting males show variable dark patches below; could cause confusion

iridescent green visible only in good light

♂

pale yellow moustachial streak

♀ **2**

violet

♂

creamy

1 Marico Sunbird *Cinnyris mariquensis*
Common resident. Male distinguished from male of (2) by **larger size** and **longer, more decurved bill**; from Neergaard's Sunbird (p. 432) also by these features plus **claret-red or maroon (not bright red) breast-band**; from the double-collared sunbirds (p. 432) by **black belly**. Female told by **long bill, dusky throat** and **orange-yellow breast**. Immature starts with yellow underparts and black bib. As the yellow fades with ageing, the plumage can resemble female Amethyst Sunbird (p. 436). The call is a brisk 'chip-chip' or a husky 'schitz-schitz', often given as a stuttering series; the song is a rapid warbling. Usually occurs in pairs in *Acacia* thornveld. **13–14 cm** (Maricosuikerbekkie)

2 Purple-banded Sunbird *Cinnyris bifasciatus*
Fairly common resident. Easily confused with (1): similar coloration to that species but **much smaller**, the **bill short and only slightly decurved**. Male differs from male of Neergaard's Sunbird (p. 432) in **claret-red or maroon (not bright red) breast-band**. The call is a distinctive 'tsikit-y-dik' plus a trill, often by two birds in unison. The song is a high-pitched, descending trill. Pairs occur in riverine forests, the fringes of coastal evergreen forests, woodland, coastal bush and occasionally mangroves, preferring dense thickets in all habitats. A restless, nomadic species. **10–11,5 cm** (Purperbandsuikerbekkie)

3 Western Violet-backed Sunbird *Anthreptes longuemarei*
Fairly common resident. The **violet upperparts** and **white underparts** of male and **violet tail** of female unmistakable. The call is a sharp 'chit' or 'skee', the song a series of chittering sounds. Pairs occur in broad-leaved woodland (especially miombo), where they frequent the tree canopies, feeding in the foliage and probing beneath loose bark. Sometimes in groups on flowering trees; especially favours *Erythrina* and *Faurea* tree blossoms. **12,5–14 cm** (Blousuikerbekkie)

long, curved bill

1

♀

♂

J ♂

broad claret-red band

heavy, dusky smudging

black belly

slightly decurved bill; shorter than (1)

♂

♀

2

narrow claret-red band

light, dusky smudging

blackish

short, nearly straight bill

3

♂

white

violet tail

♀

black wings contrast with violet upperparts

only sunbird with noticeable white eyebrow

NEAR THREATENED

1 Plain-backed Sunbird *Anthreptes reichenowi* R

Uncommon, localised resident. A small, warbler-like sunbird with a short bill. Male identified by **dark blue throat and forehead**; cf. immature White-bellied Sunbird (p. 434). Female resembles a white-eye (p. 442), but has a slightly longer, slightly decurved bill and no white eye-rings. Both sexes have **dull olive-green upperparts**. Call is 'tik-tik', song an accelerating series of notes, repeated three or four times at increasingly higher pitch. Pairs frequent coastal, montane and riverine forests, feeding unobtrusively in both the upper and lower strata. **10 cm** (Bloukeelsuikerbekkie)

2 Dusky Sunbird *Cinnyris fuscus* N E

Common, near-endemic resident. Breeding male is **blackish with white belly**, the **breast with a coppery iridescence. Pectoral tufts are bright orange.** Non-breeding male has **dull-brown upperparts**, the underparts with an **irregular blackish patch from chin to breast** (see small illustration). Female is smaller, **underparts white**; cf. female White-bellied Sunbird (p. 434). Has a loud warbling song reminiscent of that species: 'chuee-chuee-trrrrr'. Occurs in pairs in Karoo and Kalahari scrub, the riverine growth of dry river courses and even on rocky outcrops almost devoid of vegetation. **10–12 cm** (Namakwasuikerbekkie)

3 Orange-breasted Sunbird *Anthobaphes violacea* E

Common endemic resident. Male unmistakable with **orange underparts, green iridescence on head** and **elongated central tail-feathers.** Female differs from female Southern Double-collared Sunbird (p. 432) in **yellower underparts**. Call is 'sshraynk' uttered one or more times, the song a subdued, high-pitched warbling. Pairs or loose parties found on fynbos-covered hillsides. Male indulges in much chasing with conspicuous aerial manoeuvres. Male 15 cm; Female **12 cm** (Oranjeborssuikerbekkie)

4 Grey Sunbird *Cyanomitra veroxii* *aka Mouse-colored*

Common resident. Sexes are alike. A **nondescript species** best identified by distinctive song and, when visible, **red pectoral tufts.** Southern race (a) has pink-grey underparts, northern race (b) has pale green-grey underparts. Call is a husky 'zzip' or 'tsit-tswaysit' and similar brisk notes; the song is loud, starting with single slow syllables and speeding up to a stuttering finish 'styeep-styip-styip-styip, yip, yip, yip, yip, yipyipyip...'. Pairs occur in coastal forests, riverine forests and valley bush, feeding in both upper and lower strata. When singing often flicks its wings and displays its red pectoral tufts. **14 cm** (Gryssuikerbekkie)

5 Olive Sunbird *Cyanomitra olivacea*

Common resident. A **large, dull** and nondescript sunbird. Sexes are alike. **Rusty upper breast** is often absent in adult but usually present in immature. Isolated population in eastern Zimbabwe (b) sometimes considered a separate species (Western Olive Sunbird, *C. obscura*); the **yellow pectoral tufts** are absent in females of this race. Calls a sharp 'tuk, tuk, tuk', sings a reedy 'tsee-tsee-tsee-tsee, tseedlee, eedlee-id-id-id-seedle...'. Occurs singly or in pairs in coastal and montane forests, mixed woodland, valley bush, riverine forests and suburban gardens. **13–15 cm** (Olyfsuikerbekkie)

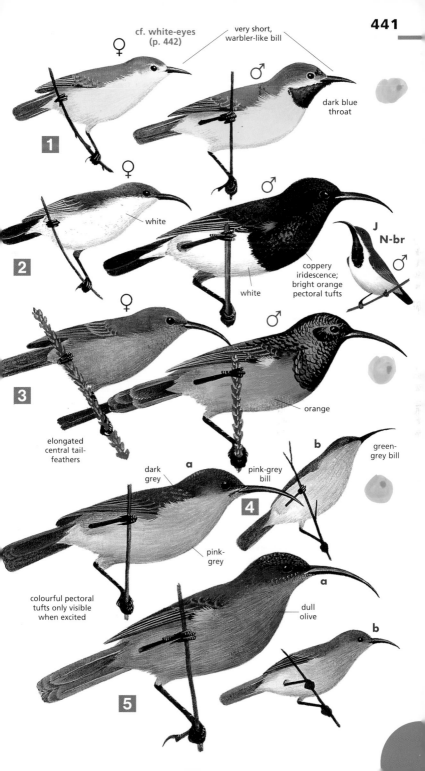

cf. white-eyes (p. 442)

very short, warbler-like bill

♀

♂

dark blue throat

1

♀

white

♂

2

white

coppery iridescence; bright orange pectoral tufts

J N-br

♂

♀

♂

3

orange

elongated central tail-feathers

dark grey

a

pink-grey bill

b

green-grey bill

4

pink-grey

colourful pectoral tufts only visible when excited

a

dull olive

b

5

WHITE-EYES

Very small yellow-green birds that **glean insects from leaves and probe flowers for nectar**. **Unless breeding**, **they occur in flocks** that go from tree to tree where they search the foliage closely, frequently in an inverted position. They are named for the **ring of small, stiff white feathers surrounding their eyes**, often mistaken for a skin-wattle. Immatures are duller and initially lack white eye-surround.

1 **Cape White-Eye** *Zosterops capensis*   **E**

Common resident. Two basic colour morphs occur, with intergradings between them: (a) in the south with **grey underparts**; (b) in eastern and highveld regions with **greener underparts**. The feeding call is a repeated melancholy 'phe' by several in a party. It also sings a loud rambling song from tree tops in summer (including much mimicry), plus a subdued warbling song from the depths of bushes. Flocks occur in almost any well-wooded habitat; often abundant in suburban gardens. **12 cm** (Kaapse Glasogie)

2 **Orange River White-Eye** *Zosterops pallidus*   **E**

Locally common. This species differs from (1) in being **paler overall**, especially the underparts. Only the **throat and vent are pale yellow**, while the **flanks are washed cinnamon**. The song is similar to that of (1) but of higher pitch; call very different and diagnostic: a harsh 'chirrit'. Replaces (1) over much of the arid western parts of the subregion. Often abundant in rural towns. **12 cm** (Gariepglasogie)

3 **African Yellow White-Eye** *Zosterops senegalensis*

Common resident. Distinguished from all morphs of (1) by **clear yellow underparts** and more **yellow-green upperparts**. Calls like (1). Occurs in riverine forests, broad-leaved woodland (miombo), forests, exotic plantations and suburbia. Behaviour and habits like (1). **10,5 cm** (Geelglasogie)

WEAVERS, SPARROWS AND QUELEAS

A very large group of conical-billed, mainly seed-eating birds. Many **breed colonially** and **weave complicated nests** that aid identification; see drawings on pp. 454–455.

4 **Red-headed Quelea** *Quelea erythrops*

Uncommon resident. Both sexes differ from Red-billed Quelea (p. 444) in **brownish-horn bill**; male in **entirely red head**; female in more **orange-yellow coloration**. Male is distinguished from male Red-headed Finch (p. 468) by lack of scaly appearance on underparts; cf. also Red-headed Weaver (p. 452). Immature resembles female. No distinctive call; flocks utter a twittering sound. Occurs in flocks, often with other small seed-eaters, in damp grassland, marshes and woodland, where they feed on grass seeds. Irregular and nomadic. **11,5 cm** (Rooikopkwelea)

5 **Cardinal Quelea** *Quelea cardinalis*   **V**

Rare vagrant. Its presence in southern Africa only recently confirmed with sightings in Zimbabwe and the Caprivi region. Similar to (4), but **red head of the male extends to the breast**. **Male's bill is blackish; female's bill is horn-coloured**. It has been seen among flocks of (4). **10–11 cm** (Kardinaalkwelea)

greenish crown

b

greenish

a

1

grey (variable)

2

cinnamon wash

3

yellow-green upperparts

yellow fore-crown

always brighter than (1)

red does not extend down hindneck

♂

5

♂

extensive red nape

♀

plain upper breast

red upper breast

4

cf. Red-headed Finch (p. 468)

1 Yellow-throated Petronia *Gymnoris superciliaris*

Fairly common resident. **Yellow throat-spot** not a field character. Best identified by **broad white eyebrows**; cf. Streaky-headed Seedeater (p. 478), which also has white eyebrows but lacks this species' **white wing-bars**. Usual call is a rapid 'chree-chree-chree-chree'. Frequently flicks wings and tail when calling. Usually found in pairs, frequenting tall woodland, thornveld and mixed bushveld. Walks; does not hop like other sparrows. **15–16 cm** (Geelvlekmossie)

2 Southern Grey-headed Sparrow *Passer diffusus*

Common resident. Identified by **grey head** and **single white shoulder-bar. Bill black when breeding**, otherwise horn-coloured. Sexes are alike. Immature has a streaked mantle. Utters a repetitive 'cheep-chirp', the first note descending, the second ascending, plus an occasional trill. Found in pairs in summer, small flocks in winter, in various wooded habitats; common in many towns. It frequents large trees but feeds on the ground. **15 cm** (Gryskopmossie)

3 Northern Grey-headed Sparrow *Passer griseus* R

Status uncertain. Closely similar to (2) but **slightly larger; bill heavier; upperparts richer brown;** the **head darker grey and extending to the upper breast; chin white** but **white shoulder-patch less obvious**. However, both species are variable (with juveniles often duller and more brownish than adults), and care must be taken with their identification. Seen in northeast Botswana and the Victoria Falls region. **16 cm** (Witkeelmossie)

4 House Sparrow *Passer domesticus* T

Very common resident. An introduced species. Male distinguished by **grey cap** and variable **black bib**; cf. larger, brighter Great Sparrow (p. 446). Female and immature are paler, **bill and legs pink**. The call is 'chissip' or 'chee-ip'. Pairs and small parties occur in association with human habitation, breeding under the eaves of houses. Found in most towns and small settlements, even isolated permanent camps. Distribution patchy but widespread. **14–15 cm** (Huismossie)

5 Red-billed Buffalo-Weaver *Bubalornis niger*

Fairly common resident. A distinctive **blackish bird** with **red bill** and **white feathers on the flanks and shoulders**. Immature is greyish with much mottling on sides of head and underparts, the bill initially horn-coloured, then dull yellow, then orange. Utters chattering sounds at the nest plus a mellow trill, 'triddlyoo-triddlyoo-triddlyoo-triddlyoo'. Pairs and small flocks occur in thornveld and mixed bushveld, especially in dry regions, in association with baobab trees and large *Acacia* trees in which they build their communal nests (see illustration on p. 454). Patchily distributed and nomadic when not breeding. **24 cm** (Buffelwewer)

6 Red-billed Quelea *Quelea quelea*

Common to locally abundant resident. **Breeding male variable** as illustrated; breeding female has **yellow bill**. Non-breeding birds all have **red bills**. Breeding colonies may be huge, involving tens of thousands, and may cover many hectares of bush. Occurs in flocks and is nomadic when not breeding, mainly in dry thornveld and mixed bushveld. Flocks utter a twittering when flying and nesting. Flying flocks resemble columns of smoke. A serious agricultural pest in some regions. **13 cm** (Rooibekkwelea)

1 Br
broad white eyebrow
yellow throat-spot difficult to see in the field
often flicks wings

3 heavy bill
rich brown above
white chin contrasts with dark head

2
conspicuous white 'shoulder'
limited white (variable)
brown tinge

4 ♂
grey cap and rump
♀
variable black bib

5 ♀
large red bill

♂
variable white flecks

6
often in sizeable flocks
N-Br ♂
red bill
Br
♀
Br ♂

white wing flashes
reddish legs

1 Scaly-feathered Weaver *Sporopipes squamifrons* N E

Common, near-endemic resident. Identified by very small size, **pink bill, 'bearded' appearance, fine 'scaling' on forehead** and **black wing-feathers boldly edged with white**. Sexes are alike; immature much duller, bill horn-coloured. When disturbed, flies off making a chattering sound. Small parties occur in dry thornveld regions, often around human settlements, frequenting fowl runs, gardens and camps. **10 cm** (Baardmannetjie)

2 Sociable Weaver *Philetairus socius* E

Common endemic resident. **Pale blueish bill** offset by **black face and throat** diagnostic; a small, pallid, highly gregarious weaver. Sexes are alike; immature similar. Groups utter an excitable twittering at nesting sites. Flocks occur in the vicinity of their communal nests in dry western regions. The huge nests are placed in a large tree, frequently a thorn, and accommodate many pairs of birds for both breeding and roosting, as well as other species such as Pygmy Falcon, Acacia Pied Barbet, Red-headed Finch, Rosy-faced Lovebird and Ashy Tit. **14 cm** (Versamelvoël)

3 Cape Sparrow *Passer melanurus* N E

Very common, near-endemic resident. **Black-and-white h**ead and breast pattern of male distinctive; female told from female House Sparrow (p. 444) by richer coloration, **greyer head** and **black bill**. Immature resembles female. Normal call is 'chirrup' or 'chissik'. Usually seen near human habitation. When not breeding, flocks occur on farmlands and in cattle kraals. Tame and confiding. **15 cm** (Gewone Mossie)

4 Great Sparrow *Passer motitensis* N E

Uncommon, near-endemic resident. Most resembles House Sparrow (p. 444) but is **larger** and **more brightly coloured**, and has a **rufous (not grey) rump** and a more **restricted black bib** (variable). The call is typically sparrow-like: 'chirrup, chirroo, t-t-t-trs'. Pairs occur in dry thornveld regions, seldom near human settlements, differing in this respect from House Sparrow and (3). **15–16 cm** (Grootmossie)

5 White-browed Sparrow-Weaver *Plocepasser mahali*

Common resident. Distinguished by **bold white eyebrow** and, in flight, **striking white rump and upper tail coverts**. The spotted-breast race (b) is found in Zimbabwe. Sexes are alike; immature has a horn-coloured bill. Call is a harsh 'chick-chick'; also a loud, rambling song of liquid notes 'cheeoo-preeoo-chop-chop, cheeoo-trroo-cheeoo-preeoo-chop-chip…'. Pairs and loose flocks occur in dry thornveld, usually near the trees containing their nests. Conspicuous and active, nest-building at all times of year. **18 cm** (Koringvoël)

Weaver nests are illustrated on pp. 454–455.

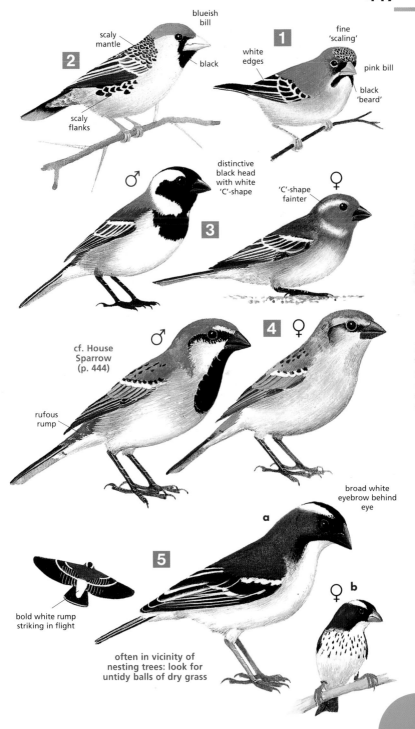

2
blueish bill
scaly mantle
black
scaly flanks

1
fine 'scaling'
white edges
pink bill
black 'beard'

3
♂
distinctive black head with white 'C'-shape
♀
'C'-shape fainter

4
♂
cf. House Sparrow (p. 444)
rufous rump
♀

5
broad white eyebrow behind eye
a
bold white rump striking in flight
♀ b
often in vicinity of nesting trees: look for untidy balls of dry grass

1 Chestnut Weaver *Ploceus rubiginosus*
Uncommon, localised summer resident. Breeding male unmistakable; female and non-breeding male best identified by **grey bill** and **brownish (not greenish) coloration**. Call is a swizzling sound like (3). Usually occurs in flocks, females outnumbering males while breeding. Frequents thornveld in the arid northwestern regions of Namibia and Botswana. **14–15 cm** (Bruinwewer)

2 Dark-backed Weaver *Ploceus bicolor* a.ka Forest...
Common, localised resident. Adults identical, maintaining the same plumage all year. Race (a) typical of southern birds, race (b) found in coastal southern Mozambique, northern Mozambique and northeastern Zimbabwe. Immatures are similar, the flanks with an olive wash. The song is a duet by both sexes, the most common phrase a high-pitched series of pleasant notes 'fweeee, foo-fwee foo-fwee…', repeated with variations plus some soft rattling sounds. A non-gregarious, insectivorous weaver usually occurring in pairs in the midstratum of coastal and inland forests, dense riverine forests and valley bush. A quiet species that creeps about branches and probes for its food beneath bark and in *Usnea* lichen ('old man's beard'). **16 cm** (Bosmusikant)

3 Cape Weaver *Ploceus capensis* E
Common endemic resident. Easily identified by **large size, long, pointed bill** and **pale eye**. Breeding male distinguished from female Spectacled Weaver (p. 450) by large size and **black eye-line not extending behind the eye**. Non-breeding male like female but **yellower on underparts** and with **pale eye**. Female distinguished from female Southern or Lesser Masked-Weavers (p. 452) by larger size and **heavier, more sharply pointed bill**. The normal sound in the vicinity of nests when breeding is a rapidly repeated swizzling 'a-zwit, a-zwit, zweeeeeee-zt-zt-zt…' similar to that of masked-weavers and Village Weavers (p. 452) but harsher. Occurs singly, in pairs or in flocks almost anywhere where there are trees, especially near water and in suburbia, where exotic trees are used for nesting. **16–18 cm** (Kaapse Wewer)

4 Olive-headed Weaver *Ploceus olivaceiceps* R
Uncommon, localised resident. Unmistakable within its restricted range and preferred habitat. Male has **golden crown, orange-brown wash on breast** and **plain olive-green ear coverts and mantle. Female has the entire head olive.** The song is 'tzee-twa-twa-twa-twa', the flight call a high-pitched 'tsa-see-see-see', unlike any other weaver. Usually in pairs in broad-leaved (miombo) woodland, where it feeds on insects in the tree canopies, often in bird parties. Quiet and unobtrusive, clambering around on trunks and branches, and inspecting patches of *Usnea* lichen (from which the nest is constructed). Currently known only from the Panda area in southern Mozambique, where continued existence threatened by logging and slash-and-burn agriculture. **14,5 cm** (Olyfkopwewer)

Weaver nests are illustrated on pp. 454–455.

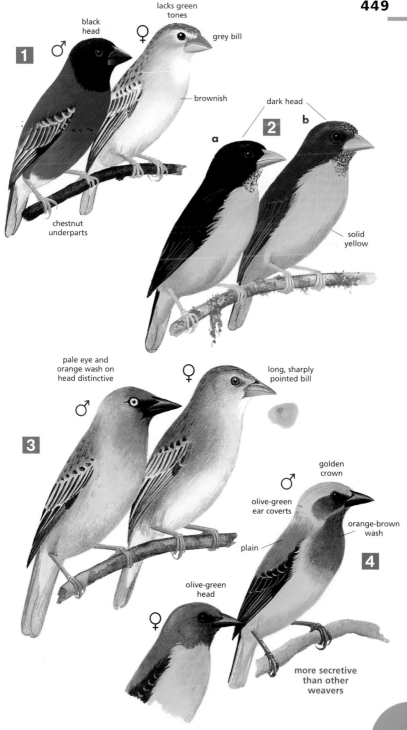

1 ♂ black head

♀ lacks green tones

grey bill

brownish

chestnut underparts

2 dark head

a

b

solid yellow

3 pale eye and orange wash on head distinctive

♂

♀ long, sharply pointed bill

4 ♂ golden crown

olive-green ear coverts

orange-brown wash

plain

♀ olive-green head

more secretive than other weavers

aka African Golden ...

1 Yellow Weaver *Ploceus subaureus*
Common resident. **Palest yellow** of the yellow weavers, **upperparts slightly greener when not breeding**. Further recognised by **stubby bill** and **red eye**. Immature resembles female. Utters a harsh 'zik' and a soft swizzling sound. Pairs and flocks occur in the eastern coastal and littoral zones, moving inland along rivers. Breeds in reed beds and trees on rivers and lagoons; when not breeding occurs in riverine bush and adjacent woodland. **16 cm** (Geelwewer)

2 Spectacled Weaver *Ploceus ocularis*
Common resident. An insectivorous weaver distinguished by **pale eyes** and **black streak through eye to ear coverts**; male also told by **black bib**; cf. Cape Weaver (p. 448). Immature has a horn-coloured bill. Call is distinctive, a descending 'tee-tee-tee-tee-tee-tee-tee'. Pairs occur in riverine forests, fringes of lowland and coastal forests, thornveld around pans and vleis, around farmsteads and in suburbia. Not a social weaver. **15–16 cm** (Brilwewer)

3 Southern Brown-throated Weaver *Ploceus xanthopterus*
Uncommon to locally common resident. A **small, short-tailed weaver.** Male has a **distinct brown patch on throat and lores** (not diffuse brown wash, cf. Cape Weaver, p. 448), female has a **pale bill**. Both sexes have **brown eyes**. Pairs and small flocks occur in large reed beds over water when breeding, in adjacent riverine forests and thickets when not breeding. Mostly on the east coast and littoral, the Zambezi River and extreme northern Botswana. Seldom far from water or swamps. **15 cm** (Bruinkeelwewer)   *aka Holub's Golden ..*

4 African Golden Weaver *Ploceus xanthops*
Uncommon to locally common resident. A **large, golden-yellow weaver** with **heavy black bill** and **pale yellow eyes**. In the Okavango region and western Zimbabwe, male has an **orange wash over the throat** (b); this not present in southern birds (a). See also (3), which has a brown throat-patch. The immature resembles the female but is greener and more streaked above. Utters a harsh chirp and a prolonged swizzling. Found in pairs or small flocks in reeds and thickets on rivers, marshes and gardens. Sparsely distributed in the south. **18 cm** (Goudwewer)

5 Thick-billed Weaver *Amblyospiza albifrons*
Common resident. **Heavy bill diagnostic**; the male's **white frontal patches** present in the breeding season only. Female recognised by thick bill and **heavily streaked underparts**. The immature resembles the female but the bill is yellower. Nesting birds (summer) utter a monotonous chattering; male occasionally sings an almost musical song. Pairs and small parties occur in reed beds and the bush adjacent to rivers, pans and swamps when breeding; at other times found in coastal bush, riverine forests and wooded valleys. Flocks frequently seen flying slowly overhead between feeding and roosting sites while giving high-pitched calls. Currently expanding its range westwards, and now common in Gauteng and surrounds. **18 cm** (Dikbekwewer)

Weaver nests are illustrated on pp. 454–455.

red eye

Br

♂

1

Br ♀

narrow black streak

slender bill

♂

black bib

2

♀

narrow black streak

Br

3

♂

distinct brown patch

Br ♀

♂

heavy bill

Br

4

a

b

♂

pale yellow eye

♀

Br

very bright yellow below

♂

♀

massive bill

heavily streaked

5

1 Southern Masked-Weaver *Ploceus velatus*

Very common resident. Breeding male distinguished from (2) by **red eyes, pointed (not rounded) bib** and **more yellow crown (black mask extends across forehead only)**; from (3) by **plain back** and **black forehead**. Non-breeding male resembles female. Breeding female has slightly more yellow underparts and redder eyes. Immature is duller, greyer on underparts. Utters prolonged swizzling sounds when breeding plus a sharp 'zik'. Gregarious at all times. Small parties and flocks occur in thornveld, riverine bush, and exotic trees around homesteads and farms. Breeds in small colonies in trees away from water, commonly in suburbia, or in large colonies in waterside bushes and reeds. Nomadic when not breeding; often on farmlands. **15 cm** (Swartkeelgeelvink)

2 Lesser Masked-Weaver *Ploceus intermedius*

Fairly common, localised resident. Noticeably smaller than (1) and (3). Breeding male differs from males of those species in **pale yellow eyes, rounded (not pointed) bib** and **black mask extending over the top of the head**; female more yellow at all times. **Legs of both sexes blue-grey**, not pinkish brown like (1) and (3). Immature is like female but whitish on belly. Utters swizzling sounds typical of most weavers, especially when nesting. Occurs in thornveld, mixed bushveld and riverine forests, being attracted to *Acacia* trees or reeds when breeding. Colonies often large and sometimes with (1) or (3). **14 cm** (Kleingeelvink)

3 Village Weaver *Ploceus cucullatus*

Common resident. Breeding male identified by **spotted back** and, in the northern race (a), by **entirely black head**; in the southern race (b) the **clear yellow crown** with **black only on face and throat**; **eyes red**. Female has **yellow breast**, **white underparts** and **brown eyes**. Non-breeding male like female but retains the red eyes. Breeds in colonies, often large, in thorn trees overhanging water, sometimes in reeds or away from water in exotic trees at farms and in suburbia. Male displays by hanging beneath the nest, swinging from side to side with quivering wings while making husky swizzling sounds. Nomadic in flocks when not breeding. **17 cm** (Bontrugwewer)

4 Red-headed Weaver *Anaplectes melanotis*

Fairly common resident. Breeding male has **red head and mantle**; female recognised by **bright yellow head** contrasting with **white belly**, and **pointed salmon-coloured bill**. Non-breeding male and immature like female. Small illustration (a) shows male in transitional plumage. Normally silent but utters a squeaky chattering at the nest and high-pitched calls while foraging. Pairs or males with several females occur in broad-leaved woodland, breeding in isolation. Nomadic when not breeding. **15 cm** (Rooikopwewer)

5 Yellow-crowned Bishop *Euplectes afer*

Common resident. Breeding male conspicuous, displaying by flying about puffed up with rapidly whirring wings while making various buzzing sounds. Female and non-breeding male difficult to distinguish from other bishops and widowbirds, but rather **small and compact**, with **dark mantle** and **whitish belly**. Found in vleis, near dams, in grassland and cultivations when breeding, otherwise in nomadic flocks that wander widely, often with other weavers. **12 cm** (Goudgeelvink)

Weaver nests are illustrated on pp. 454–455.

1
black on neck forms pointed shape
red eye, yellow crown
Br
♂
N-Br
♀

2
blue-grey bill
black on neck forms rounded shape
pale yellow eye
Br
♂
♀
blue-grey legs

3
a
b
spotted back
Br
♂
N-Br
♀
pinkish-brown legs

5
yellow forehead, cap and nape
♂
♀
whitish belly

4
a
sharp, salmon-coloured bill
yellow head
Br
♂
♀
whitish belly

SOME COMMON WEAVER NESTS

◀ **RED-BILLED BUFFALO-WEAVER**
Stick nests in large trees. Small colonies. (See also photograph in introduction, p. 12.)

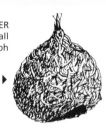

YELLOW WEAVER ▶
Suspended from reeds or trees. Large colonies.

SOUTHERN BROWN-THROATED WEAVER ▶
Suspended from reeds or bushes. Solitary.

◀ **LESSER MASKED-WEAVER**
Suspended from reeds or trees. Large colonies.

◀ **SPECTACLED WEAVER**
Suspended from bushes or trees. Spout often longer. Small colonies.

▲
CAPE WEAVER
Suspended from trees or in reeds over water or from trees away from water. Small colonies.

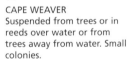

AFRICAN GOLDEN WEAVER ▶
Suspended from bushes, trees or reeds. Solitary.

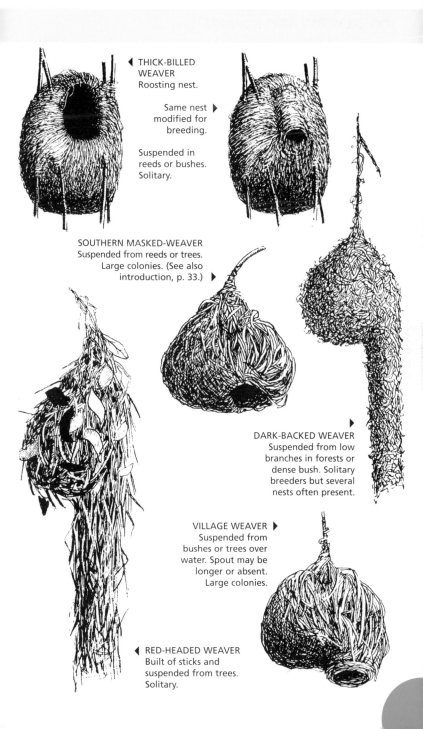

◀ THICK-BILLED
WEAVER
Roosting nest.

Same nest ▶
modified for
breeding.

Suspended in
reeds or bushes.
Solitary.

SOUTHERN MASKED-WEAVER
Suspended from reeds or trees.
Large colonies. (See also
introduction, p. 33.) ▶

DARK-BACKED WEAVER
Suspended from low
branches in forests or
dense bush. Solitary
breeders but several
nests often present.

VILLAGE WEAVER ▶
Suspended from
bushes or trees over
water. Spout may be
longer or absent.
Large colonies.

◀ RED-HEADED WEAVER
Built of sticks and
suspended from trees.
Solitary.

WIDOWBIRDS AND BISHOPS

Reed- and grass-loving seed-eaters, differing from other Ploceidae in that **males are predominantly black when breeding**, some with long tails. They habitually **puff out their plumage** in display. **Non-breeding males and immatures resemble females**, and can be very difficult to identify.

1 Fan-tailed Widowbird   *Euplectes axillaris*

Common resident. Breeding male identified by **pale bill, short tail** and **red shoulders**. Male utters a husky 'tseek, wirra, wirra, wirra, wirra' when displaying. Occurs in grass and coarse vegetation fringing marshes, riverine reed beds and papyrus, cultivated fields, fallow lands and even cane fields. In summer, male flies about conspicuously over its territory, otherwise inconspicuous and in flocks. **19 cm (Kortstertflap)**

2 Red-collared Widowbird   *Euplectes ardens*

Common, localised resident. Breeding male has only a **narrow red collar** (can be difficult to see) and is much smaller than Long-tailed Widowbird (p. 458); **tail thinner**. When displaying, male utters a weak 'kizz-zizz-zizz-zizz' as well as a blowing sound. Occurs in well-grassed bushveld, vleis, streams, rank grass in old cultivations and on hillsides. In summer, male flies about with spread tail or perches conspicuously on bushes. **15–40 cm** (Rooikeelflap)

3 White-winged Widowbird   *Euplectes albonotatus*

Common resident. Breeding male is recognised by **yellow-and-white wings, blueish bill** and **broad tail**, which is frequently fanned. Utters a twittering sound when displaying. Frequents marshes or damp vleis in otherwise dry thornveld and mixed bushveld; also rank vegetation bordering cultivations. Male displays and perches conspicuously during summer. **15–19 cm** (Witvlerkflap)

4 Southern Red Bishop   *Euplectes orix*

Common resident. Well-known and conspicuous colonial nester in reed beds, even in urban environments. Breeding male could only be mistaken in northeastern regions for (5), but differs in **black (not red) crown**. Female and non-breeding male difficult to identify, but typically rather **warm brown** with **streaked breast**. In summer, male calls a wheezy, spluttering 'zik-zik-zik… zayzayzayzayzay'. Occurs in flocks in association with reeds, rank grassland and cultivations; common in vleis. In summer, male displays by puffing out its plumage while perched or flying over its territory (see illustration); usually several visible at a time. In winter, forms flocks and is nomadic. **14 cm** (Rooivink)

5 Black-winged Red Bishop   *Euplectes hordeaceus*   **R**

Uncommon localised resident. Breeding male differs from (4) in having an **entirely red crown, black flight-feathers and upper tail plus a whitish vent**. When not breeding, the **black wing-feathers and central upper tail-feathers remain**. Female more yellowish but distinguished at all times by black central upper tail-feathers. Usually occurs in pairs; behaviour and habitat otherwise very similar to (4), both species often nesting in close proximity. Found in eastern Zimbabwe and Mozambique. **13–15 cm** (Vuurkopvink)

1

♂

red

♀

pale
bill

2

no
colour

red
collar

♂

♀

shorter, narrower
than Long-tailed
Widowbird (p. 458)

3

blueish
bill

♂

yellow

white

♀

streaked

♀

5

♂ black

♀

dark
brown
wings

4

red

♂

black
wings

1 Long-tailed Widowbird *Euplectes progne*

Common resident. Breeding males easily recognisable when displaying over Highveld grasslands in summer. Male has **longer and fuller tail** than Red-collared Widowbird (p. 456). **Red shoulder-patch, whitish wing-edges** and **pale bill** good field features. Non-breeding male has same wing pattern, but is much larger than female and all other widowbirds. Female and immature normally seen in a flock with male. Normal call is a repeated 'chip… chip… chip…'; breeding male utters a subdued, swizzling song. A grassland species, especially in vleis and valleys with rich growth. When breeding (summer), males perch prominently on a tall weed near the nest, or patrol the territory in low flight, wings flapping slowly and deliberately. Joins mixed flocks when not breeding. Male **19–60 cm**; Female **15 cm** (Langstertflap)

2 Yellow Bishop *Euplectes capensis*

Common resident. Non-breeding male resembles female but **retains the yellow rump and shoulders**. Female and immature have a **dull-yellow rump**; cf. also Yellow-crowned Bishop (p. 452). Breeding male calls 'skeet' from the top of a tree and has an exceptionally sharp, high-pitched trilling song. Family groups or flocks (when not breeding) occur in vleis and marshy regions near streams in foothills and bracken slopes near montane forests and plantations. Displaying male makes audible wing flutters both at rest and in flight. At these times the plumage is puffed out, the yellow rump conspicuous. **15 cm** (Kaapse Flap)

3 Yellow-mantled Widowbird *Euplectes macrourus*

Locally common resident. Breeding male has **yellow shoulders and back**; cf. (2), from which it is also identified by **longer tail**. Non-breeding male resembles female but **retains yellow shoulders**. Distinguished from White-winged Widowbird (p. 456) by lack of white in wings. Immature resembles female. Call is a thin, buzzing sound. Occurs in grassland near water. Breeding male displays with a jerky flight, the tail jerking up and down. When not breeding, forms flocks, often with other grassland species. **14–22 cm** (Geelrugflap)

1

♂ **Br**

pale bill

black crown

black mantle

Br

♂

cf. Yellow-crowned Bishop (p. 452)

2

♀

yellow rump

short tail

heavily streaked below

♂ **N-Br**

conspicuous black flight-feathers

♀

yellow mantle

♀

♂ **Br**

3

black rump

long, broad tail (cf. (2))

exceptionally long tail when breeding

FINCHES, WAXBILLS, TWINSPOTS AND MANNIKINS

Small, conical-billed, ground- or grass-feeding seed-eaters, although some will also eat insects. They usually have **colourful plumage**, although females are usually more drab than males. They generally occur in pairs, or are gregarious when not breeding.

1 Green-winged Pytilia *Pytilia melba*

Common resident. Both sexes differ from (2) in **black-and-white-barred underparts**, **all-green wings** and **longer, predominantly red bill**. Usual call is a single, low 'wick'; also utters a plaintive whistle and has an attractive short song. Pairs frequent thorny thickets, often near water, and associate with other waxbills and firefinches, feeding on open ground. Is host to Long-tailed Paradise-Whydah (p. 472). **12–13 cm** (Gewone Melba)

2 Orange-winged Pytilia *Pytilia afra*

Locally common resident. Differs from (1) mainly in the **underparts being barred green and buff (not black and white)** and in having **orange-edged wing-feathers**, which appear as an orange patch on the folded wing. The **bill is shorter and mostly brown on the upper mandible**. **Red mask of male extends over lores**, unlike (1). Call is a single, flat 'seee' and a two-note, piping whistle. Behaviour and habitat preferences very similar to (1). Is host to Broad-tailed Paradise-Whydah (p. 474). **11 cm** (Oranjevlerkmelba)

3 Red-faced Crimsonwing *Cryptospiza reichenovii* 🇷

Uncommon, localised resident. A distinctive species with **dark olive underparts**, **deep crimson wings and back**; cf. (4), which is predominantly brown. Only the **male has a red mask**. The call is a high-pitched 'zeet'; also utters a descending song of four notes followed by a chirp. A very shy, mostly silent species found in forests. Small parties feed on the ground in dense shade by forest streams and at forest fringes, seldom flying more than a few metres when disturbed. **12 cm** (Rooiwangwoudsysie)

4 Lesser Seedcracker *Pyrenestes minor* 🇷

Uncommon, localised resident. Both sexes have **red foreheads and faces**, the **red colour extending onto the breast in the male**. Differs from (3) in being generally **earth-brown (not green)** and **lacking deep crimson wings**. Call is 'tzeet', plus a sharp clicking when alarmed. Pairs frequent thick woodland along streams or forest fringes, preferring hilly regions with high rainfall. Stays low down in the vegetation but not in dense cover. **13 cm** (Oostelike Saadbrekertjie)

♀

♂

1

grey lores

grey ear coverts

green upperparts

black-and-white barring

black-and-white barring

♀

♂

full red mask and throat

2

green-and-buff barring

green-and-buff barring

orange-edged wing-feathers

♀

♂

3

deep crimson upperparts and wing edges

red mask

black tail-feathers

♀

♂

4

heavy bill

earth-brown upperparts

red face and breast

red rump and tail-feathers

1 Brown Firefinch *Lagonosticta nitidula* R

Fairly common, localised resident. Might be confused with (2), but the **red is confined to the face, throat and upper breast**; no red on rump. Sexes are alike. The call is a flat, unmusical 'tsiep, tsiep' or 'chick, chick'. Occurs in thickets and reeds near water in the extreme north of southern Africa, but groups feed on open ground, often on termite hills. **10 cm** (Bruinvuurvinkie)

2 Red-billed Firefinch *Lagonosticta senegala*

Common resident. Both sexes have a **red rump**; cf. (1). Male has more **extensive red on head and underparts**. Distinguished from other firefinches by **reddish bill, yellowish eye-ring** or, in mixed parties, by the **grey-brown females**. The call is a nasal 'fweet, fweet'. Occurs in pairs or small parties in mixed bushveld, especially near watercourses and, in the north, in suburbia. Is host to Village Indigobird (p. 474). **10 cm** (Rooibekvuurvinkie)

3 African Firefinch *Lagonosticta rubricata*

Common resident. The **bill appears black** in the field. Identified by **grey crown and nape** plus **blackish belly** in the male. In Zimbabwe, crown and nape are **washed with pink**; then differs from (4) in distinctly **browner wings and mantle**. Has a trilling, bell-like call involving 'chit-chit-chit' sounds and ending with 'wink-wink-wink'; also a stuttering alarm call. Pairs and small parties occur in dense bushveld, forest fringes and in thorn and grass tangles. Prefers moister, shadier situations than (4). Is host to Dusky Indigobird (p. 474). **11 cm** (Kaapse Vuurvinkie)

4 Jameson's Firefinch *Lagonosticta rhodopareia*

Common resident. The **reddest firefinch**; **bill blackish** in both sexes. Male has the **crown, nape and mantle washed pink**. Rest of upperparts less dark than (3); **underparts rose-pink. Female more orange-pink on underparts.** Immature male (see illustration) more uniformly brown above; below rose-pink with a brownish wash on lateral breast. Has a tinkling 'trrr-trrr' alarm note plus various musical calls 'tewee-tewee…', 'fweeee' or 'zik, zik'. Frequents thickets and rank grass in thornveld, and riparian and secondary growth around cultivated lands. Mostly found in drier situations than (3). Is host to Purple Indigobird (p. 474). **11 cm** (Jamesonvuurvinkie)

1
no red on rump
uniform coloration
red limited to face, throat and upper breast
brownish

2
narrow, yellowish eye-ring
reddish bill
♂
pink lores
♀
red

3
grey crown and nape
blue-black bill
dark brown
♂
brown tinge
♀
occurs in moist eastern regions

4
washed pink
blackish bill
♂
orange-pink tinge
♀
occurs in miombo woodland and bushveld
J

1 Locust Finch *Ortygospiza locustella* **R**
Uncommon, localised resident and visitor. A **very small, ground-feeding bird**. Female has much darker upperparts than (2), and **flame-red edges to wing-feathers**. Best told from (2) by call: a querulous 'pink-pink'. Frequents wet grassland in dense flocks except when breeding (late summer). Flocks usually fly only a short distance before resettling, but flight fast and dipping. Very difficult to see on the ground. **9 cm** (Rooivlerkkwartelvinkie)

2 African Quail-Finch *Ortygospiza fuscocrissa*
Common resident. Differs from (1) in **paler, less striking coloration, barred breast and flanks** plus **white facial markings around the eye**. Call is a diagnostic, querulous, metallic 'tirrilink', given in flight and often the only clue to the species' presence. Very difficult to see on the ground and usually noticed only when put to flight; birds coming to drink from muddy puddles present the best viewing opportunities. Pairs or small parties frequent short grassland, especially overgrazed regions, pan fringes and other damp localities. Occasionally takes off in brief flight, suddenly descending again. In courtship the male towers to a great height and then descends like a falling object while making a clicking sound; cf. 'cloud' cisticolas (pp. 388–390). **9,5 cm** (Gewone Kwartelvinkie)

3 Green Twinspot *Mandingoa nitidula*
Uncommon resident. Mature adult differs from other small green birds in having **white-spotted underparts**, but immature has plain green underparts. Sexes differ as illustrated. Call is a chirping 'tzeet' and a soft trill; also has a subdued song. An elusive, shy species, which frequents the fringes of forests and coastal bush, feeding in areas of open ground, but darting into thick cover if disturbed. **10 cm** (Groenkolpensie)

4 Pink-throated Twinspot *Hypargos margaritatus* **E**
Common, localised endemic resident. Most resembles (5), but the deep crimson area in (5) is **dull rose-pink** in this species; female has **only the rump and tail pink** and has a **grey breast and throat**. Call is a trilling 'tit-it-it-it-it-it-it' or 'trrr-it'. Pairs or small groups frequent dense, tangled scrub in patches of open ground and forest fringes, darting into cover when alarmed. **12 cm** (Rooskeelkolpensie)

NEAR THREATENED

aka Peter's

5 Red-throated Twinspot *Hypargos niveoguttatus*
Common, localised resident. Male differs from (4) in **deep crimson coloration,** female in more **rusty breast**. Call is a stuttering, grasshopper-like trill 'trree-rree'. Pairs and small parties occur on open ground near forests, dense bush and streams or in dry, open country. **12,5 cm** (Rooikeelkolpensie)

difficult to see on the ground

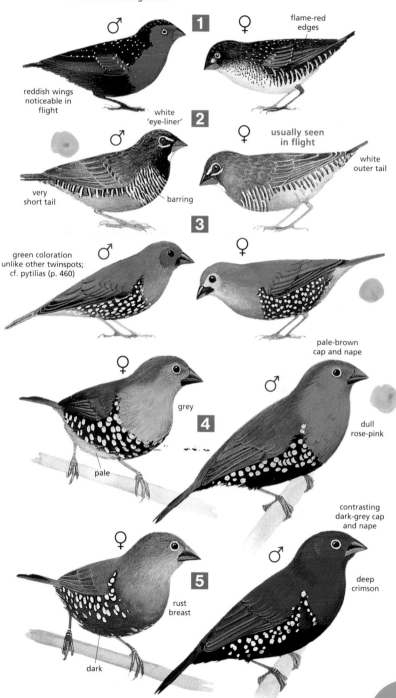

1 ♂ ♀ flame-red edges

reddish wings noticeable in flight

white 'eye-liner'

2 ♂ ♀ usually seen in flight

very short tail

barring

white outer tail

3 ♂ ♀

green coloration unlike other twinspots; cf. pytilias (p. 460)

pale-brown cap and nape

4 ♀ ♂

grey

dull rose-pink

pale

contrasting dark-grey cap and nape

5 ♀ ♂

rust breast

deep crimson

dark

1 Orange-breasted Waxbill *Amandava subflava*
Common resident. The male's **orange breast** is variable, sometimes absent. Both sexes recognised by **barring on yellowish background, orange undertail, red rump** and **red bill and face mask**. Immature like female but has black bill. Call is a quiet, metallic tinkling often made in flight. Pairs and small flocks occur in waterside grass and reeds, especially in vleis and other marshy regions plus cultivated fields. Very active, mobile little birds that make off in straggling sequence at low height, then suddenly drop down again. A secondary host to the parasitic Pin-tailed Whydah. **8,5–9 cm** (Rooiassie)

2 Black-faced Waxbill *Estrilda erythronotos*
Fairly common resident. Identifying characteristics include **black mask, barred wings** and **deep-red underparts**. Female is slightly duller; less red. Immature is like female. Call is an ascending whistle 'fwooee'. In pairs; flocks occur when not breeding. Found in dry and semi-arid thornveld and thick riverine scrub. Feeds mainly on the ground but flies into trees if disturbed. Seldom plentiful and probably nomadic much of the year. **12–13 cm** (Swartwangsysie)

aka Blue-breasted Cordon bleu

3 Blue Waxbill *Uraeginthus angolensis*
Very common resident. Easily identified by **powder-blue underparts** (extent variable). Immature paler than female, bill black. Calls frequently on the ground and in flight, a high-pitched 'weet-weet'; also has a complicated song. Pairs and small parties – frequently with other small seedeaters – occur in dry thornveld, often in dry watercourses and bare patches of ground under bushes and in kraals. Flies into bushes when disturbed. Never far from water. Nomadic, moving into suburbia in dry winters. **12–14 cm** (Gewone Blousysie)

4 Common Waxbill *Estrilda astrild*
Common resident. **Red bill, facial skin and underbelly** distinctive; immature has blackish bill. The call is 'chik-chik-ZEEE, chik-chik-ZEEE', descending on the third syllable. Small or large flocks occur on grassy riverbanks, reed beds, vleis and rank vegetation bordering cultivated lands. Very active birds, flocks always flying off in straggling procession from place to place. Feeds on the ground and on seeding grasses. Is the primary host of Pin-tailed Whydah (p. 472). **13 cm** (Rooibeksysie)

5 Violet-eared Waxbill *Uraeginthus granatinus*
Common resident. When seen clearly, both sexes are unmistakable. Can be identified in flight by **long tail** (often appears broad). Immature is duller than female. The often-repeated call is 'tiu-woowee'; also has a buzzy flight call. Pairs, often in company with (3), occur in dry thornveld, especially sandveld. Feeds on the ground, flying into thickets when disturbed. Is host to Shaft-tailed Whydah (p. 472). **13–15 cm** (Koningblousysie)

red bill and mask

red rump conspicuous in flight

♂

♀

1

coarse barring

black face

barred

2

deep red

orange undertail

3 ♂

♀

powder-blue breast

red bill and facial skin

fine barring

red

4

unmistakeable

chestnut

5

♂

♀

violet ear coverts

long tail and deep-blue rump conspicuous in flight

1 Swee Waxbill *Coccopygia melanotis*   E

Common, endemic resident. The ranges of this species and (2) are mutually exclusive. The **crimson rump and upper tail coverts** and the **yellow belly** of both sexes are distinctive in the field. Adult male easily identified by **black face**. Usual call is a soft 'swee-swee'. An inconspicuous little bird that occurs in flocks, feeding in tall grass near forest fringes and thick bush, and in montane regions usually near wooded streams. When flushed the flock makes off, calling, and settles briefly in a bush before again flying to feed in the grass. **9–10 cm** (Suidelike Swie)

2 Yellow-bellied Waxbill *Estrilda quartina*   R

Uncommon, localised resident. Both sexes are **virtually identical to the female of (1)**; often regarded as a race of that species. However, ranges mutually exclusive and thus unlikely to be confused. Habits, habitat and voice identical. Occurs only on the eastern Zimbabwe–Mozambique border. **10 cm** (Tropiese Swie)

3 Grey Waxbill *Estrilda perreini* *a.k.a. Black-tailed*

Uncommon resident. Similar to (4) but **darker grey** with a **black bill**; **no red on the flanks**. Ranges mutually exclusive, and confusion highly unlikely. Call is a thin 'pseeu, pseeu'. An inconspicuous species of woodland and forest edges where thick bush tangles with tall grass. Usually in pairs, which seldom venture far from dense cover. **11 cm** (Gryssysie)

4 Cinderella Waxbill *Estrilda thomensis*   R

Uncommon localised resident. Superficially resembles (3), but the **grey is paler with a rosy flush on the upperparts and belly**. The **bill is red with a black tip**; the **flanks are red and black**. Small parties occur in low bushes along the Kunene River in northern Namibia. The call is 'seee' or 'see-eh see-eh sueee'. Can be very elusive and never numerous. **11 cm** (Angolasysie)

NEAR THREATENED

5 Cut-throat Finch *Amadina fasciata*

Common resident. Both sexes identified by the **fine scaling on the head and underparts** and extensive **chestnut belly patch**. Male has small **red band across throat**. Female has a generally scaly appearance with a **pale bill**; smaller and darker than female of (6). A thin 'kee-air' call is uttered in flight. Occurs in pairs when nesting, otherwise in flocks in dry, broad-leaved woodland, often near villages and cultivations. Takes over old nests of weavers and often in the vicinity of weaver colonies. **12 cm** (Bandkeelvink)

6 Red-headed Finch *Amadina erythrocephala*   NE

Common, near-endemic resident. Larger than (5), male with an **entirely red head**, female **paler, plainer on the upperparts, lightly barred below, bill dark horn**. Call is a distinctive double note 'chuck-chuck'. Mostly seen in small flocks in dry thornveld or grassland, feeding on the ground, often with other species. A frequent visitor to waterholes and common in suburbia, especially in rural towns in arid areas. **12–13 cm** (Rooikopvink)

very similar to female (1), but belly brighter yellow

pale grey

2

♂

black face

1

crimson rump

♀

grey head

grey head

lower mandible red

no red

dark grey

grey underparts

3

pale grey

red bill with black tip

4

red-and-black flanks and vent

♂

dense scaling

♀

pale bill

fine barring

extensive chestnut belly patch

hybrids have been recorded

5

♀

♂

plain

broad white scaling edged black

6

1 Bronze Mannikin *Lonchura cucullata*
Very common resident. Adult differs from (2) in **earth-brown upper-parts** grading to **blackish over the head, face, throat and upper breast**. All **blackish areas washed with bottle-green or bronze**, with some bottle-green feathers present on the mantle. The **bill has dark upper mandible. Flanks finely barred.** Immature as illustrated; upperparts less rufous than immature of (2); bill all-dark. Call is a wheezy 'chik, chik, chikka'. Found in a wide variety of mixed grass and bushveld, forest fringes, coastal scrub and old cultivated lands. A very small, highly gregarious bird. Feeds in flocks, clambering about grass stems to obtain the seeds. When flushed, all fly into a bush, eventually returning to feed in ones and twos. **9 cm** (Gewone Fret)

2 Black-and-white Mannikin *Lonchura bicolor*
Fairly common resident. Differs from (1) in **red-brown upperparts** and **more extensive area of black over the sides of head and breast; bill uniformly blue-grey;** and **broader barring on flanks**. Immature is duller. Utters a clear whistling note in flight. Small flocks occur in open bushveld and coastal dune forests, feeding on the seeds of grasses. **9,5–10 cm** (Rooirugfret)

3 Magpie Mannikin *Lonchura fringilloides* 🅁
Rare, localised resident. **Much larger than (1) and (2)**, with distinctly **pied appearance** and **heavy black bill**. Immature also told by robust build and black bill. Utters a chirruping 'pee-oo-pee-oo'. Small flocks occur in clearings in coastal bush and riverine woodland, usually near bamboo thickets. Rare in South Africa, but range apparently expanding, especially into northeastern Lowveld. More common in Zimbabwe and Mozambique. **12–13 cm** (Dikbekfret)

NEAR THREATENED

CUCKOO WEAVERS

A parasitic bird related to the whydahs and indigobirds, but resembling a finch in size and weaver in plumage (previously known as Cuckoo Finch); cf. weavers on pp 444–452. They occur throughout sub-Saharan Africa, and are water-dependent.

a.k.a. Parasitic ...

4 Cuckoo Weaver *Anomalospiza imberbis*
Fairly common resident. The **black bill is shorter and stouter** than in weavers. Juvenile (a) and immature (b) have a two-coloured bill and more orange-brown appearance. Male calls 'tsileu, tsileu, tsileu' or, in display, utters a weaver-like swizzling. Usually occurs in small flocks in well-vegetated vleis, grassland or grassland with scattered bushes. Parasitises cisticolas and prinias. It is migratory in its southern range. **12–13 cm** (Koekoekvink)

earth-brown with bottle-green or bronze sheen

bi-coloured bill

J

dark bill

1

narrow bars

red-brown

pale blue-grey bill

J

pale bill

broad bars

2

chocolate brown

heavy bill

J

very broad bars

3

large size

stubby, deep-based black bill

J **b**

J **a**

4

bright yellow

WHYDAHS

Small, ground-feeding, seed-eating finches that are brood parasites, **laying their eggs in waxbill, firefinch, twinspot and pytilia nests**. Male whydahs in breeding plumage have **very long tails**, different in all species, but when not breeding they **resemble the confusingly similar females**. At times males may be seen in transient plumage with traces of the breeding colours visible. Immatures are very plainly coloured and are probably indistinguishable.

1 **Pin-tailed Whydah** *Vidua macroura*
Common resident. Breeding male distinctive; the **red bill is retained in non-breeding plumage**. Female has **pinkish-brown bill**, but told from similar female (3) by **bolder head stripes**. Courting male hovers over the females, describing a circle in the vertical plane, while calling a continuous wispy 'peetzy-peetzy-peetzy…'. In normal flight calls 'tseet-tseet-tseet'. Male is pugnacious, chasing other small birds and dominating at food sources. Usually in parties of one male and several females, which frequent a wide variety of habitats including suburbia. Parasitises Common Waxbill (p. 466). **12–34 cm** (Koningrooibekkie)

2 **Long-tailed Paradise-Whydah** *Vidua paradisaea*
Common resident. Distinctive plumage of breeding male (a) similar only to Broad-tailed Paradise-Whydah (p. 474), but differs in **tapering tail-feathers**; transitional plumage (b) frequently seen. Female and non-breeding male have bolder **black-and-white head-stripes** than (1). Has a short, sparrow-like song and utters an occasional 'chit'. Small flocks occur mainly in thornveld. Breeding male has a display flight in which the two short tail-feathers are held erect (see illustration of Broad-tailed Paradise-Whydah on p. 475). Also hovers over females in slow, bobbing flight causing the tail to undulate. Parasitises Green-winged Pytilia (p. 460). **12–38 cm** (Gewone Paradysvink)

3 **Shaft-tailed Whydah** *Vidua regia*   NE
Common, near-endemic resident. Breeding male distinguished by **creamy buff underparts** plus **thin tail-shafts with broadened ends**. Female and non-breeding male have **less distinctive head markings** than other whydahs. The voice is 'chit-chit-chit…'; male has a scratchy song like that of an indigobird. Occurs singly or in small flocks, females predominating, in dry thornveld, sandveld with sparse vegetation and grassland with scattered thorn bushes. Male chases other small birds at feeding assemblies. Parasitises Violet-eared Waxbill (p. 466). **12–34 cm** (Pylstertrooibekkie)

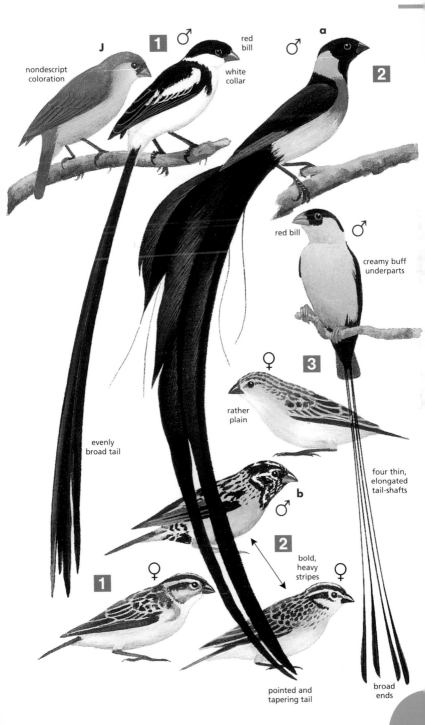

nondescript
coloration

J

1 ♂

red
bill

white
collar

♂

a

♂

2

red bill

♂

creamy buff
underparts

♀

3

rather
plain

evenly
broad tail

four thin,
elongated
tail-shafts

♂

b

2

bold,
heavy
stripes

♀

1 ♀

pointed and
tapering tail

broad
ends

1 Broad-tailed Paradise-Whydah *Vidua obtusa*
Common resident. Male differs from Long-tailed Paradise-Whydah (p. 472) only in the **wide tail-feathers that do not taper**. Females and immatures of the two species are virtually indistinguishable. Male, like Long-tailed Paradise-Whydah, has a display flight as in (a); also identical in other respects, and often occurs in mixed flocks with that species. Its distribution is linked to that of its host, the Orange-winged Pytilia (p. 460). **12–38 cm** (Breëstertparadysvink)

INDIGOBIRDS

Brood parasites of firefinches (p. 462) and, in the case of the Zambezi Indigobird, the Red-throated Twinspot (p. 464). They appear to be so **strictly host-specific** that their presence in a region is an indication of the presence of the species they parasitise. Breeding males are black with a blue, green or mauve iridescence. **Non-breeding males resemble females**; see illustration (2). Immatures are more russet-brown, especially on the underparts; crowns unstreaked. Males are identified by **bill and leg coloration** plus **song, which mimics that of the host.**

a.k.a. Variable...

2 Dusky Indigobird *Vidua funerea*
Common resident. Has **whitish bill** and **reddish legs**. Male has a grating song interspersed with the notes of African Firefinch (p. 462), which the female parasitises. Male may bob up and down in front of the female calling a harsh 'cha, cha'. Occurs mostly in moist savanna, around villages, near cultivation and at forest fringes; decidedly uncommon (as is its host) in drier bushveld regions. **11 cm** (Gewone Blouvinkie)

3 Purple Indigobird *Vidua purpurascens*
Fairly common resident. Male told by **whitish or pale pink bill and legs**, female by **whitish bill** and **pink legs**. Parasitises Jameson's Firefinch (p. 462) and mimics the bell-like call-note of that species. Habits as for other indigobirds. It frequents thickets and rank grass in thornveld, plus riparian and old cultivated lands like its host. Much more common in dry bushveld regions than (2). **11 cm** (Witpootblouvinkie)

4 Village Indigobird *Vidua chalybeata*
Common resident. Male told by **red bill and legs**; in the female the **bill is pink, legs red**. In Botswana and western Zimbabwe, the male's **bill is white** like (2), but ranges do not overlap. It parasitises the Red-billed Firefinch (p. 462) and mimics the call of that species. Occurs in the same habitat as its host: mixed bushveld near watercourses and suburbia. **11 cm** (Staalblouvinkie)

5 Zambezi Indigobird *Vidua codringtoni* **R**
Fairly common resident. Has a **whitish bill** and **orange legs and feet**, the **black body plumage** showing a **green gloss in good light**; otherwise appears all-black. The female is similar to other female indigobirds. Occurs in the eastern regions of Zimbabwe and adjacent Mozambique. Unusual in that it parasitises the Red-throated Twinspot (p. 464). Its call imitates the call of the twinspot. **11 cm** (Groenblouvinkie)

burnt orange loops around the nape

1

a

cf. Long-tailed Paradise Whydah (p. 472)

♂

♀

tail broader, shorter and less tapering than that of Long-tailed Paradise-Whydah (p. 472)

2

♂

whitish bill

reddish legs

angle of light influences colour of legs and bills of indigobirds

3

♂

white or pale pink bill

whitish legs

4

♂

red bill

red legs

green gloss

♂

5

orange legs

rounded, bulbous tail-ends

CANARIES, SISKINS AND BUNTINGS

Sparrow-sized or smaller songbirds. Canaries and siskins have **strong conical bills, usually notched tails** and **undulating flight**. Buntings are **strongly terrestrial** and have **weaker, narrower bills**. Many species are nomadic.

1 Yellow-fronted Canary *Crithagra mozambica*

Common resident. A small canary with **bold facial markings, greyish crown and nape, yellow rump** and **white tail-tip**. The **eyes are brown** (contrary to alternative name of Yellow-eyed Canary). Sexes are alike. Immature is duller. Has a lively song delivered in short bursts. Occurs in small parties and flocks in all types of woodland, bushveld, forest and plantation fringes and suburbia. Feeds both in the grass and in trees. **12 cm** (Geeloogkanarie)

2 Forest Canary *Crithagra scotops* E

Common endemic resident. **Heavily streaked appearance** diagnostic, boldest in northern birds. Also shows a **small, dark mask**. Immature resembles adult. Normal call is a thin, plaintive 'tweetoo, twee-ee' given frequently, often the first clue to its presence (similar to co-occurring Swee Waxbill, p. 468). Also has a brisk warbling song of sibilant quality. Pairs and small parties frequent tree canopies in forests at all altitudes, as well as adjacent forested kloofs and plantation fringes. **13 cm** (Gestreepte Kanarie)

3 Yellow Canary *Crithagra flaviventris* NE

Common, near-endemic resident. Shows marked differences between the sexes. **Palest, yellowest males with bright yellow rumps** (a) occur in the northwest (cf. 5); **darkest males with greenish rumps** (b) in the southeast, with intergrading elsewhere. Females of (b) duskier about the breast, streaking less obvious than in females of (a). Immatures are like females, upperparts greener. Males sing well and vigorously from tree tops. Small parties and flocks occur in semi-arid regions, frequenting low-growing bushes of mountain sides, and Karoo and coastal scrub, especially along watercourses; they also enter small towns. Nomadic in some regions. **13–14 cm** (Geelkanarie)

4 Cape Canary *Serinus canicollis* E

Common endemic resident. Identified by **grey nape, ear coverts and sides of neck**. Female duller than male, and immature streaked below. Song is a series of loud, rolling warbles and trills. Occurs singly or in flocks in a wide variety of habitats, from coastal scrub to montane grassland and protea-covered slopes, plantations and farmlands. Feeds mostly on the ground. **13–14 cm** (Kaapse Kanarie)

5 Brimstone Canary *Crithagra sulphuratus*

Common resident. A **thickset, heavy-billed species**. Southern birds (a) mainly **dull olive-green** with **dark-streaked upperparts**; northern birds (b) much paler, more yellow and smaller; other races between these extremes. Race (b) differs from (3a) in lack of white edges to wing coverts, plus **dark crown extending to base of bill**. Immature is duller than adult. Song slower, huskier, less tuneful than other canaries. Occurs singly, in pairs or in small flocks in various bushy habitats including hillsides, kloofs, forest fringes, bracken-briar patches and riverside thickets. **14–15 cm** (Dikbekkanarie)

bold grey facial markings

1

white terminal edge

small dark mask

2

streaked

♂ a

3

♀

b ♂

yellow rump

grey nape and ear coverts

4

no white on tail-tip

5

dark crown reaches base of bill

large bill

a

b

olive-green wash on breast and flanks

no white on tail-tip

1 Black-headed Canary *Crithagra alario* E

Common endemic resident. Male distinctive with **chestnut wings** and **bold black head** (a). In northwestern part of range, males have much **white on the face and throat** (b); this race sometimes considered a separate species: Damara Canary (*Serinus leucolaemus*). **Females sparrow-like**, but usually in association with the easily identified males. Immatures duller, more streaky above. Calls 'sweea' and has a subdued song. Pairs and flocks occur in dry regions, frequenting scrubby vegetation, rocky hillsides, cultivated lands and suburbia. **12–15 cm** (Swartkopkanarie, Bontkopkanarie)

2 Black-eared Seedeater *Crithagra mennelli*

Fairly common, localised resident. Distinguished from (3) by **darker upperparts** plus **breast streaking**. Male has **bold black mask**, browner in female and immature. In summer, male sings for long periods 'teeu-twee-teu, twiddy-twee-twee'. Pairs and small parties occur in broad-leaved woodland, often in bird parties, feeding in trees or on the ground. **13–14 cm** (Swartoorkanarie)

3 Streaky-headed Seedeater *Crithagra gularis*

Common resident. Identified by **bold white eyebrows** and **streaked crown**. Told from (2) by lack of a distinct mask or any breast streaking; cf. Yellow-throated Petronia (p. 444), which has similar bold eyebrows. Has a pleasant song, rendered in short bursts 'wit-chee-chee-chee-cha, cha, cha, cha, cha, chip', rising to a crescendo. When nest-building, utters a repetitive 'tweu, tweu, tirrirrit-tirik'. Occurs singly, in pairs or in small parties in woodland, fallow farmlands and suburbia. Inconspicuous and seldom numerous. **16 cm** (Streepkopkanarie)

4 White-throated Canary *Crithagra albogularis* NE

Common, near-endemic resident. Distinguished from all brown canaries except (6) by **yellow rump**. Palest birds with brightest rump occur in Namibia (b); darkest with greenish-yellow rump occur in south (a), with intergrading elsewhere. Distinguished from (6) by **white throat**; could also be mistaken for smaller female Yellow Canary (p. 476). Has a strong, tuneful song 'weetle, weetle, frrra, weetle, frree, tee, chipchipchipchip…'. Occurs singly or in small flocks in dry thornveld, Karoo, desert and coastal dunes, generally not far from water. **14–15 cm** (Witkeelkanarie)

5 Protea Canary *Crithagra leucoptera* R E

Fairly common, localised endemic resident. A **large, drab canary** with a **pale bill** and **two distinct light wing-bars on the folded wing**; cf. (3). Distinctive call is 'tree-lee-loo', the song soft, sweet and varied; an excellent mimic. Small, scattered parties occur in protea bush on southern mountains, occasionally in wooded kloofs and forest fringes. Shy and retiring, the flight swift and direct. **16 cm** (Witvlerkkanarie)

6 Black-throated Canary *Crithagra atrogularis*

Common resident. A **small canary** with **yellow rump**. **Black throat** diagnostic when present but may be absent or vestigial. Shows a **bright yellow rump** in flight and a **white tail-tip**. Gives a strong and sustained rambling song from a tree top. Small flocks feed on grass and weed seeds in woodland, fallow farmlands, waste ground and on roadside verges. **11–12 cm** (Bergkanarie)

1
a ♂
b ♂
♀

2
very finely streaked, grey-brown head
streaked
bold black mask
greyish streaking

3
bold white eyebrow
streaked
no streaking

4
a
white
b
no streaking (cf. Yellow Canary, p. 476)
lemon-yellow rump

5
distinct, light wing-bars
contrasting pale bill on dark face
no yellow

6
variable dark mottling
yellow rump obvious in flight

1 Cape Siskin *Crithagra totta*   E

Common, localised endemic resident. Male told from male of (2) mainly by **white tips to primary feathers and tail**. Immature resembles female. The call is a high-pitched, metallic 'tchwing, tchwing, tchwing, tchwing'; also calls 'pitchee' during each dip of its pronouncedly undulating flight. Pairs and small parties occur on fynbos-covered mountain slopes, or in valleys and forest clearings. Feeds on the ground and in bushes, but is shy. **13 cm** (Kaapse Pietjiekanarie)

2 Drakensberg Siskin *Crithagra symonsi*   E

Common, localised endemic resident. Male **lacks any white in the wings**, but shows clear **white panels on its outer tail-feathers**. Female is much browner than female of (1). Sings well. Pairs and small parties occur on high grassy slopes of the Drakensberg, moving to lower levels in winter. Common around villages and agricultural fields in the Lesotho highlands. Habits much like (1). **13 cm** (Bergpietjiekanarie)

3 Lemon-breasted Canary *Crithagra citrinipecta*   NE

Fairly common, localised near-endemic resident. Told by **very small size**, male with **buffy flanks and belly**; cf. Yellow-fronted Canary (p. 476). Female has **buffy underparts** and **yellow rump**. Has a pretty song of sparrow-like quality. Flocks, often with Yellow-fronted Canaries, occur in dry woodland, cultivated lands and coastal grassland. Like Yellow-fronted Canary is attracted to seeding grasses. Somewhat nomadic when not breeding. **9,5–10 cm** (Geelborskanarie)

NEAR THREATENED

4 Common Chaffinch *Fringilla coelebs*   I

Uncommon, localised resident. An introduced species. Male unmistakable with **deep-pink underparts, striking white wing-bars** and **grey nape**. Female similar, but duller. Calls 'chink, chink' and has a distinctive, frequently repeated song 'chip-chip-chip-tell-tell-tell-cherry-erry-erry-tissi-cheweeoo'. Occurs singly or in pairs in suburban gardens, parks and pine plantations around Cape Town. **15 cm** (Gryskoppie)

ranges do not overlap

1

♀

2

♂

♀

♂

white feather-tips

white panels on outer tail-feathers

♀

white 'shoulder'

white wing-bar

4

grey cap

white or yellow

♂

lemon-yellow

deep pink

♂

3

pale buffy flanks

1 Lark-like Bunting *Emberiza impetuani*

Common, near-endemic resident. A small, pale, **cinnamon-washed** bunting, mostly **lacking in diagnostic features**. Sexes are alike. Immature is closely similar to adult. Call, uttered at take-off, is a nasal 'chut'; the song is a rapidly delivered 'trrrooo-cheeoo-cheepp-trree' repeated frequently with variations. Usually in **small flocks** in grassland, Karoo and semi-arid woodland, often in rocky regions with sparse bushes and in exotic plantations. Nomadic, in very cold periods sometimes erupting into new areas in large numbers. **13–14 cm** (Vaalstreepkoppie)

2 Cabanis's Bunting *Emberiza cabanisi*

Uncommon, localised resident. Distinguished from (4) by black face and ear coverts, **no white line below eyes**, plus **greyer mantle**. Female is like male but head markings are more brown than black. Immature has brownish (not white) head-streaks and browner flanks. Has a soft 'tureee' call and a sweet but variable song 'wee-chidderchidder, chidder-wee' or 'her-ip-ip-ip ... her-hee'. Usually singly or in pairs in **miombo woodland**. **15 cm** (Geelstreepkoppie)

3 Cinnamon-breasted Bunting *Emberiza tahapisi*

Common resident. Distinguished by **cinnamon colouring of body** with **black, white-streaked head**. Immature resembles female. The short, distinctive song is repeated at frequent intervals, 'tee-trrr, chirri-chee' or 'swiddle-swiddle-saaa'. In pairs, occasionally flocks, on **rocky or stony ground** with or without bushes, often on soil-eroded ground or in broad-leaved woodland and mixed bushveld. **13–14 cm** (Klipstreepkoppie)

4 Golden-breasted Bunting *Emberiza flaviventris*

Common resident. Distinguished from (2) by **white stripe below eyes, browner mantle** and more **orange breast**. Female has **yellowish head-streaks**, brown in immature. The normal call is 'pret-ty-boyeee', sometimes answered by the mate 'sitee'. The song is a frequently repeated 'chipchipchipchipchip-teee, teeu-teeu-teeu-teeu'. Pairs occur in mixed bushveld, thornveld, broad-leaved woodland and exotic plantations. **16 cm** (Rooirugstreepkoppie)

5 Cape Bunting *Emberiza capensis*

Common, near-endemic resident. Regionally variable, but differs from (3) in **pale throat** and **paler, duller underparts**. Sexes are alike. Immature is duller. Call is a distinctive 'cheriowee'. The song, uttered from a rock or bush top, is 'cheep, cheep, tip, cheeucheeu, tip-cheeu-tip-cheeu'. Occurs singly, in pairs or in flocks in a variety of semi-arid, coastal montane regions, coastal sand dunes with sparse scrub, rocky hillsides in the Karoo and Zimbabwe, broad-leaved woodland in Zimbabwe plus suburbia in many regions. **16 cm** (Rooivlerkstreepkoppie)

1

hint of typical bunting head-pattern

cinnamon wash

cinnamon-edged feathers

stripe above eye and black cheeks

greyish mantle

♂

2

yellow

♀

3

♂

black head with white streaks

cinnamon

♂

white stripe above and below eye

brown mantle

4

orange (variable; less so in female)

throat paler than breast

5

GLOSSARY OF TERMS

Acacia Deciduous trees of the genus *Acacia*. In Africa these are thorny, with bipinnately compound leaves (each leaf is again divided into small leaflets) and small, powderpuff-like or elongated flowers.

Accipiter Sparrowhawks and goshawks. Long-tailed, short-winged raptors with long, unfeathered legs and long toes. They specialise in catching small birds (or small mammals in the larger species) in swift pursuit from a standing start.

Afrotropical Region Africa south of the Palaearctic Region, the Tropic of Cancer roughly forming its northern limit. Formerly called the Ethiopian Region.

Aggregation A gathering (of birds) brought about by some common interest such as a temporary food availability, after which individuals disperse separately.

Albinistic White or partially white plumage resulting from a lack of normal colour pigmentation.

Altitudinal migrant A bird that moves seasonally from one altitude to another.

Brood parasite A bird that deposits its eggs in the nest of another species; e.g. cuckoos, honeyguides, whydahs.

Broad-leaved woodland Woodland comprising trees with broad leaves as opposed to thornveld where trees of the genus Acacia are dominant.

Bush Refers to any terrain with trees of moderate height as opposed to the taller, more luxuriant growth of woodland or riparian forest; see Bushveld.

Bushveld A terrain with mixed trees of moderate height (5–10 m) where the trees frequently touch each other below canopy height; sometimes in dense thickets and usually with a grassy groundcover.

Coastal bush Dense, humid, evergreen bush found on coastal dunes; mainly along the east coast.

Coastal forest Larger trees than in coastal bush and frequently extending inland in dense patches with grassland in between.

Conspecific Being of the same species.

Crepuscular Active at dusk. Applied to birds, it usually infers that they are active in the half-light hours, dawn and dusk.

Dam An artificial water impoundment, usually with a retaining wall at the end opposite the inflow.

Damaraland Plateau The inland plateau region of north-central Namibia, the home of many endemic bird species. The habitat varies from semi-desert transition in the south to thornveld in the north-east and mopane and teak woodland in the north.

Delta A river mouth with several diverging branches forming a triangle. In the context of this fieldguide, usually refers to the inland delta of the Okavango River drainage system (also known as the Okavango Swamps) in northern Botswana.

Desert A region of extremely low rainfall, usually less than 25 mm. In southern Africa the driest desert is the Namib, comprising sand dunes in the southern and coastal regions and stony plains elsewhere, with isolated patches of thornbush in some lower-lying areas or on hillsides. The Kalahari Desert in central Botswana consists of dunes in the south and sandy or stony plains, with sparse thorn scrub elsewhere, merging into Kalahari thornveld further north.

Dispersal A more or less random centrifugal movement away from a locality.

Display Actions that have become specialised in the course of evolution: threat display, courtship display, social displays, etc.

Donga A gully caused by erosion.

Egg-dumping The habit among secondary females in such social species as the Ostrich and guineafowls, of laying their eggs in the nest of another female of the same species, usually the dominant female in a flock. Also refers to random egg-laying in places other than nests by immature or unmated hens of any species.

Endemic A species found only in a specific region or country.

Estuary The tidal mouth of a large river, an important feeding area for many water-associated birds because of its food-rich mud flats and floodplains.

Escarpment The long, steep face of a plateau. In southern Africa usually refers to the eastern escarpment, which forms the edge of the inland plateau or highveld.

Ethiopian Region Old name for Africa south of the Palaearctic Region, now replaced by the term Afrotropical Region.

Falcon Small, swift-flying raptor with pointed wings; specialises in catching flying birds by means of a rapid descent from above, known as a 'stoop'.

F Female.

Flats Level grassland.

Fledgling A young bird that has recently acquired its first feathers.

Flock A group of birds that moves as a more or less cohesive unit.

Floodplain Grassland, especially that adjacent to estuaries, which becomes inundated by river spillage.

Forest A tract of land covered by tall evergreen trees with interlocking canopies.

Fynbos A natural habitat occurring in the south-eastern and south-western coastal regions of South Africa: a Mediterranean-type scrub composed of proteas, ericas and legumes, among other plants.

Gamebird An outdated term used by hunters. Refers to ducks, geese, pheasants, partridges, guineafowls and others. In the past bustards were included in this category.

Graduated tail A tail in which the central feathers are longest and all others progressively shorter, the outermost being shortest.

Grassland Any region with extensive grass coverage, especially the plateau or highveld regions of southern Africa, but can also refer to grass-covered foothills or montane grassland.

Gregarious Living in flocks or communities.

Highveld The plateau region of inland southern Africa; consists mainly of grassland above c. 1 500 m.

Immature In the context of this fieldguide, refers to any bird beyond the nestling stage.

Intra-Africa migrant A bird that migrates regularly within the African continent.

Irruption An irregular migration into a new area, often brought about by unfavourable conditions in the normal range of a species, and usually of a temporary nature.

Juvenile A young bird below sub-adult stage.

Kalahari thornveld Thornveld with stunted, scattered or more or less continuous Acacia or Dichrostachys tree species on Kalahari sand and calcareous soil with tufty grasses.

Karoo veld Stony plains with little soil, dotted with dwarf trees and succulent plants, or undulating stony plains with numerous grasses and shrubs but few succulents and trees, or rocky hills with scrub. Annual rainfall 150–300 mm. The driest region is known as the arid Karoo, where desert grasses predominate. Annual rainfall 50–200 mm.

Kloof A cleft or valley, usually with steeply inclined or rocky sides, often well-wooded.

Koppie A small hill, often with a rocky summit.

Lagoon A stretch of salt water separated from the sea by a low sandbank.

Leaf-gleaner A bird that seeks insects from the leaves of the tree canopy.

Littoral The region of land lying along the sea shore.

Local movement A mass movement, not necessarily regular, within a comparatively small area.

Lowland Those regions lying below c. 900 m. Mixed bush and grassland.

Lowveld The eastern part of southern Africa, which lies between c. 100 m and 900 m and comprises bushveld.

Mangrove A forest, comprising mainly trees of the family Rhizophoraceae, which grows in tidal estuaries. The trees produce air roots, which protrude upwards from the mud.

Melanistic Darkness of plumage colour resulting from abnormal development of black pigmentation.

Migration A regular movement of birds (or other animals) between two alternative regions inhabited by them at different times of the year, one region in which they breed and the other region used by them when not breeding.

Miombo Broad-leaved woodland in which trees of the genus Brachystegia dominate; common in Zimbabwe.

Mist-belt The eastern region of southern Africa at 900–1 350 m above sea level (otherwise known as the escarpment) where the rainfall is between 900 mm and 1 150 mm per annum and the conditions are frequently misty during easterly maritime winds: of mostly hilly or montane grassland with isolated forest patches and, these days, with exotic plantations.

Mixed bushveld A region of mixed tree types, including both broad-leaved and thorny species, growing more or less continually or in clumps, to an average height of about 7–10 m. This form of bush covers much of the eastern lowveld of South Africa and Mozambique plus the northern lowlands of Mozambique where various palms become dominant. Soils may be sandy or stony, with good grass cover.

M Male.

Monoculture Extensive planting of one crop, e.g. sugarcane.

Montane Mountainous country.

Mopane A broad-leaved, deciduous tree, *Colophospermum mopane*. In some regions remains a smallish bush, in others grows to a height of c. 12 m. Leaves are rounded, heart-shaped and reddish when young.

Morph An alternative but permanent plumage colour.

Nomad A species with no fixed territory when not breeding.

Palaearctic Region The northern hemisphere, incorporating North Africa, Europe, Scandinavia and Asia.

Pan (or floodpan) A natural depression that fills with water as the result of rainfall or river spillage.

Parkland Regions of woodland with well-spaced trees, little secondary growth and a grassy groundcover.

Passerine A bird that habitually sings or calls and that has 'normal' feet, with three toes facing forward and one facing backward; excludes birds with webbed, lobbed or zygodactylous feet.

Pectoral The breast region; in birds especially the lateral breast regions.

Pelagic seabird A bird of the open seas as opposed to one that roosts or breeds on mainland shores.

Plantation Trees, usually exotic species (gums, wattles or pines) planted for timber; closely planted and devoid of groundcover, their interiors unattractive to most birds.

Range expansion The process in which a species increases its breeding range; a spread into regions not previously occupied.

Raptor A bird of prey; one that hunts and kills other animals for food.

Retrices The main tail feathers of a bird (rectrix in the singular).

Recurved bill A bill that bends upwards, e.g. Avocet.

Remiges The primary and secondary wing feathers of a bird (remex in the singular).

Riparian Of or on riverbanks.

Riverine forest The trees fringing a river, usually evergreen and more luxuriant than trees of the surrounding country and often with an understorey of dense thickets and secondary growth. In the more arid regions growth is less well developed, then often referred to as riverine bush.

Scrub Brushwood or stunted bushes.

Sexual dimorphism Difference in appearance between male and female of a species.

Soft parts A bird's bill, legs and feet, eye-surround and bare facial skin if present.

Speculum A patch of iridescent colour on the wings of some birds, notably ducks.

Still-hunt Watching for prey (usually on the ground) while perched.

Subantarctic The southern oceans between 45 °S and the Antarctic Circle.

Sub-song A birdsong of lower than normal pitch, sometimes of longer than normal duration.

Tail streamer Elongated tail feathers, often the central or outer feathers.

Teak The tree *Baikiaea plurijuga* (Rhodesian teak), which grows extensively in the northern parts of southern Africa.

Thicket A number of shrubs or trees growing very close together.

Thornveld A bush habitat or woodland comprising Acacia, Albizia or Dichrostachys trees, all of which are thorny.

Understorey The lowest stratum in (usually) forest or woodland; secondary growth consisting of young trees, small bushes and annual plants.

Upland High-altitude regions, but below montane.

Valley bush Narrow belts of dense bush, often thorny and with succulent plant species, found in hot river valleys that drain into the Indian Ocean. Rainfall 500–900 mm per annum.

Veld A term used loosely in reference to various types of terrain, thus grassveld, bushveld, etc.

Vlei A marshy area, usually in grassland.

Watercourse The dry course of a river that flows only during good rains.

Waterhole Any natural or artificial water-point used by animals for drinking.

Woodland Regions with trees of moderate height and well-developed canopies that are so spaced as not to interlock; may cover flat ground or hillside, with or without well-developed secondary growth or groundcover.

Zygodactyl Feet which, in certain non-passerine birds, have two toes directed forward and two backward: cuckoos, barbets, woodpeckers, honeyguides and others.

REFERENCES

GENERAL IDENTIFICATION

Chittenden, H. *Roberts Bird Guide*. John Voelcker Bird Book Fund, 2007. Condensed version of the voluminous Roberts Birds of Southern Africa (VII), focusing on field identification.

Ginn, P.J., McIlleron, W.G. & Milstein, P. le S. *The Complete Book of Southern African Birds*. Struik Winchester, 1989. Large format coffee table book discussing each of the region's species, accompanied by high quality photographs.

Mullarney, K., Svensson, L., Zetterström, D. & Grant, P.J. *Collins Bird Guide*. HarperCollins Publishers, 1999. Widely considered to be the most complete field guide to the birds of Britain and Europe, but includes extensive information on migratory species visiting our region, as well as potential vagrants.

Newman, K. *Newman's Birds by Colour*. Struik Publishers, 2008. Simplifies the complicated bird identification process by grouping species according to their basic colours.

Newman, K. *What's that Bird? A starter's guide to birds of southern Africa*. Struik Publishers, 2003. Introduces the reader to the region's rich bird diversity by highlighting the main bird groups.

Newman, K. & Solomon, D. *Look-alike Birds*. Southern Book Publishers, 1994. Points out critical identification characters in diagrammatic form for some of the most frequently misidentified species.

Newman, K., Solomon, D., Johnson, D. & Masterson, A. *LBJs – Little Brown Jobs Made Easier*. Southern Book Publishers, 1998. Supplementary information on the identification of larks, cisticolas, warblers and other LBJs.

Oberprieler, U. & Cillié, B. *The Bird Guide of Southern Africa*. Game Parks Publishing, 2008. Photographic guide to the birds of the region.

Sinclair, I. & Davidson, I. *Southern African Birds: A Photographic Guide*. Struik Publishers,

2006. A4-size, hard-cover photographic guide originally published in 1993.

Sinclair, I. & Hockey, P. *Larger Illustrated Guide to Birds of Southern Africa*. Struik Publishers, 2006. Popular field guide covering all Southern African species. Large format also includes identification essays on similar species.

Sinclair, I. & Ryan, P. *The Complete Photographic Guide: Birds of Southern Africa*. Struik Nature, 2009. Large format guide featuring the most comprehensive collection of bird photographs to date.

Sinclair, I. *Field Guide - Birds of Southern Africa*. Struik Publishers, 1994. Popular photographic field guide to the birds of Southern Africa.

Sinclair, I. *Pocket Guide: Birds of Southern Africa*. Struik Nature, 2009. Covers 500 more common species, in a portable, pocket-size format.

BIRD DISTRIBUTION

Harrison, J.A., Allan, D.G., Underhill, L.G., Herremans, M., Tree, A.J., Parker, V. & Brown, C.J. (eds). *The Atlas of Southern African Birds*. BirdLife South Africa, Johannesburg, 1997. Fine-scale distribution and abundance data presented in two volumes. The results of the first SABAP survey. Also available online at http://sabap2.adu.org.za.

Parker, V. *The Atlas of the Birds of Sul do Save*, Southern Mozambique. Endangered Wildlife Trust and Avian Demography Unit, Johannesburg & Cape Town, 1999. Distribution and abundance of birds in Mozambique south of the Save River.

Parker, V. *The Atlas of the Birds of Central Mozambique*. Endangered Wildlife Trust and Avian Demography Unit, Johannesburg & Cape Town, 2005. Distribution and abundance of birds in Mozambique north of the Save River.

BIRDING LOCALITIES

Cohen, C., Spottiswoode C. & Rossouw, J. *Southern African Birdfinder*. Struik Publishers, 2006. A guide to over 330 birding sites in southern Africa, as well as Angola, Zambia, Malawi and Madagascar. Includes pull-out map.

Hardaker, T. & Sinclair, I. *Birding Map of Southern Africa*. Struik Publishers, 2000. Fold-out map of Southern Africa, with summarised information on 200 key birding sites.

Marais, E. & Peacock, F. *The Chamberlain Guide to Birding Gauteng*. Mirafra Publishing, 2008. A detailed guide to 101 prime birding sites in and around Johannesburg and Pretoria, as well as top weekend and further afield sites. Includes detailed site maps and annotated checklist.

BIOLOGY & CONSERVATION

Barnes, K.N. (ed). *The Important Bird Areas of Southern Africa*. BirdLife South Africa, Johannesburg, 1998. Reference framework presenting estimated numbers of threatened species in the region's most important bird conservation localities.

Barnes, K.N. (ed). *The Eskom Red Data Book of Birds of South Africa, Lesotho and Swaziland*. BirdLife South Africa, Johannesburg, 2000. Focuses on the conservation of and threats facing the region's endangered species.

Carnaby, T. *Beat About The Bush: Birds*. Jacana Media, 2008. This comprehensive reference guide provides answers to everyday questions pertaining to a myriad southern African bird-related topics.

Hockey, P.A.R., Dean, W.R.J. & Ryan, P.G. *Roberts — Birds of Southern Africa VIIth Edition*. John Voelcker Bird Book Fund, 2005. The latest update of this trusted name that has been in print for more than 65 years. The seventh edition includes detailed information on the breeding biology, movements, diet, moult and measurements of all Southern African species, spanning nearly 1300 pages.

Little, R., Crowe, T. & Barlow, S. *Gamebirds of Southern Africa*. Struik Publishers, 2000. Discussion of the region's sandgrouse, francolins, spurfowls, guineafowls and quails, accompanied by beautiful painting by Simon Barlow.

Loon, R. & Loon, R. *Birds – The Inside Story*. Struik Publishers, 2005. Explores Southern African birds and their behaviour.

Maclean, G.L. *Ornithology for Africa*. University of Natal Press, 1990. Fascinating insights into a wide range of topics relating to the ecology, behaviour, biology and physiology of birds.

Steyn, P. *Nesting Birds*. Fernwood Press, 1996. Beautifully illustrated coffee table book detailing the breeding habits of Southern African birds.

Tarboton, W. *A Guide to the Nests & Eggs of Southern African Birds*. Struik Publishers, 2001. Details the breeding habits of each locally breeding species, accompanied by photographs of nests and eggs at actual size.

MISCELLANEOUS

Newman, K. *Beating About The Bush — The Idiot's Guide to Birdwatching*. Southern Book Publishers, 1992. Humorous yet informative introductory guide to birding as a pastime, as well as bird groups.

Ryan, P. *Birdwatching in Southern Africa*. Struik Publishers, 2006. An excellent introduction to birds and birding – what you need, where to go, what to look for and the basics of identification. Also available as *Practical Birding*.

Trendler, R & Hes, L. *Attracting Birds to your Garden*. Struik Publishers, 2000. Gardening strategies aimed at attracting birds by providing feeding and nesting opportunities.

BIRD GROUPS

Brooke, M. *Albatrosses and Petrels across the World*. Oxford University Press, 2004. Guide to these enigmatic oceanic wanderers.

Cleere, N. & Nurney, D. *Nightjars: A guide to the Nightjars and Related Birds*. Pica Press, 1998. Information on this cryptic and challenging, yet fascinating nocturnal bird group.

Enticott, J. & Tipling, D. *Photographic Handbook to the Seabirds of the World*. New Holland, 1997. Photographic identification guide to world's pelagic and coastal seabirds.

Erasmus, R. & Tarboton, W. *Owls & Owling in Southern Africa*. Struik Publishers, 2004. Insights into the fascinating world of this enigmatic group of birds.

Forsman, D. *The Raptors of Europe and The Middle East*. Christopher Helm/A&C Black Publishers, 2003. Extensive guide to field identification of Palearctic raptors, including several Southern African species and migrants.

Harris, T. & Arnott, G. *Shrikes of Southern Africa*. Struik Publishers, 1988. Dedicated to the region's shrikes, tchagras, boubous, bush-shrikes, helmet-shrikes and allies.

Harrison, P. *Seabirds: An Identification Guide*. Croom Helm, 1983. The quintessential guide to the identification of the world's seabirds.

Hayman, P., Marchant, J. & Prater, T. *Shorebirds – An identification guide*. Trusted handbook for wader-enthusiasts around the world.

Hockey, P. & Douie, C. *Waders of Southern Africa*. Struik Winchester, 1995. Large format, coffee table book outlining the biology, conservation and fascinating migration of this diverse bird group.

Kemp, A. & Kemp, M. *Sasol Birds of Prey of Africa and its Islands*. Struik Publishers, 2002. Provides essential supplementary information on the identification of this diverse and challenging group.

Message, S. & Taylor, D. *Waders of Europe, Asia and North America*. Christopher Helm/A&C Black Publishers, 2005. Identification guide to Northern Hemisphere waders, including many migratory species occurring in Southern Africa during the southern summer.

Oatley, T. & Arnott, G. *Robins of Africa*. Acorn Books & Russel Friedman Books, 1998. Large format, coffee table book on the African continent's robin-chats, scrub-robins and akalats.

Olsen, K.M. & Larsson, H. *Skuas and Jaegers*. Pica Press, 1997. Essential reference guide for anyone interested in mastering the identification of this difficult group.

Peacock, F. *Pipits of southern Africa*. Published by the author, Pretoria, 2006. www. pipits.co.za. Additional information on the identification and biology of pipits – considered by many to be Africa's ultimate LBJs.

Rosair, D. & Cottridge, D. *Photographic Guide to the Waders of the World*. Hamlyn, 1995. Descriptions and photographs of the world's 212 wader species.

Rowan, M.K. *The Doves, Parrots, Louries and Cuckoos of Southern Africa*. David Phillip Publishers, 1983. Information on the identification and biology of the local representatives of these four groups.

Skead, C.J. (ed). *The Canaries, Seedeaters and Buntings of Southern Africa*. South African Bird Book Fund, 1960. Although difficult to obtain nowadays, this detailed book provides in-depth information on these fascinating species.

Taylor, B. & Van Perlo, B. *Rails: A guide to the Rails, Crakes, Gallinules and Coots of the World*. Pica Press, 1998. Comprehensive guide to the Rallidae family, many of which are threatened, poorly known and highly secretive, not to mention sought after by birders.

BIRD CLUBS AND ORGANISATIONS

BirdLife South Africa is the local partner of BirdLife International, a worldwide organization that promotes bird research, conservation of birds and their habitats and general enjoyment of wild birds. BirdLife South Africa boasts a membership of 8 000 birders and has more than 40 branches nationwide. It is highly recommended that you join your local regional BirdLife branch, which will give you the opportunity to join birding outings, participate in conservation projects and attend fascinating courses on birds' ecology and identification. Contact details for the BirdLife branches in Zimbabwe and Botswana are also provided.

BirdLife South Africa
P.O. Box 515, Randburg, 2125, Johannesburg, South Africa
Tel: 011-789-1122 / 0861-BIRDER/247337
www.birdlife.org.za

BirdLife Botswana
Private Bag 003, Suite 348, Mogoditshane, Gaborone, Botswana
Tel: 0267-319-0540/1
www.birdlifebotswana.org.bw

BirdLife Zimbabwe
P.O. Box RVL 100, Runiville, Harare, Zimbabwe
Tel: 0263-4-481496/490208
http://birdlife.mweb.co.zw/

SABAP2
The second Southern African Bird Atlas Project (SABAP2) aims to map the distribution and abundance of birds throughout South Africa, Lesotho and Swaziland in 5x5 minute grids ('pentads') for biodiversity planning and conservation. SABAP2 welcomes the participation of all birders. Visit **http://saba2.adu.org.za** to register.

RARITIES
There are few aspects of birding quite as exciting as finding a rarity. However, for rare bird records in South Africa, Lesotho and Swaziland (including sightings up to 200 nautical miles offshore) to be officially accepted and published, you will need to submit the record (along with detailed notes and preferably photographs) to the South African National Rarities Committee (forms available at **www.birdlife.org.za**).

EMAIL NEWSGROUPS
Several specialised email newsgroups have been established to facilitate contact between birders wishing to share their sightings, discuss issues pertaining to birds, or request information and advice from others. SABirdNet is a good starting point: to subscribe, send a message with only the word subscribe in the body of the message to **sabirdnet-request@lists.ukzn.ac.za**. Local newsgroups such as PretoriaBirds and CapeBirdNet focus on more limited geographical areas. If you are interested in receiving information about the occurrence of rarities, joining the SA Rare Bird News Google Group is recommended.

MULTIMEDIA
In recent years, electronic media have become an invaluable tool in birding. A range of video, audio and electronic products are available, e.g. at **www.sabirding.co.za**.

USEFUL WEBSITES
African Bird Club: **www.africanbirdclub.org**
Animal Demography Unit: **www.adu.org.za**
Birding Africa: **www.birdingafrica.com**
Birding Route through South Africa: **www.birdingroutes.co.za**
Bird Info: **www.birdinfo.co.za**
Endangered Wildlife Trust: **www.ewt.org.za**
Gauteng Birding: **www.gautengbirding.co.za**
Indicator Birding: **www.birding.co.za**
Internet Bird Collection: **http://ibc.lynxeds.com**
Natural World: www.natworld.org
Percy FitzPatrick Institute of African Ornithology: **http://web.uct.ac.za/depts/fitzpatrick**
Photography: **www.birdpics.co.za**; **www.hardaker.co.za**; **www.warwicktarboton.co.za**
South African Bird Ringing Unit: **www.birds.sanbi.org/safring/safring.php**
Simply Birding: **www.simplybirding.com**
South African National Parks Forums: **www.sanparks.org/forums**
Wildlife and Environment Society of SA: **www.wessa.org.za**
WWF South Africa: **www.panda.org.za**
ZestForBirds: **www.zestforbirds.co.za**

INDEX TO SCIENTIFIC NAMES

INDEX TO AFRIKAANS NAMES

INDEX TO ENGLISH NAMES AND LIFE LIST

	PLACE	DATE

	PLACE	DATE

	PLACE	DATE

	PLACE	DATE

		PLACE	DATE

	PLACE	DATE

	PLACE	DATE

		PLACE	DATE
Rockjumper, Cape	354		
Rockjumper, Drakensberg	354		
Rockrunner	388		
Roller, Broad-billed	286		
Roller, European	286		
Roller, Lilac-breasted	286		
Roller, Purple	286		
Roller, Racket-tailed	286		
Ruff	136		
Sanderling	144		
Sandgrouse, Burchell's	224		
Sandgrouse, Double-banded	224		
Sandgrouse, Namaqua	224		
Sandgrouse, Yellow-throated	224		
Sandpiper, Baird's	140		
Sandpiper, Broad-billed	140		
Sandpiper, Buff-breasted	146		
Sandpiper, Common	142		
Sandpiper, Curlew	142		
Sandpiper, Green	136		
Sandpiper, Marsh	134		
Sandpiper, Pectoral	142		
Sandpiper, Terek	144		
Sandpiper, White-rumped	140		
Sandpiper, Wood	136		
Saw-wing, Black	264		
Saw-wing, Eastern	264		
Saw-wing, White-headed	264		
Scimitarbill, Common	288		
Secretarybird	178		
Seedcracker, Lesser	460		
Seedeater, Black-eared	478		
Seedeater, Streaky-headed	478		
Shearwater, Balearic	60		

	PLACE	DATE

	PLACE	DATE

	PLACE	DATE

	PLACE	DATE

	PLACE	DATE